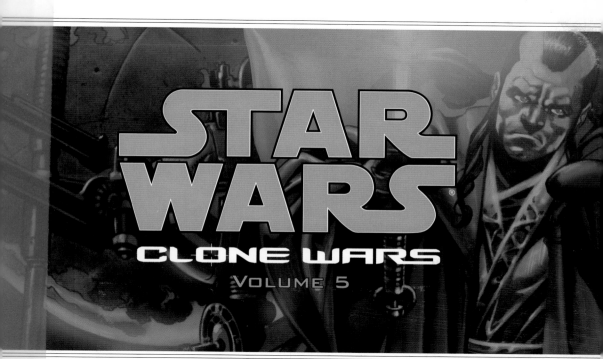

# STAR WARS®

## CLONE WARS

### VOLUME 5

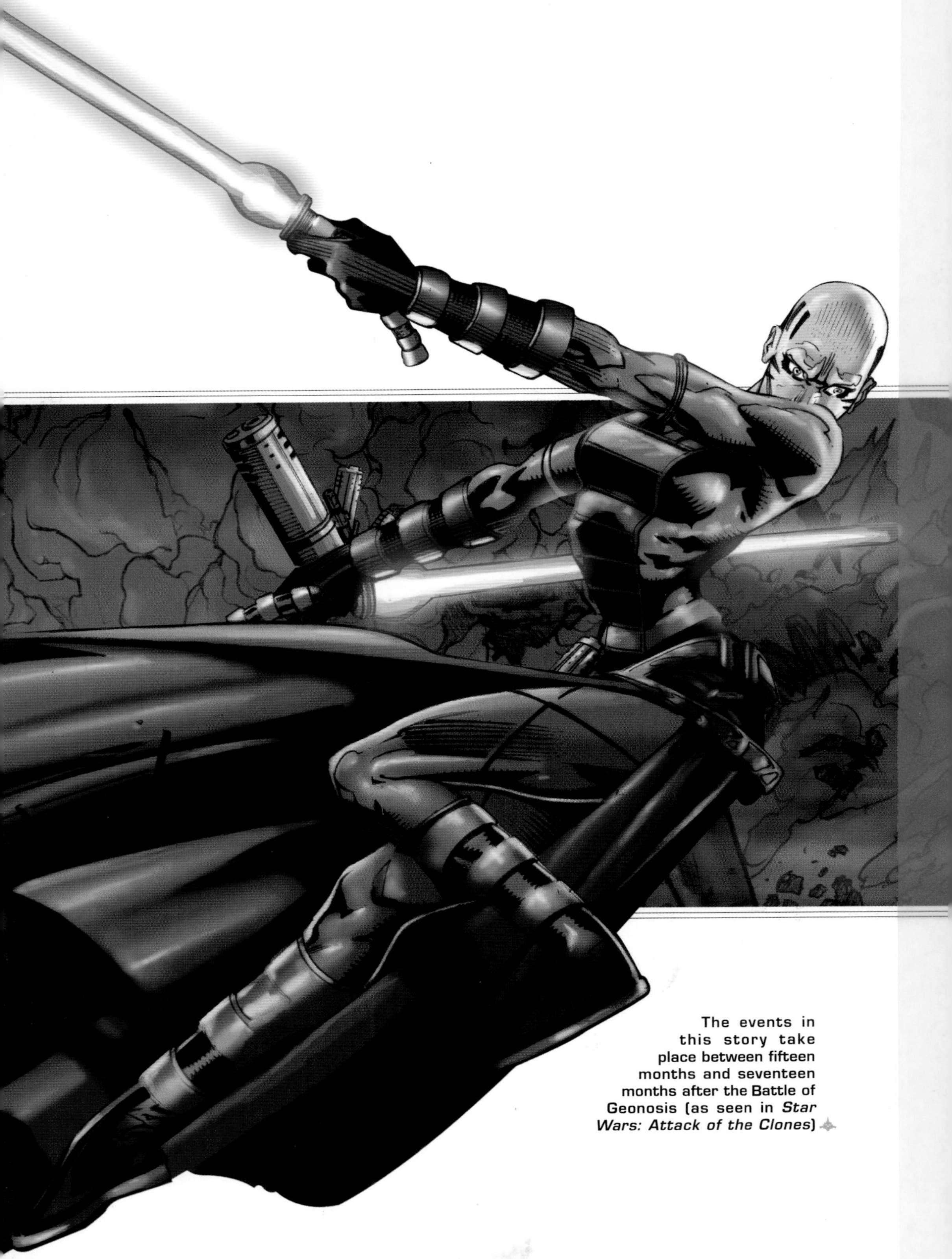

The events in this story take place between fifteen months and seventeen months after the Battle of Geonosis (as seen in *Star Wars: Attack of the Clones*)

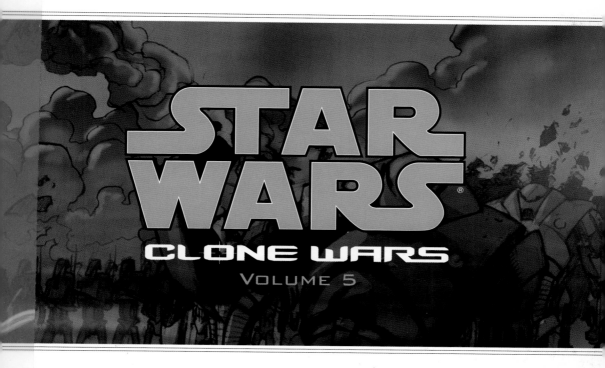

# STAR WARS®
## CLONE WARS
### VOLUME 5

## The Best Blades

Dark Horse Books™

colors by **Brad Anderson**

lettering by **Michael David Thomas & Sno Cone Studios**

cover illustration by **Tomás Giorello**

*(YAGRAPH)*
*YA*
*STAR WARS*
*364-2843*

publisher **Mike Richardson**

collection designer **Darin Fabrick**

art director **Lia Ribacchi**

assistant editor **Jeremy Barlow**

editor **Randy Stradley**

special thanks to **Sue Rostoni** and
**Amy Gary** at Lucas Licensing

**STAR WARS®:CLONE WARS VOLUME 5**

**THIS VOLUME COLLECTS ISSUES SIXTY-ONE, SIXTY-FOUR, SIXTY, AND SIXTY-TWO OF THE DARK HORSE COMIC BOOK SERIES *STAR WARS: REBUBLIC* AND THE DARK HORSE COMIC BOOK *STAR WARS: JEDI — YODA*.**

**PUBLISHED BY DARK HORSE BOOKS, A DIVISION OF DARK HORSE COMICS, INC.**
**10956 SE MAIN STREET · MILWAUKIE, OR 97222**

WWW.DARKHORSE.COM   WWW.STARWARS.COM
To find a comics shop in your area, call the Comic Shop Locator Service
toll-free at 1-888-266-4226

**FIRST EDITION: NOVEMBER 2004**
**ISBN: 1-59307-273-2**
5 7 9 10 8 6 4
**PRINTED IN CHINA**

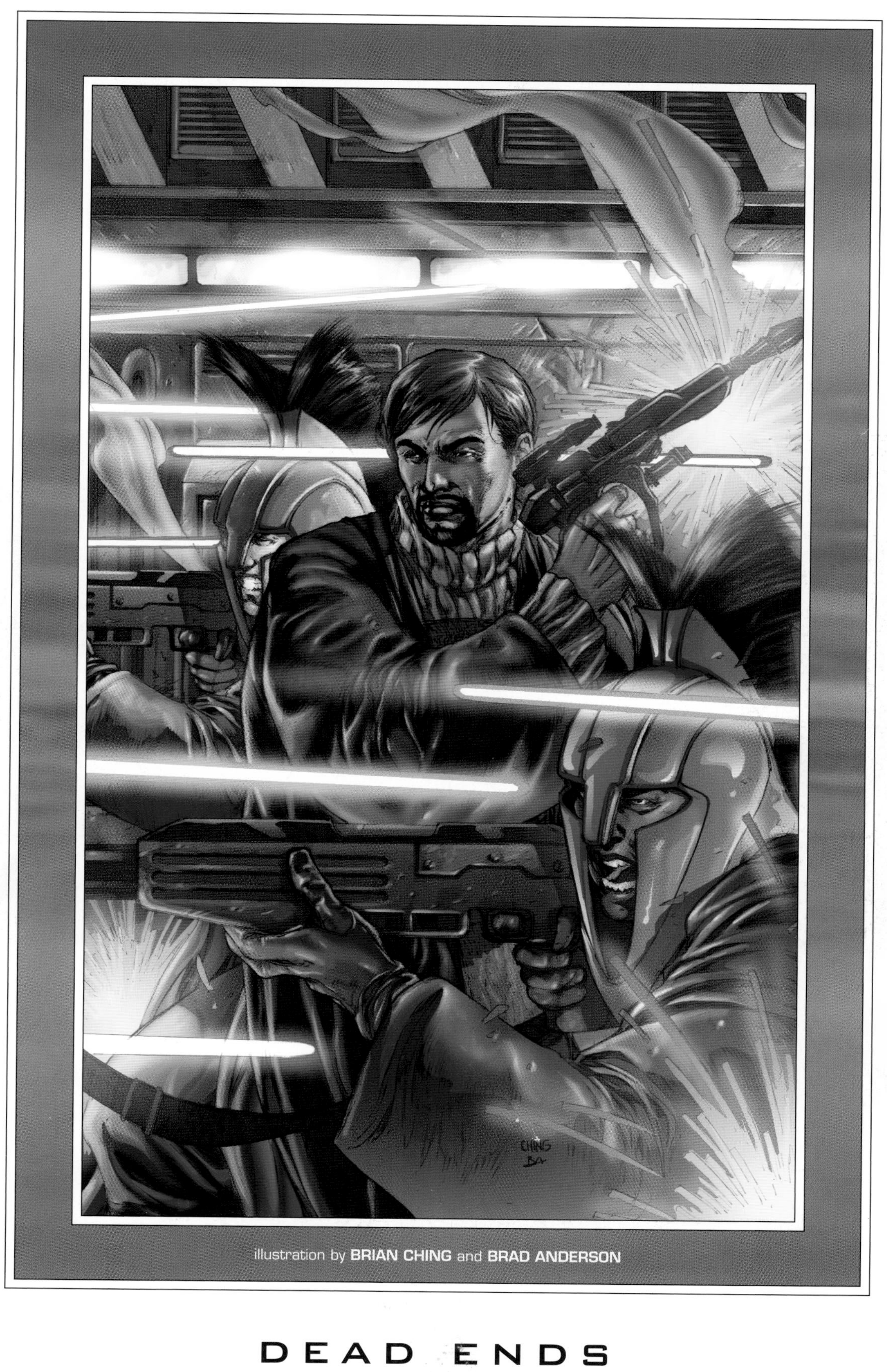

illustration by **BRIAN CHING** and **BRAD ANDERSON**

# DEAD ENDS

APPROXIMATELY SIXTEEN MONTHS
AFTER THE BATTLE OF GEONOSIS...

**"Dead Ends"**
written by **John Ostrander**
pencilled by **Brandon Badeaux**
inked by **Armando Durruthy**

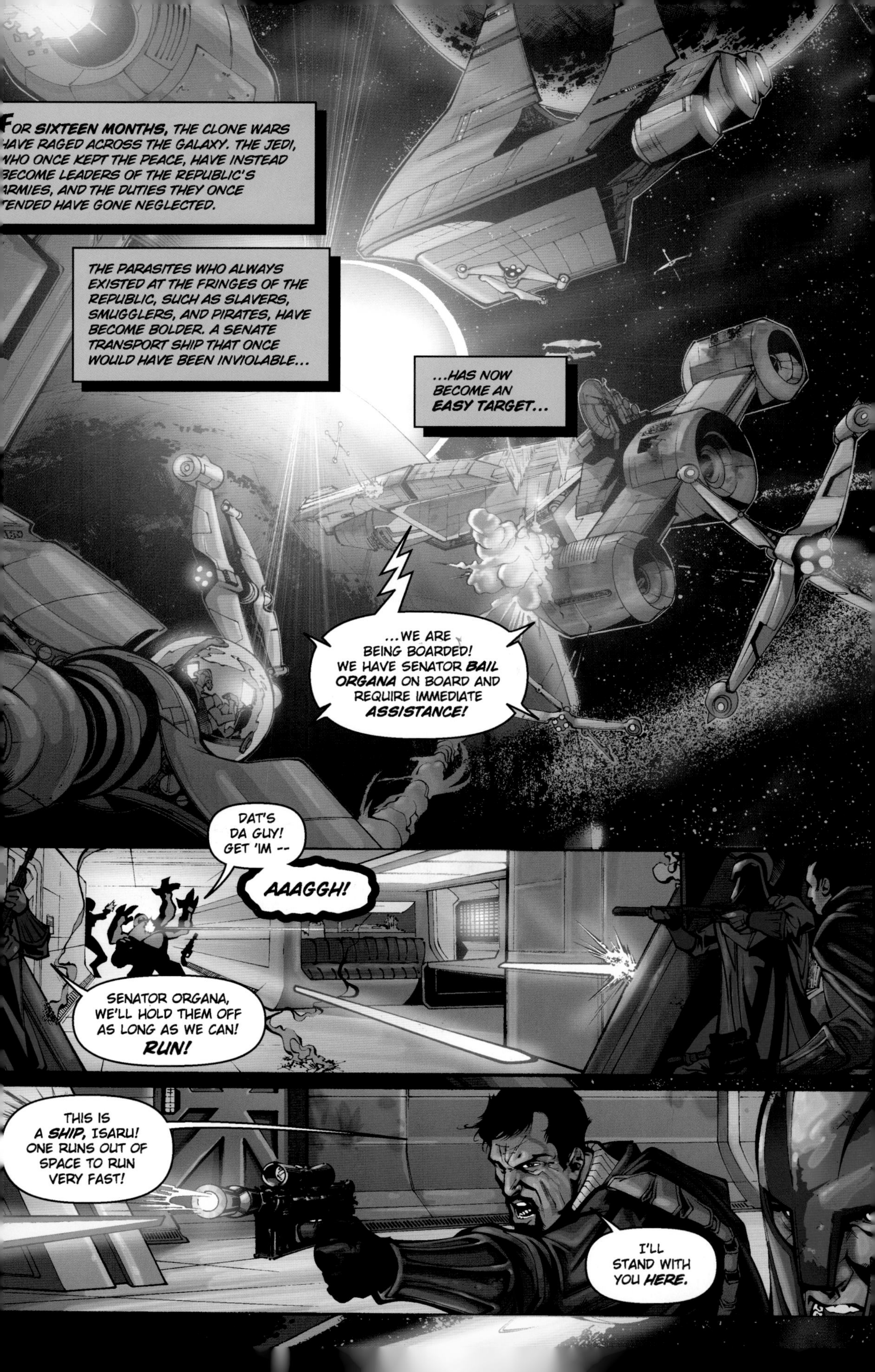
FOR SIXTEEN MONTHS, THE CLONE WARS HAVE RAGED ACROSS THE GALAXY. THE JEDI, WHO ONCE KEPT THE PEACE, HAVE INSTEAD BECOME LEADERS OF THE REPUBLIC'S ARMIES, AND THE DUTIES THEY ONCE TENDED HAVE GONE NEGLECTED.
THE PARASITES WHO ALWAYS EXISTED AT THE FRINGES OF THE REPUBLIC, SUCH AS SLAVERS, SMUGGLERS, AND PIRATES, HAVE BECOME BOLDER. A SENATE TRANSPORT SHIP THAT ONCE WOULD HAVE BEEN INVIOLABLE...
...HAS NOW BECOME AN EASY TARGET...
...WE ARE BEING BOARDED! WE HAVE SENATOR BAIL ORGANA ON BOARD AND REQUIRE IMMEDIATE ASSISTANCE!
DAT'S DA GUY! GET 'IM --
AAAGGH!
SENATOR ORGANA, WE'LL HOLD THEM OFF AS LONG AS WE CAN! RUN!
THIS IS A SHIP, ISARU! ONE RUNS OUT OF SPACE TO RUN VERY FAST!
I'LL STAND WITH YOU HERE.

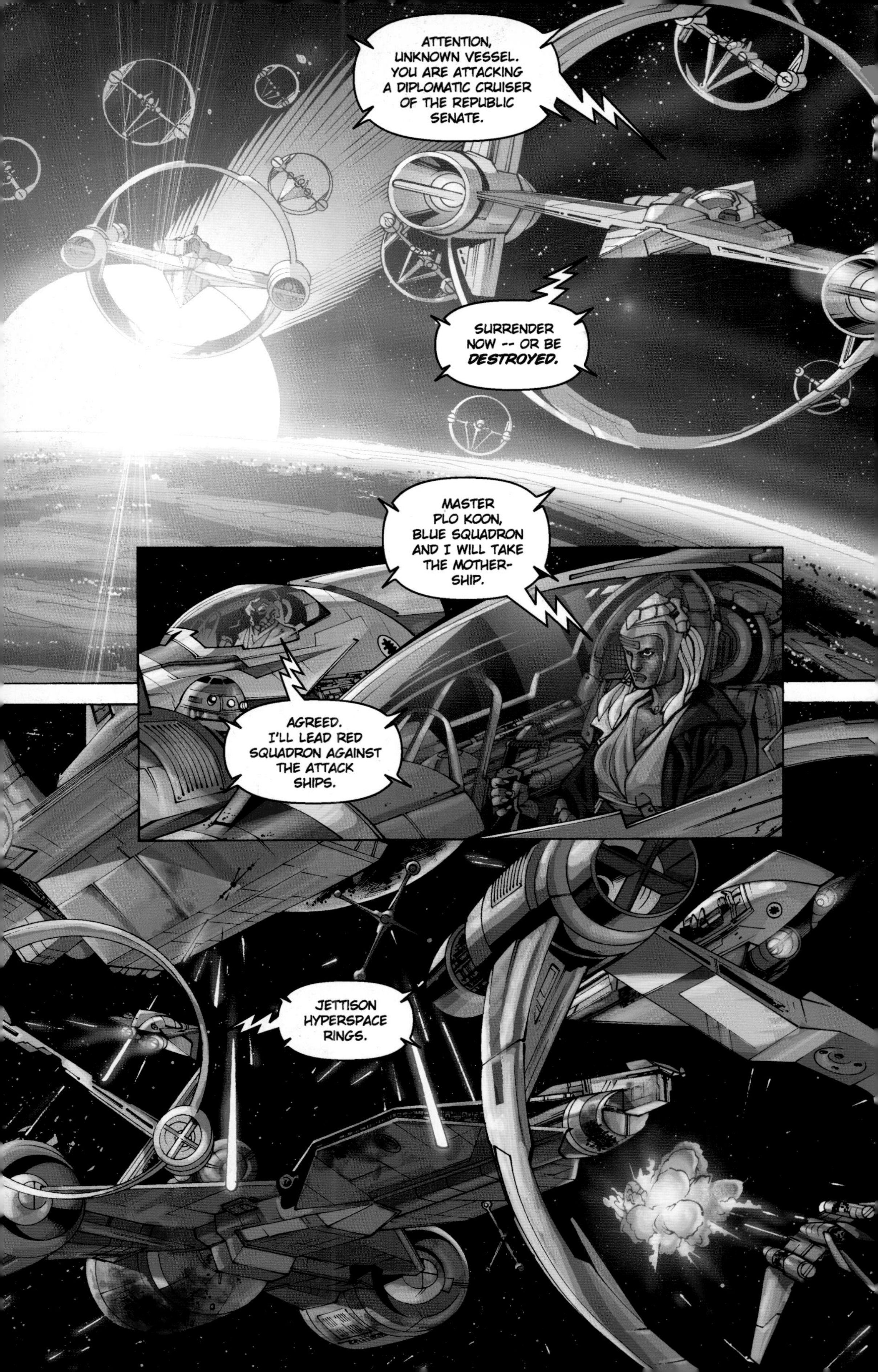
ATTENTION, UNKNOWN VESSEL. YOU ARE ATTACKING A DIPLOMATIC CRUISER OF THE REPUBLIC SENATE.
SURRENDER NOW -- OR BE *DESTROYED.*
MASTER PLO KOON, BLUE SQUADRON AND I WILL TAKE THE MOTHER-SHIP.
AGREED. I'LL LEAD RED SQUADRON AGAINST THE ATTACK SHIPS.
JETTISON HYPERSPACE RINGS.

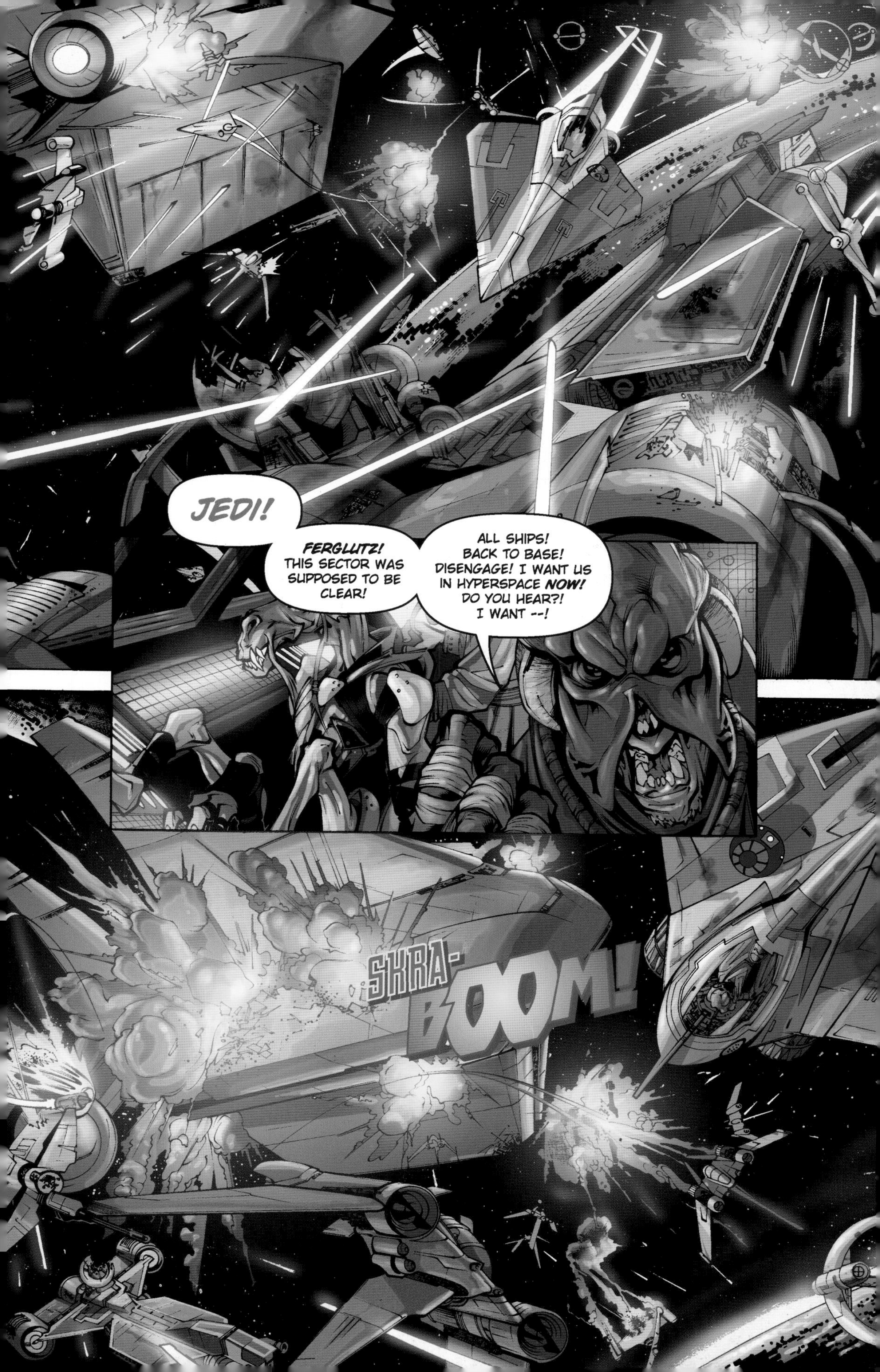
JEDI!
FERGLUTZ! THIS SECTOR WAS SUPPOSED TO BE CLEAR!
ALL SHIPS! BACK TO BASE! DISENGAGE! I WANT US IN HYPERSPACE NOW! DO YOU HEAR?! I WANT --!
SHRA-BOOM!!

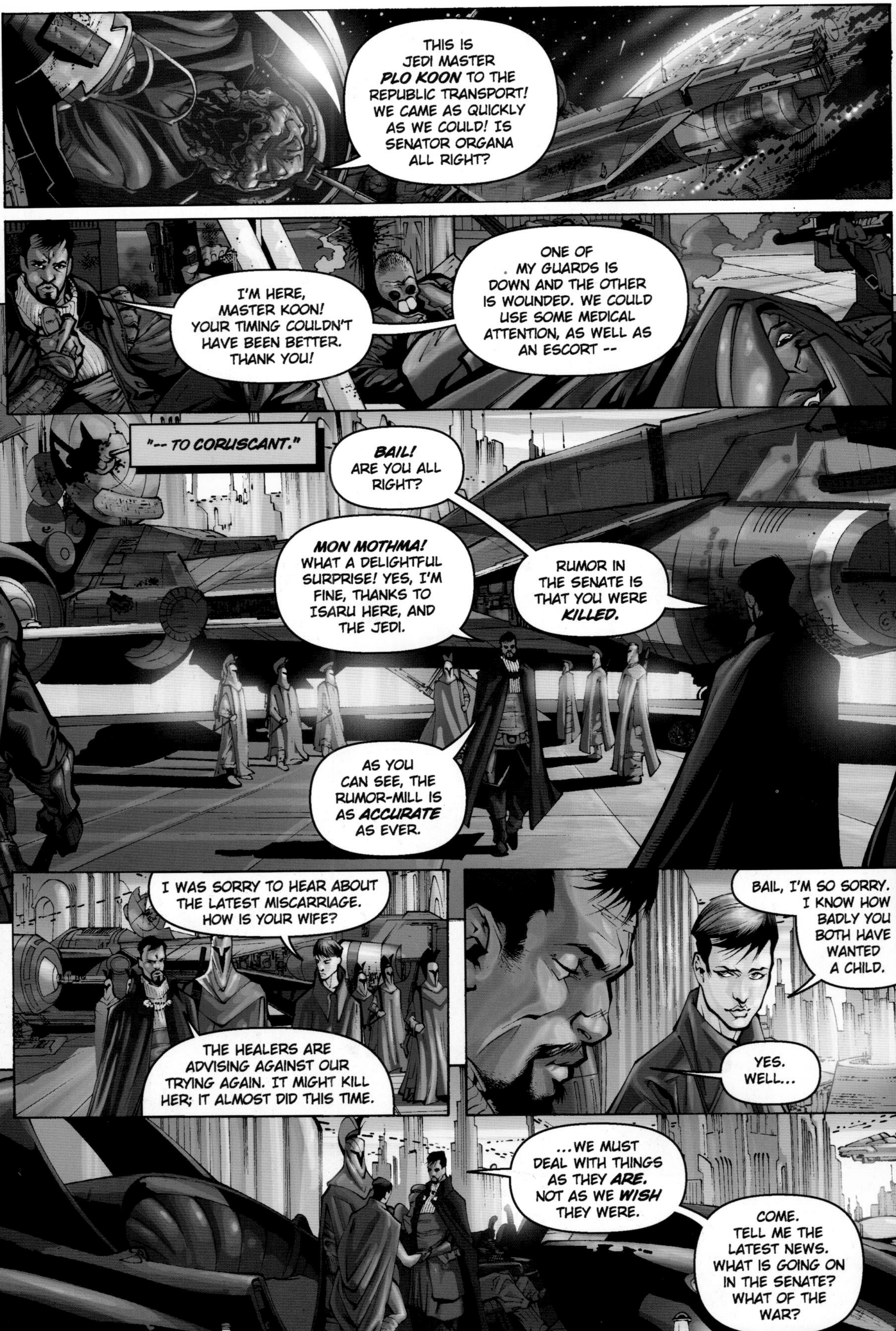

THIS IS JEDI MASTER PLO KOON TO THE REPUBLIC TRANSPORT! WE CAME AS QUICKLY AS WE COULD! IS SENATOR ORGANA ALL RIGHT?
I'M HERE, MASTER KOON! YOUR TIMING COULDN'T HAVE BEEN BETTER. THANK YOU!
ONE OF MY GUARDS IS DOWN AND THE OTHER IS WOUNDED. WE COULD USE SOME MEDICAL ATTENTION, AS WELL AS AN ESCORT --
"-- TO CORUSCANT."
BAIL! ARE YOU ALL RIGHT?
MON MOTHMA! WHAT A DELIGHTFUL SURPRISE! YES, I'M FINE, THANKS TO ISARU HERE, AND THE JEDI.
RUMOR IN THE SENATE IS THAT YOU WERE KILLED.
AS YOU CAN SEE, THE RUMOR-MILL IS AS ACCURATE AS EVER.
I WAS SORRY TO HEAR ABOUT THE LATEST MISCARRIAGE. HOW IS YOUR WIFE?
THE HEALERS ARE ADVISING AGAINST OUR TRYING AGAIN. IT MIGHT KILL HER; IT ALMOST DID THIS TIME.
BAIL, I'M SO SORRY. I KNOW HOW BADLY YOU BOTH HAVE WANTED A CHILD.
YES. WELL...
...WE MUST DEAL WITH THINGS AS THEY ARE. NOT AS WE WISH THEY WERE.
COME. TELL ME THE LATEST NEWS. WHAT IS GOING ON IN THE SENATE? WHAT OF THE WAR?

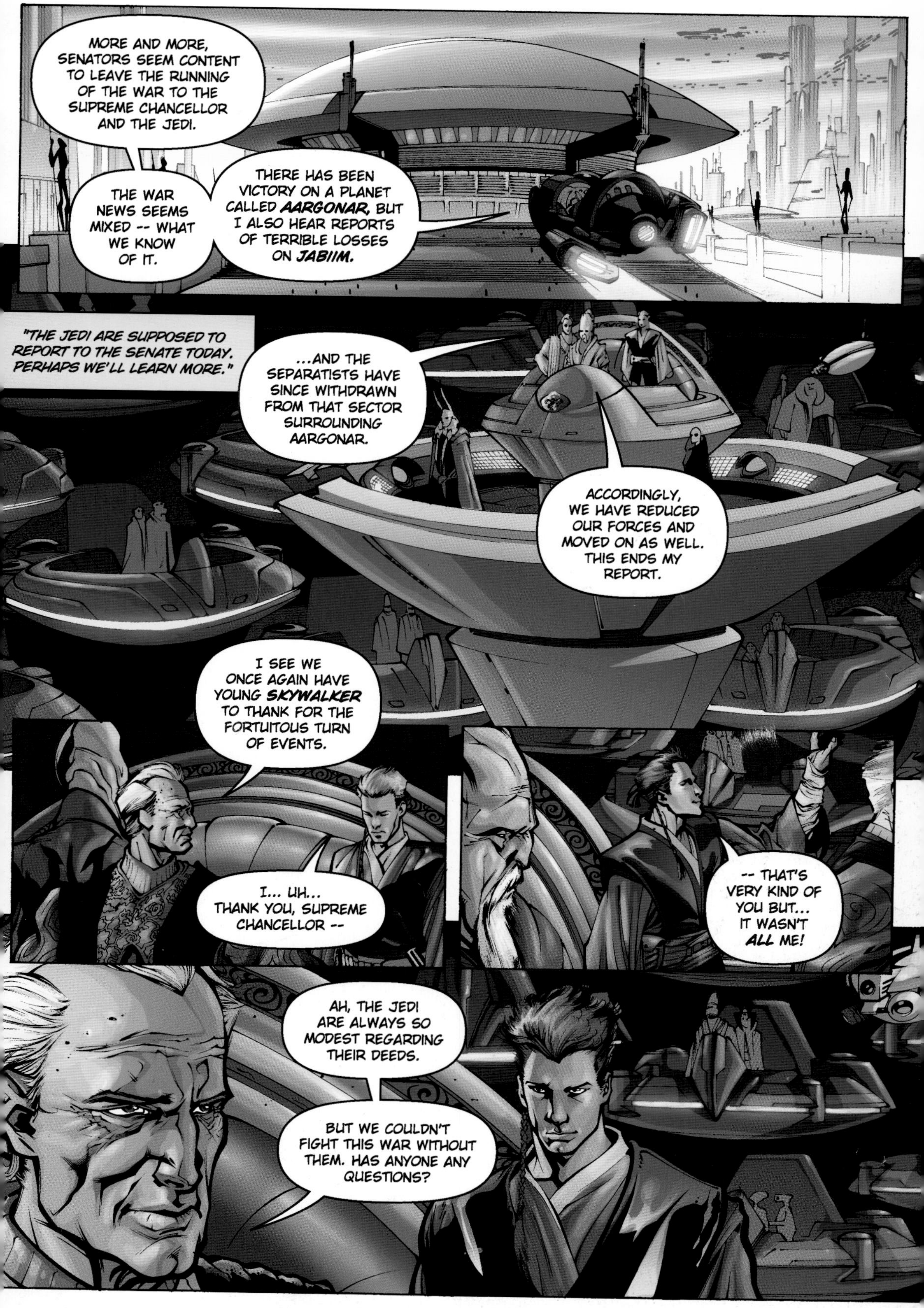
MORE AND MORE, SENATORS SEEM CONTENT TO LEAVE THE RUNNING OF THE WAR TO THE SUPREME CHANCELLOR AND THE JEDI.
THE WAR NEWS SEEMS MIXED -- WHAT WE KNOW OF IT.
THERE HAS BEEN VICTORY ON A PLANET CALLED AARGONAR, BUT I ALSO HEAR REPORTS OF TERRIBLE LOSSES ON JABIIM.
"THE JEDI ARE SUPPOSED TO REPORT TO THE SENATE TODAY. PERHAPS WE'LL LEARN MORE."
...AND THE SEPARATISTS HAVE SINCE WITHDRAWN FROM THAT SECTOR SURROUNDING AARGONAR.
ACCORDINGLY, WE HAVE REDUCED OUR FORCES AND MOVED ON AS WELL. THIS ENDS MY REPORT.
I SEE WE ONCE AGAIN HAVE YOUNG SKYWALKER TO THANK FOR THE FORTUITOUS TURN OF EVENTS.
I... UH... THANK YOU, SUPREME CHANCELLOR --
-- THAT'S VERY KIND OF YOU BUT... IT WASN'T ALL ME!
AH, THE JEDI ARE ALWAYS SO MODEST REGARDING THEIR DEEDS.
BUT WE COULDN'T FIGHT THIS WAR WITHOUT THEM. HAS ANYONE ANY QUESTIONS?

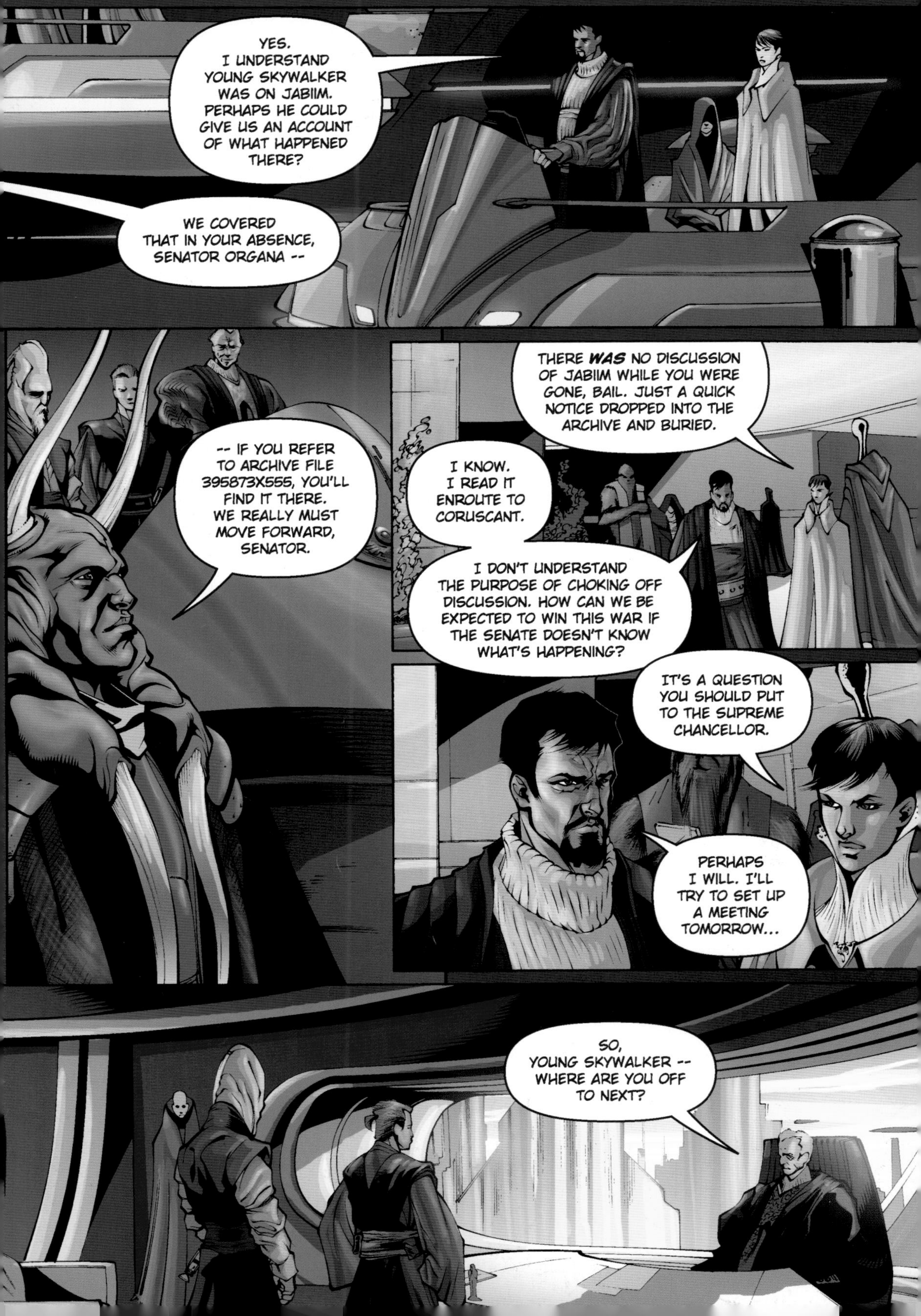
YES. I UNDERSTAND YOUNG SKYWALKER WAS ON JABIIM. PERHAPS HE COULD GIVE US AN ACCOUNT OF WHAT HAPPENED THERE?
WE COVERED THAT IN YOUR ABSENCE, SENATOR ORGANA --
-- IF YOU REFER TO ARCHIVE FILE 395873X555, YOU'LL FIND IT THERE. WE REALLY MUST MOVE FORWARD, SENATOR.
THERE **WAS** NO DISCUSSION OF JABIIM WHILE YOU WERE GONE, BAIL. JUST A QUICK NOTICE DROPPED INTO THE ARCHIVE AND BURIED.
I KNOW. I READ IT ENROUTE TO CORUSCANT.
I DON'T UNDERSTAND THE PURPOSE OF CHOKING OFF DISCUSSION. HOW CAN WE BE EXPECTED TO WIN THIS WAR IF THE SENATE DOESN'T KNOW WHAT'S HAPPENING?
IT'S A QUESTION YOU SHOULD PUT TO THE SUPREME CHANCELLOR.
PERHAPS I WILL. I'LL TRY TO SET UP A MEETING TOMORROW...
SO, YOUNG SKYWALKER -- WHERE ARE YOU OFF TO NEXT?

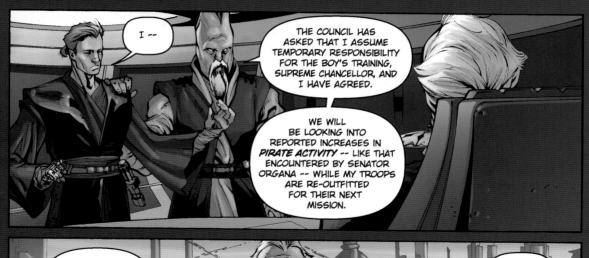

I --

THE COUNCIL HAS ASKED THAT I ASSUME TEMPORARY RESPONSIBILITY FOR THE BOY'S TRAINING, SUPREME CHANCELLOR, AND I HAVE AGREED.

WE WILL BE LOOKING INTO REPORTED INCREASES IN *PIRATE ACTIVITY* -- LIKE THAT ENCOUNTERED BY SENATOR ORGANA -- WHILE MY TROOPS ARE RE-OUTFITTED FOR THEIR NEXT MISSION.

MASTER KENOBI'S DEATH ... A TERRIBLE LOSS! AND HOW TERRIBLE FOR *YOU*, ANAKIN! YOU MUST MISS HIM A GREAT DEAL.

YES...

WE JEDI BELIEVE THERE IS NO DEATH, SUPREME CHANCELLOR. ONLY THE FORCE.

OF COURSE. THE CONCEPT IS A LITTLE HARD FOR WE WHO ARE NOT JEDI TO GRASP, HOWEVER. TO US, DEATH SEEMS VERY REAL. VERY *PAINFUL*. I ADMIRE YOUR DETACHMENT, KI-ADI-MUNDI. I WISH I SHARED IT. GOOD LUCK TO YOU ALL.

MASTER, HOW LONG BEFORE WE LEAVE CORUSCANT?

WHY?

WELL, I WAS HOPING TO LOOK UP A FRIEND BEFORE I LEAVE.

SENATOR AMIDALA FROM NABOO...

I DON'T BELIEVE SHE'S ON CORUSCANT, ANAKIN. BESIDES, WE LEAVE IMMEDIATELY.

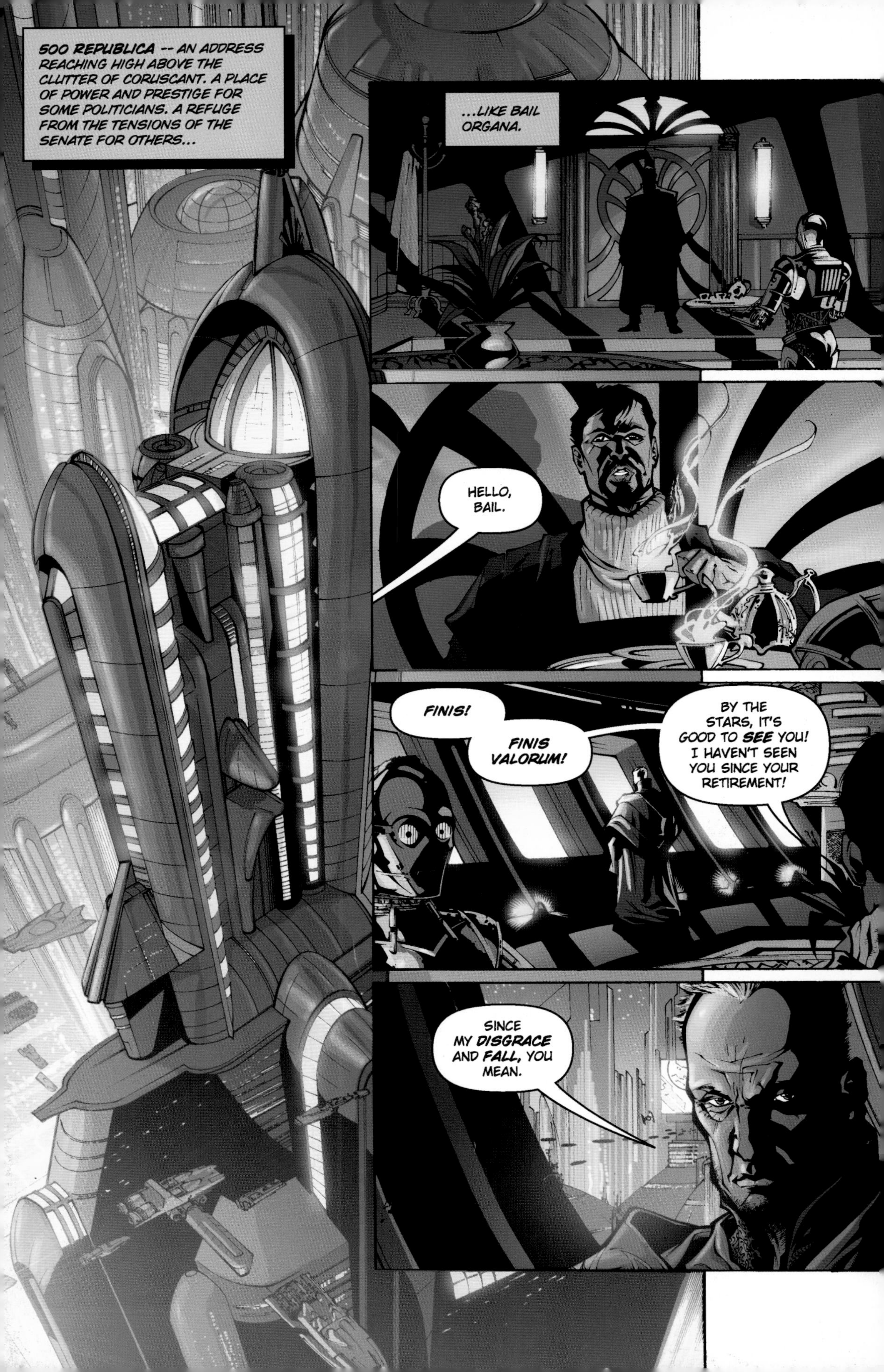

500 REPUBLICA -- AN ADDRESS REACHING HIGH ABOVE THE CLUTTER OF CORUSCANT. A PLACE OF POWER AND PRESTIGE FOR SOME POLITICIANS. A REFUGE FROM THE TENSIONS OF THE SENATE FOR OTHERS...
...LIKE BAIL ORGANA.
HELLO, BAIL.
FINIS!
FINIS VALORUM!
BY THE STARS, IT'S GOOD TO SEE YOU! I HAVEN'T SEEN YOU SINCE YOUR RETIREMENT!
SINCE MY DISGRACE AND FALL, YOU MEAN.

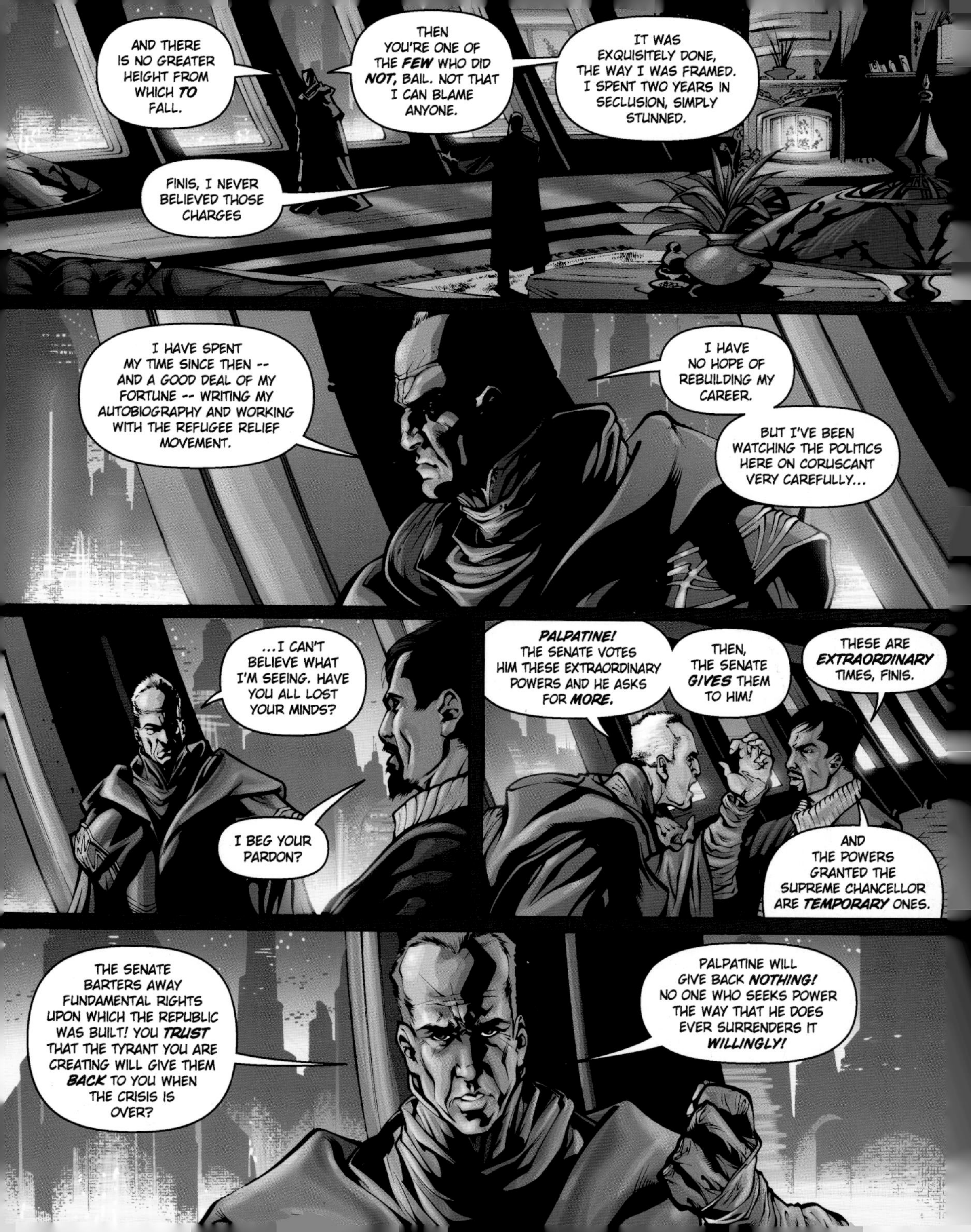
AND THERE IS NO GREATER HEIGHT FROM WHICH *TO* FALL.
FINIS, I NEVER BELIEVED THOSE CHARGES
THEN YOU'RE ONE OF THE *FEW* WHO DID *NOT,* BAIL. NOT THAT I CAN BLAME ANYONE.
IT WAS EXQUISITELY DONE, THE WAY I WAS FRAMED. I SPENT TWO YEARS IN SECLUSION, SIMPLY STUNNED.
I HAVE SPENT MY TIME SINCE THEN -- AND A GOOD DEAL OF MY FORTUNE -- WRITING MY AUTOBIOGRAPHY AND WORKING WITH THE REFUGEE RELIEF MOVEMENT.
I HAVE NO HOPE OF REBUILDING MY CAREER.
BUT I'VE BEEN WATCHING THE POLITICS HERE ON CORUSCANT VERY CAREFULLY...
...I CAN'T BELIEVE WHAT I'M SEEING. HAVE YOU ALL LOST YOUR MINDS?
I BEG YOUR PARDON?
*PALPATINE!* THE SENATE VOTES HIM THESE EXTRAORDINARY POWERS AND HE ASKS FOR *MORE.*
THEN, THE SENATE *GIVES* THEM TO HIM!
THESE ARE *EXTRAORDINARY* TIMES, FINIS.
AND THE POWERS GRANTED THE SUPREME CHANCELLOR ARE *TEMPORARY* ONES.
THE SENATE BARTERS AWAY FUNDAMENTAL RIGHTS UPON WHICH THE REPUBLIC WAS BUILT! YOU *TRUST* THAT THE TYRANT YOU ARE CREATING WILL GIVE THEM *BACK* TO YOU WHEN THE CRISIS IS OVER?
PALPATINE WILL GIVE BACK *NOTHING!* NO ONE WHO SEEKS POWER THE WAY THAT HE DOES EVER SURRENDERS IT *WILLINGLY!*

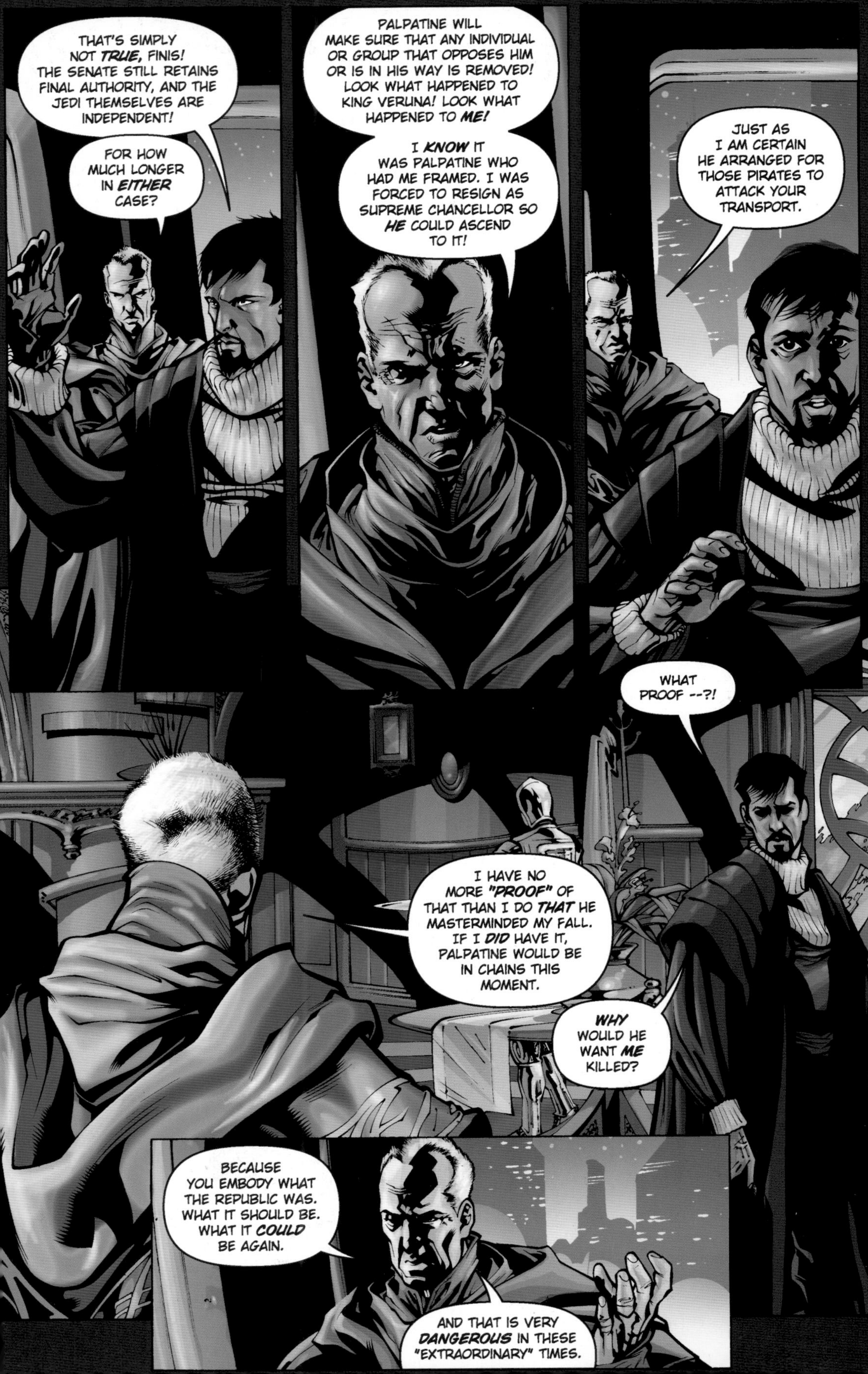
THAT'S SIMPLY NOT TRUE, FINIS! THE SENATE STILL RETAINS FINAL AUTHORITY, AND THE JEDI THEMSELVES ARE INDEPENDENT!
FOR HOW MUCH LONGER IN EITHER CASE?
PALPATINE WILL MAKE SURE THAT ANY INDIVIDUAL OR GROUP THAT OPPOSES HIM OR IS IN HIS WAY IS REMOVED! LOOK WHAT HAPPENED TO KING VERUNA! LOOK WHAT HAPPENED TO ME!
I KNOW IT WAS PALPATINE WHO HAD ME FRAMED. I WAS FORCED TO RESIGN AS SUPREME CHANCELLOR SO HE COULD ASCEND TO IT!
JUST AS I AM CERTAIN HE ARRANGED FOR THOSE PIRATES TO ATTACK YOUR TRANSPORT.
WHAT PROOF --?!
I HAVE NO MORE "PROOF" OF THAT THAN I DO THAT HE MASTERMINDED MY FALL. IF I DID HAVE IT, PALPATINE WOULD BE IN CHAINS THIS MOMENT.
WHY WOULD HE WANT ME KILLED?
BECAUSE YOU EMBODY WHAT THE REPUBLIC WAS. WHAT IT SHOULD BE. WHAT IT COULD BE AGAIN.
AND THAT IS VERY DANGEROUS IN THESE "EXTRAORDINARY" TIMES.

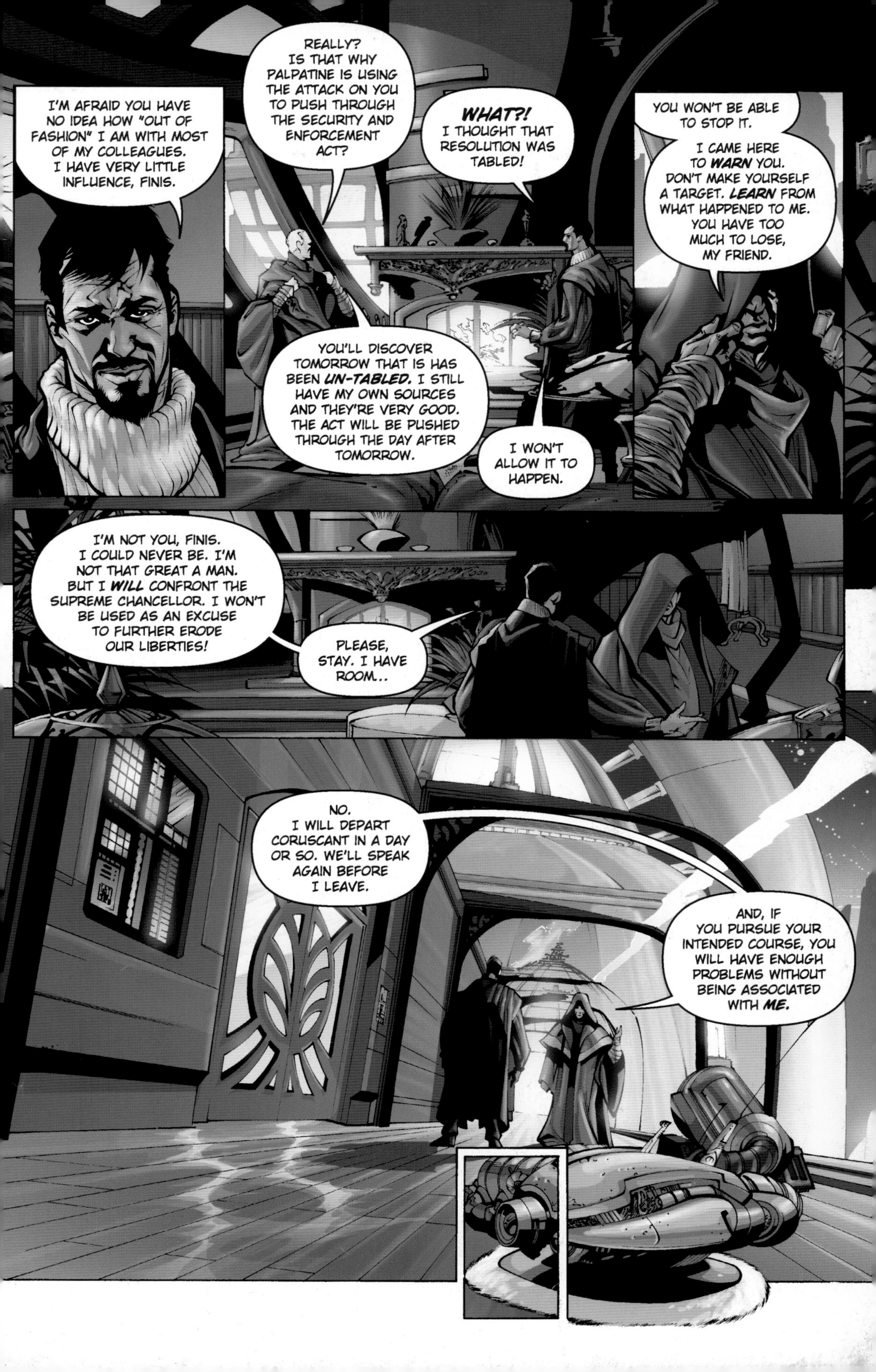
I'M AFRAID YOU HAVE NO IDEA HOW "OUT OF FASHION" I AM WITH MOST OF MY COLLEAGUES. I HAVE VERY LITTLE INFLUENCE, FINIS.
REALLY? IS THAT WHY PALPATINE IS USING THE ATTACK ON YOU TO PUSH THROUGH THE SECURITY AND ENFORCEMENT ACT?
WHAT?! I THOUGHT THAT RESOLUTION WAS TABLED!
YOU'LL DISCOVER TOMORROW THAT IS HAS BEEN UN-TABLED. I STILL HAVE MY OWN SOURCES AND THEY'RE VERY GOOD. THE ACT WILL BE PUSHED THROUGH THE DAY AFTER TOMORROW.
I WON'T ALLOW IT TO HAPPEN.
YOU WON'T BE ABLE TO STOP IT.
I CAME HERE TO WARN YOU. DON'T MAKE YOURSELF A TARGET. LEARN FROM WHAT HAPPENED TO ME. YOU HAVE TOO MUCH TO LOSE, MY FRIEND.
I'M NOT YOU, FINIS. I COULD NEVER BE. I'M NOT THAT GREAT A MAN. BUT I WILL CONFRONT THE SUPREME CHANCELLOR. I WON'T BE USED AS AN EXCUSE TO FURTHER ERODE OUR LIBERTIES!
PLEASE, STAY. I HAVE ROOM...
NO. I WILL DEPART CORUSCANT IN A DAY OR SO. WE'LL SPEAK AGAIN BEFORE I LEAVE.
AND, IF YOU PURSUE YOUR INTENDED COURSE, YOU WILL HAVE ENOUGH PROBLEMS WITHOUT BEING ASSOCIATED WITH ME.

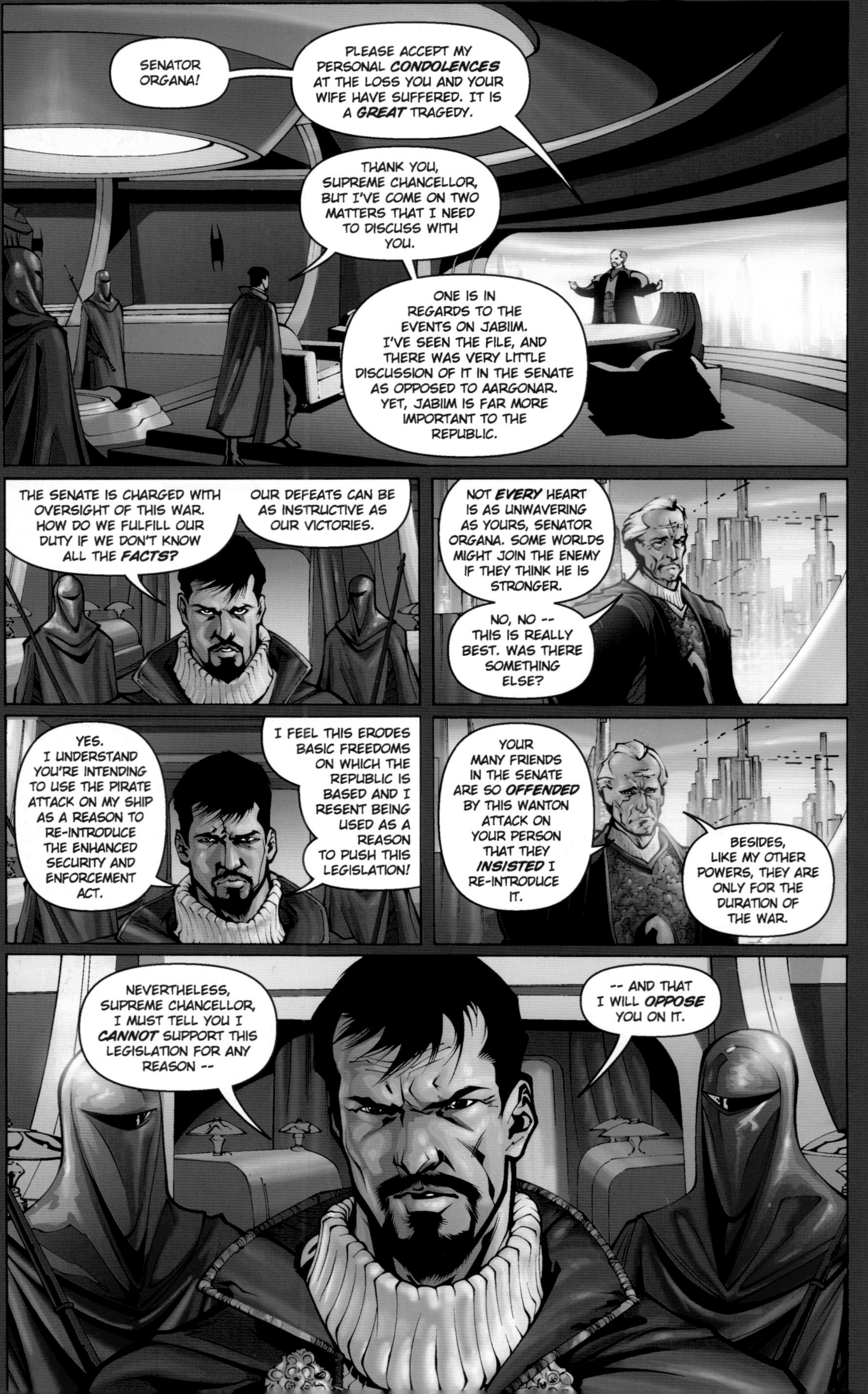
SENATOR ORGANA!
PLEASE ACCEPT MY PERSONAL CONDOLENCES AT THE LOSS YOU AND YOUR WIFE HAVE SUFFERED. IT IS A GREAT TRAGEDY.
THANK YOU, SUPREME CHANCELLOR, BUT I'VE COME ON TWO MATTERS THAT I NEED TO DISCUSS WITH YOU.
ONE IS IN REGARDS TO THE EVENTS ON JABIIM. I'VE SEEN THE FILE, AND THERE WAS VERY LITTLE DISCUSSION OF IT IN THE SENATE AS OPPOSED TO AARGONAR. YET, JABIIM IS FAR MORE IMPORTANT TO THE REPUBLIC.
THE SENATE IS CHARGED WITH OVERSIGHT OF THIS WAR. HOW DO WE FULFILL OUR DUTY IF WE DON'T KNOW ALL THE FACTS?
OUR DEFEATS CAN BE AS INSTRUCTIVE AS OUR VICTORIES.
NOT EVERY HEART IS AS UNWAVERING AS YOURS, SENATOR ORGANA. SOME WORLDS MIGHT JOIN THE ENEMY IF THEY THINK HE IS STRONGER.
NO, NO -- THIS IS REALLY BEST. WAS THERE SOMETHING ELSE?
YES. I UNDERSTAND YOU'RE INTENDING TO USE THE PIRATE ATTACK ON MY SHIP AS A REASON TO RE-INTRODUCE THE ENHANCED SECURITY AND ENFORCEMENT ACT.
I FEEL THIS ERODES BASIC FREEDOMS ON WHICH THE REPUBLIC IS BASED AND I RESENT BEING USED AS A REASON TO PUSH THIS LEGISLATION!
YOUR MANY FRIENDS IN THE SENATE ARE SO OFFENDED BY THIS WANTON ATTACK ON YOUR PERSON THAT THEY INSISTED I RE-INTRODUCE IT.
BESIDES, LIKE MY OTHER POWERS, THEY ARE ONLY FOR THE DURATION OF THE WAR.
NEVERTHELESS, SUPREME CHANCELLOR, I MUST TELL YOU I CANNOT SUPPORT THIS LEGISLATION FOR ANY REASON --
-- AND THAT I WILL OPPOSE YOU ON IT.

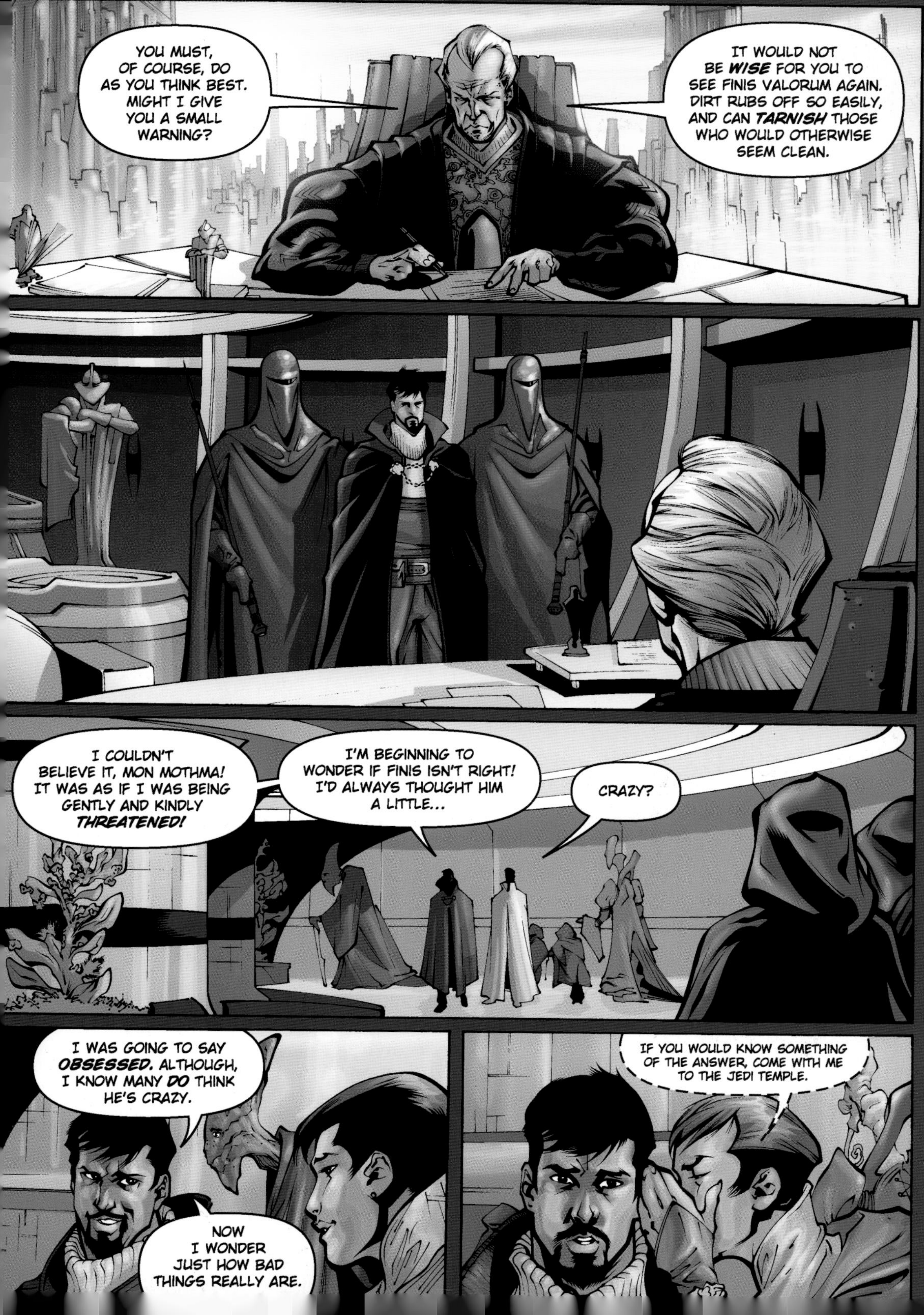

YOU MUST, OF COURSE, DO AS YOU THINK BEST. MIGHT I GIVE YOU A SMALL WARNING?
IT WOULD NOT BE WISE FOR YOU TO SEE FINIS VALORUM AGAIN. DIRT RUBS OFF SO EASILY, AND CAN TARNISH THOSE WHO WOULD OTHERWISE SEEM CLEAN.
I COULDN'T BELIEVE IT, MON MOTHMA! IT WAS AS IF I WAS BEING GENTLY AND KINDLY THREATENED!
I'M BEGINNING TO WONDER IF FINIS ISN'T RIGHT! I'D ALWAYS THOUGHT HIM A LITTLE...
CRAZY?
I WAS GOING TO SAY OBSESSED. ALTHOUGH, I KNOW MANY DO THINK HE'S CRAZY.
NOW I WONDER JUST HOW BAD THINGS REALLY ARE.
IF YOU WOULD KNOW SOMETHING OF THE ANSWER, COME WITH ME TO THE JEDI TEMPLE.

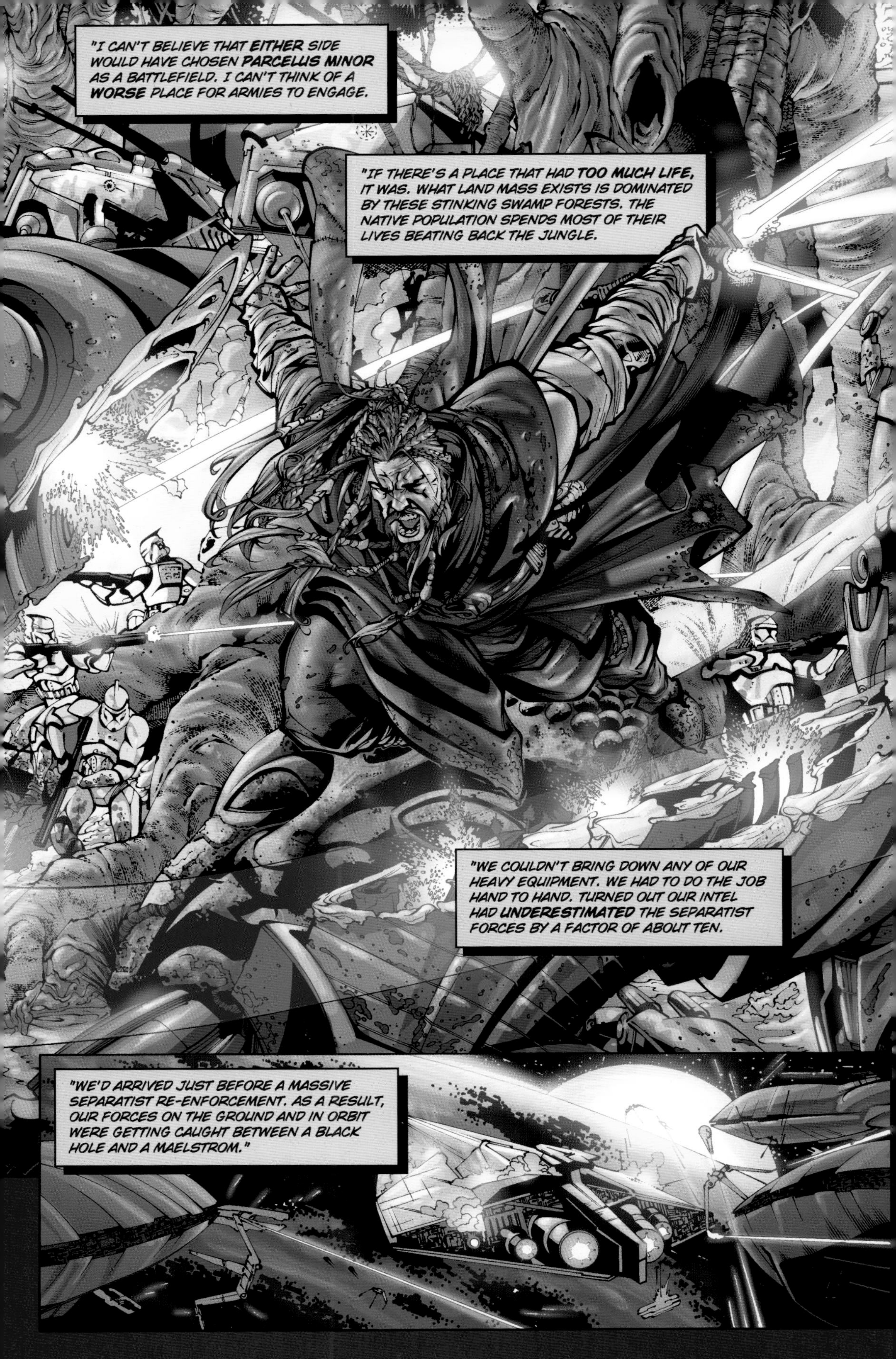
"I CAN'T BELIEVE THAT EITHER SIDE WOULD HAVE CHOSEN PARCELUS MINOR AS A BATTLEFIELD. I CAN'T THINK OF A WORSE PLACE FOR ARMIES TO ENGAGE.
"IF THERE'S A PLACE THAT HAD TOO MUCH LIFE, IT WAS. WHAT LAND MASS EXISTS IS DOMINATED BY THESE STINKING SWAMP FORESTS. THE NATIVE POPULATION SPENDS MOST OF THEIR LIVES BEATING BACK THE JUNGLE.
"WE COULDN'T BRING DOWN ANY OF OUR HEAVY EQUIPMENT. WE HAD TO DO THE JOB HAND TO HAND. TURNED OUT OUR INTEL HAD UNDERESTIMATED THE SEPARATIST FORCES BY A FACTOR OF ABOUT TEN.
"WE'D ARRIVED JUST BEFORE A MASSIVE SEPARATIST RE-ENFORCEMENT. AS A RESULT, OUR FORCES ON THE GROUND AND IN ORBIT WERE GETTING CAUGHT BETWEEN A BLACK HOLE AND A MAELSTROM."

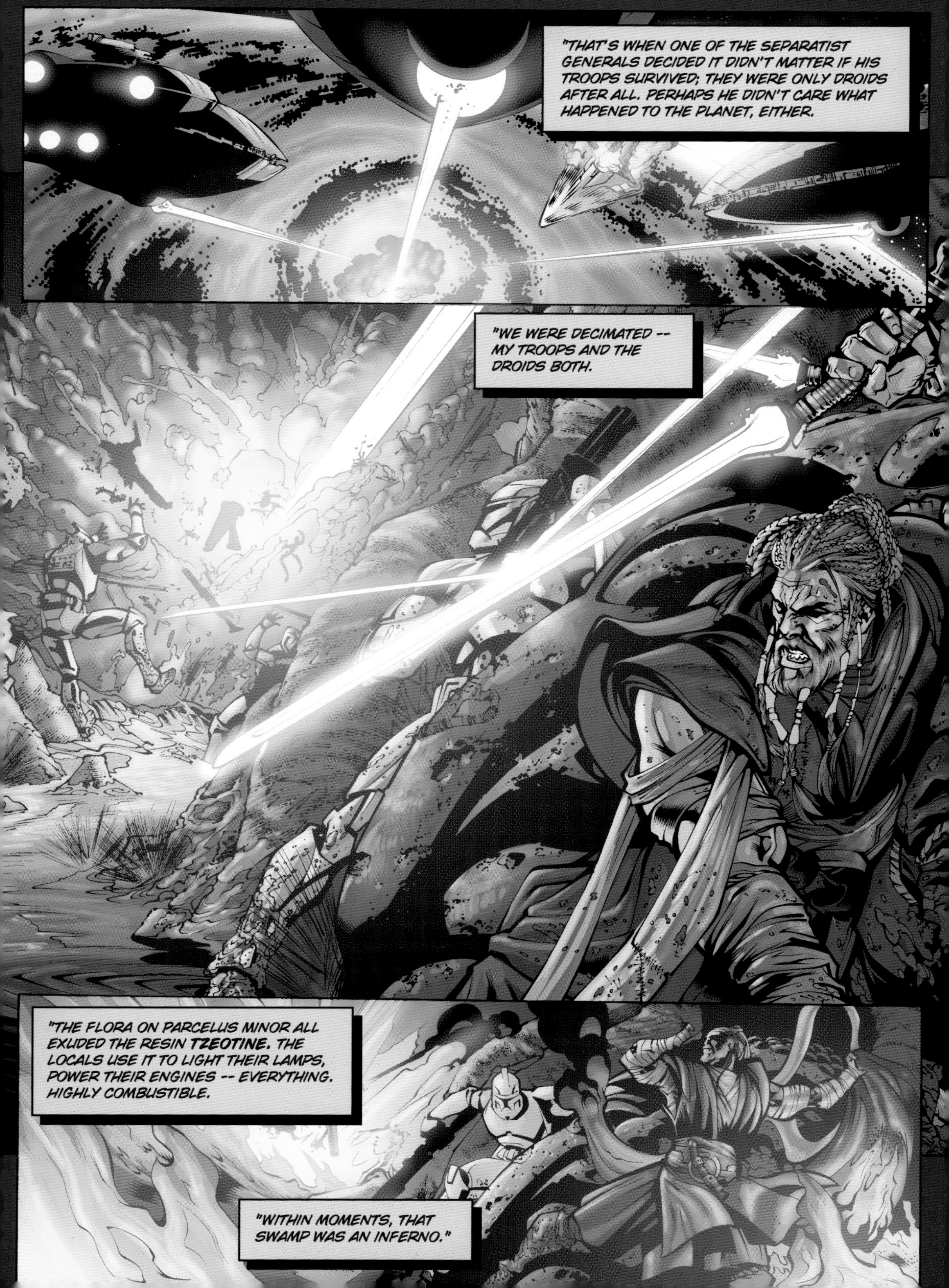
"THAT'S WHEN ONE OF THE SEPARATIST GENERALS DECIDED IT DIDN'T MATTER IF HIS TROOPS SURVIVED; THEY WERE ONLY DROIDS AFTER ALL. PERHAPS HE DIDN'T CARE WHAT HAPPENED TO THE PLANET, EITHER.
"WE WERE DECIMATED -- MY TROOPS AND THE DROIDS BOTH.
"THE FLORA ON PARCELUS MINOR ALL EXUDED THE RESIN TZEOTINE. THE LOCALS USE IT TO LIGHT THEIR LAMPS, POWER THEIR ENGINES -- EVERYTHING. HIGHLY COMBUSTIBLE.
"WITHIN MOMENTS, THAT SWAMP WAS AN INFERNO."

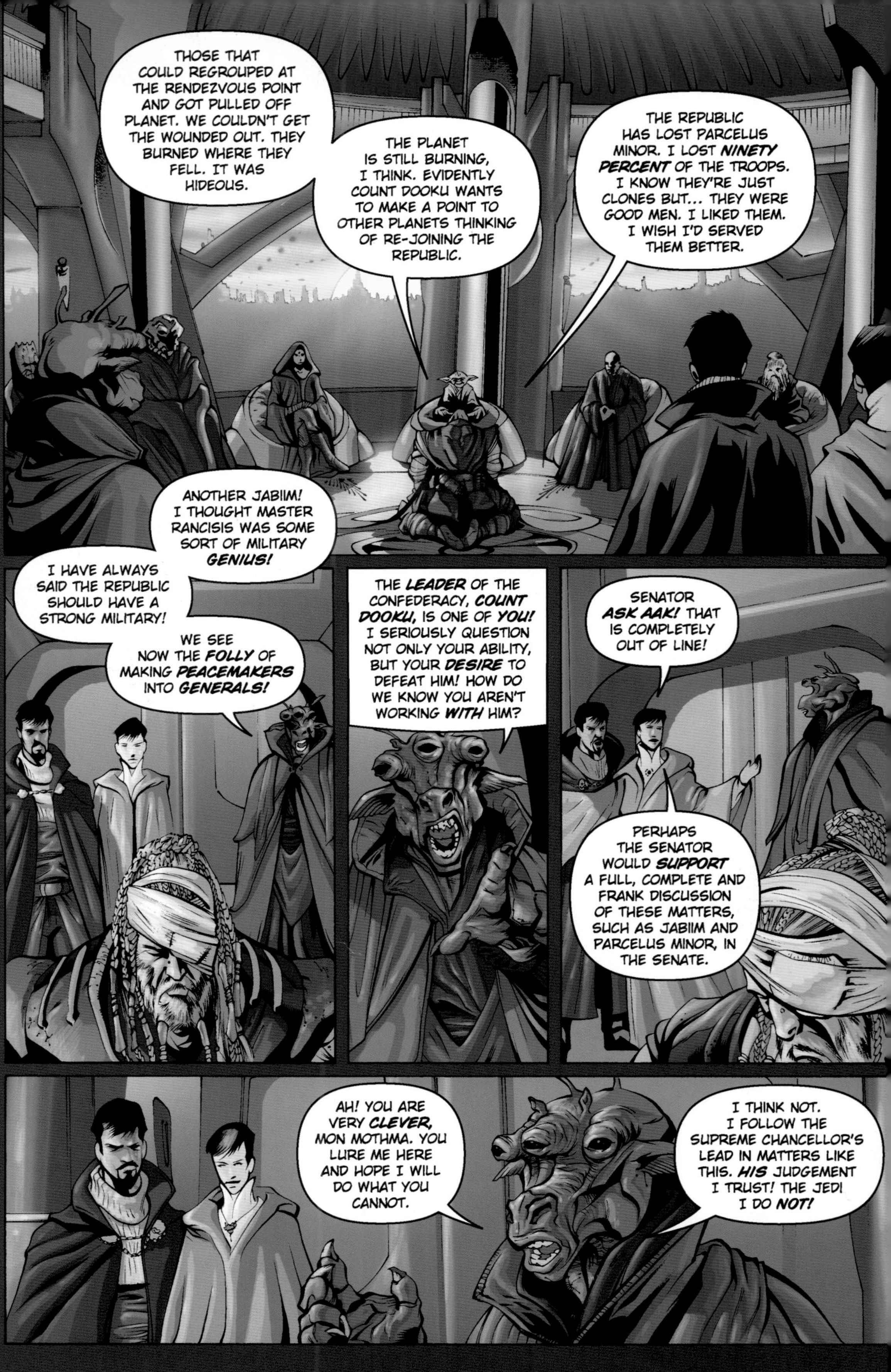
THOSE THAT COULD REGROUPED AT THE RENDEZVOUS POINT AND GOT PULLED OFF PLANET. WE COULDN'T GET THE WOUNDED OUT. THEY BURNED WHERE THEY FELL. IT WAS HIDEOUS.
THE PLANET IS STILL BURNING, I THINK. EVIDENTLY COUNT DOOKU WANTS TO MAKE A POINT TO OTHER PLANETS THINKING OF RE-JOINING THE REPUBLIC.
THE REPUBLIC HAS LOST PARCELUS MINOR. I LOST NINETY PERCENT OF THE TROOPS. I KNOW THEY'RE JUST CLONES BUT... THEY WERE GOOD MEN. I LIKED THEM. I WISH I'D SERVED THEM BETTER.
ANOTHER JABIIM! I THOUGHT MASTER RANCISIS WAS SOME SORT OF MILITARY GENIUS!
I HAVE ALWAYS SAID THE REPUBLIC SHOULD HAVE A STRONG MILITARY!
WE SEE NOW THE FOLLY OF MAKING PEACEMAKERS INTO GENERALS!
THE LEADER OF THE CONFEDERACY, COUNT DOOKU, IS ONE OF YOU! I SERIOUSLY QUESTION NOT ONLY YOUR ABILITY, BUT YOUR DESIRE TO DEFEAT HIM! HOW DO WE KNOW YOU AREN'T WORKING WITH HIM?
SENATOR ASK AAK! THAT IS COMPLETELY OUT OF LINE!
PERHAPS THE SENATOR WOULD SUPPORT A FULL, COMPLETE AND FRANK DISCUSSION OF THESE MATTERS, SUCH AS JABIIM AND PARCELUS MINOR, IN THE SENATE.
AH! YOU ARE VERY CLEVER, MON MOTHMA. YOU LURE ME HERE AND HOPE I WILL DO WHAT YOU CANNOT.
I THINK NOT. I FOLLOW THE SUPREME CHANCELLOR'S LEAD IN MATTERS LIKE THIS. HIS JUDGEMENT I TRUST! THE JEDI I DO NOT!

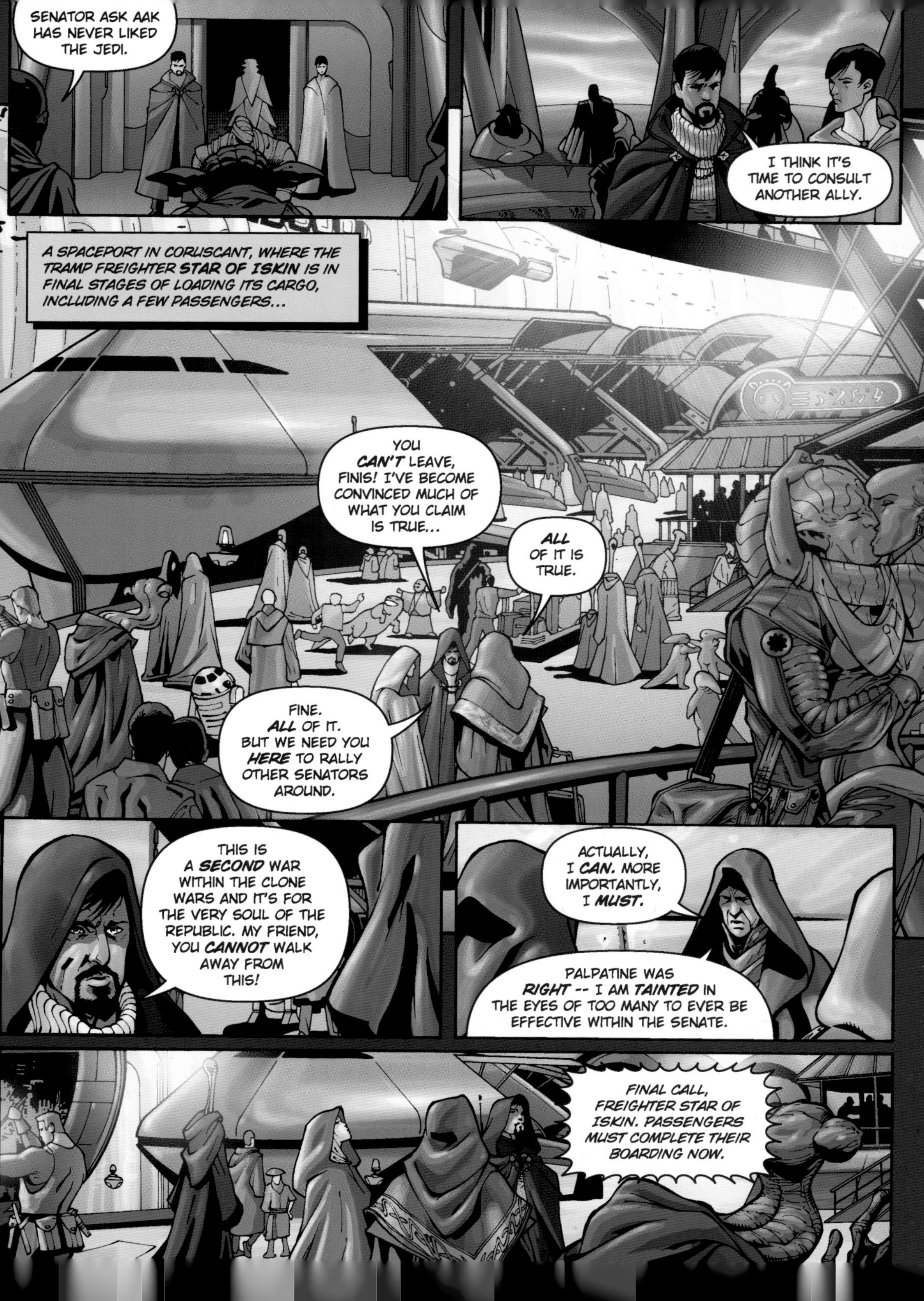

SENATOR ASK AAK HAS NEVER LIKED THE JEDI.
I THINK IT'S TIME TO CONSULT ANOTHER ALLY.
A SPACEPORT IN CORUSCANT, WHERE THE TRAMP FREIGHTER STAR OF ISKIN IS IN FINAL STAGES OF LOADING ITS CARGO, INCLUDING A FEW PASSENGERS...
YOU CAN'T LEAVE, FINIS! I'VE BECOME CONVINCED MUCH OF WHAT YOU CLAIM IS TRUE...
ALL OF IT IS TRUE.
FINE. ALL OF IT. BUT WE NEED YOU HERE TO RALLY OTHER SENATORS AROUND.
THIS IS A SECOND WAR WITHIN THE CLONE WARS AND IT'S FOR THE VERY SOUL OF THE REPUBLIC. MY FRIEND, YOU CANNOT WALK AWAY FROM THIS!
ACTUALLY, I CAN. MORE IMPORTANTLY, I MUST.
PALPATINE WAS RIGHT -- I AM TAINTED IN THE EYES OF TOO MANY TO EVER BE EFFECTIVE WITHIN THE SENATE.
FINAL CALL, FREIGHTER STAR OF ISKIN. PASSENGERS MUST COMPLETE THEIR BOARDING NOW.

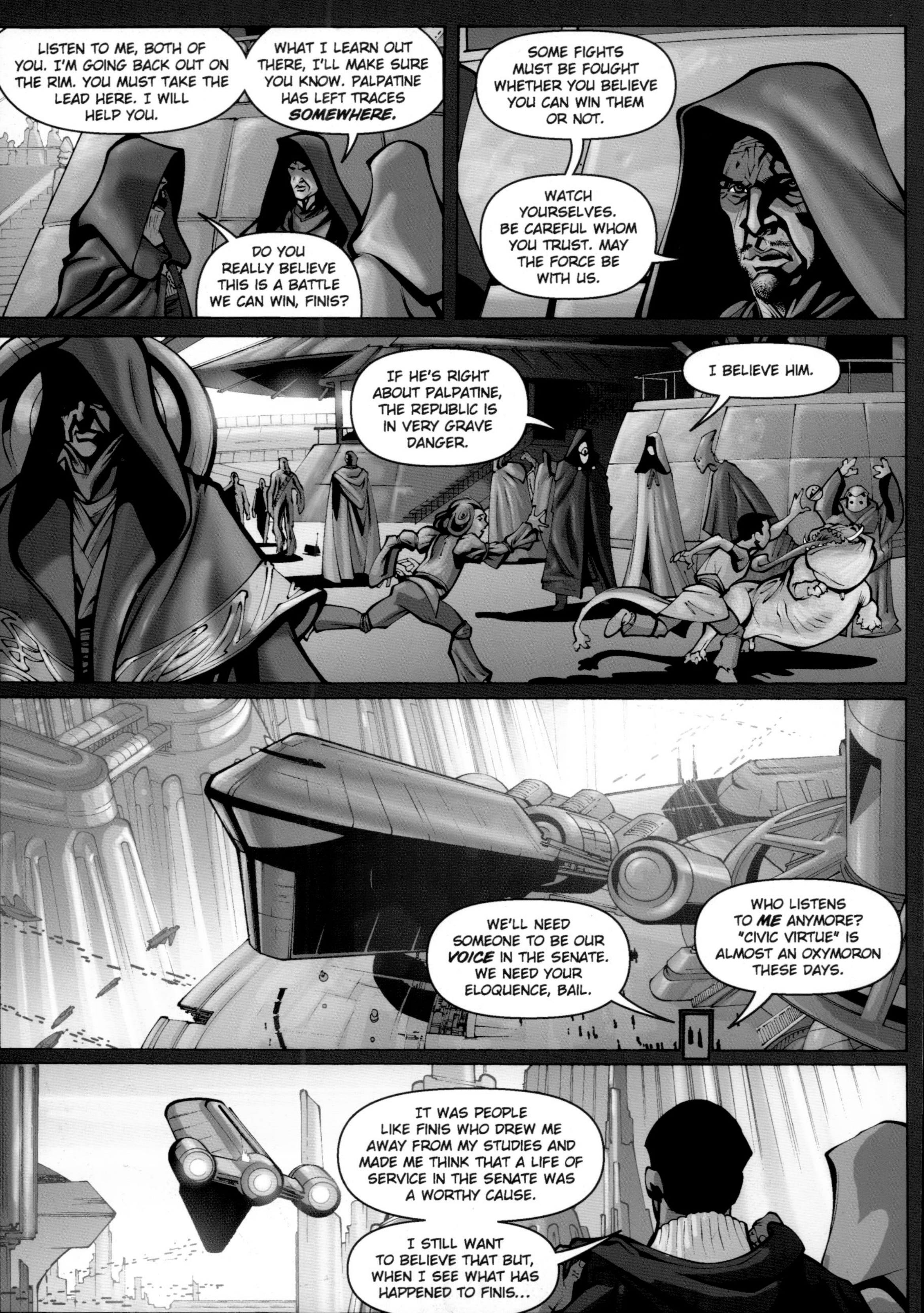
LISTEN TO ME, BOTH OF YOU. I'M GOING BACK OUT ON THE RIM. YOU MUST TAKE THE LEAD HERE. I WILL HELP YOU.
WHAT I LEARN OUT THERE, I'LL MAKE SURE YOU KNOW. PALPATINE HAS LEFT TRACES SOMEWHERE.
DO YOU REALLY BELIEVE THIS IS A BATTLE WE CAN WIN, FINIS?
SOME FIGHTS MUST BE FOUGHT WHETHER YOU BELIEVE YOU CAN WIN THEM OR NOT.
WATCH YOURSELVES. BE CAREFUL WHOM YOU TRUST. MAY THE FORCE BE WITH US.
IF HE'S RIGHT ABOUT PALPATINE, THE REPUBLIC IS IN VERY GRAVE DANGER.
I BELIEVE HIM.
WE'LL NEED SOMEONE TO BE OUR VOICE IN THE SENATE. WE NEED YOUR ELOQUENCE, BAIL.
WHO LISTENS TO ME ANYMORE? "CIVIC VIRTUE" IS ALMOST AN OXYMORON THESE DAYS.
IT WAS PEOPLE LIKE FINIS WHO DREW ME AWAY FROM MY STUDIES AND MADE ME THINK THAT A LIFE OF SERVICE IN THE SENATE WAS A WORTHY CAUSE.
I STILL WANT TO BELIEVE THAT BUT, WHEN I SEE WHAT HAS HAPPENED TO FINIS...

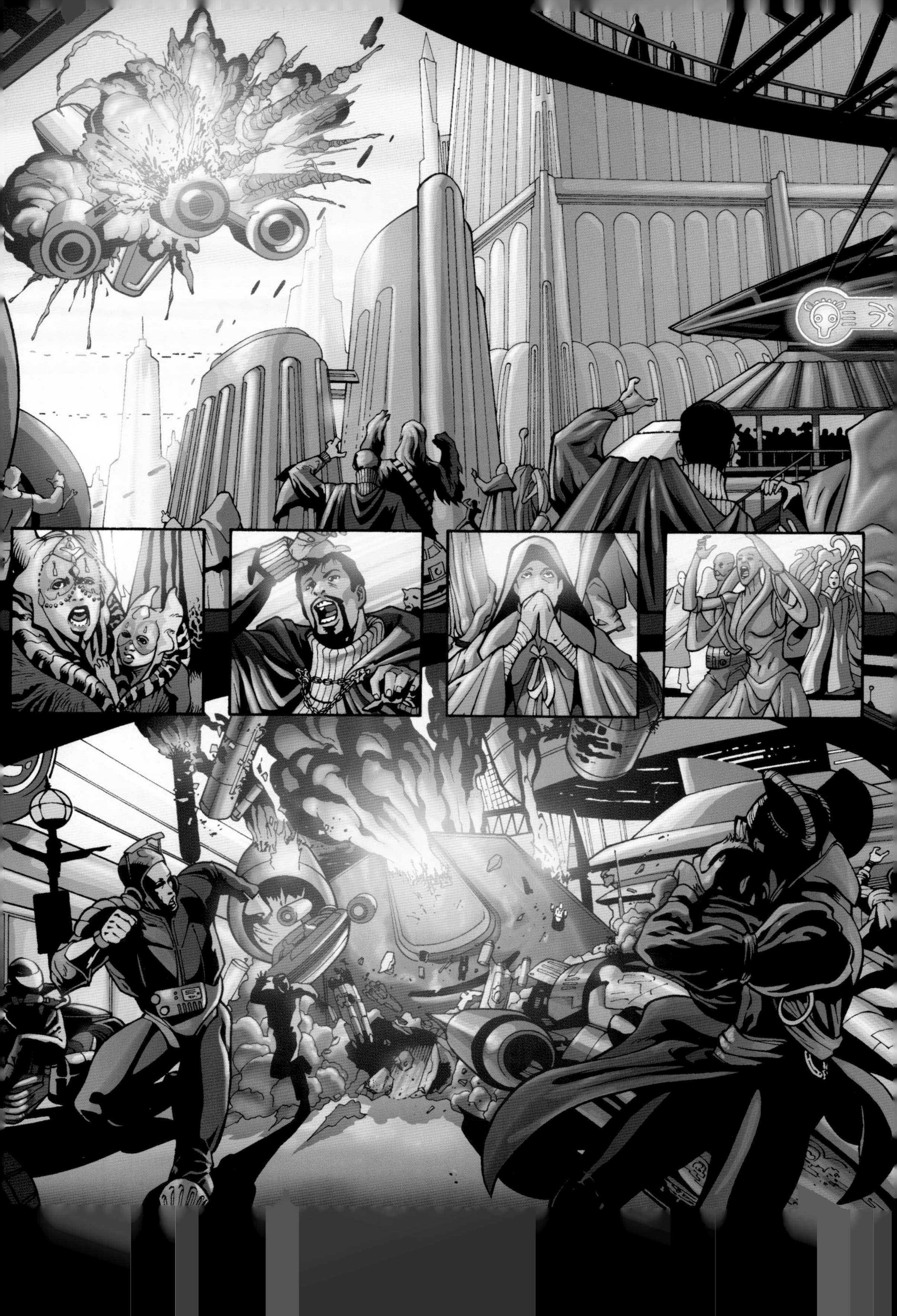

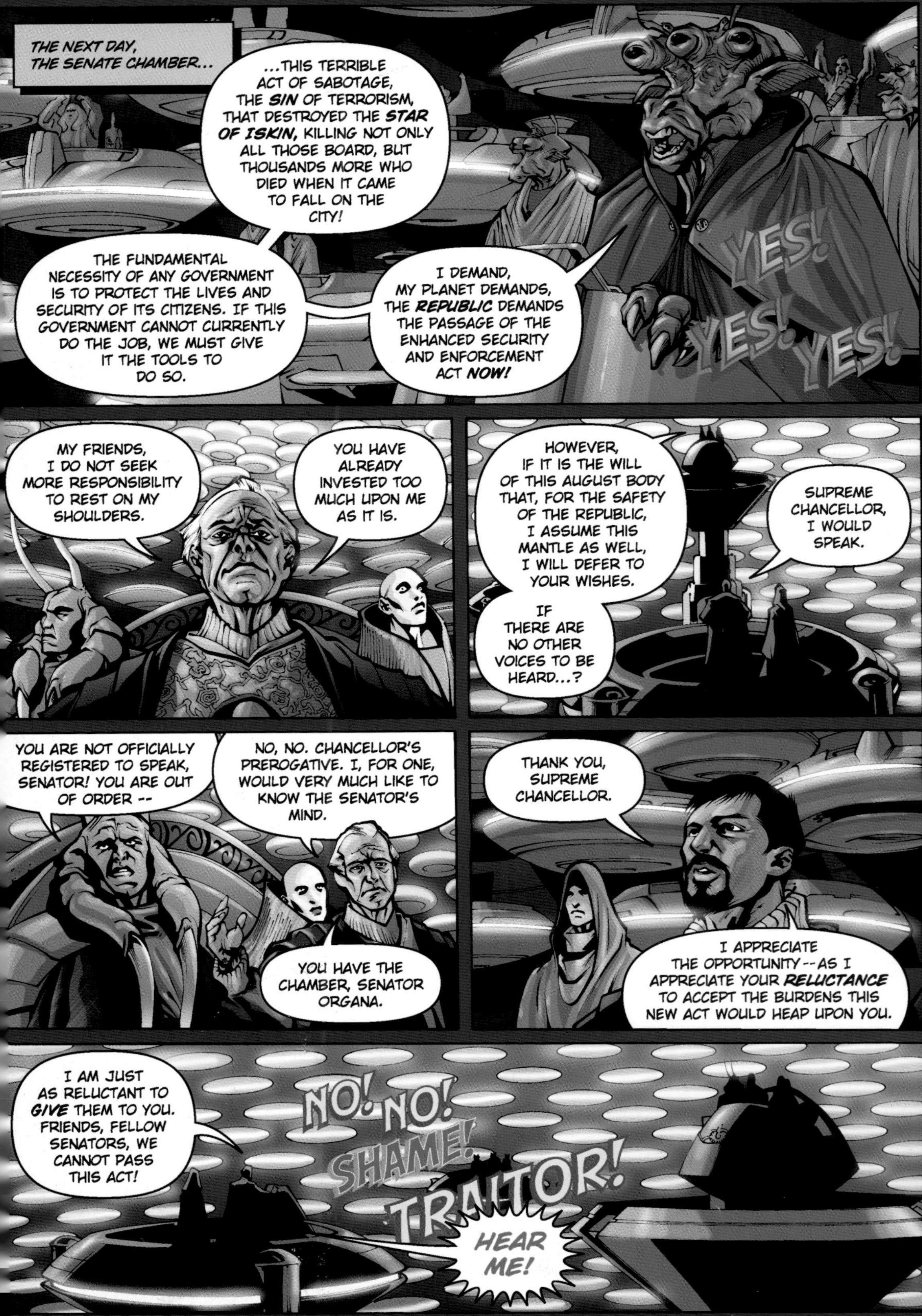
THE NEXT DAY, THE SENATE CHAMBER...
...THIS TERRIBLE ACT OF SABOTAGE, THE SIN OF TERRORISM, THAT DESTROYED THE STAR OF ISKIN, KILLING NOT ONLY ALL THOSE BOARD, BUT THOUSANDS MORE WHO DIED WHEN IT CAME TO FALL ON THE CITY!
THE FUNDAMENTAL NECESSITY OF ANY GOVERNMENT IS TO PROTECT THE LIVES AND SECURITY OF ITS CITIZENS. IF THIS GOVERNMENT CANNOT CURRENTLY DO THE JOB, WE MUST GIVE IT THE TOOLS TO DO SO.
I DEMAND, MY PLANET DEMANDS, THE REPUBLIC DEMANDS THE PASSAGE OF THE ENHANCED SECURITY AND ENFORCEMENT ACT NOW!
YES! YES! YES!
MY FRIENDS, I DO NOT SEEK MORE RESPONSIBILITY TO REST ON MY SHOULDERS.
YOU HAVE ALREADY INVESTED TOO MUCH UPON ME AS IT IS.
HOWEVER, IF IT IS THE WILL OF THIS AUGUST BODY THAT, FOR THE SAFETY OF THE REPUBLIC, I ASSUME THIS MANTLE AS WELL, I WILL DEFER TO YOUR WISHES.
IF THERE ARE NO OTHER VOICES TO BE HEARD...?
SUPREME CHANCELLOR, I WOULD SPEAK.
YOU ARE NOT OFFICIALLY REGISTERED TO SPEAK, SENATOR! YOU ARE OUT OF ORDER --
NO, NO. CHANCELLOR'S PREROGATIVE. I, FOR ONE, WOULD VERY MUCH LIKE TO KNOW THE SENATOR'S MIND.
YOU HAVE THE CHAMBER, SENATOR ORGANA.
THANK YOU, SUPREME CHANCELLOR.
I APPRECIATE THE OPPORTUNITY -- AS I APPRECIATE YOUR RELUCTANCE TO ACCEPT THE BURDENS THIS NEW ACT WOULD HEAP UPON YOU.
I AM JUST AS RELUCTANT TO GIVE THEM TO YOU. FRIENDS, FELLOW SENATORS, WE CANNOT PASS THIS ACT!
NO! NO! SHAME! TRAITOR!
HEAR ME!

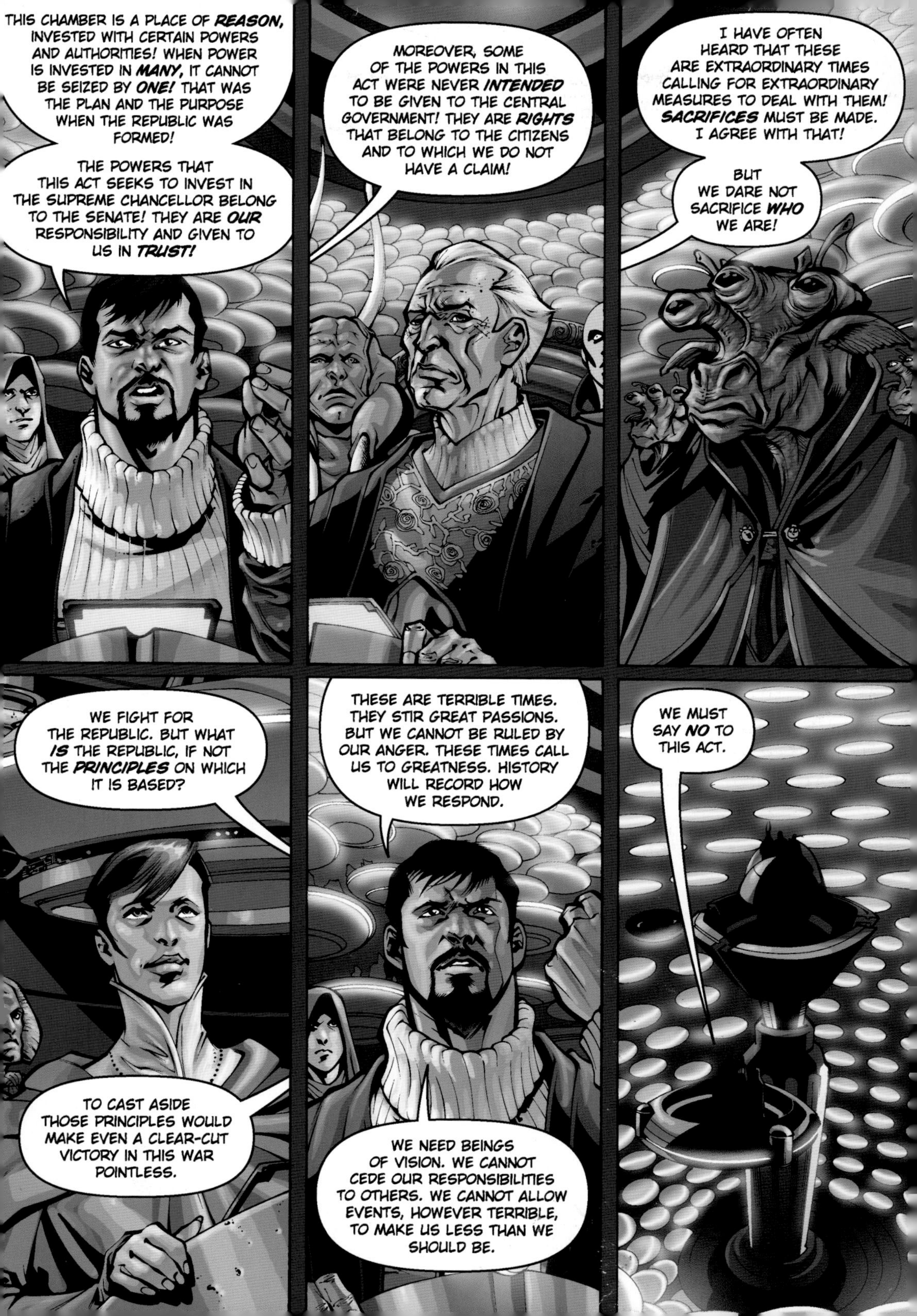
THIS CHAMBER IS A PLACE OF REASON, INVESTED WITH CERTAIN POWERS AND AUTHORITIES! WHEN POWER IS INVESTED IN MANY, IT CANNOT BE SEIZED BY ONE! THAT WAS THE PLAN AND THE PURPOSE WHEN THE REPUBLIC WAS FORMED!
THE POWERS THAT THIS ACT SEEKS TO INVEST IN THE SUPREME CHANCELLOR BELONG TO THE SENATE! THEY ARE OUR RESPONSIBILITY AND GIVEN TO US IN TRUST!
MOREOVER, SOME OF THE POWERS IN THIS ACT WERE NEVER INTENDED TO BE GIVEN TO THE CENTRAL GOVERNMENT! THEY ARE RIGHTS THAT BELONG TO THE CITIZENS AND TO WHICH WE DO NOT HAVE A CLAIM!
I HAVE OFTEN HEARD THAT THESE ARE EXTRAORDINARY TIMES CALLING FOR EXTRAORDINARY MEASURES TO DEAL WITH THEM! SACRIFICES MUST BE MADE. I AGREE WITH THAT!
BUT WE DARE NOT SACRIFICE WHO WE ARE!
WE FIGHT FOR THE REPUBLIC. BUT WHAT IS THE REPUBLIC, IF NOT THE PRINCIPLES ON WHICH IT IS BASED?
TO CAST ASIDE THOSE PRINCIPLES WOULD MAKE EVEN A CLEAR-CUT VICTORY IN THIS WAR POINTLESS.
THESE ARE TERRIBLE TIMES. THEY STIR GREAT PASSIONS. BUT WE CANNOT BE RULED BY OUR ANGER. THESE TIMES CALL US TO GREATNESS. HISTORY WILL RECORD HOW WE RESPOND.
WE NEED BEINGS OF VISION. WE CANNOT CEDE OUR RESPONSIBILITIES TO OTHERS. WE CANNOT ALLOW EVENTS, HOWEVER TERRIBLE, TO MAKE US LESS THAN WE SHOULD BE.
WE MUST SAY NO TO THIS ACT.

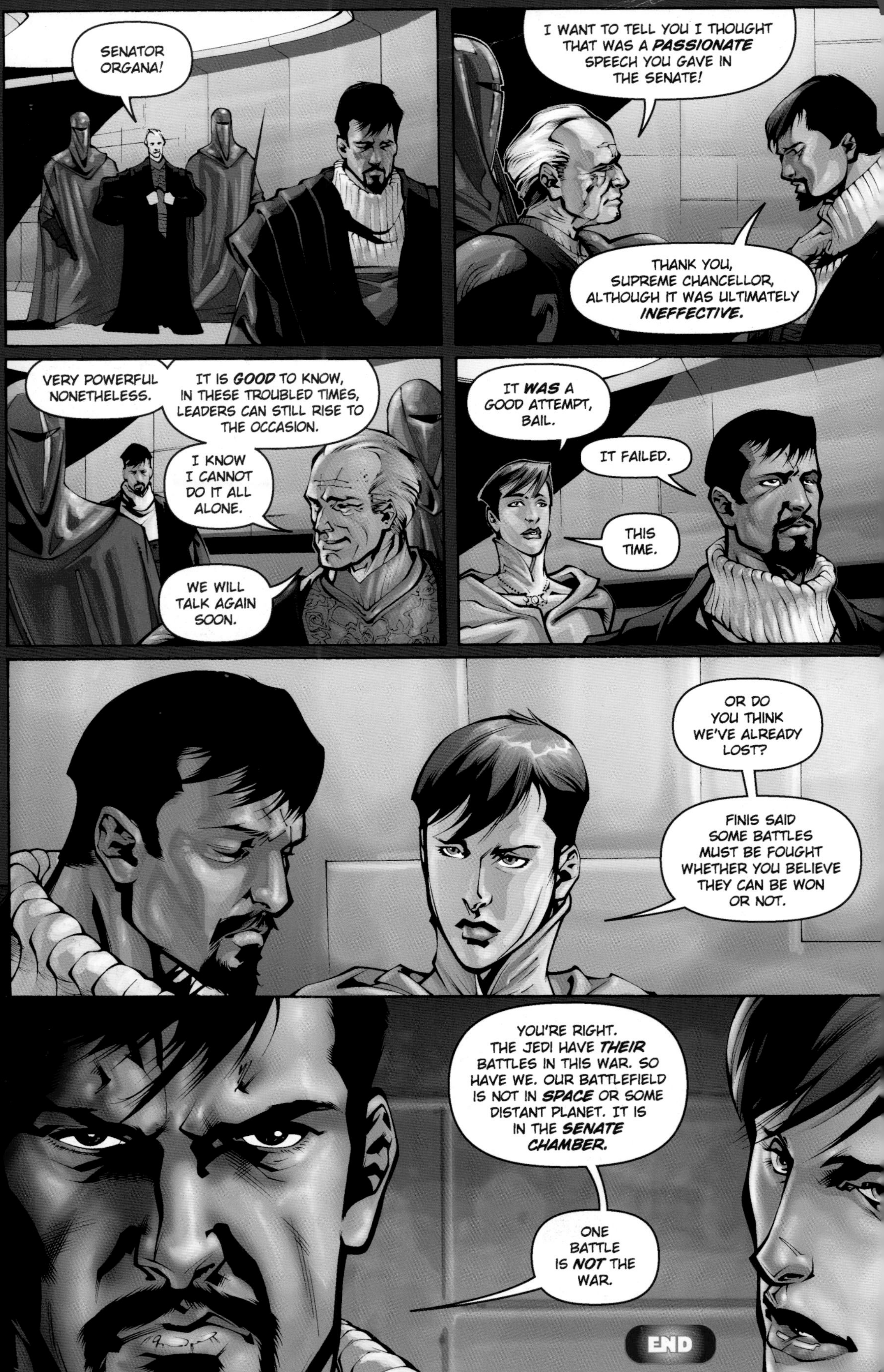
SENATOR ORGANA!
I WANT TO TELL YOU I THOUGHT THAT WAS A PASSIONATE SPEECH YOU GAVE IN THE SENATE!
THANK YOU, SUPREME CHANCELLOR, ALTHOUGH IT WAS ULTIMATELY INEFFECTIVE.
VERY POWERFUL NONETHELESS.
IT IS GOOD TO KNOW, IN THESE TROUBLED TIMES, LEADERS CAN STILL RISE TO THE OCCASION.
I KNOW I CANNOT DO IT ALL ALONE.
WE WILL TALK AGAIN SOON.
IT WAS A GOOD ATTEMPT, BAIL.
IT FAILED.
THIS TIME.
OR DO YOU THINK WE'VE ALREADY LOST?
FINIS SAID SOME BATTLES MUST BE FOUGHT WHETHER YOU BELIEVE THEY CAN BE WON OR NOT.
YOU'RE RIGHT. THE JEDI HAVE THEIR BATTLES IN THIS WAR. SO HAVE WE. OUR BATTLEFIELD IS NOT IN SPACE OR SOME DISTANT PLANET. IT IS IN THE SENATE CHAMBER.
ONE BATTLE IS NOT THE WAR.
END

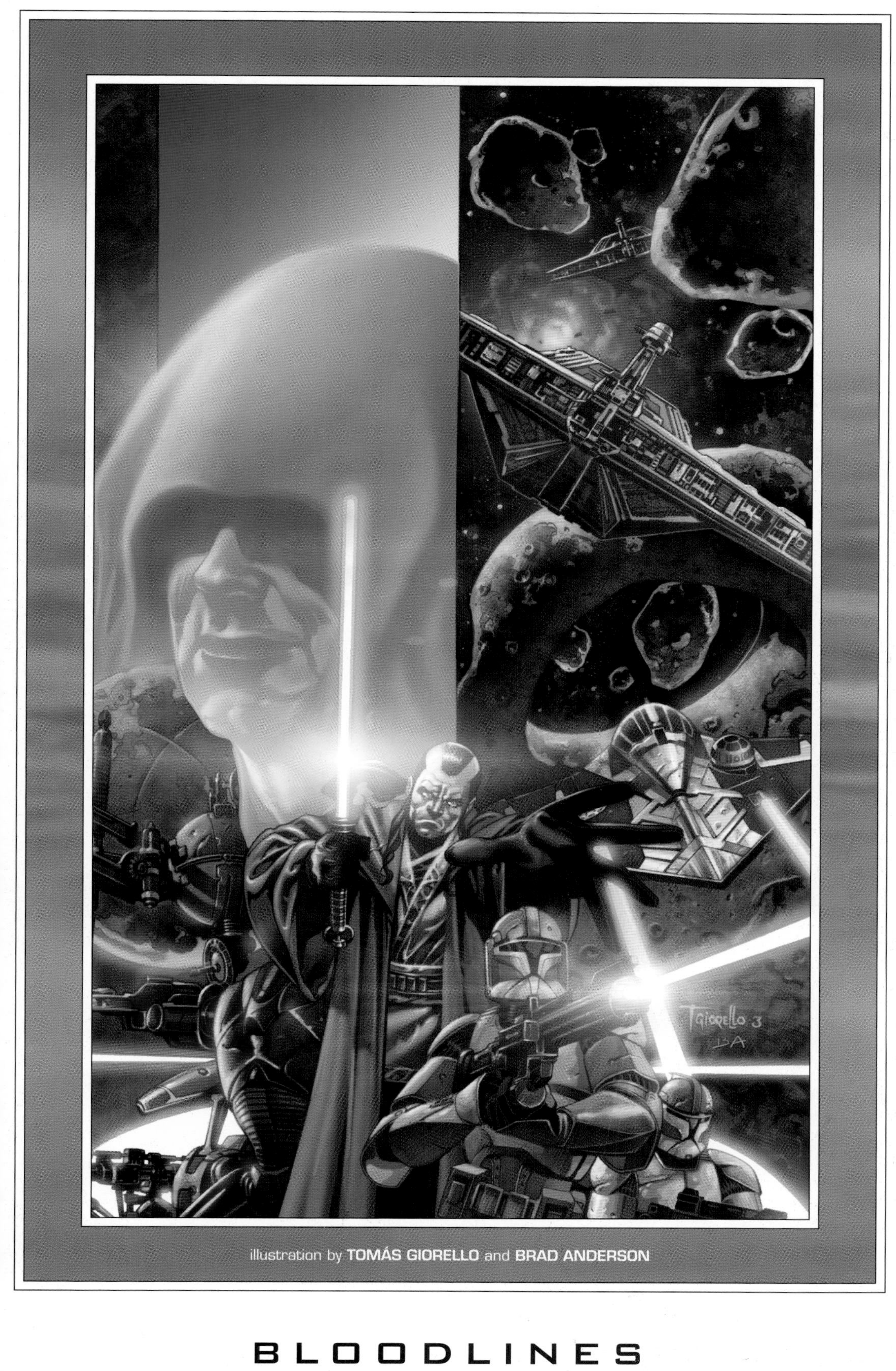

illustration by **TOMÁS GIORELLO** and **BRAD ANDERSON**

# BLOODLINES

**"Bloodlines"**
written by **John Ostrander**
art by **Brandon Badeaux**

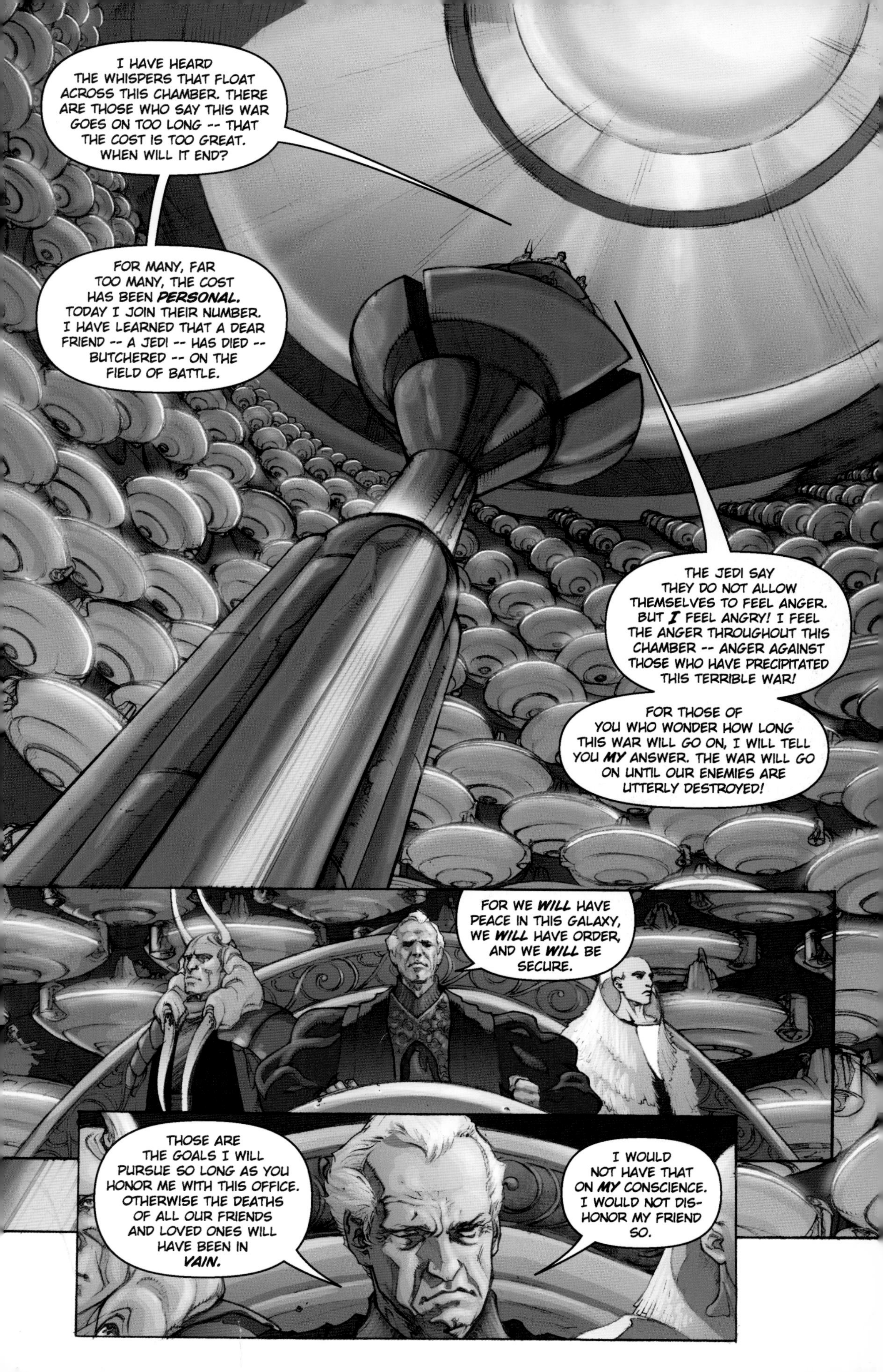
I HAVE HEARD THE WHISPERS THAT FLOAT ACROSS THIS CHAMBER. THERE ARE THOSE WHO SAY THIS WAR GOES ON TOO LONG -- THAT THE COST IS TOO GREAT. WHEN WILL IT END?
FOR MANY, FAR TOO MANY, THE COST HAS BEEN ***PERSONAL.*** TODAY I JOIN THEIR NUMBER. I HAVE LEARNED THAT A DEAR FRIEND -- A JEDI -- HAS DIED -- BUTCHERED -- ON THE FIELD OF BATTLE.
THE JEDI SAY THEY DO NOT ALLOW THEMSELVES TO FEEL ANGER. BUT ***I*** FEEL ANGRY! I FEEL THE ANGER THROUGHOUT THIS CHAMBER -- ANGER AGAINST THOSE WHO HAVE PRECIPITATED THIS TERRIBLE WAR!
FOR THOSE OF YOU WHO WONDER HOW LONG THIS WAR WILL GO ON, I WILL TELL YOU ***MY*** ANSWER. THE WAR WILL GO ON UNTIL OUR ENEMIES ARE UTTERLY DESTROYED!
FOR WE ***WILL*** HAVE PEACE IN THIS GALAXY, WE ***WILL*** HAVE ORDER, AND WE ***WILL*** BE SECURE.
THOSE ARE THE GOALS I WILL PURSUE SO LONG AS YOU HONOR ME WITH THIS OFFICE. OTHERWISE THE DEATHS OF ALL OUR FRIENDS AND LOVED ONES WILL HAVE BEEN IN ***VAIN.***
I WOULD NOT HAVE THAT ON ***MY*** CONSCIENCE. I WOULD NOT DIS-HONOR MY FRIEND SO.

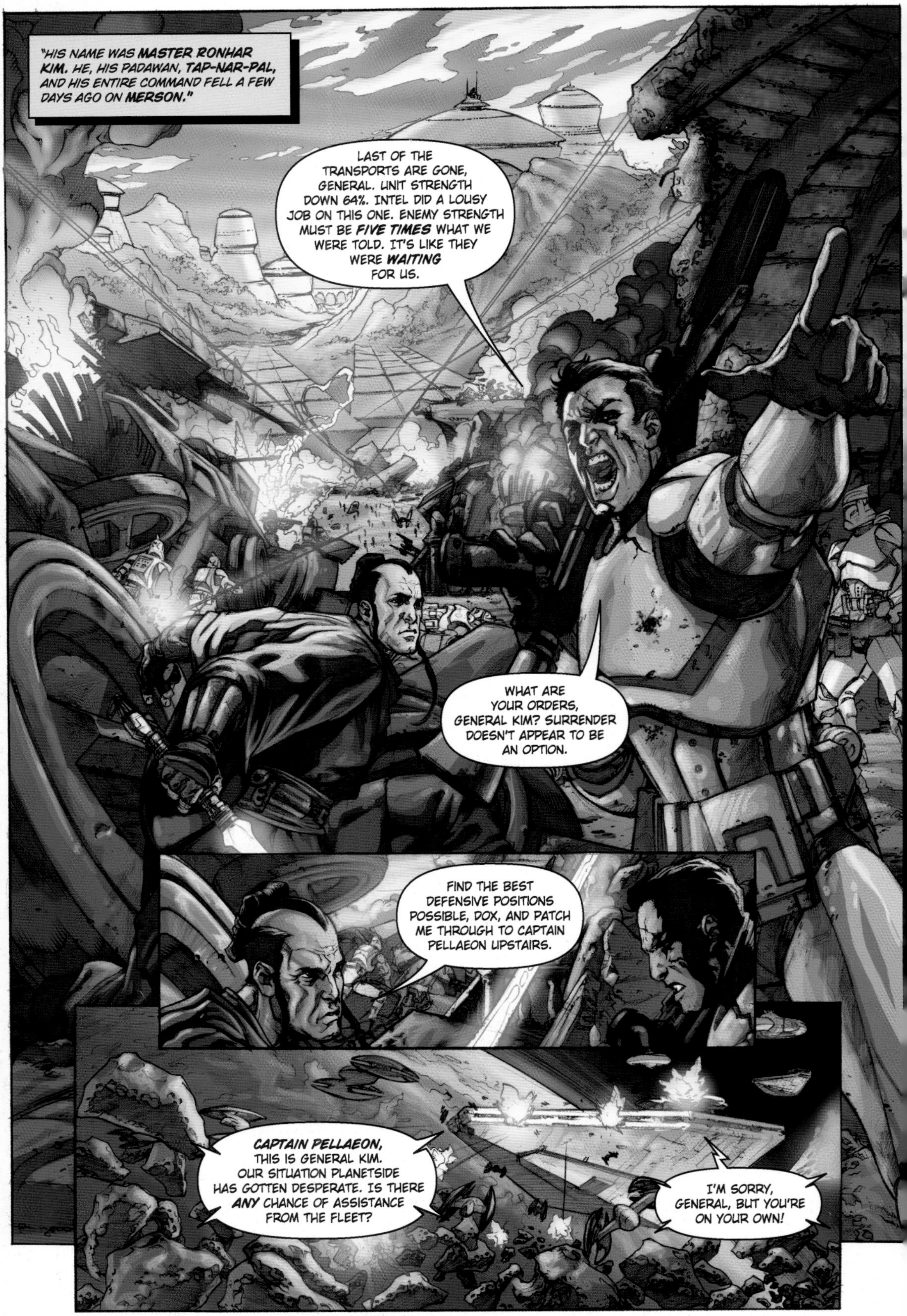
"HIS NAME WAS MASTER RONHAR KIM. HE, HIS PADAWAN, TAP-NAR-PAL, AND HIS ENTIRE COMMAND FELL A FEW DAYS AGO ON MERSON."
LAST OF THE TRANSPORTS ARE GONE, GENERAL. UNIT STRENGTH DOWN 64%. INTEL DID A LOUSY JOB ON THIS ONE. ENEMY STRENGTH MUST BE FIVE TIMES WHAT WE WERE TOLD. IT'S LIKE THEY WERE WAITING FOR US.
WHAT ARE YOUR ORDERS, GENERAL KIM? SURRENDER DOESN'T APPEAR TO BE AN OPTION.
FIND THE BEST DEFENSIVE POSITIONS POSSIBLE, DOX, AND PATCH ME THROUGH TO CAPTAIN PELLAEON UPSTAIRS.
CAPTAIN PELLAEON, THIS IS GENERAL KIM. OUR SITUATION PLANETSIDE HAS GOTTEN DESPERATE. IS THERE ANY CHANCE OF ASSISTANCE FROM THE FLEET?
I'M SORRY, GENERAL, BUT YOU'RE ON YOUR OWN!

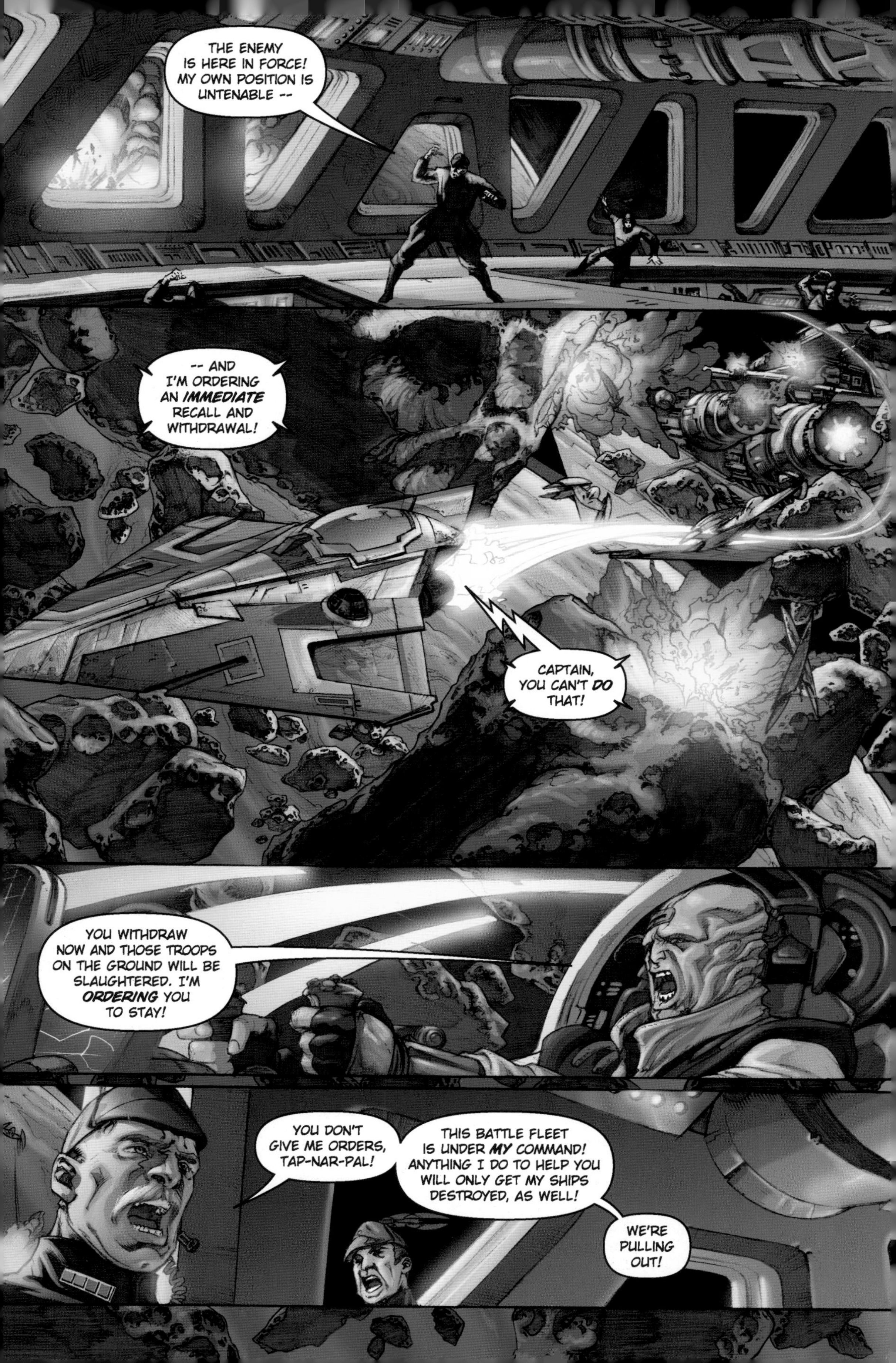
THE ENEMY IS HERE IN FORCE! MY OWN POSITION IS UNTENABLE --
-- AND I'M ORDERING AN IMMEDIATE RECALL AND WITHDRAWAL!
CAPTAIN, YOU CAN'T DO THAT!
YOU WITHDRAW NOW AND THOSE TROOPS ON THE GROUND WILL BE SLAUGHTERED. I'M ORDERING YOU TO STAY!
YOU DON'T GIVE ME ORDERS, TAP-NAR-PAL!
THIS BATTLE FLEET IS UNDER MY COMMAND! ANYTHING I DO TO HELP YOU WILL ONLY GET MY SHIPS DESTROYED, AS WELL!
WE'RE PULLING OUT!

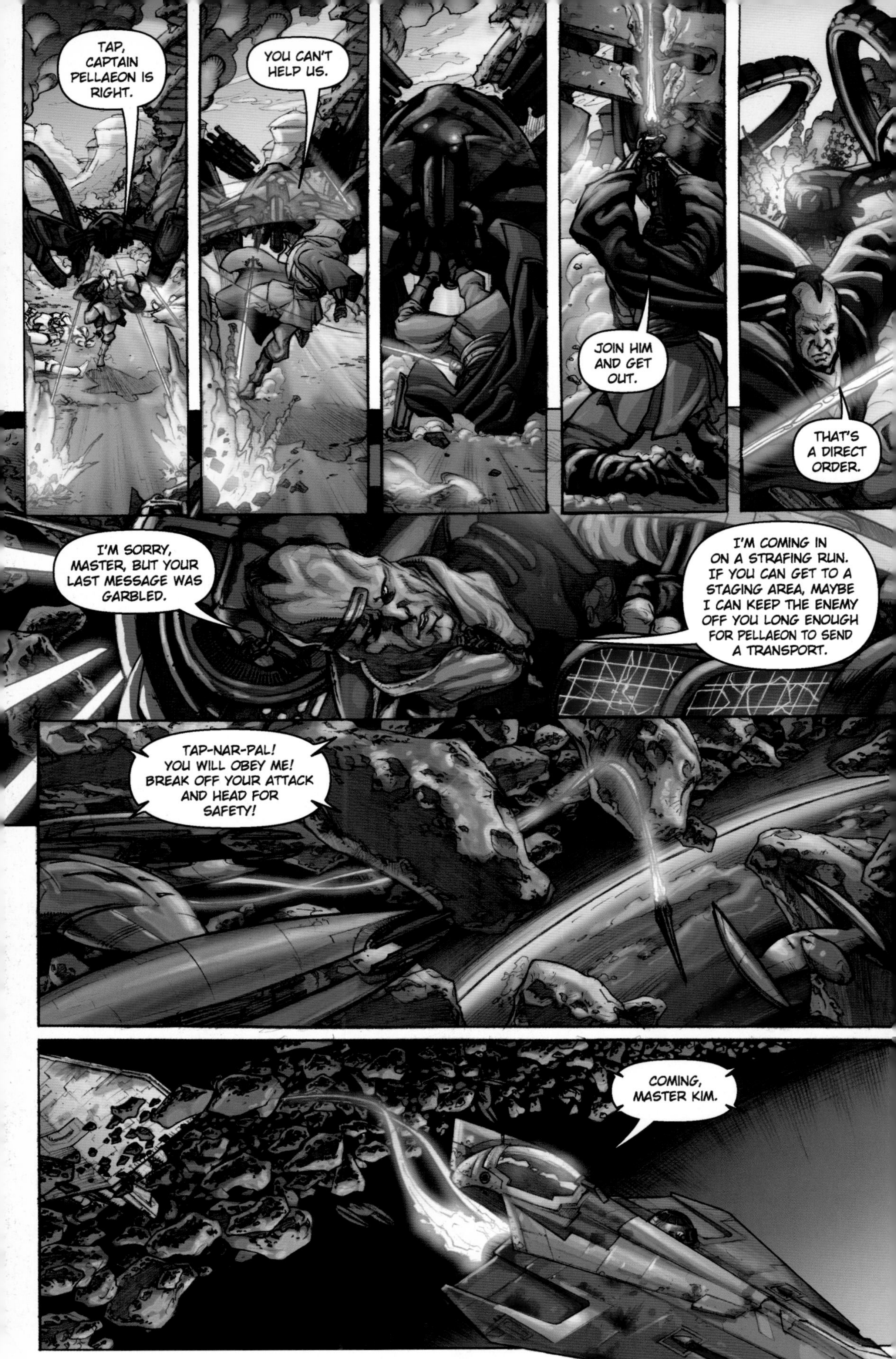

TAP, CAPTAIN PELLAEON IS RIGHT.
YOU CAN'T HELP US.
JOIN HIM AND GET OUT.
THAT'S A DIRECT ORDER.
I'M SORRY, MASTER, BUT YOUR LAST MESSAGE WAS GARBLED.
I'M COMING IN ON A STRAFING RUN. IF YOU CAN GET TO A STAGING AREA, MAYBE I CAN KEEP THE ENEMY OFF YOU LONG ENOUGH FOR PELLAEON TO SEND A TRANSPORT.
TAP-NAR-PAL! YOU WILL OBEY ME! BREAK OFF YOUR ATTACK AND HEAD FOR SAFETY!
COMING, MASTER KIM.

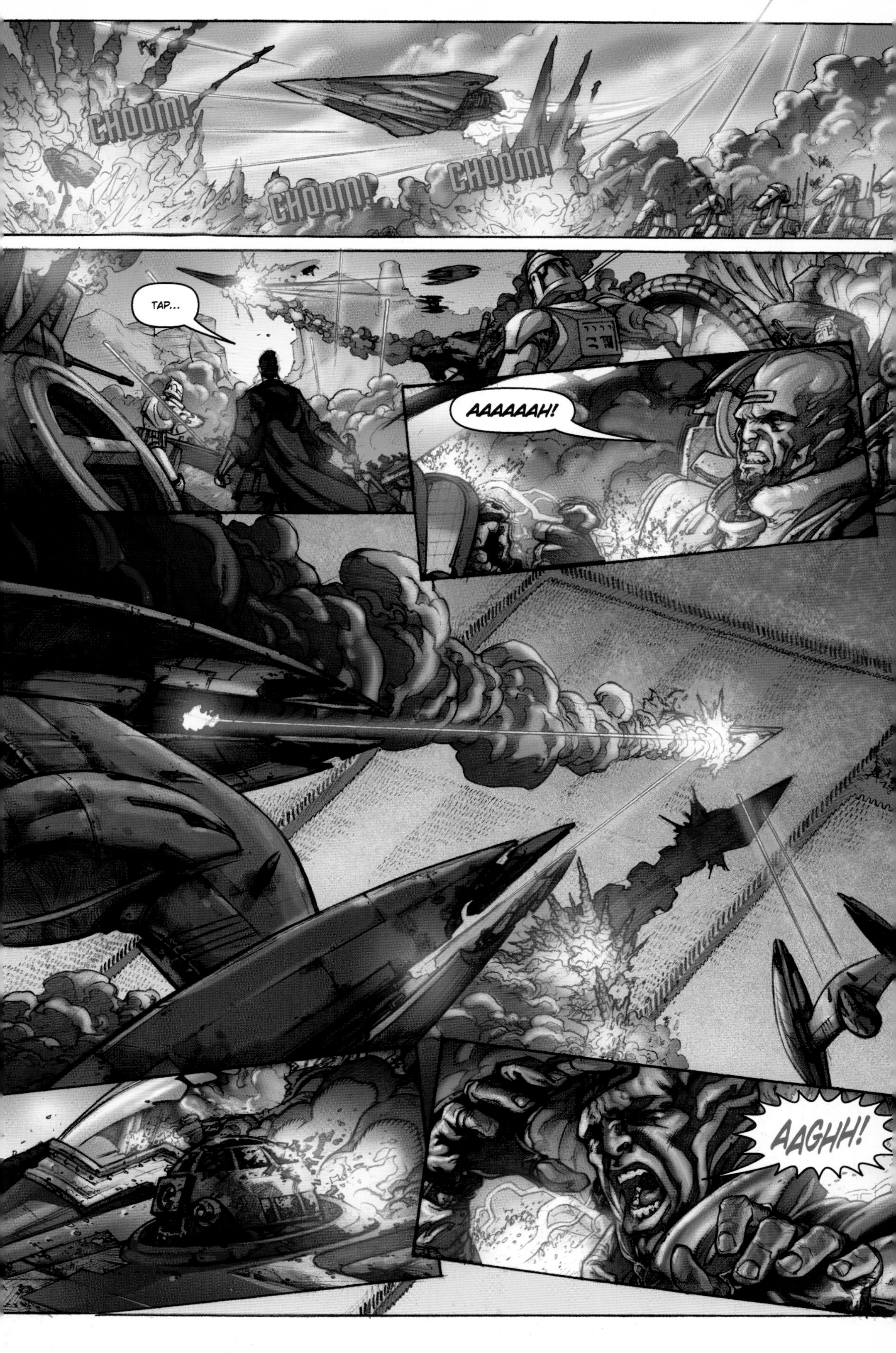
CHOOM!
CHOOM!
CHOOM!
TAP...
AAAAAAH!
AAGHH!

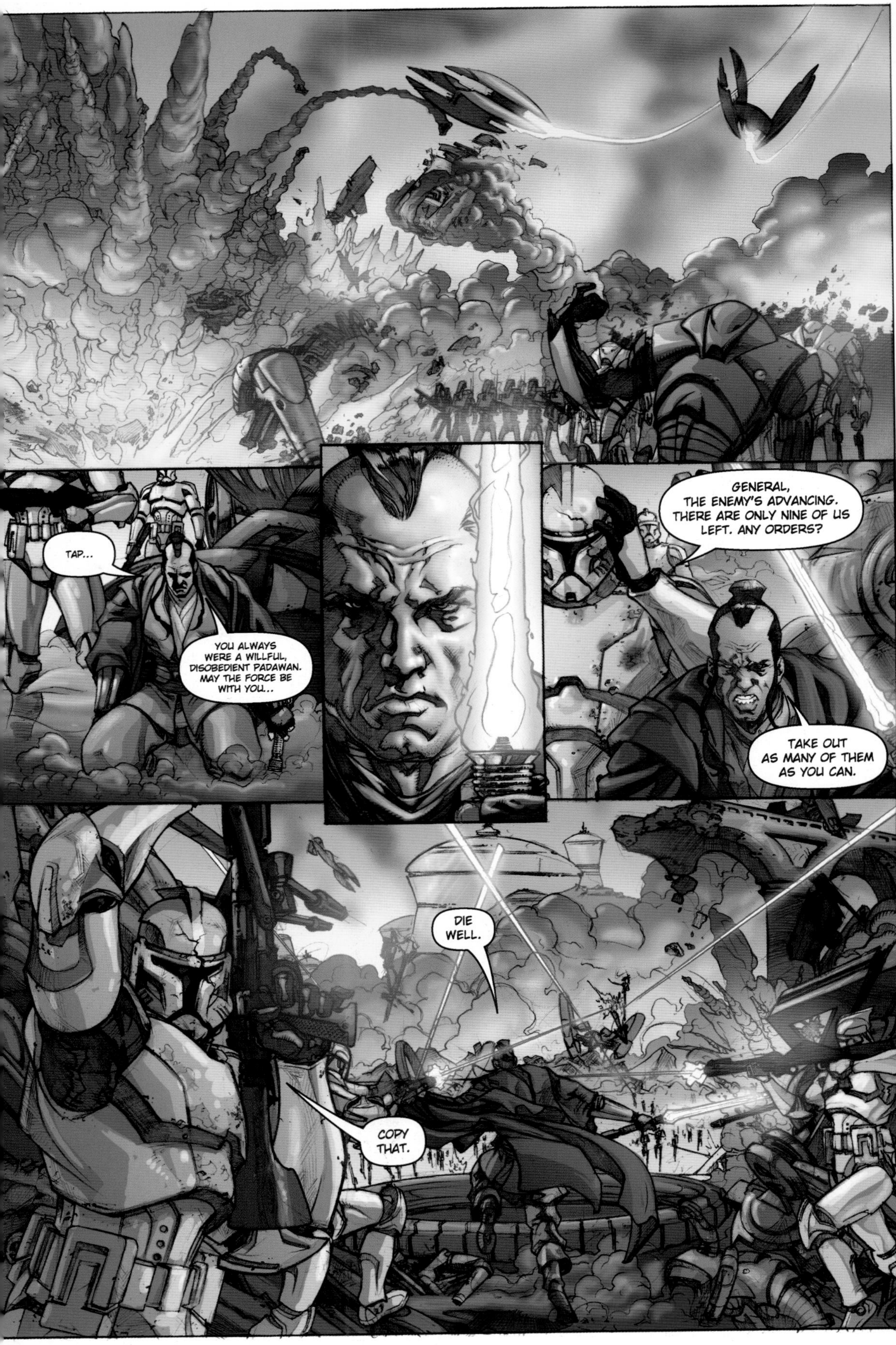
TAP...
YOU ALWAYS WERE A WILLFUL, DISOBEDIENT PADAWAN. MAY THE FORCE BE WITH YOU...
GENERAL, THE ENEMY'S ADVANCING. THERE ARE ONLY NINE OF US LEFT. ANY ORDERS?
TAKE OUT AS MANY OF THEM AS YOU CAN.
DIE WELL.
COPY THAT.

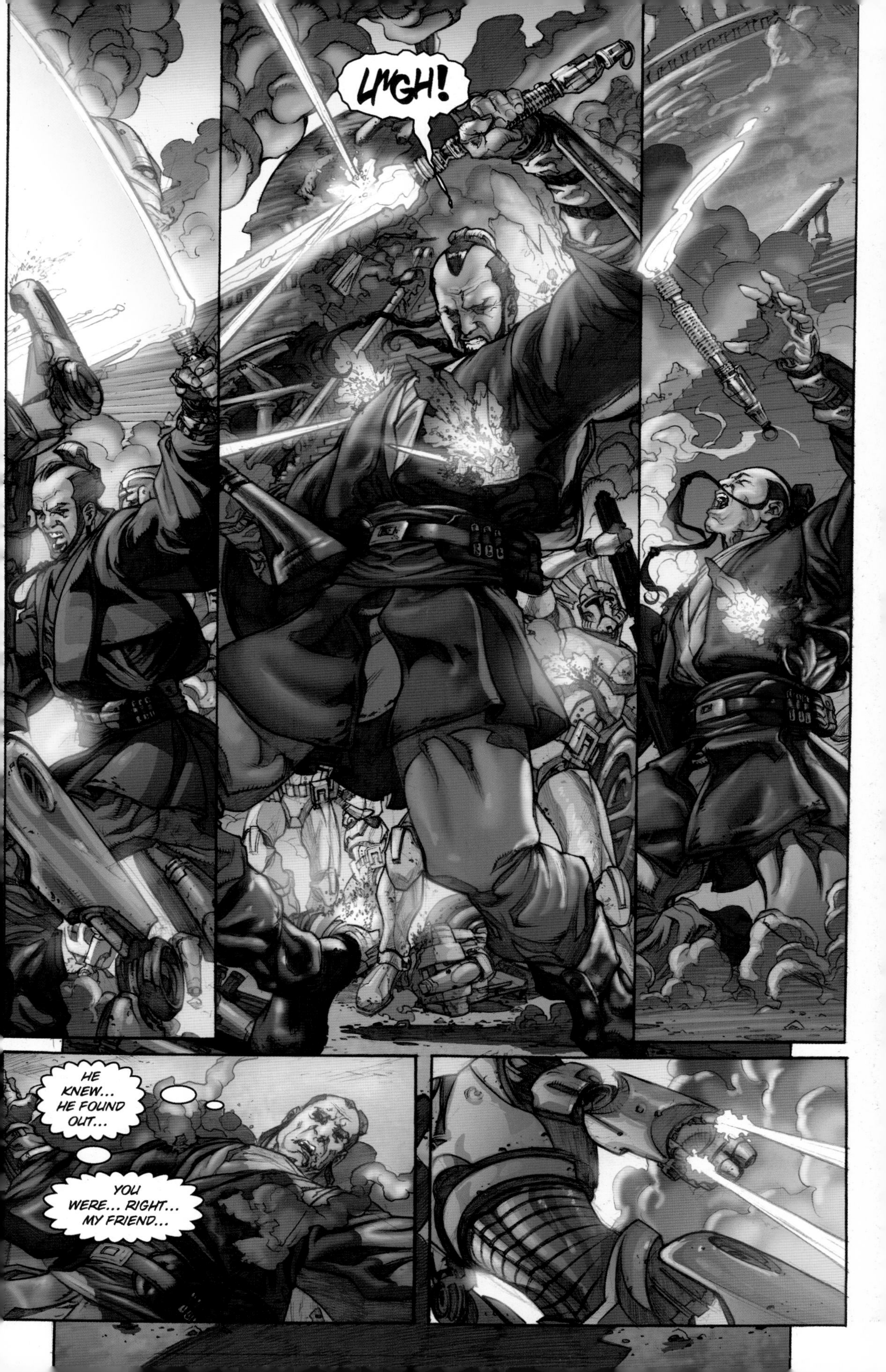
UNGH!
HE KNEW... HE FOUND OUT...
YOU WERE... RIGHT... MY FRIEND...

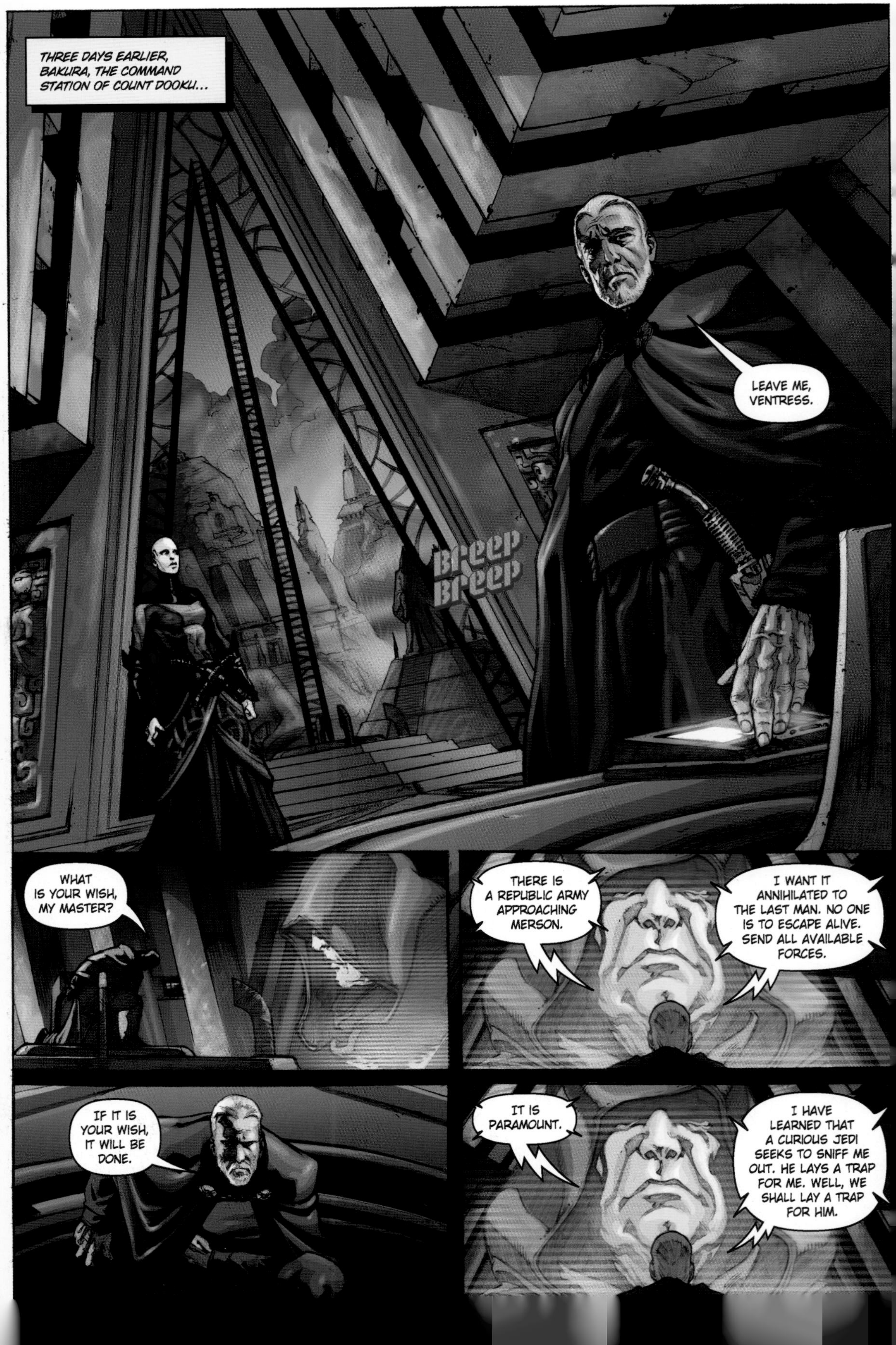
THREE DAYS EARLIER, BAKURA, THE COMMAND STATION OF COUNT DOOKU...
LEAVE ME, VENTRESS.
BREEP BREEP
WHAT IS YOUR WISH, MY MASTER?
THERE IS A REPUBLIC ARMY APPROACHING MERSON.
I WANT IT ANNIHILATED TO THE LAST MAN. NO ONE IS TO ESCAPE ALIVE. SEND ALL AVAILABLE FORCES.
IF IT IS YOUR WISH, IT WILL BE DONE.
IT IS PARAMOUNT.
I HAVE LEARNED THAT A CURIOUS JEDI SEEKS TO SNIFF ME OUT. HE LAYS A TRAP FOR ME. WELL, WE SHALL LAY A TRAP FOR HIM.

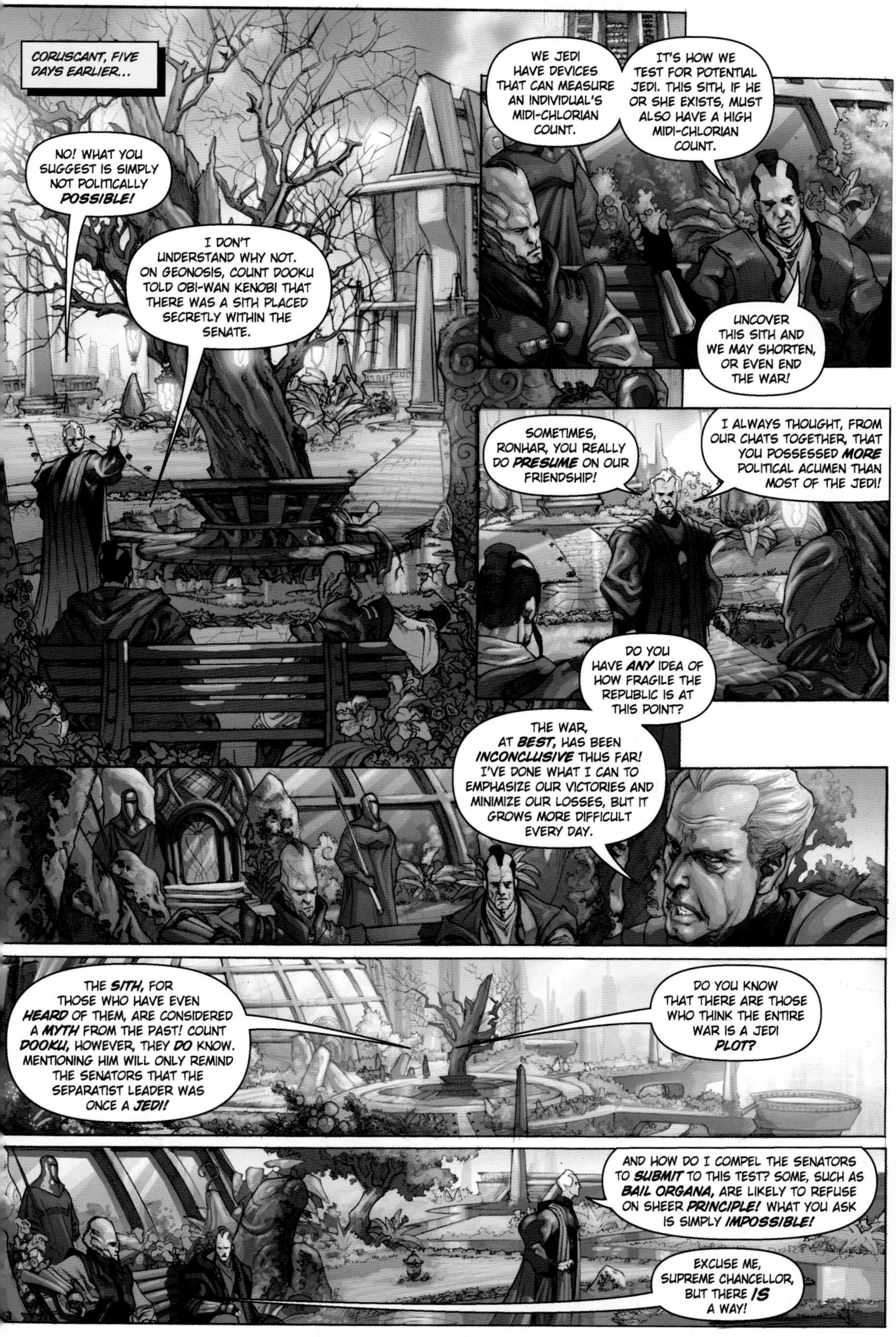
CORUSCANT, FIVE DAYS EARLIER...
NO! WHAT YOU SUGGEST IS SIMPLY NOT POLITICALLY POSSIBLE!
I DON'T UNDERSTAND WHY NOT. ON GEONOSIS, COUNT DOOKU TOLD OBI-WAN KENOBI THAT THERE WAS A SITH PLACED SECRETLY WITHIN THE SENATE.
WE JEDI HAVE DEVICES THAT CAN MEASURE AN INDIVIDUAL'S MIDI-CHLORIAN COUNT.
IT'S HOW WE TEST FOR POTENTIAL JEDI. THIS SITH, IF HE OR SHE EXISTS, MUST ALSO HAVE A HIGH MIDI-CHLORIAN COUNT.
UNCOVER THIS SITH AND WE MAY SHORTEN, OR EVEN END THE WAR!
SOMETIMES, RONHAR, YOU REALLY DO PRESUME ON OUR FRIENDSHIP!
I ALWAYS THOUGHT, FROM OUR CHATS TOGETHER, THAT YOU POSSESSED MORE POLITICAL ACUMEN THAN MOST OF THE JEDI!
DO YOU HAVE ANY IDEA OF HOW FRAGILE THE REPUBLIC IS AT THIS POINT?
THE WAR, AT BEST, HAS BEEN INCONCLUSIVE THUS FAR! I'VE DONE WHAT I CAN TO EMPHASIZE OUR VICTORIES AND MINIMIZE OUR LOSSES, BUT IT GROWS MORE DIFFICULT EVERY DAY.
THE SITH, FOR THOSE WHO HAVE EVEN HEARD OF THEM, ARE CONSIDERED A MYTH FROM THE PAST! COUNT DOOKU, HOWEVER, THEY DO KNOW. MENTIONING HIM WILL ONLY REMIND THE SENATORS THAT THE SEPARATIST LEADER WAS ONCE A JEDI!
DO YOU KNOW THAT THERE ARE THOSE WHO THINK THE ENTIRE WAR IS A JEDI PLOT?
AND HOW DO I COMPEL THE SENATORS TO SUBMIT TO THIS TEST? SOME, SUCH AS BAIL ORGANA, ARE LIKELY TO REFUSE ON SHEER PRINCIPLE! WHAT YOU ASK IS SIMPLY IMPOSSIBLE!
EXCUSE ME, SUPREME CHANCELLOR, BUT THERE IS A WAY!

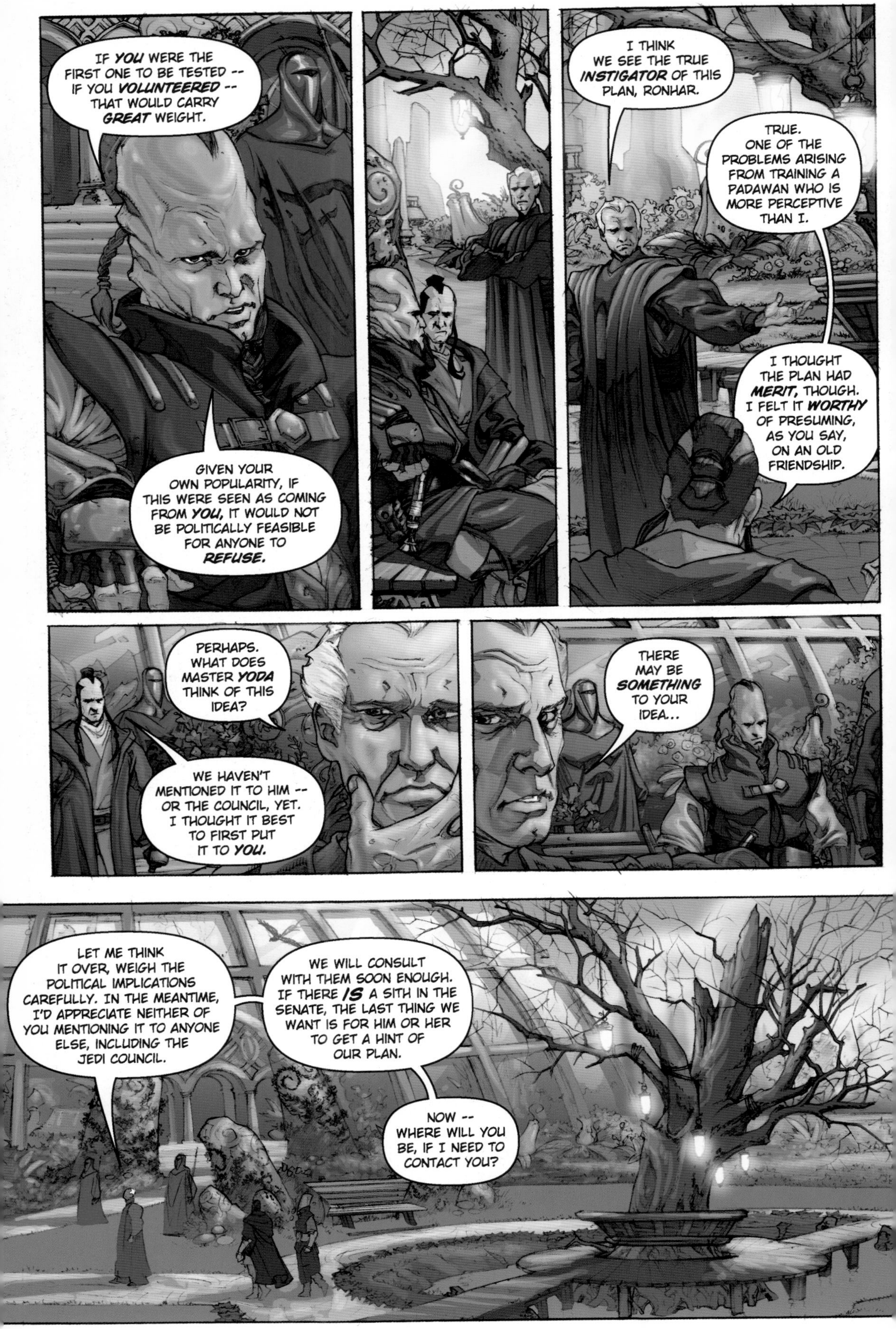
IF YOU WERE THE FIRST ONE TO BE TESTED -- IF YOU VOLUNTEERED -- THAT WOULD CARRY GREAT WEIGHT.
GIVEN YOUR OWN POPULARITY, IF THIS WERE SEEN AS COMING FROM YOU, IT WOULD NOT BE POLITICALLY FEASIBLE FOR ANYONE TO REFUSE.
I THINK WE SEE THE TRUE INSTIGATOR OF THIS PLAN, RONHAR.
TRUE. ONE OF THE PROBLEMS ARISING FROM TRAINING A PADAWAN WHO IS MORE PERCEPTIVE THAN I.
I THOUGHT THE PLAN HAD MERIT, THOUGH. I FELT IT WORTHY OF PRESUMING, AS YOU SAY, ON AN OLD FRIENDSHIP.
PERHAPS. WHAT DOES MASTER YODA THINK OF THIS IDEA?
WE HAVEN'T MENTIONED IT TO HIM -- OR THE COUNCIL, YET. I THOUGHT IT BEST TO FIRST PUT IT TO YOU.
THERE MAY BE SOMETHING TO YOUR IDEA...
LET ME THINK IT OVER, WEIGH THE POLITICAL IMPLICATIONS CAREFULLY. IN THE MEANTIME, I'D APPRECIATE NEITHER OF YOU MENTIONING IT TO ANYONE ELSE, INCLUDING THE JEDI COUNCIL.
WE WILL CONSULT WITH THEM SOON ENOUGH. IF THERE IS A SITH IN THE SENATE, THE LAST THING WE WANT IS FOR HIM OR HER TO GET A HINT OF OUR PLAN.
NOW -- WHERE WILL YOU BE, IF I NEED TO CONTACT YOU?

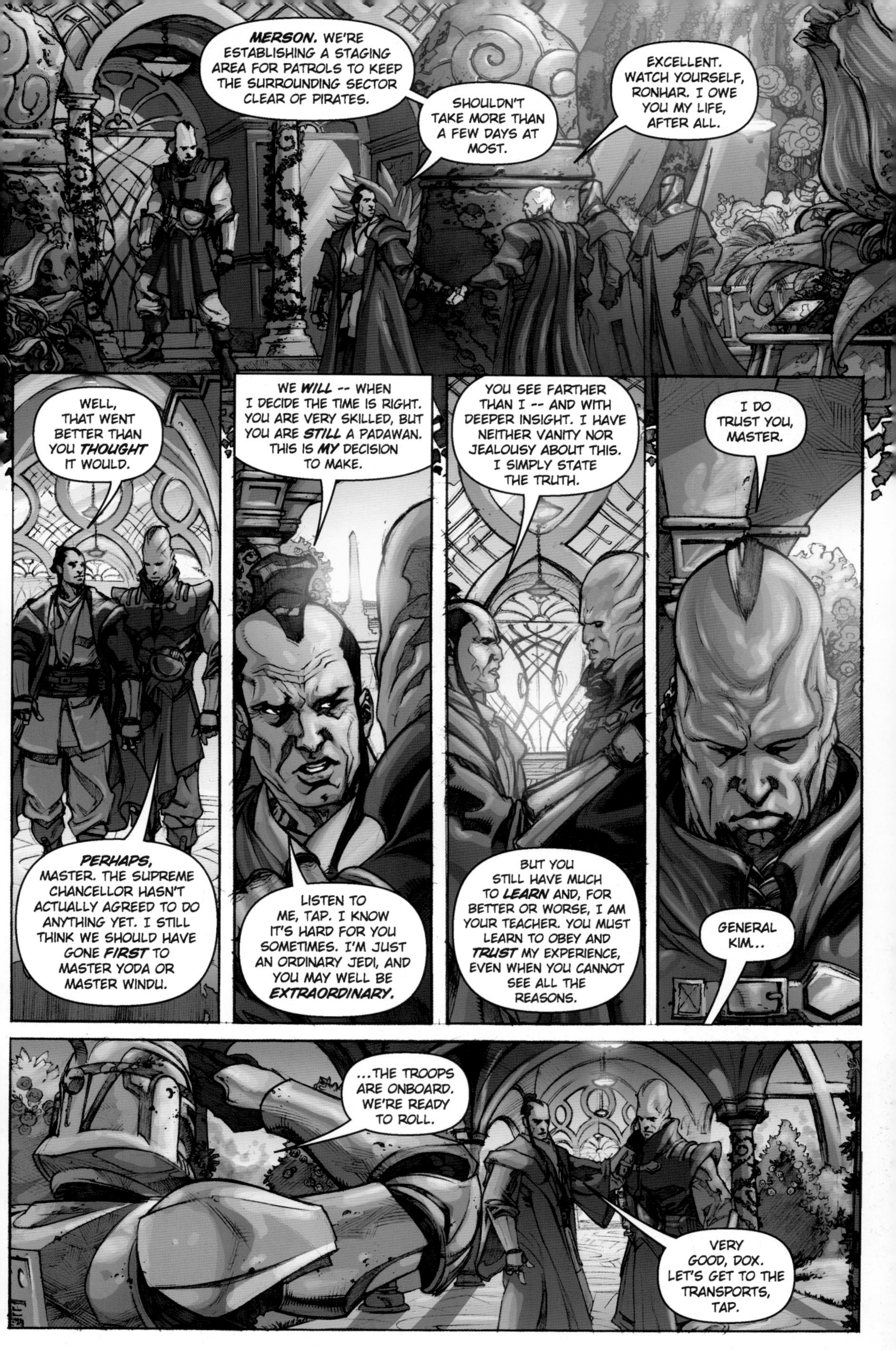

MERSON. WE'RE ESTABLISHING A STAGING AREA FOR PATROLS TO KEEP THE SURROUNDING SECTOR CLEAR OF PIRATES.
SHOULDN'T TAKE MORE THAN A FEW DAYS AT MOST.
EXCELLENT. WATCH YOURSELF, RONHAR. I OWE YOU MY LIFE, AFTER ALL.
WELL, THAT WENT BETTER THAN YOU THOUGHT IT WOULD.
PERHAPS, MASTER. THE SUPREME CHANCELLOR HASN'T ACTUALLY AGREED TO DO ANYTHING YET. I STILL THINK WE SHOULD HAVE GONE FIRST TO MASTER YODA OR MASTER WINDU.
WE WILL -- WHEN I DECIDE THE TIME IS RIGHT. YOU ARE VERY SKILLED, BUT YOU ARE STILL A PADAWAN. THIS IS MY DECISION TO MAKE.
LISTEN TO ME, TAP. I KNOW IT'S HARD FOR YOU SOMETIMES. I'M JUST AN ORDINARY JEDI, AND YOU MAY WELL BE EXTRAORDINARY.
YOU SEE FARTHER THAN I -- AND WITH DEEPER INSIGHT. I HAVE NEITHER VANITY NOR JEALOUSY ABOUT THIS. I SIMPLY STATE THE TRUTH.
BUT YOU STILL HAVE MUCH TO LEARN AND, FOR BETTER OR WORSE, I AM YOUR TEACHER. YOU MUST LEARN TO OBEY AND TRUST MY EXPERIENCE, EVEN WHEN YOU CANNOT SEE ALL THE REASONS.
I DO TRUST YOU, MASTER.
GENERAL KIM...
...THE TROOPS ARE ONBOARD. WE'RE READY TO ROLL.
VERY GOOD, DOX. LET'S GET TO THE TRANSPORTS, TAP.

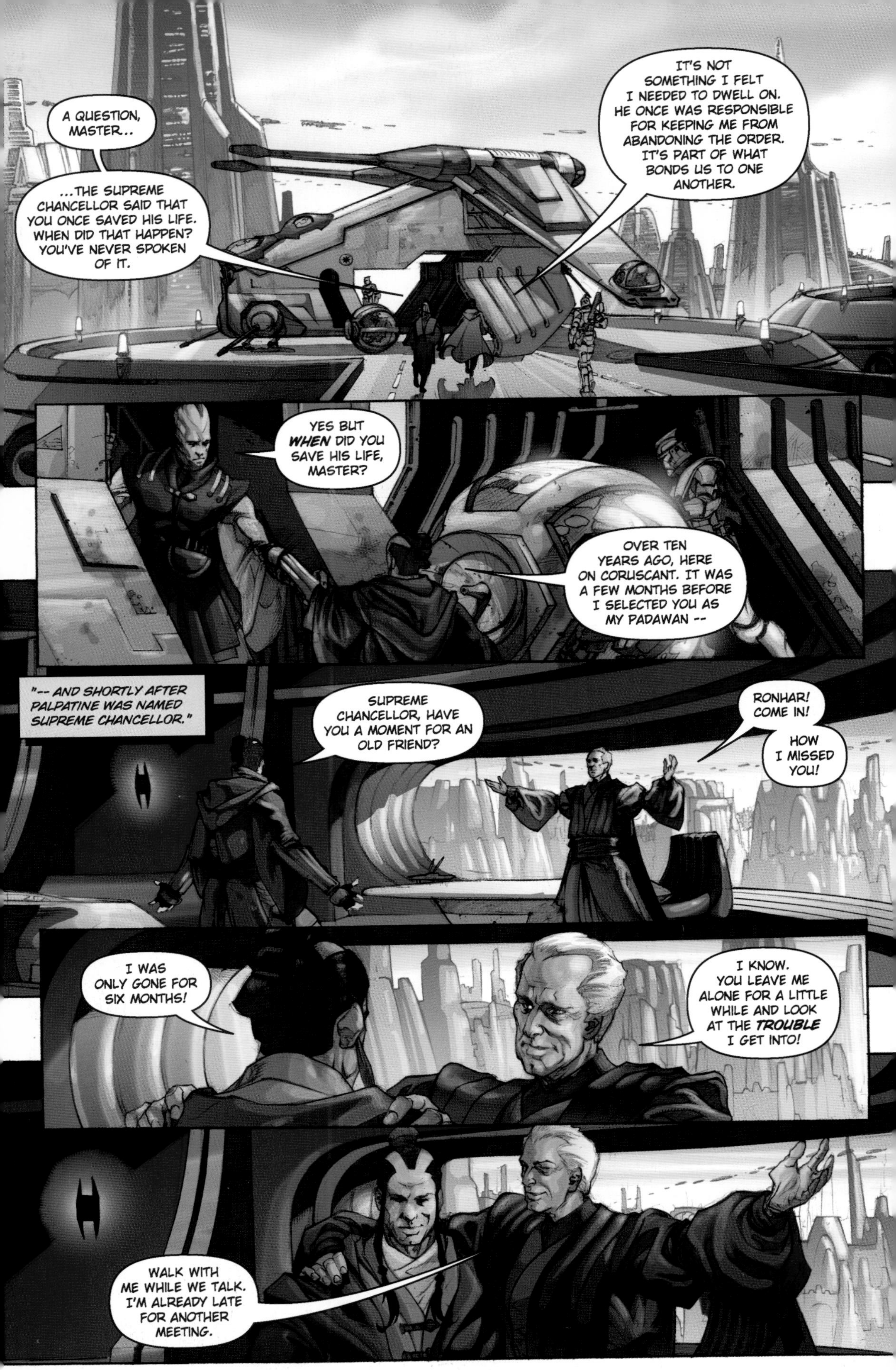
A QUESTION, MASTER...
...THE SUPREME CHANCELLOR SAID THAT YOU ONCE SAVED HIS LIFE. WHEN DID THAT HAPPEN? YOU'VE NEVER SPOKEN OF IT.
IT'S NOT SOMETHING I FELT I NEEDED TO DWELL ON. HE ONCE WAS RESPONSIBLE FOR KEEPING ME FROM ABANDONING THE ORDER. IT'S PART OF WHAT BONDS US TO ONE ANOTHER.
YES BUT WHEN DID YOU SAVE HIS LIFE, MASTER?
OVER TEN YEARS AGO, HERE ON CORUSCANT. IT WAS A FEW MONTHS BEFORE I SELECTED YOU AS MY PADAWAN --
"-- AND SHORTLY AFTER PALPATINE WAS NAMED SUPREME CHANCELLOR."
SUPREME CHANCELLOR, HAVE YOU A MOMENT FOR AN OLD FRIEND?
RONHAR! COME IN!
HOW I MISSED YOU!
I WAS ONLY GONE FOR SIX MONTHS!
I KNOW. YOU LEAVE ME ALONE FOR A LITTLE WHILE AND LOOK AT THE TROUBLE I GET INTO!
WALK WITH ME WHILE WE TALK. I'M ALREADY LATE FOR ANOTHER MEETING.

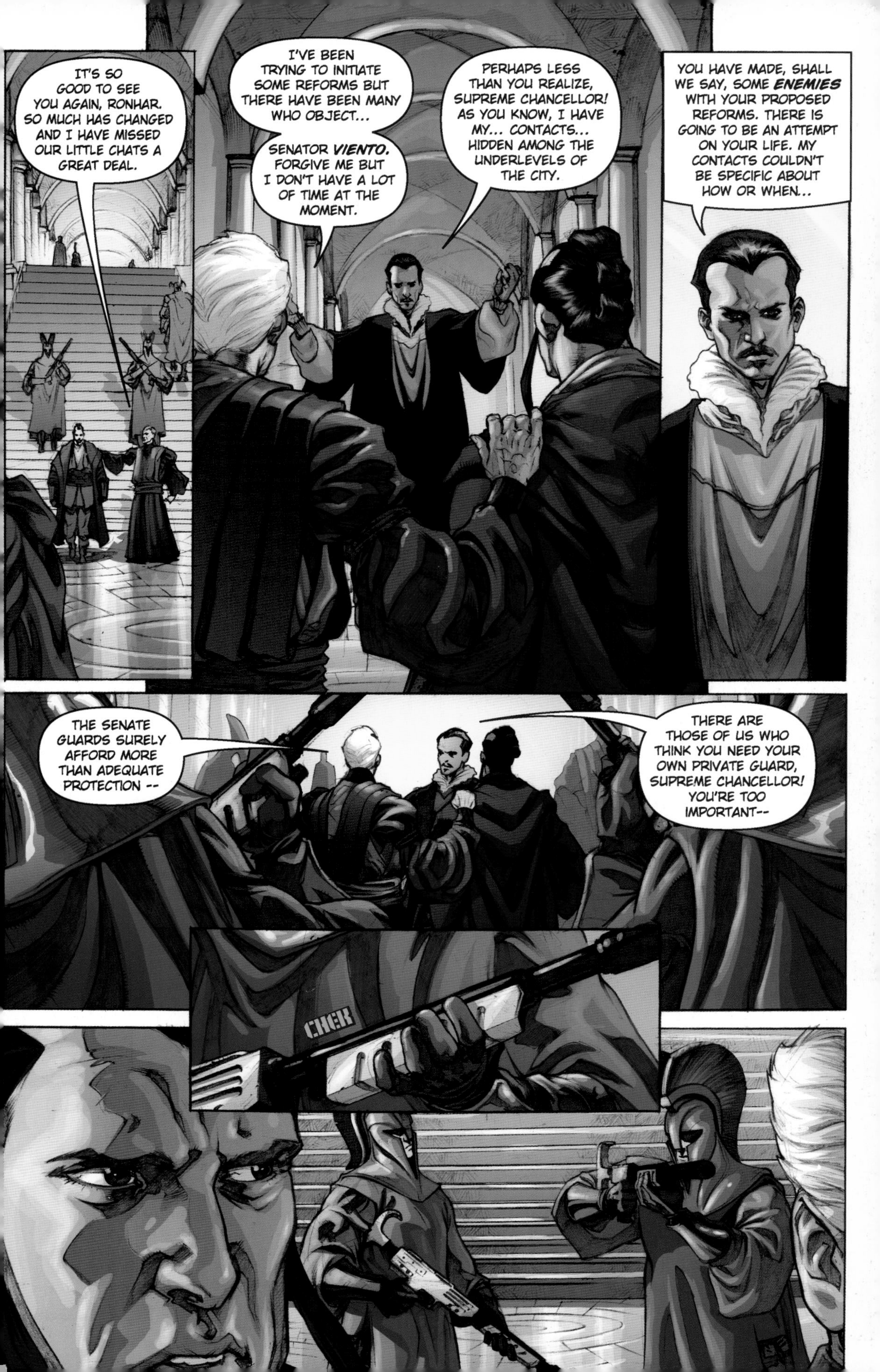

IT'S SO GOOD TO SEE YOU AGAIN, RONHAR. SO MUCH HAS CHANGED AND I HAVE MISSED OUR LITTLE CHATS A GREAT DEAL.
I'VE BEEN TRYING TO INITIATE SOME REFORMS BUT THERE HAVE BEEN MANY WHO OBJECT...
SENATOR VIENTO. FORGIVE ME BUT I DON'T HAVE A LOT OF TIME AT THE MOMENT.
PERHAPS LESS THAN YOU REALIZE, SUPREME CHANCELLOR! AS YOU KNOW, I HAVE MY... CONTACTS... HIDDEN AMONG THE UNDERLEVELS OF THE CITY.
YOU HAVE MADE, SHALL WE SAY, SOME ENEMIES WITH YOUR PROPOSED REFORMS. THERE IS GOING TO BE AN ATTEMPT ON YOUR LIFE. MY CONTACTS COULDN'T BE SPECIFIC ABOUT HOW OR WHEN...
THE SENATE GUARDS SURELY AFFORD MORE THAN ADEQUATE PROTECTION --
THERE ARE THOSE OF US WHO THINK YOU NEED YOUR OWN PRIVATE GUARD, SUPREME CHANCELLOR! YOU'RE TOO IMPORTANT--
CHER

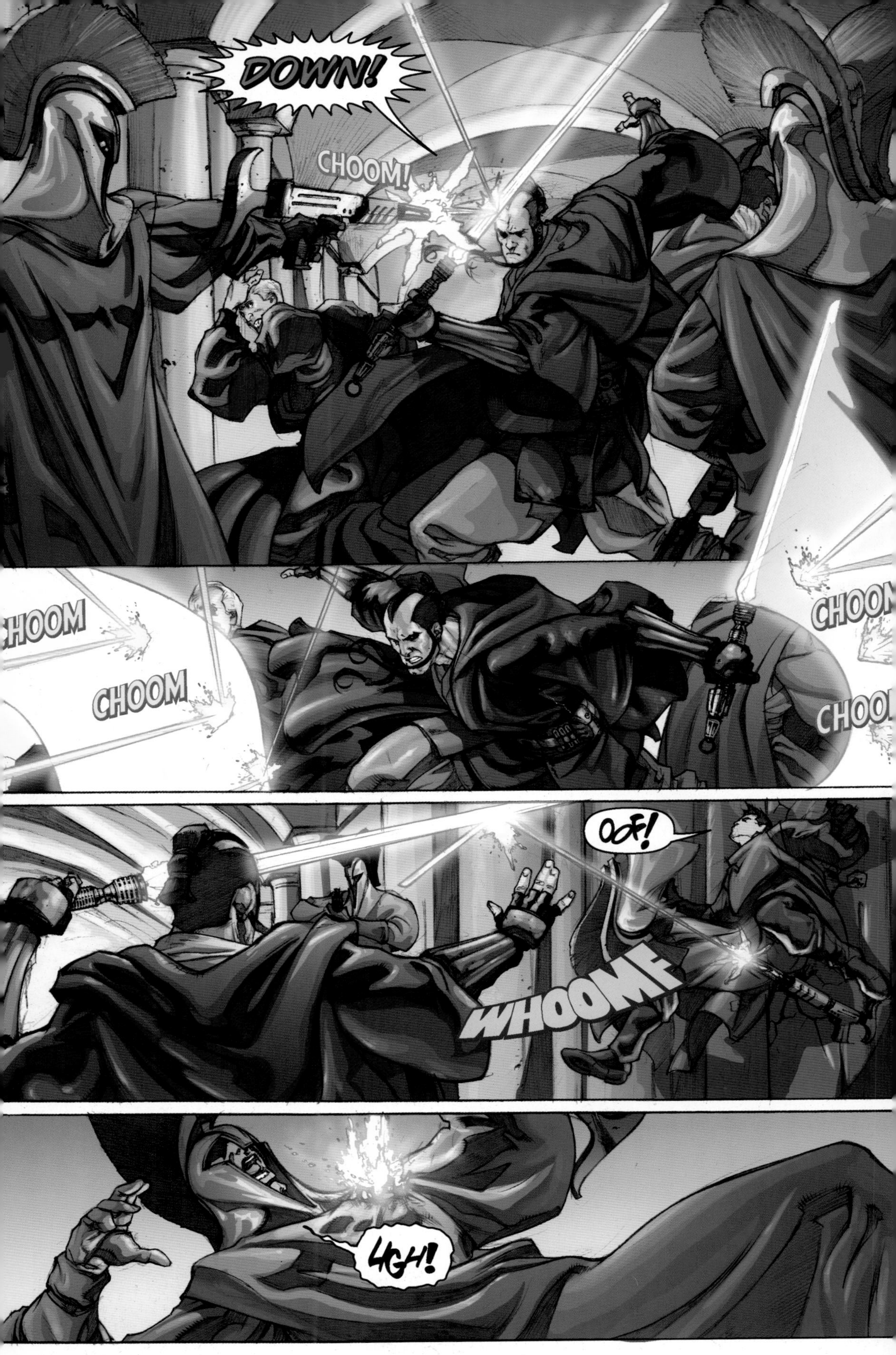
DOWN!
CHOOM!
CHOOM
CHOOM
CHOOM
CHOOM
OOF!
WHOOMF
UGH!

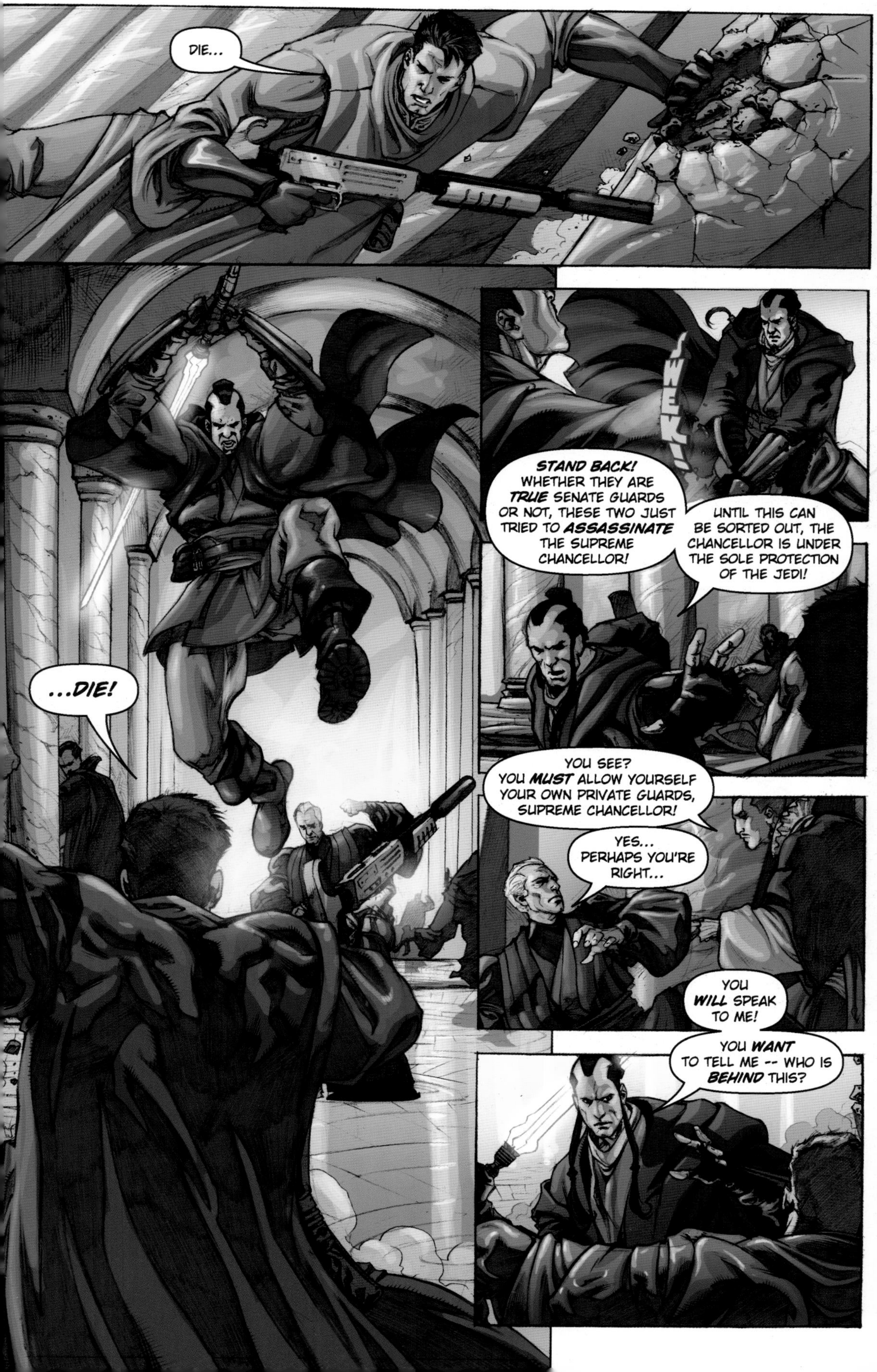

DIE...
...DIE!
SWEK!
STAND BACK! WHETHER THEY ARE TRUE SENATE GUARDS OR NOT, THESE TWO JUST TRIED TO ASSASSINATE THE SUPREME CHANCELLOR!
UNTIL THIS CAN BE SORTED OUT, THE CHANCELLOR IS UNDER THE SOLE PROTECTION OF THE JEDI!
YOU SEE? YOU MUST ALLOW YOURSELF YOUR OWN PRIVATE GUARDS, SUPREME CHANCELLOR!
YES... PERHAPS YOU'RE RIGHT...
YOU WILL SPEAK TO ME!
YOU WANT TO TELL ME -- WHO IS BEHIND THIS?

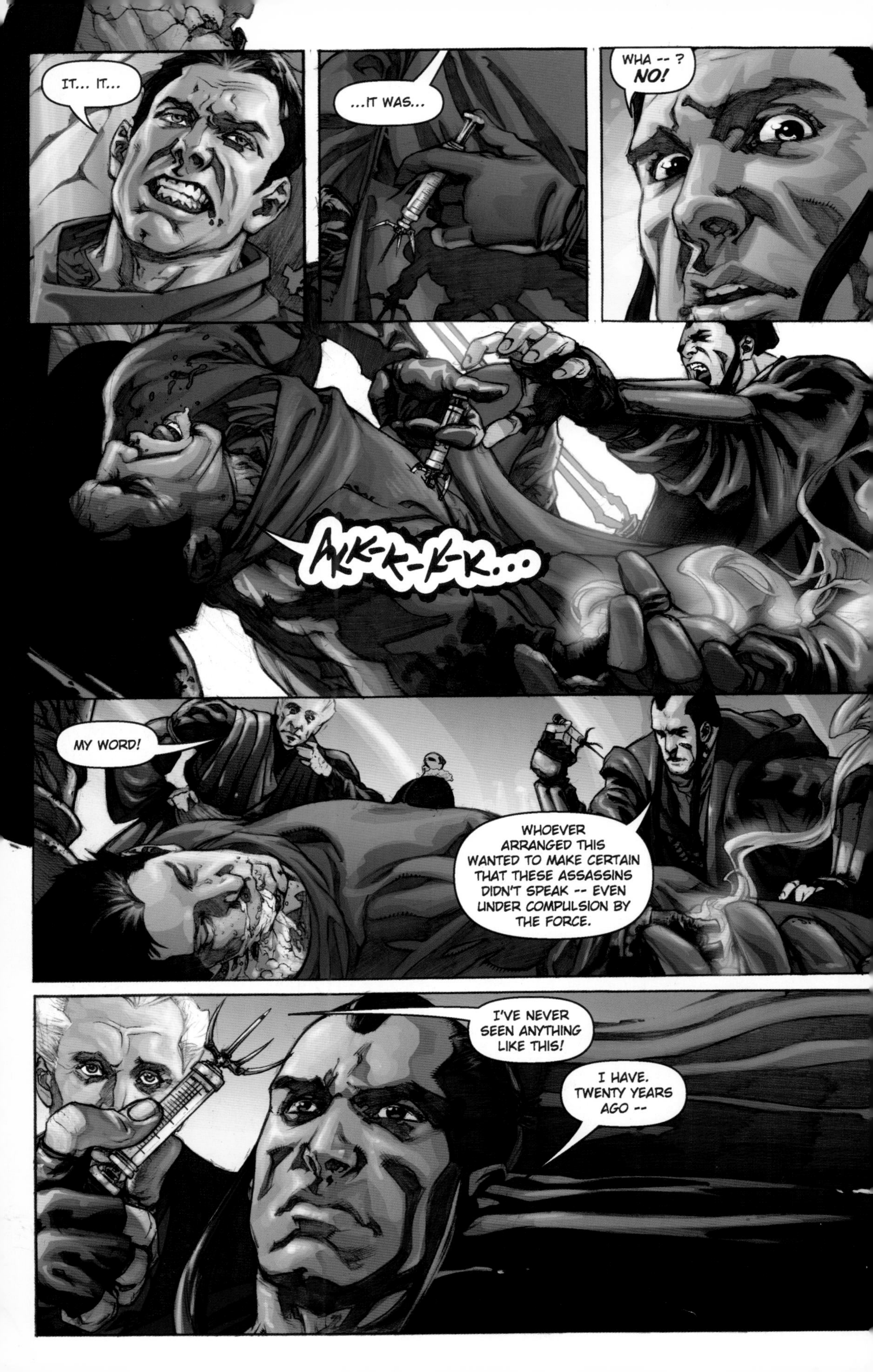
IT... IT...
...IT WAS...
WHA -- ?
NO!
AKK-K-K-K...
MY WORD!
WHOEVER ARRANGED THIS WANTED TO MAKE CERTAIN THAT THESE ASSASSINS DIDN'T SPEAK -- EVEN UNDER COMPULSION BY THE FORCE.
I'VE NEVER SEEN ANYTHING LIKE THIS!
I HAVE. TWENTY YEARS AGO --

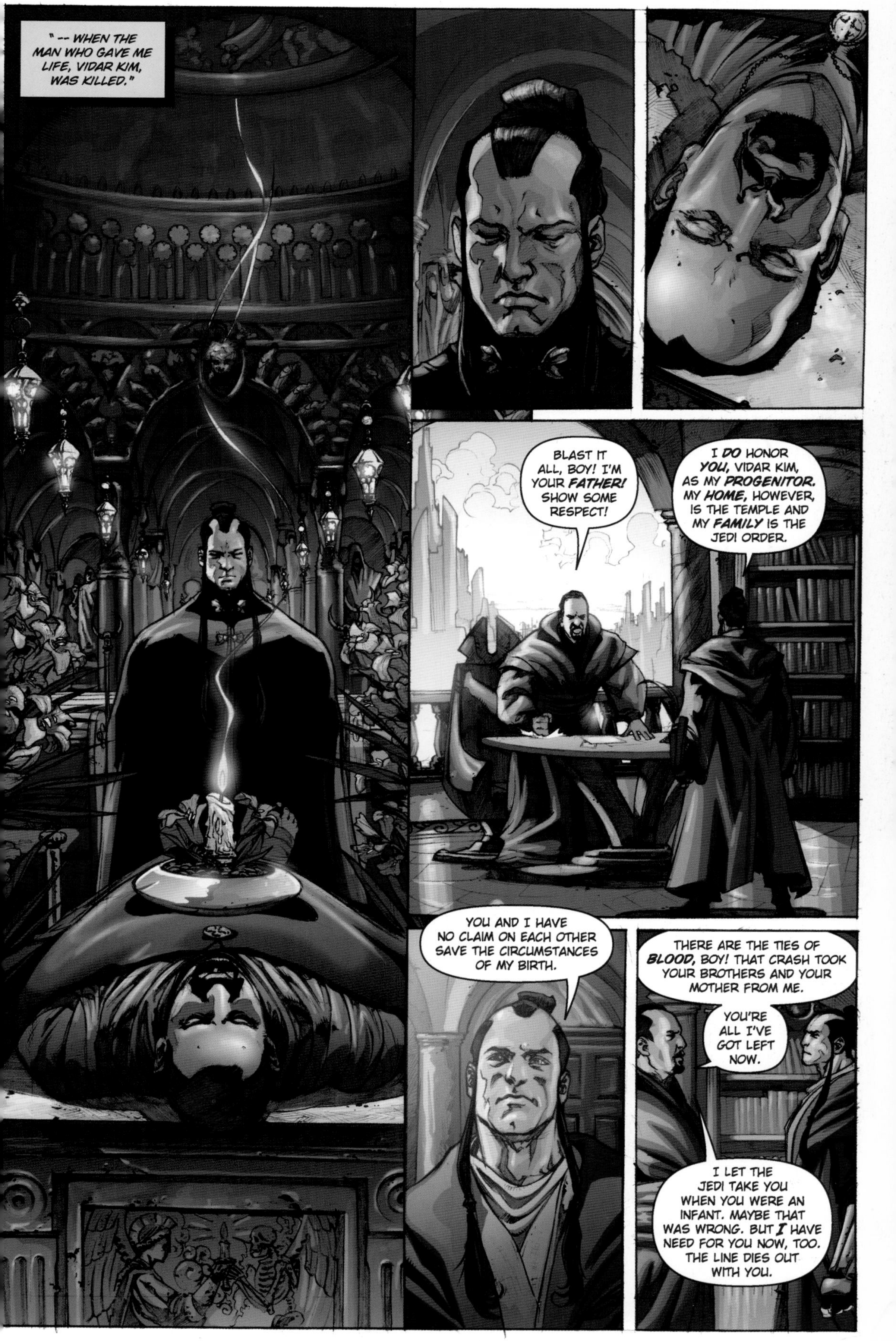
" -- WHEN THE MAN WHO GAVE ME LIFE, VIDAR KIM, WAS KILLED."
BLAST IT ALL, BOY! I'M YOUR FATHER! SHOW SOME RESPECT!
I DO HONOR YOU, VIDAR KIM, AS MY PROGENITOR. MY HOME, HOWEVER, IS THE TEMPLE AND MY FAMILY IS THE JEDI ORDER.
YOU AND I HAVE NO CLAIM ON EACH OTHER SAVE THE CIRCUMSTANCES OF MY BIRTH.
THERE ARE THE TIES OF BLOOD, BOY! THAT CRASH TOOK YOUR BROTHERS AND YOUR MOTHER FROM ME.
YOU'RE ALL I'VE GOT LEFT NOW.
I LET THE JEDI TAKE YOU WHEN YOU WERE AN INFANT. MAYBE THAT WAS WRONG. BUT I HAVE NEED FOR YOU NOW, TOO. THE LINE DIES OUT WITH YOU.

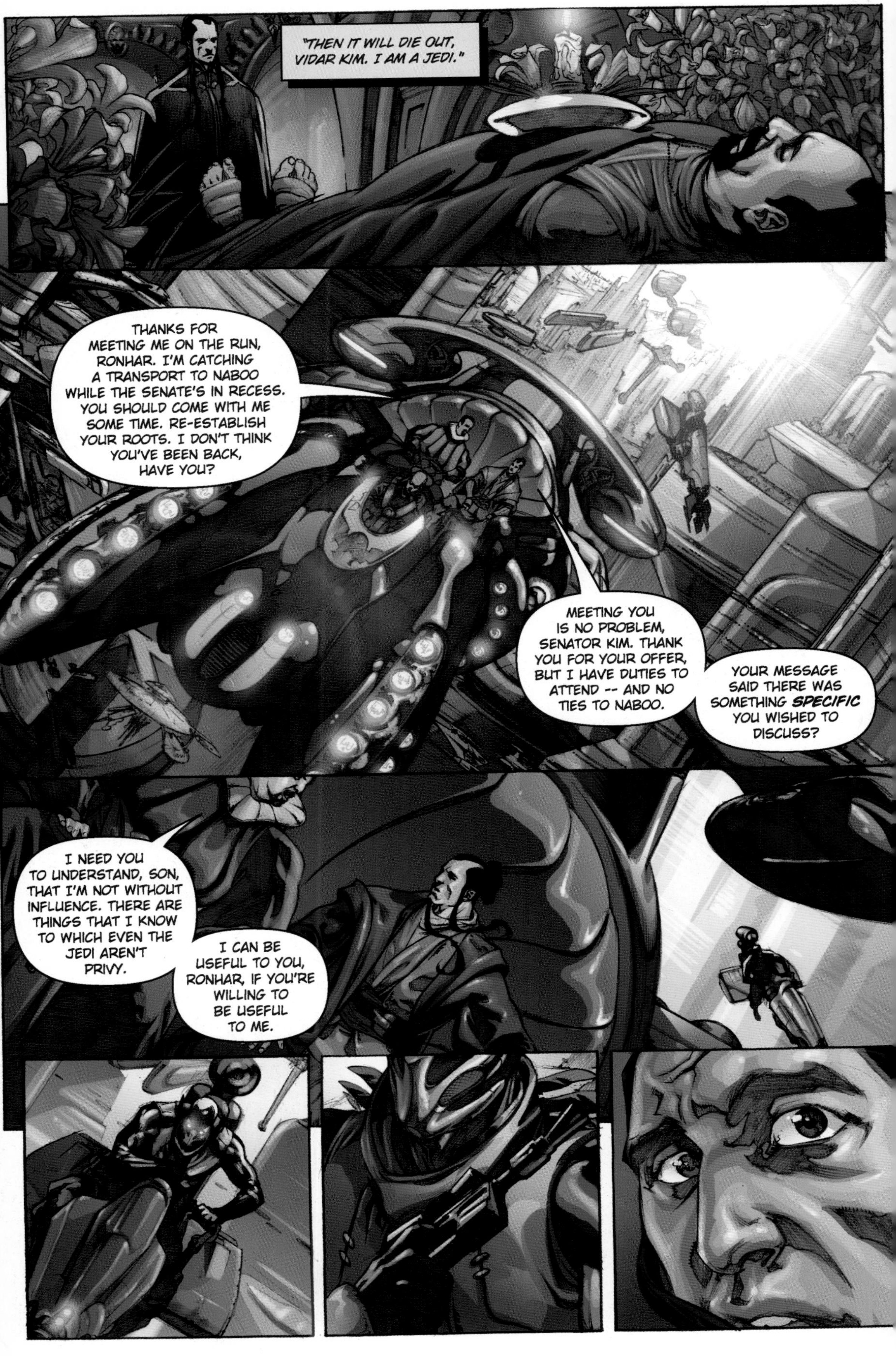
"THEN IT WILL DIE OUT, VIDAR KIM. I AM A JEDI."
THANKS FOR MEETING ME ON THE RUN, RONHAR. I'M CATCHING A TRANSPORT TO NABOO WHILE THE SENATE'S IN RECESS. YOU SHOULD COME WITH ME SOME TIME. RE-ESTABLISH YOUR ROOTS. I DON'T THINK YOU'VE BEEN BACK, HAVE YOU?
MEETING YOU IS NO PROBLEM, SENATOR KIM. THANK YOU FOR YOUR OFFER, BUT I HAVE DUTIES TO ATTEND -- AND NO TIES TO NABOO.
YOUR MESSAGE SAID THERE WAS SOMETHING SPECIFIC YOU WISHED TO DISCUSS?
I NEED YOU TO UNDERSTAND, SON, THAT I'M NOT WITHOUT INFLUENCE. THERE ARE THINGS THAT I KNOW TO WHICH EVEN THE JEDI AREN'T PRIVY.
I CAN BE USEFUL TO YOU, RONHAR, IF YOU'RE WILLING TO BE USEFUL TO ME.

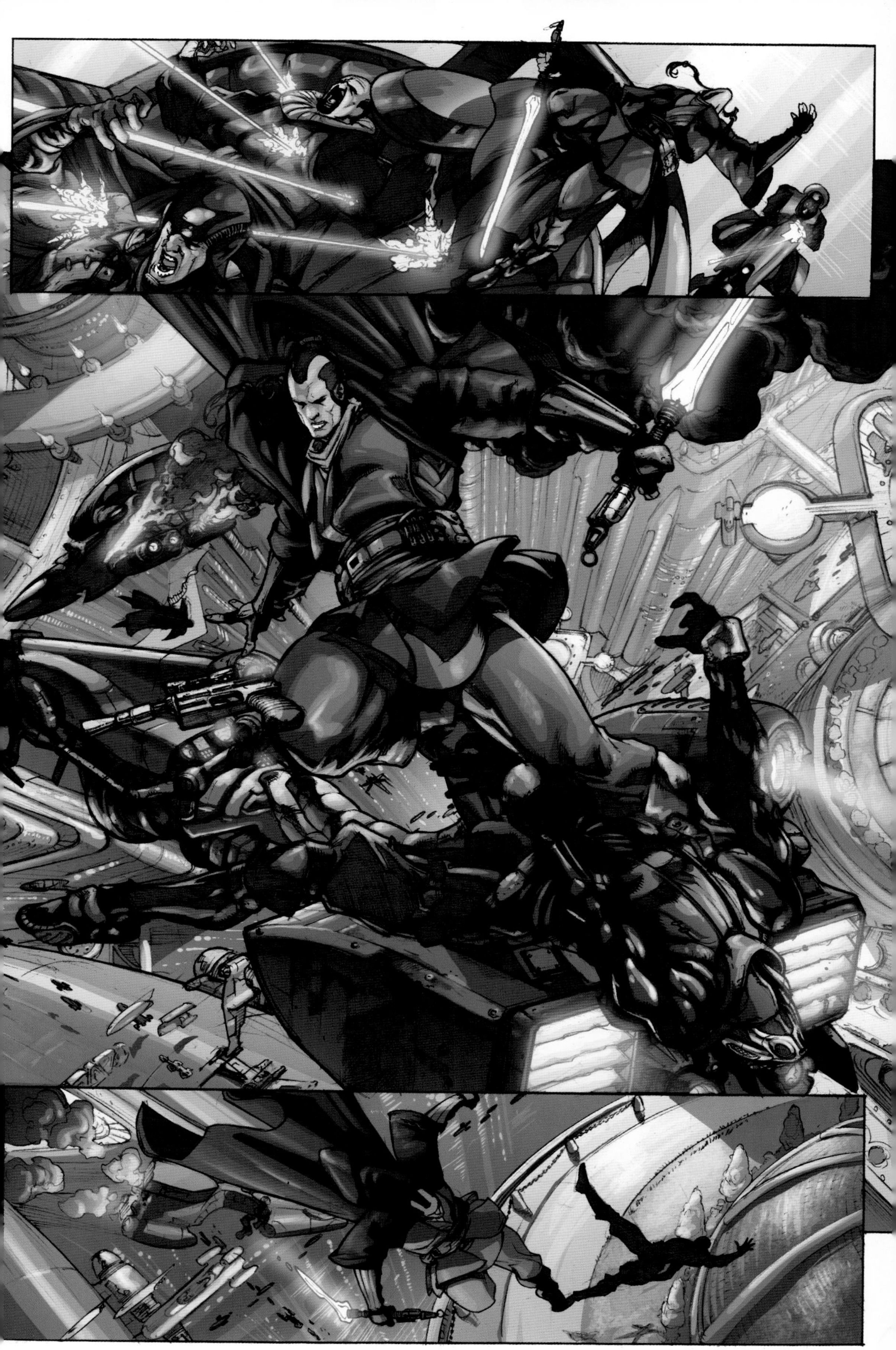

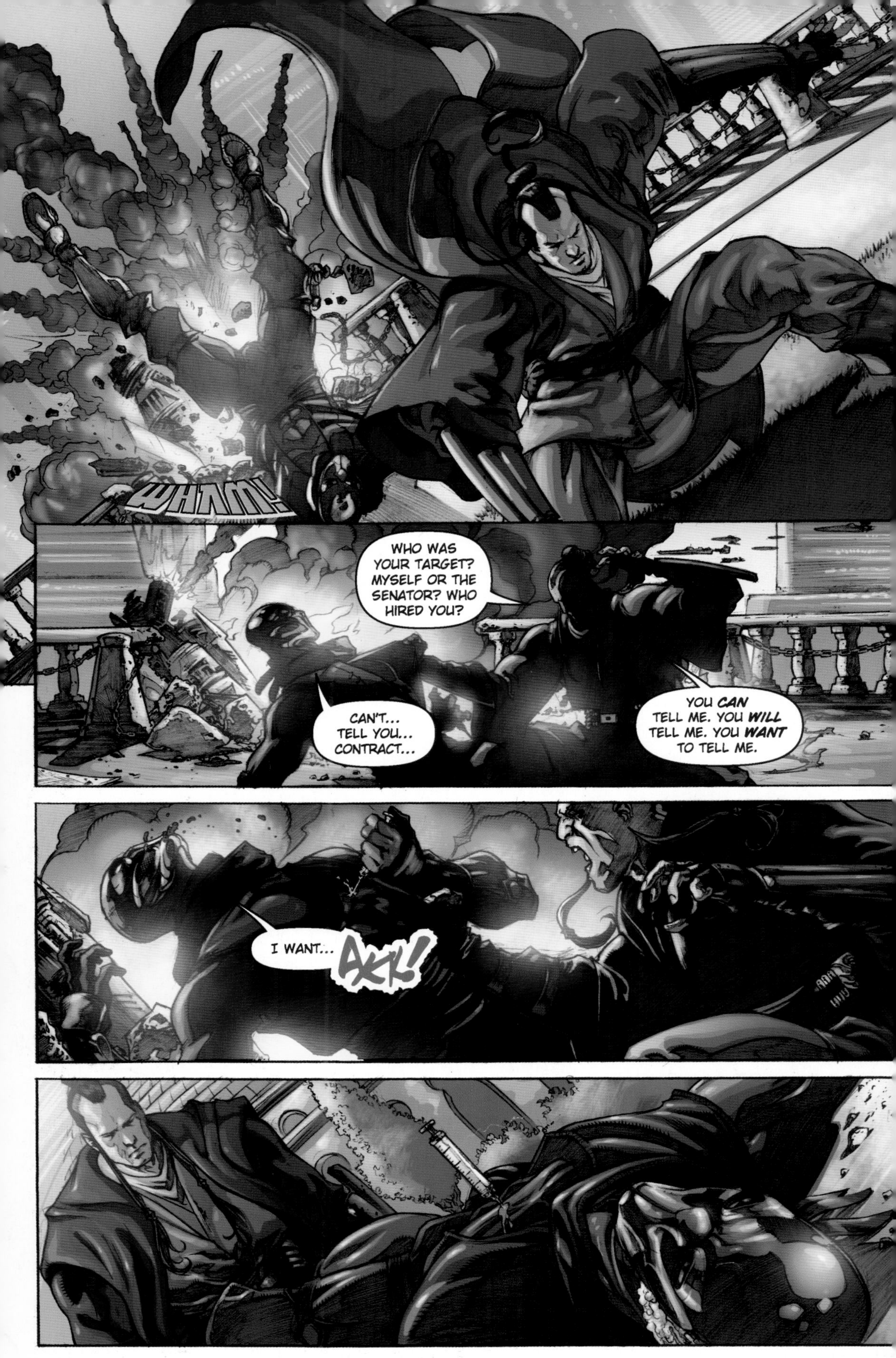
WHAM!
WHO WAS YOUR TARGET? MYSELF OR THE SENATOR? WHO HIRED YOU?
CAN'T... TELL YOU... CONTRACT...
YOU *CAN* TELL ME. YOU *WILL* TELL ME. YOU *WANT* TO TELL ME.
I WANT...
AKK!

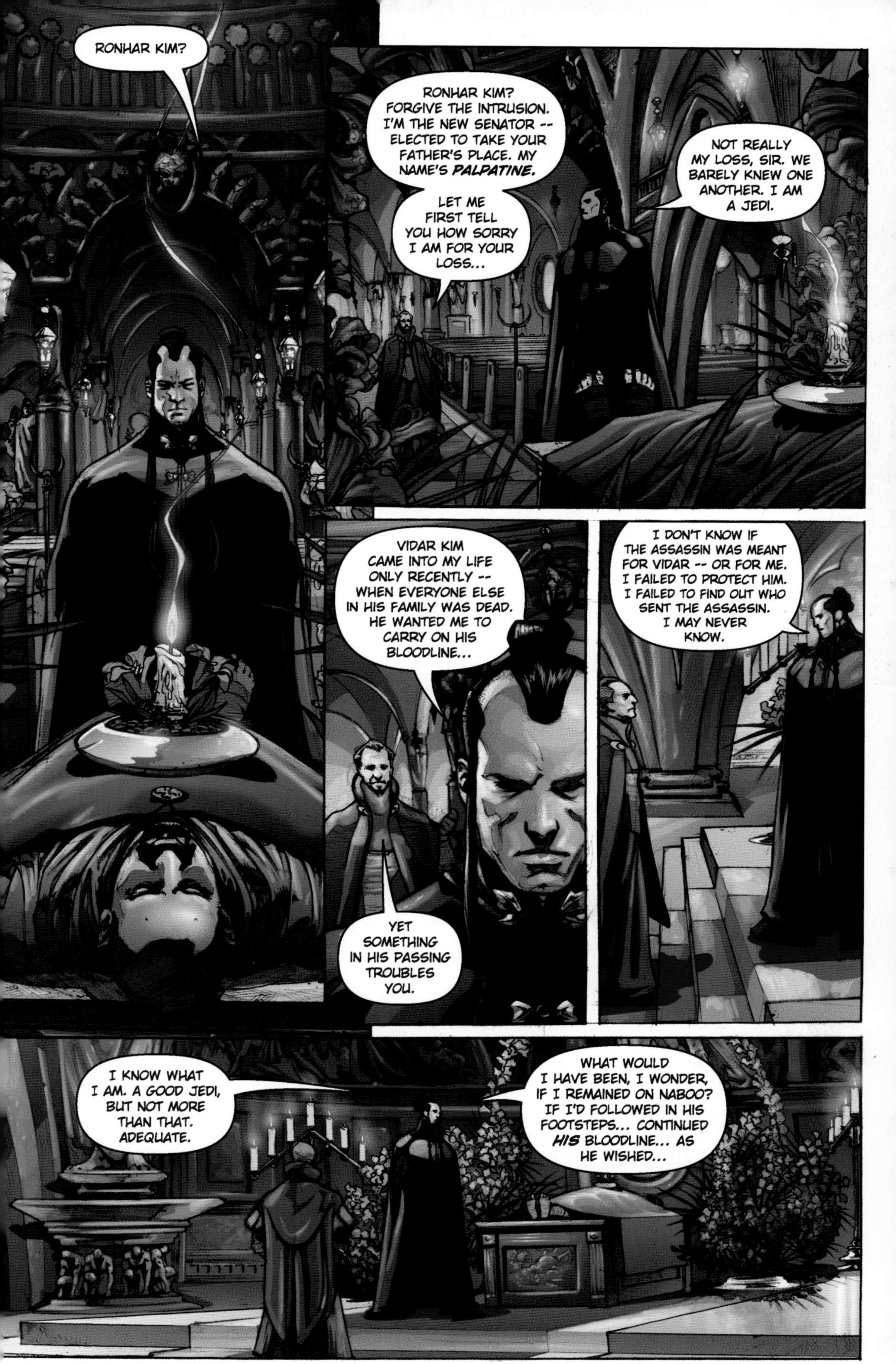
RONHAR KIM?
RONHAR KIM? FORGIVE THE INTRUSION. I'M THE NEW SENATOR -- ELECTED TO TAKE YOUR FATHER'S PLACE. MY NAME'S *PALPATINE.*
LET ME FIRST TELL YOU HOW SORRY I AM FOR YOUR LOSS...
NOT REALLY MY LOSS, SIR. WE BARELY KNEW ONE ANOTHER. I AM A JEDI.
VIDAR KIM CAME INTO MY LIFE ONLY RECENTLY -- WHEN EVERYONE ELSE IN HIS FAMILY WAS DEAD. HE WANTED ME TO CARRY ON HIS BLOODLINE...
YET SOMETHING IN HIS PASSING TROUBLES YOU.
I DON'T KNOW IF THE ASSASSIN WAS MEANT FOR VIDAR -- OR FOR ME. I FAILED TO PROTECT HIM. I FAILED TO FIND OUT WHO SENT THE ASSASSIN. I MAY NEVER KNOW.
I KNOW WHAT I AM. A GOOD JEDI, BUT NOT MORE THAN THAT. ADEQUATE.
WHAT WOULD I HAVE BEEN, I WONDER, IF I REMAINED ON NABOO? IF I'D FOLLOWED IN HIS FOOTSTEPS... CONTINUED *HIS* BLOODLINE... AS HE WISHED...

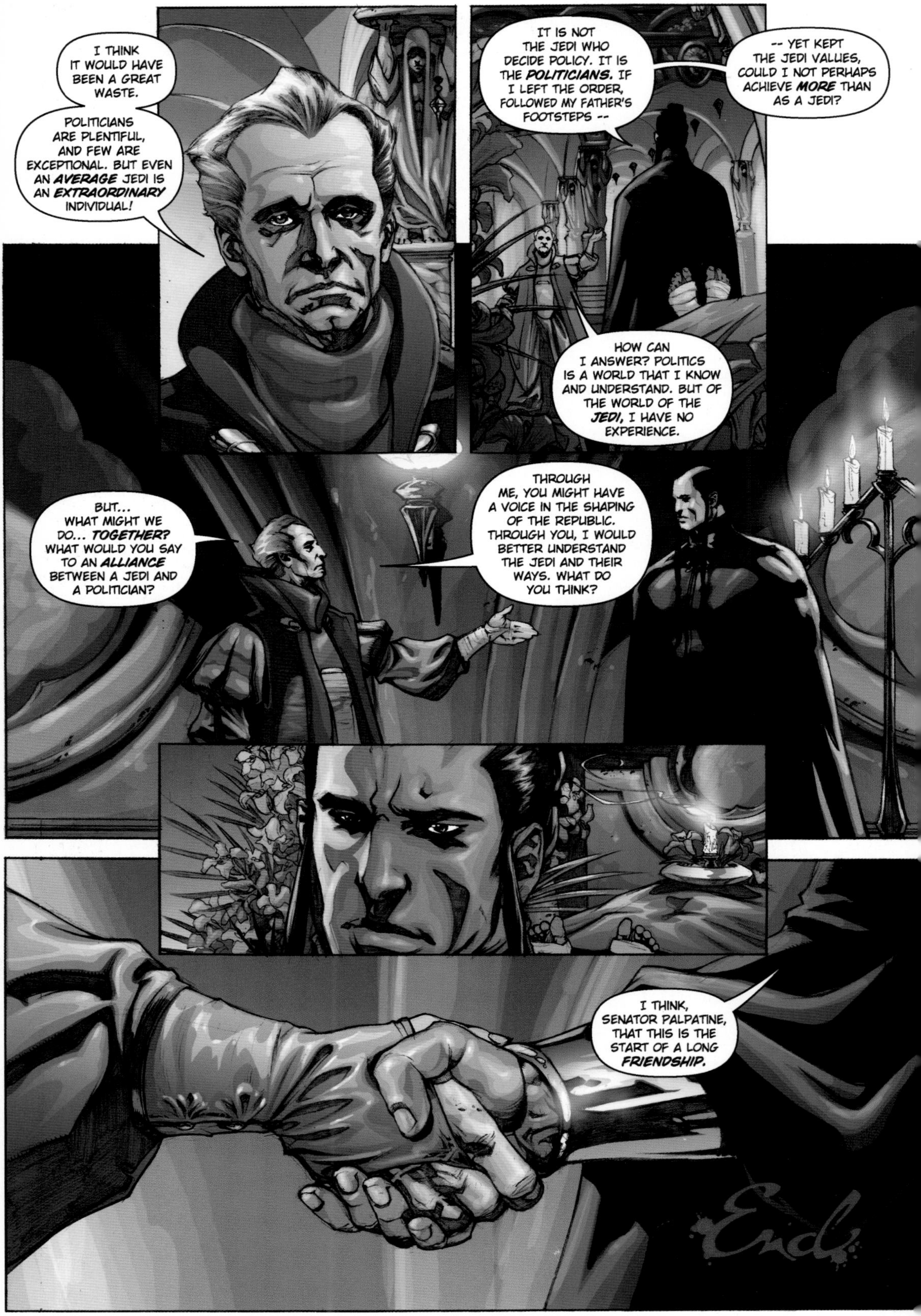
I THINK IT WOULD HAVE BEEN A GREAT WASTE.
POLITICIANS ARE PLENTIFUL, AND FEW ARE EXCEPTIONAL. BUT EVEN AN *AVERAGE* JEDI IS AN *EXTRAORDINARY* INDIVIDUAL!
IT IS NOT THE JEDI WHO DECIDE POLICY. IT IS THE *POLITICIANS.* IF I LEFT THE ORDER, FOLLOWED MY FATHER'S FOOTSTEPS --
-- YET KEPT THE JEDI VALUES, COULD I NOT PERHAPS ACHIEVE *MORE* THAN AS A JEDI?
HOW CAN I ANSWER? POLITICS IS A WORLD THAT I KNOW AND UNDERSTAND. BUT OF THE WORLD OF THE *JEDI,* I HAVE NO EXPERIENCE.
BUT... WHAT MIGHT WE DO... *TOGETHER?* WHAT WOULD YOU SAY TO AN *ALLIANCE* BETWEEN A JEDI AND A POLITICIAN?
THROUGH ME, YOU MIGHT HAVE A VOICE IN THE SHAPING OF THE REPUBLIC. THROUGH YOU, I WOULD BETTER UNDERSTAND THE JEDI AND THEIR WAYS. WHAT DO YOU THINK?
I THINK, SENATOR PALPATINE, THAT THIS IS THE START OF A LONG *FRIENDSHIP.*
End

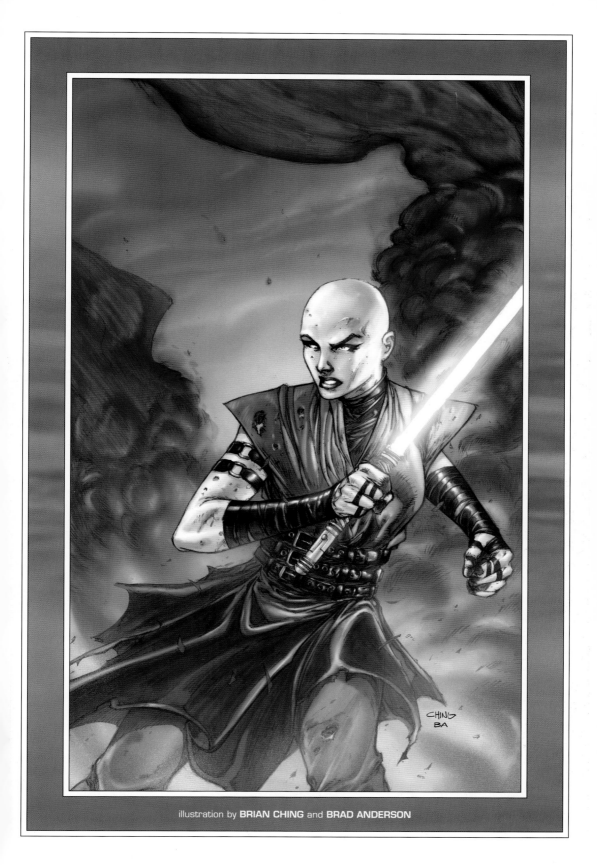

illustration by **BRIAN CHING** and **BRAD ANDERSON**

# HATE AND FEAR

MISSING IN ACTION AND BELIEVED KILLED DURING THE REPUBLIC'S FAILED DEFENSE OF THE PLANET JABIIM, OBI-WAN KENOBI AND THE CLONE ARC TROOPER KNOWN AS ALPHA WERE ACTUALLY CAPTURED BY DARK JEDI ASAJJ VENTRESS AND TAKEN TO HER HOMEWORLD RATTATAK...

**"Hate and Fear"**
written by **Haden Blackman**
art by **Tomás Giorello**

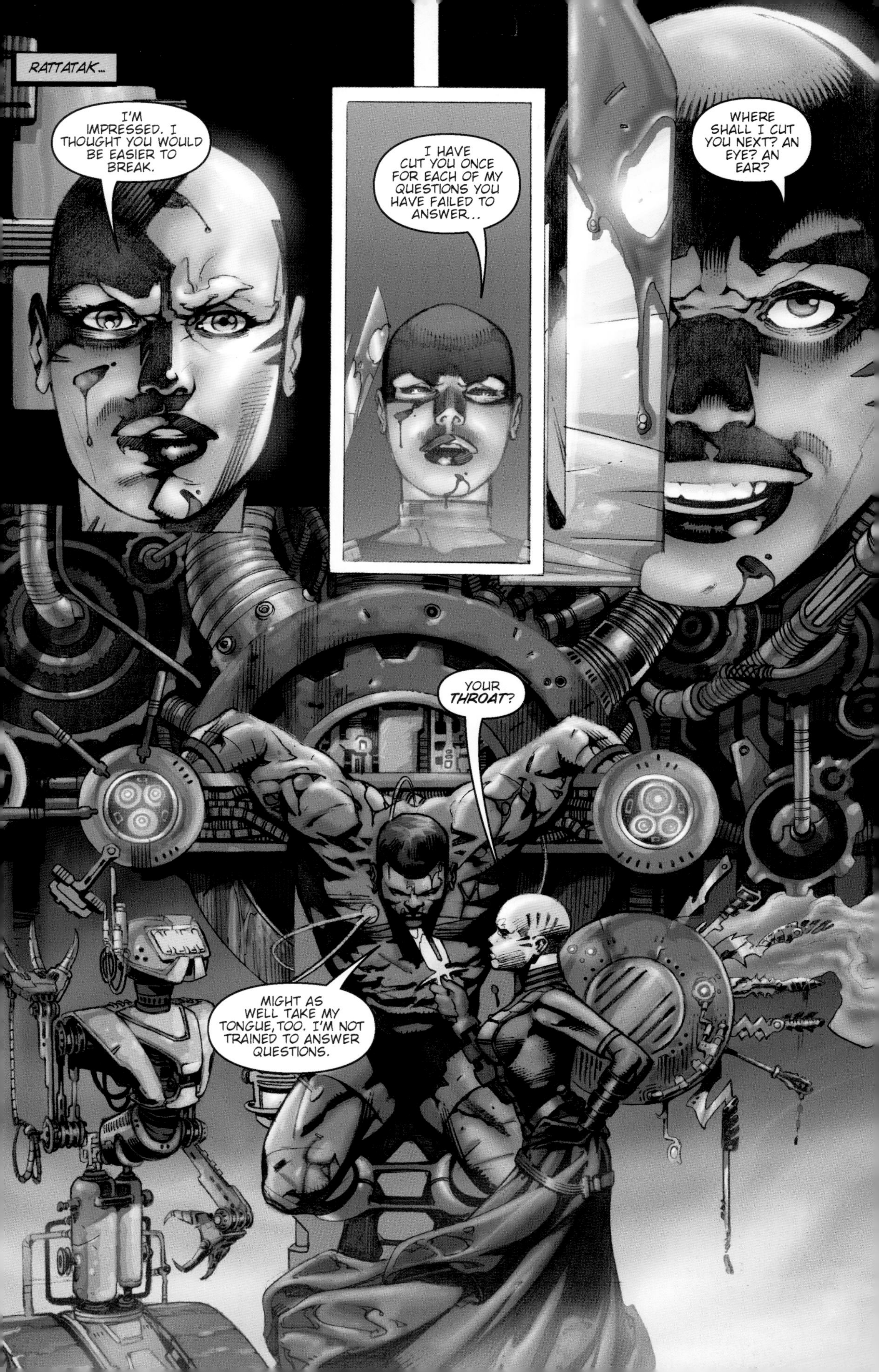
RATTATAK...
I'M IMPRESSED. I THOUGHT YOU WOULD BE EASIER TO BREAK.
I HAVE CUT YOU ONCE FOR EACH OF MY QUESTIONS YOU HAVE FAILED TO ANSWER...
WHERE SHALL I CUT YOU NEXT? AN EYE? AN EAR?
YOUR THROAT?
MIGHT AS WELL TAKE MY TONGUE, TOO. I'M NOT TRAINED TO ANSWER QUESTIONS.

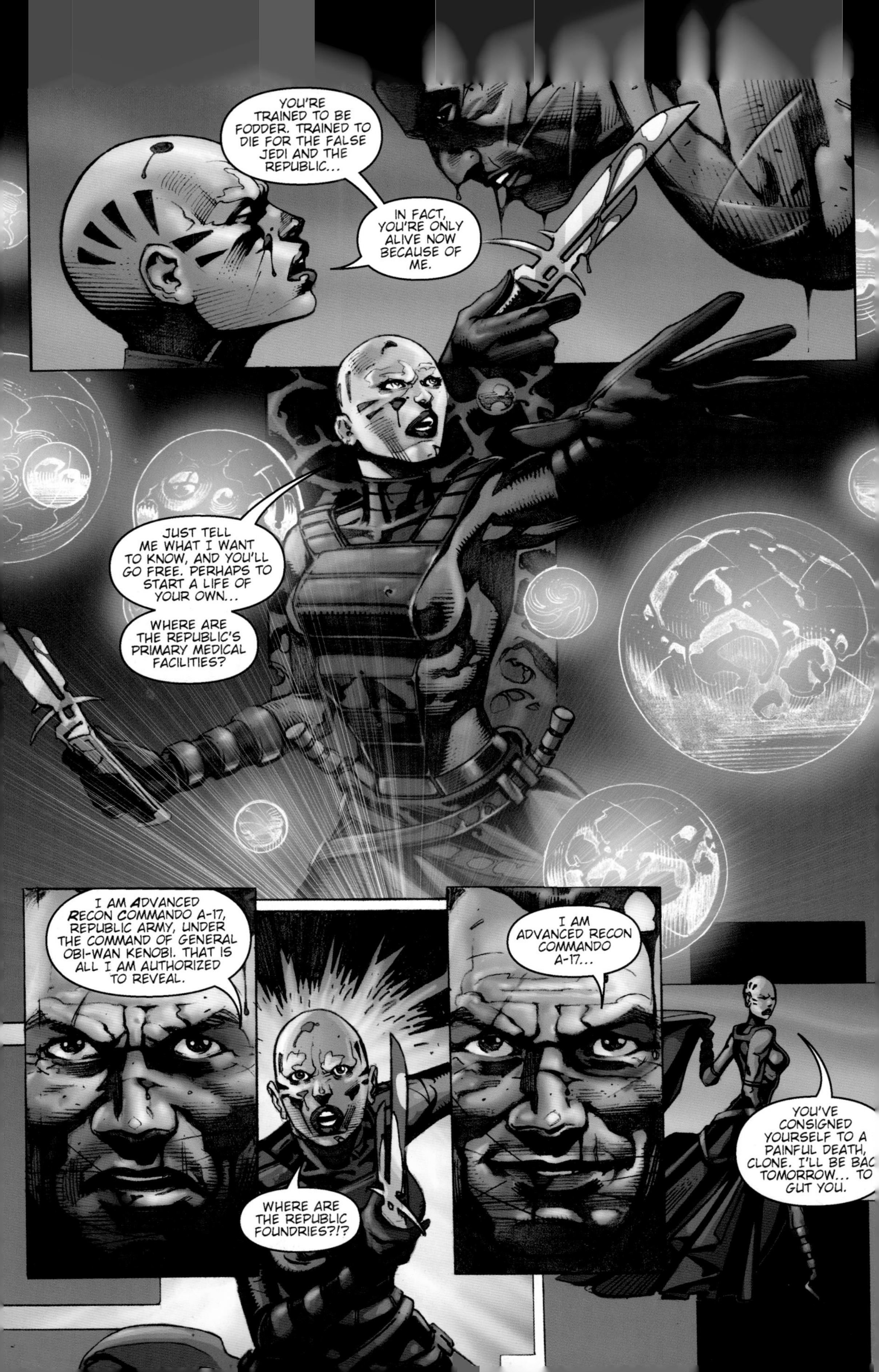

YOU'RE TRAINED TO BE FODDER. TRAINED TO DIE FOR THE FALSE JEDI AND THE REPUBLIC...
IN FACT, YOU'RE ONLY ALIVE NOW BECAUSE OF ME.
JUST TELL ME WHAT I WANT TO KNOW, AND YOU'LL GO FREE. PERHAPS TO START A LIFE OF YOUR OWN...
WHERE ARE THE REPUBLIC'S PRIMARY MEDICAL FACILITIES?
I AM ADVANCED RECON COMMANDO A-17, REPUBLIC ARMY, UNDER THE COMMAND OF GENERAL OBI-WAN KENOBI. THAT IS ALL I AM AUTHORIZED TO REVEAL.
WHERE ARE THE REPUBLIC FOUNDRIES?!?
I AM ADVANCED RECON COMMANDO A-17...
YOU'VE CONSIGNED YOURSELF TO A PAINFUL DEATH, CLONE. I'LL BE BAC TOMORROW... TO GUT YOU.

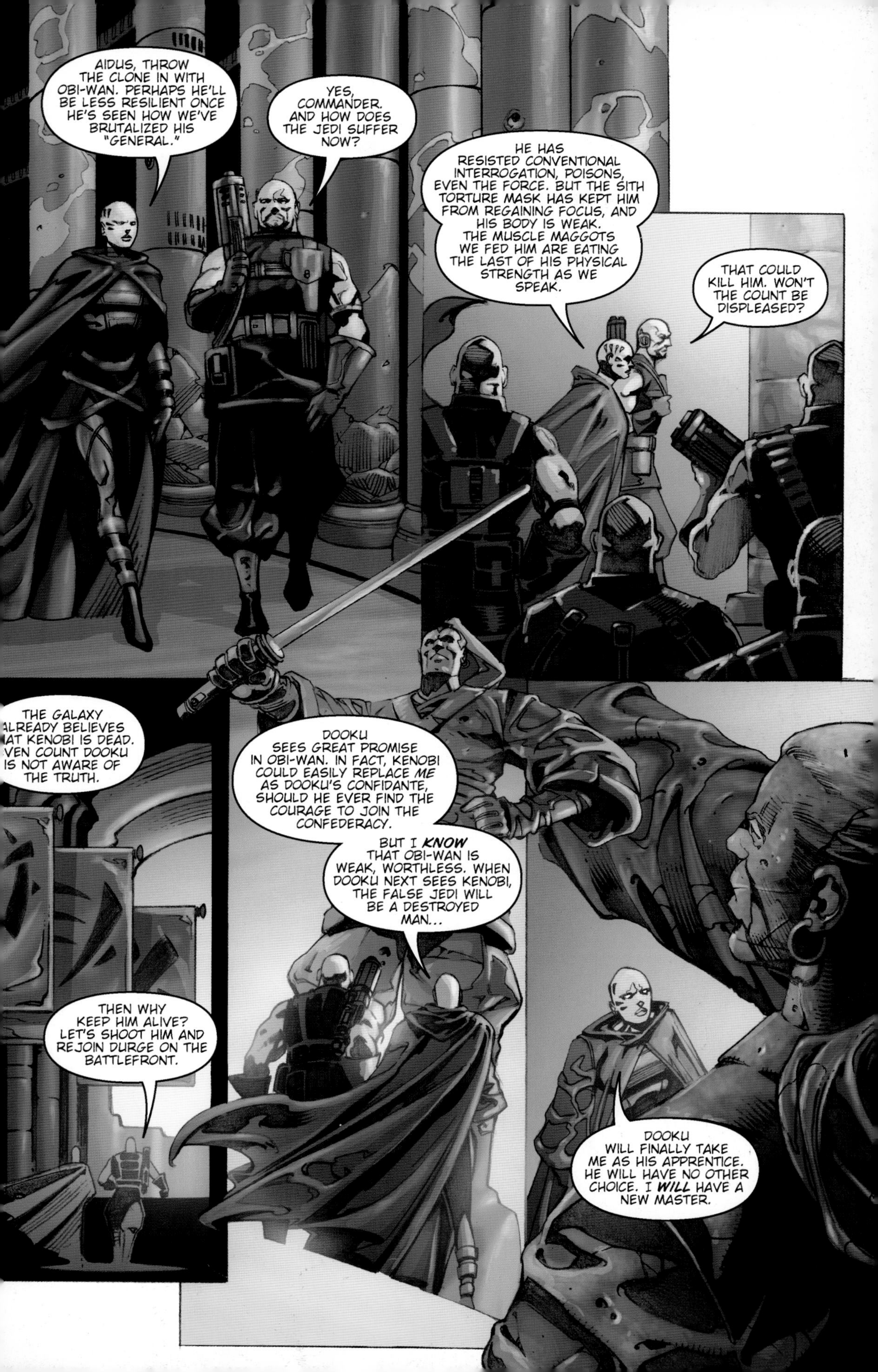
AIDUS, THROW THE CLONE IN WITH OBI-WAN. PERHAPS HE'LL BE LESS RESILIENT ONCE HE'S SEEN HOW WE'VE BRUTALIZED HIS "GENERAL."
YES, COMMANDER. AND HOW DOES THE JEDI SUFFER NOW?
HE HAS RESISTED CONVENTIONAL INTERROGATION, POISONS, EVEN THE FORCE. BUT THE SITH TORTURE MASK HAS KEPT HIM FROM REGAINING FOCUS, AND HIS BODY IS WEAK. THE MUSCLE MAGGOTS WE FED HIM ARE EATING THE LAST OF HIS PHYSICAL STRENGTH AS WE SPEAK.
THAT COULD KILL HIM. WON'T THE COUNT BE DISPLEASED?
THE GALAXY ALREADY BELIEVES THAT KENOBI IS DEAD. EVEN COUNT DOOKU IS NOT AWARE OF THE TRUTH.
THEN WHY KEEP HIM ALIVE? LET'S SHOOT HIM AND REJOIN DURGE ON THE BATTLEFRONT.
DOOKU SEES GREAT PROMISE IN OBI-WAN. IN FACT, KENOBI COULD EASILY REPLACE ME AS DOOKU'S CONFIDANTE, SHOULD HE EVER FIND THE COURAGE TO JOIN THE CONFEDERACY.
BUT I KNOW THAT OBI-WAN IS WEAK, WORTHLESS. WHEN DOOKU NEXT SEES KENOBI, THE FALSE JEDI WILL BE A DESTROYED MAN...
DOOKU WILL FINALLY TAKE ME AS HIS APPRENTICE. HE WILL HAVE NO OTHER CHOICE. I WILL HAVE A NEW MASTER.

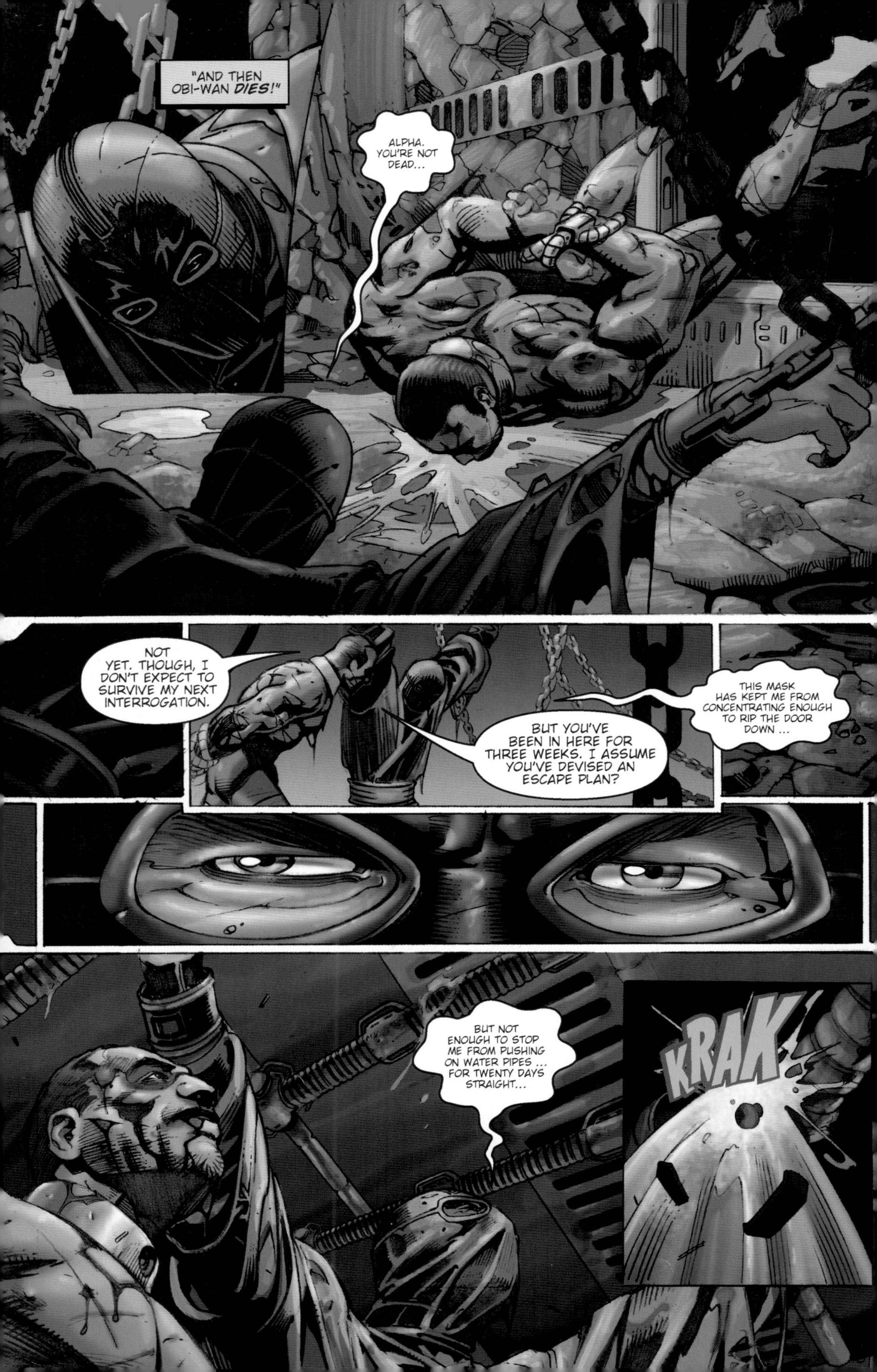
"AND THEN OBI-WAN *DIES*!"
ALPHA. YOU'RE NOT DEAD...
NOT YET. THOUGH, I DON'T EXPECT TO SURVIVE MY NEXT INTERROGATION.
BUT YOU'VE BEEN IN HERE FOR THREE WEEKS. I ASSUME YOU'VE DEVISED AN ESCAPE PLAN?
THIS MASK HAS KEPT ME FROM CONCENTRATING ENOUGH TO RIP THE DOOR DOWN ...
BUT NOT ENOUGH TO STOP ME FROM PUSHING ON WATER PIPES ... FOR TWENTY DAYS STRAIGHT...
KRAK

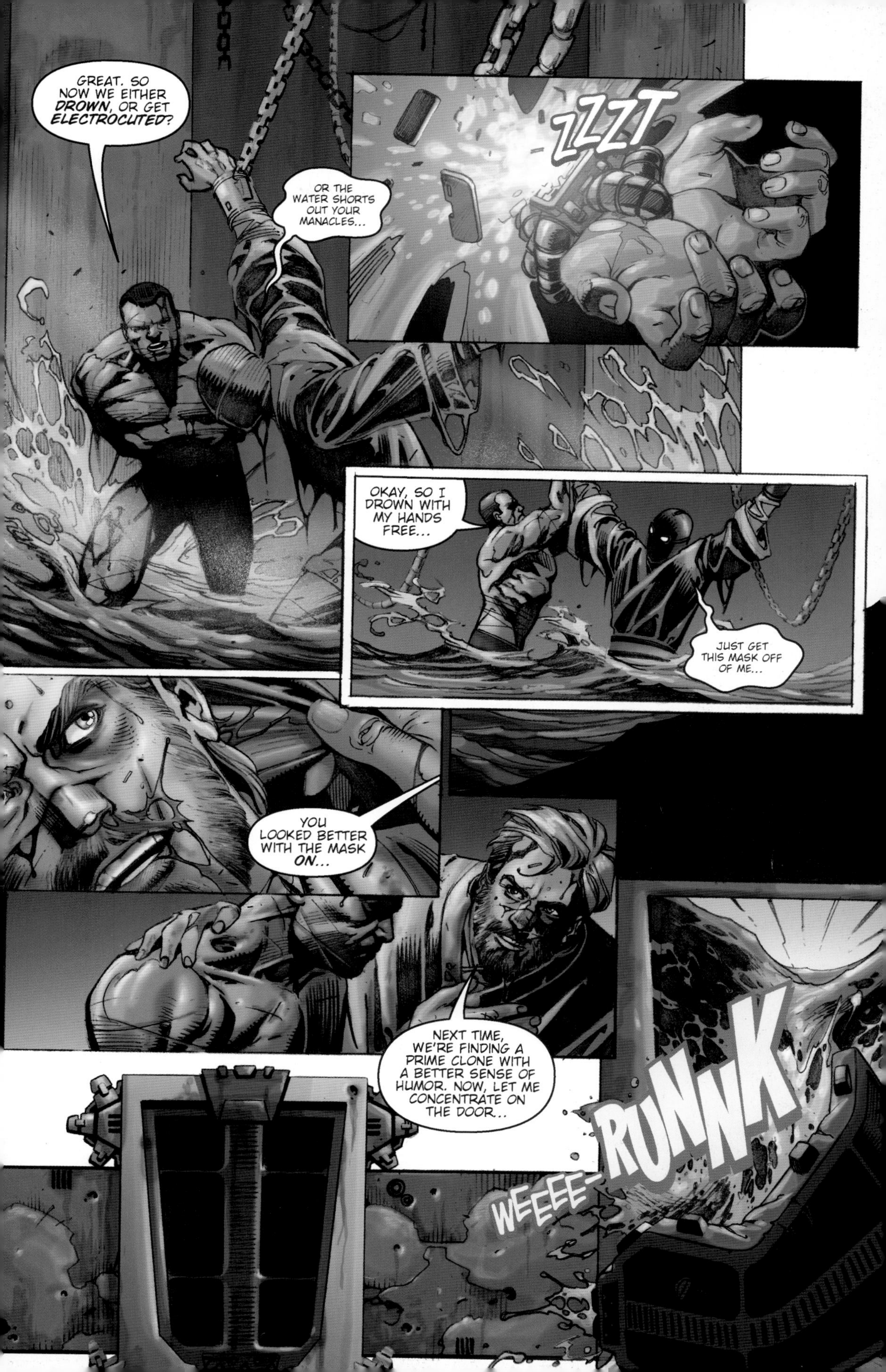
GREAT. SO NOW WE EITHER DROWN, OR GET ELECTROCUTED?
OR THE WATER SHORTS OUT YOUR MANACLES...
ZZZT
OKAY, SO I DROWN WITH MY HANDS FREE...
JUST GET THIS MASK OFF OF ME...
YOU LOOKED BETTER WITH THE MASK ON...
NEXT TIME, WE'RE FINDING A PRIME CLONE WITH A BETTER SENSE OF HUMOR. NOW, LET ME CONCENTRATE ON THE DOOR..
WEEEEE-RUNNK

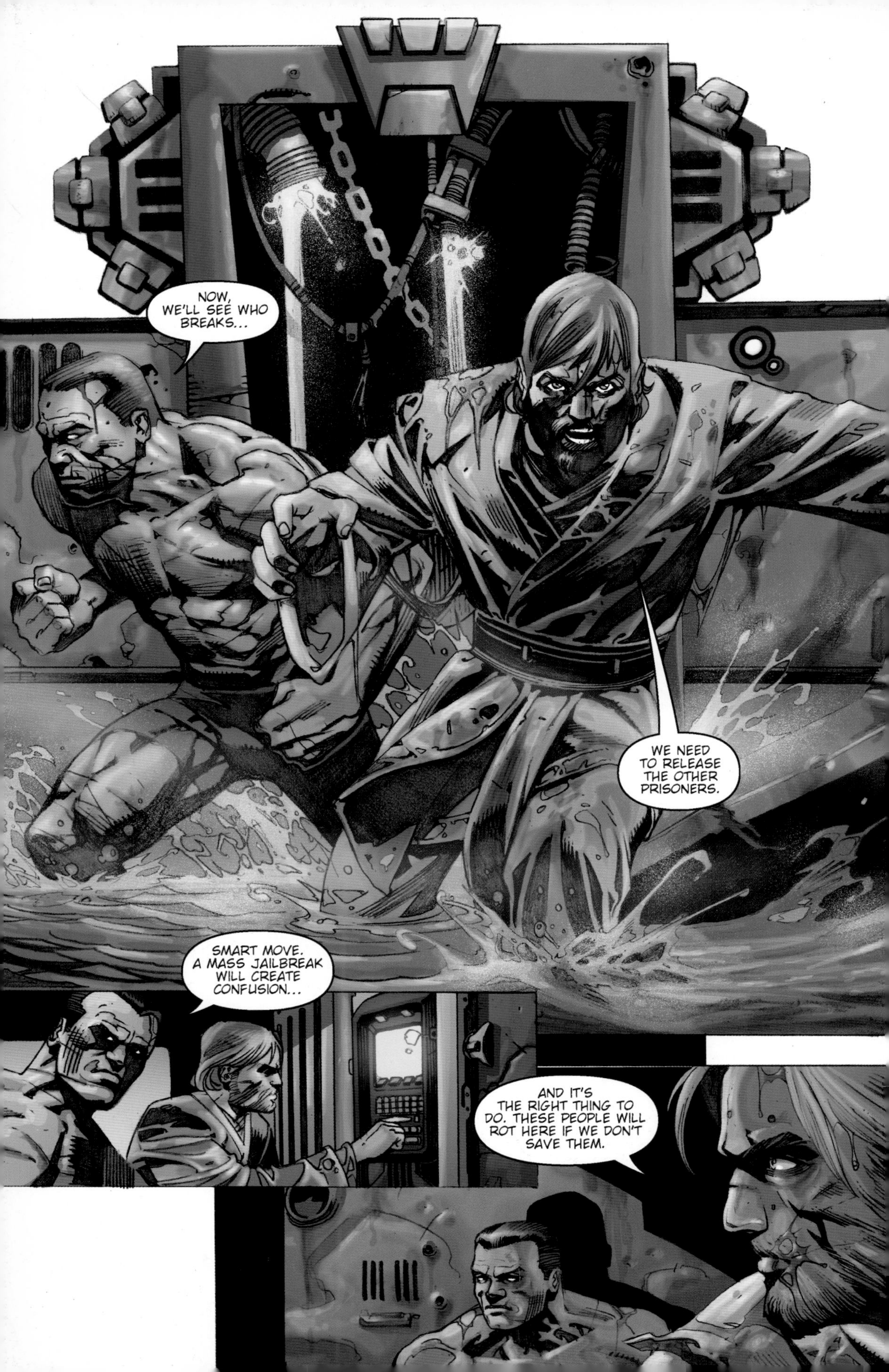
NOW, WE'LL SEE WHO BREAKS...
WE NEED TO RELEASE THE OTHER PRISONERS.
SMART MOVE. A MASS JAILBREAK WILL CREATE CONFUSION...
AND IT'S THE RIGHT THING TO DO. THESE PEOPLE WILL ROT HERE IF WE DON'T SAVE THEM.

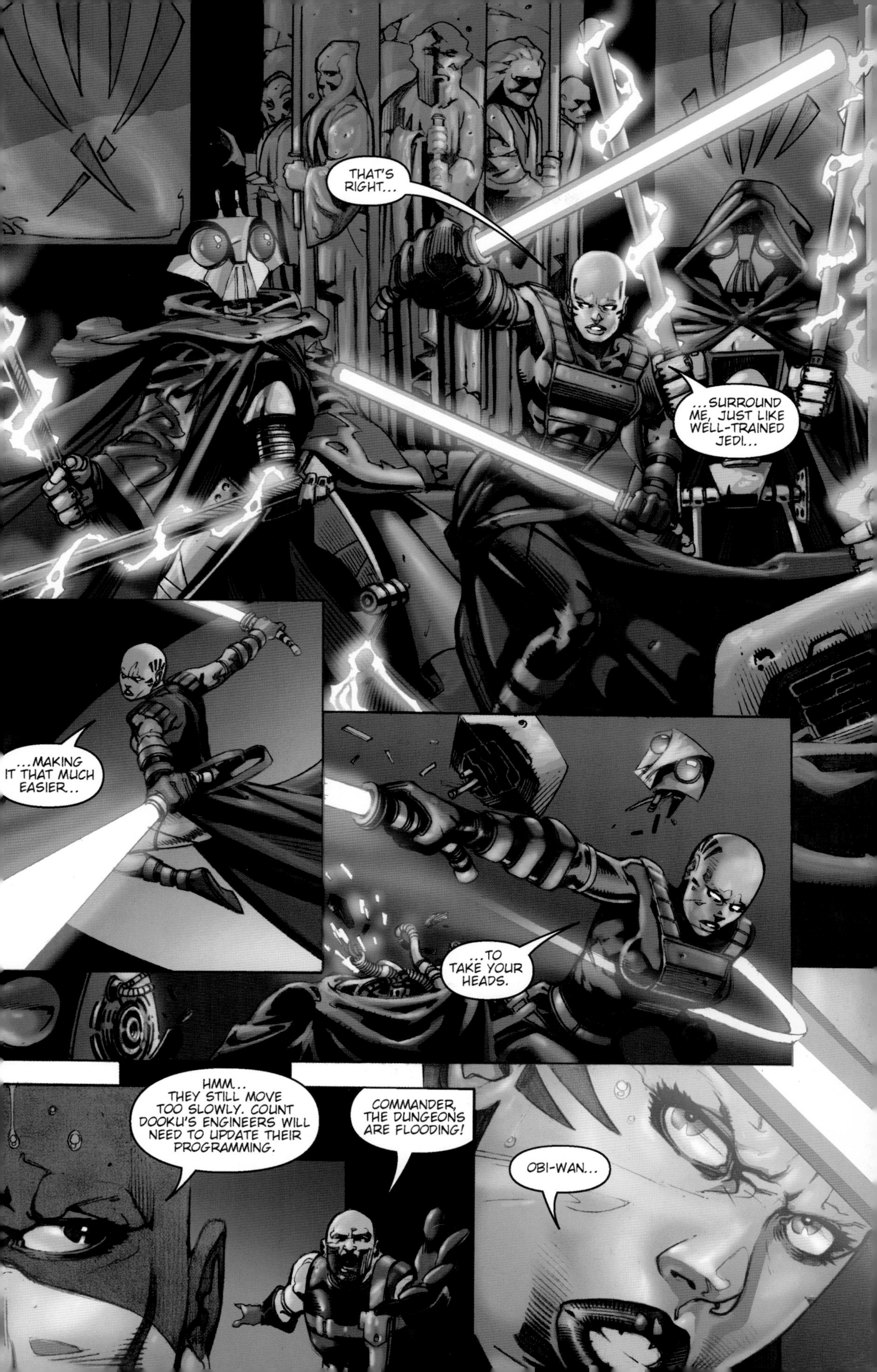
THAT'S RIGHT...
...SURROUND ME, JUST LIKE WELL-TRAINED JEDI...
...MAKING IT THAT MUCH EASIER...
...TO TAKE YOUR HEADS.
HMM... THEY STILL MOVE TOO SLOWLY. COUNT DOOKU'S ENGINEERS WILL NEED TO UPDATE THEIR PROGRAMMING.
COMMANDER, THE DUNGEONS ARE FLOODING!
OBI-WAN...

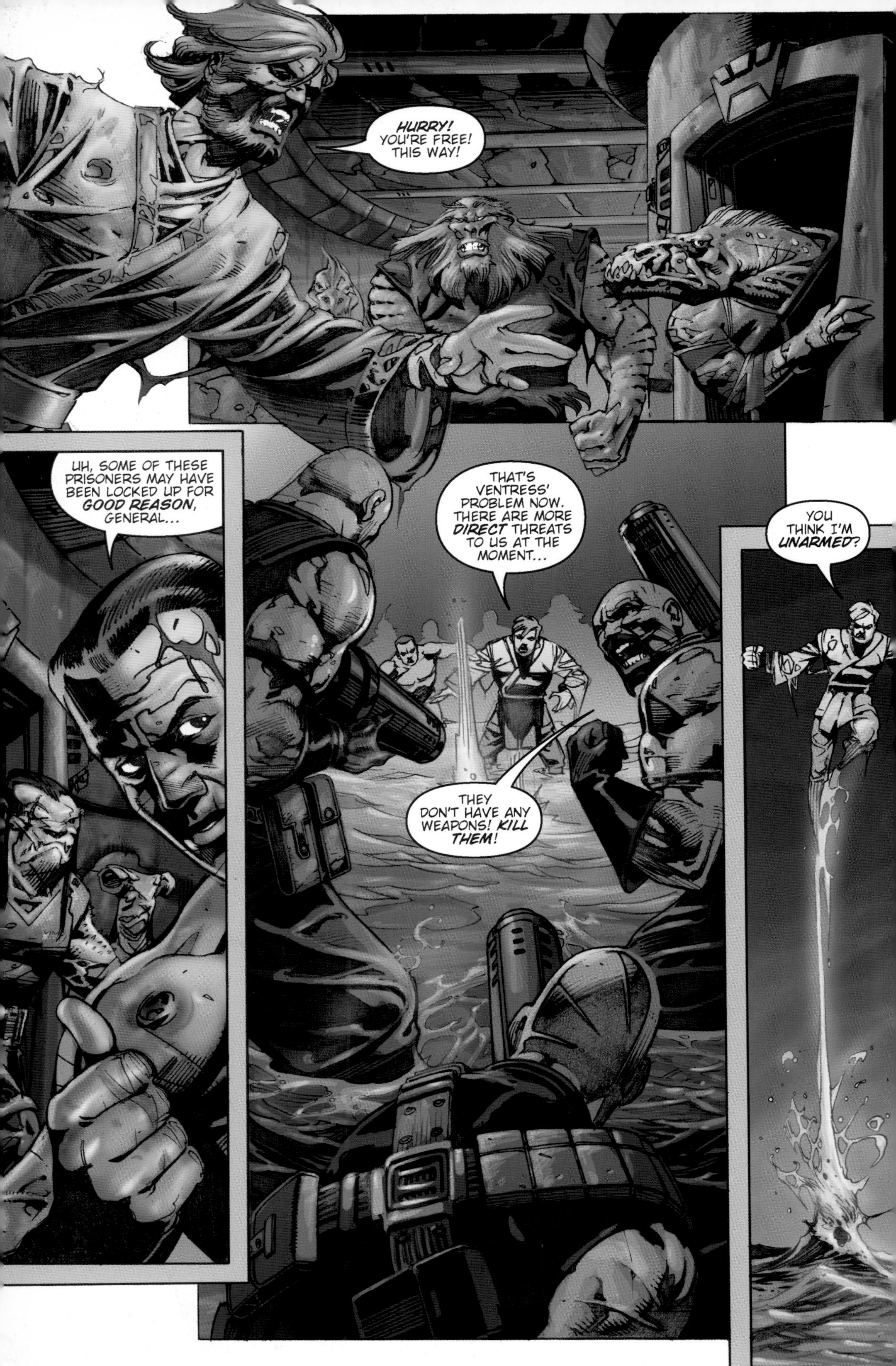
HURRY! YOU'RE FREE! THIS WAY!
UH, SOME OF THESE PRISONERS MAY HAVE BEEN LOCKED UP FOR GOOD REASON, GENERAL...
THAT'S VENTRESS' PROBLEM NOW. THERE ARE MORE DIRECT THREATS TO US AT THE MOMENT...
THEY DON'T HAVE ANY WEAPONS! KILL THEM!
YOU THINK I'M UNARMED?

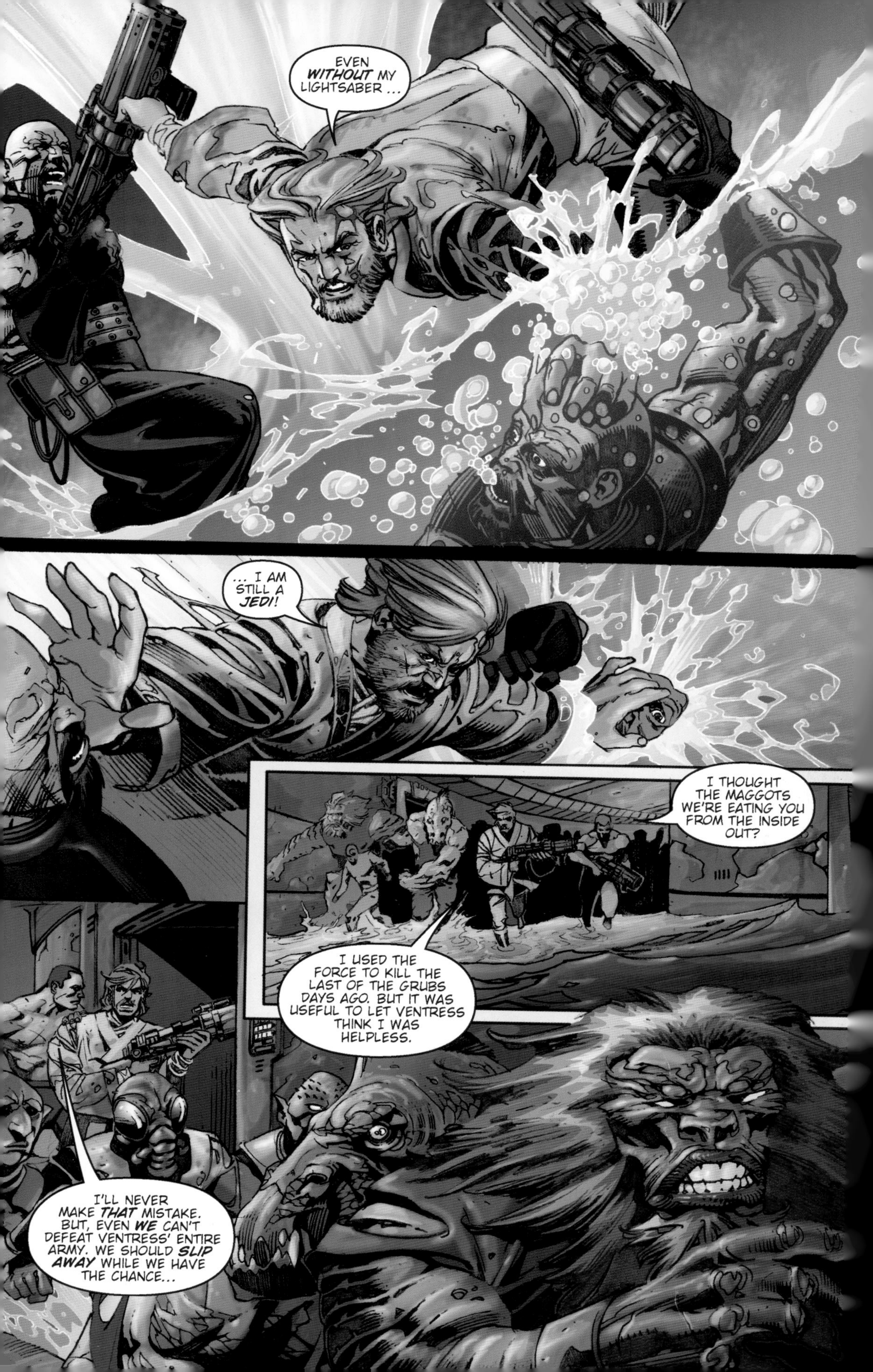

EVEN WITHOUT MY LIGHTSABER ...
... I AM STILL A JEDI!
I THOUGHT THE MAGGOTS WE'RE EATING YOU FROM THE INSIDE OUT?
I USED THE FORCE TO KILL THE LAST OF THE GRUBS DAYS AGO. BUT IT WAS USEFUL TO LET VENTRESS THINK I WAS HELPLESS.
I'LL NEVER MAKE THAT MISTAKE. BUT, EVEN WE CAN'T DEFEAT VENTRESS' ENTIRE ARMY. WE SHOULD SLIP AWAY WHILE WE HAVE THE CHANCE...

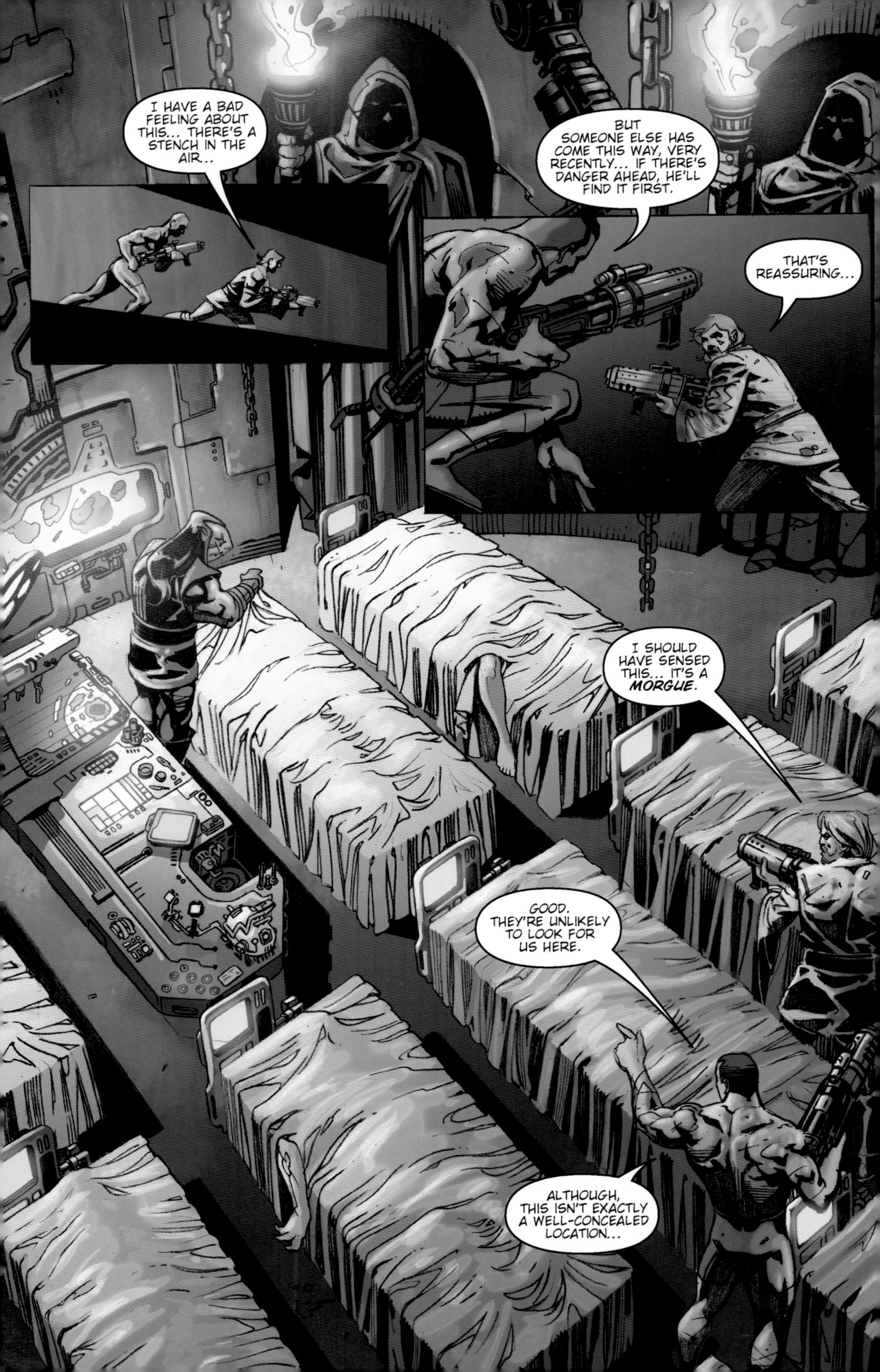
I HAVE A BAD FEELING ABOUT THIS... THERE'S A STENCH IN THE AIR...
BUT SOMEONE ELSE HAS COME THIS WAY, VERY RECENTLY... IF THERE'S DANGER AHEAD, HE'LL FIND IT FIRST.
THAT'S REASSURING...
I SHOULD HAVE SENSED THIS... IT'S A **MORGUE**.
GOOD. THEY'RE UNLIKELY TO LOOK FOR US HERE.
ALTHOUGH, THIS ISN'T EXACTLY A WELL-CONCEALED LOCATION...

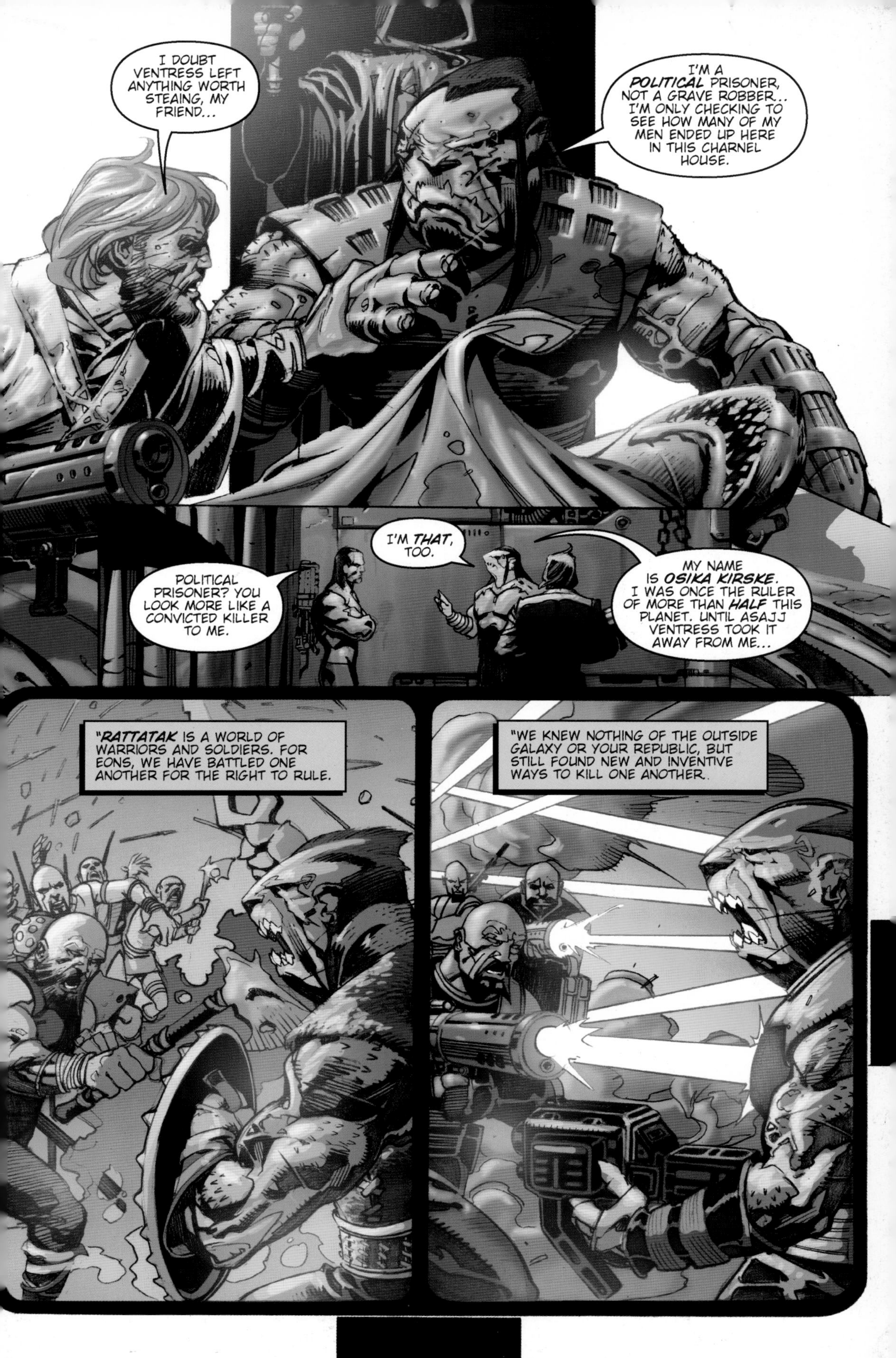
I DOUBT VENTRESS LEFT ANYTHING WORTH STEAING, MY FRIEND...
I'M A POLITICAL PRISONER, NOT A GRAVE ROBBER... I'M ONLY CHECKING TO SEE HOW MANY OF MY MEN ENDED UP HERE IN THIS CHARNEL HOUSE.
POLITICAL PRISONER? YOU LOOK MORE LIKE A CONVICTED KILLER TO ME.
I'M THAT, TOO.
MY NAME IS OSIKA KIRSKE. I WAS ONCE THE RULER OF MORE THAN HALF THIS PLANET. UNTIL ASAJJ VENTRESS TOOK IT AWAY FROM ME...
"RATTATAK IS A WORLD OF WARRIORS AND SOLDIERS. FOR EONS, WE HAVE BATTLED ONE ANOTHER FOR THE RIGHT TO RULE.
"WE KNEW NOTHING OF THE OUTSIDE GALAXY OR YOUR REPUBLIC, BUT STILL FOUND NEW AND INVENTIVE WAYS TO KILL ONE ANOTHER.

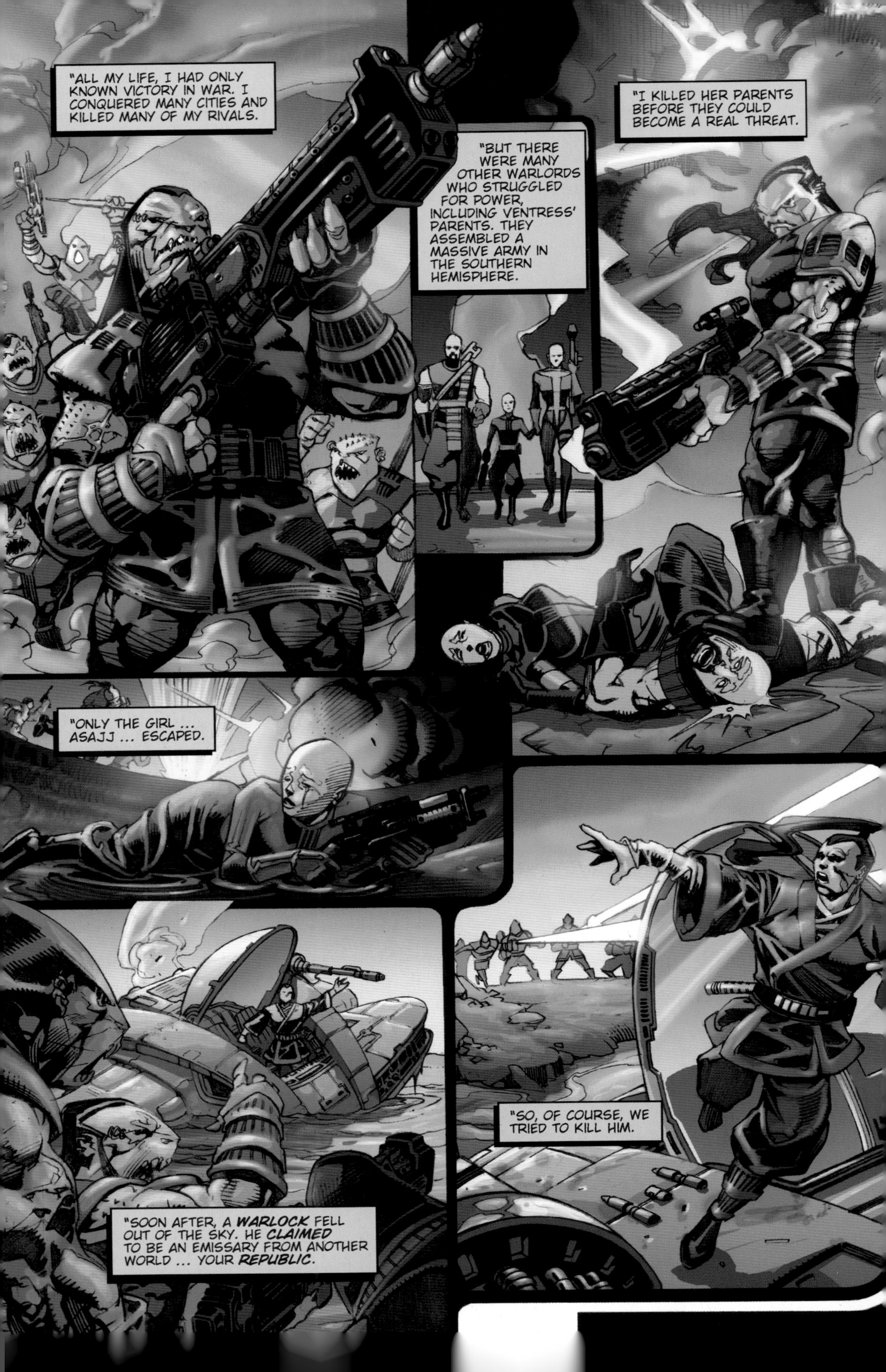
"ALL MY LIFE, I HAD ONLY KNOWN VICTORY IN WAR. I CONQUERED MANY CITIES AND KILLED MANY OF MY RIVALS.
"BUT THERE WERE MANY OTHER WARLORDS WHO STRUGGLED FOR POWER, INCLUDING VENTRESS' PARENTS. THEY ASSEMBLED A MASSIVE ARMY IN THE SOUTHERN HEMISPHERE.
"I KILLED HER PARENTS BEFORE THEY COULD BECOME A REAL THREAT.
"ONLY THE GIRL ... ASAJJ ... ESCAPED.
"SOON AFTER, A WARLOCK FELL OUT OF THE SKY. HE CLAIMED TO BE AN EMISSARY FROM ANOTHER WORLD ... YOUR REPUBLIC.
"SO, OF COURSE, WE TRIED TO KILL HIM.

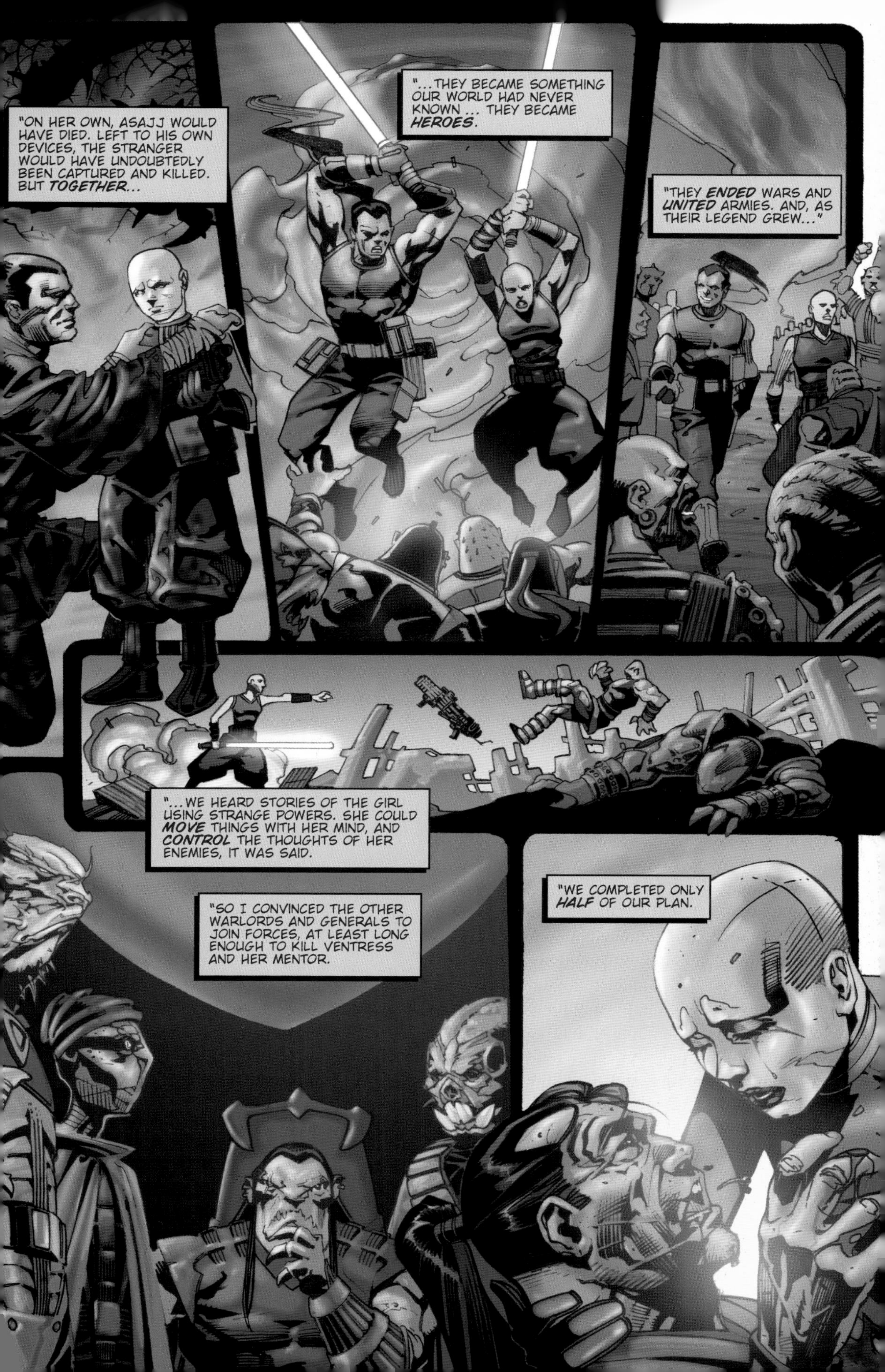
"ON HER OWN, ASAJJ WOULD HAVE DIED. LEFT TO HIS OWN DEVICES, THE STRANGER WOULD HAVE UNDOUBTEDLY BEEN CAPTURED AND KILLED. BUT TOGETHER...
"...THEY BECAME SOMETHING OUR WORLD HAD NEVER KNOWN ... THEY BECAME HEROES.
"THEY ENDED WARS AND UNITED ARMIES. AND, AS THEIR LEGEND GREW..."
"...WE HEARD STORIES OF THE GIRL USING STRANGE POWERS. SHE COULD MOVE THINGS WITH HER MIND, AND CONTROL THE THOUGHTS OF HER ENEMIES, IT WAS SAID.
"SO I CONVINCED THE OTHER WARLORDS AND GENERALS TO JOIN FORCES, AT LEAST LONG ENOUGH TO KILL VENTRESS AND HER MENTOR.
"WE COMPLETED ONLY HALF OF OUR PLAN.

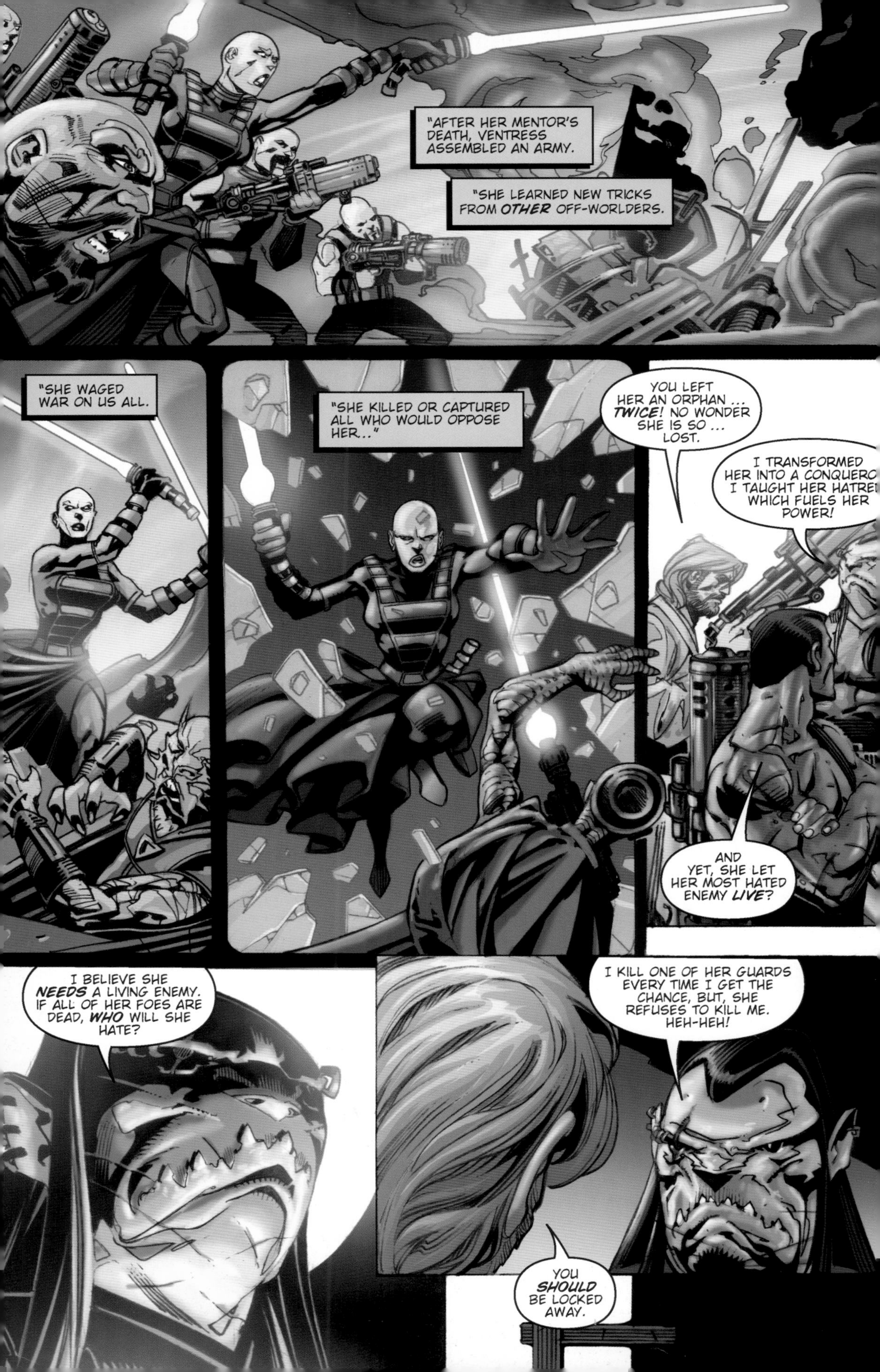
"AFTER HER MENTOR'S DEATH, VENTRESS ASSEMBLED AN ARMY.
"SHE LEARNED NEW TRICKS FROM OTHER OFF-WORLDERS.
"SHE WAGED WAR ON US ALL.
"SHE KILLED OR CAPTURED ALL WHO WOULD OPPOSE HER..."
YOU LEFT HER AN ORPHAN ... TWICE! NO WONDER SHE IS SO ... LOST.
I TRANSFORMED HER INTO A CONQUERO I TAUGHT HER HATRE WHICH FUELS HER POWER!
AND YET, SHE LET HER MOST HATED ENEMY LIVE?
I BELIEVE SHE NEEDS A LIVING ENEMY. IF ALL OF HER FOES ARE DEAD, WHO WILL SHE HATE?
I KILL ONE OF HER GUARDS EVERY TIME I GET THE CHANCE, BUT, SHE REFUSES TO KILL ME. HEH-HEH!
YOU SHOULD BE LOCKED AWAY.

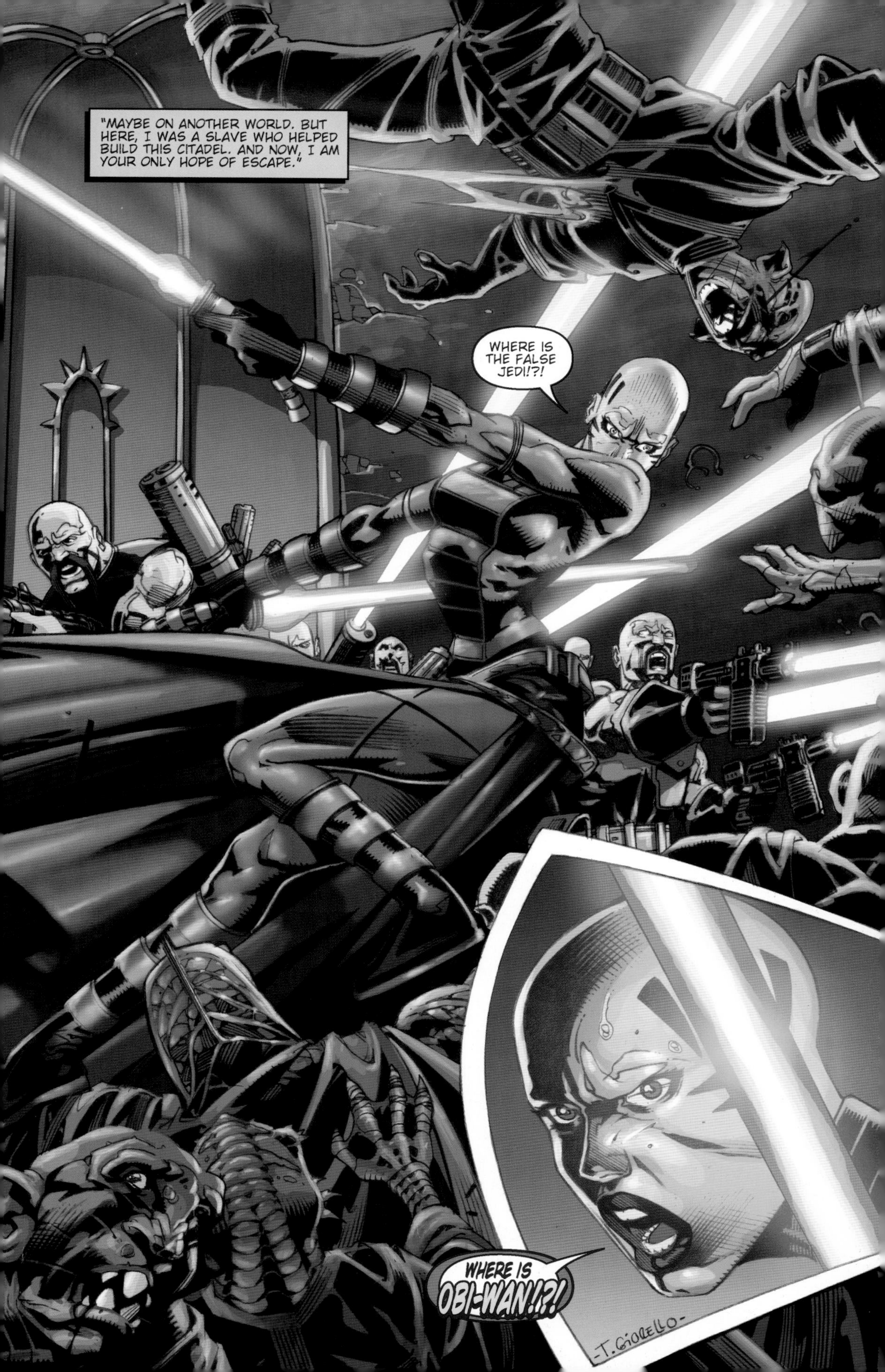
"MAYBE ON ANOTHER WORLD. BUT HERE, I WAS A SLAVE WHO HELPED BUILD THIS CITADEL. AND NOW, I AM YOUR ONLY HOPE OF ESCAPE."
WHERE IS THE FALSE JEDI!?!
WHERE IS OBI-WAN!?!
-T. GIORELLO-

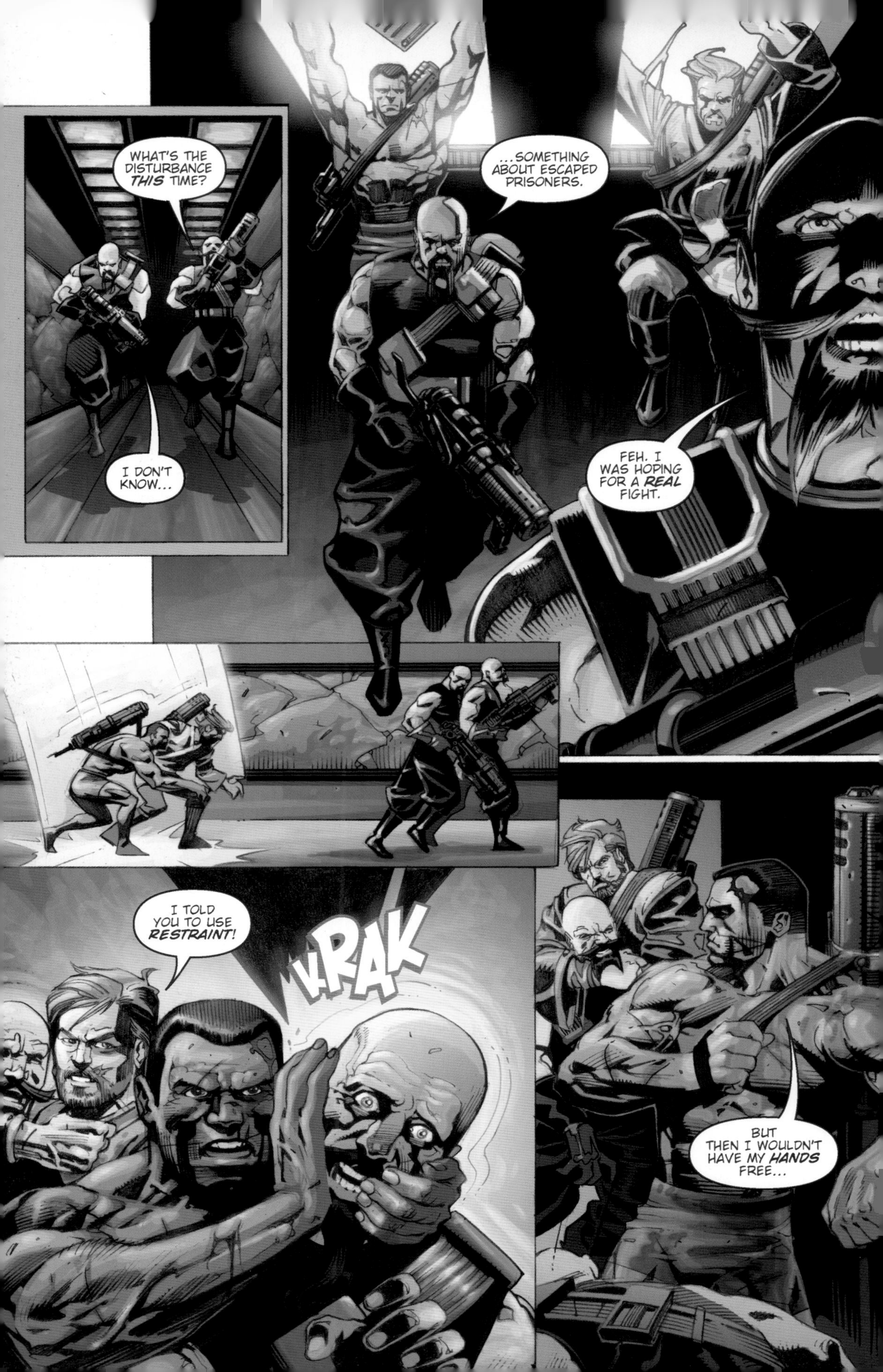
WHAT'S THE DISTURBANCE *THIS* TIME?
I DON'T KNOW...
...SOMETHING ABOUT ESCAPED PRISONERS.
FEH. I WAS HOPING FOR A *REAL* FIGHT.
I TOLD YOU TO USE *RESTRAINT*!
KRAK
BUT THEN I WOULDN'T HAVE MY *HANDS* FREE...

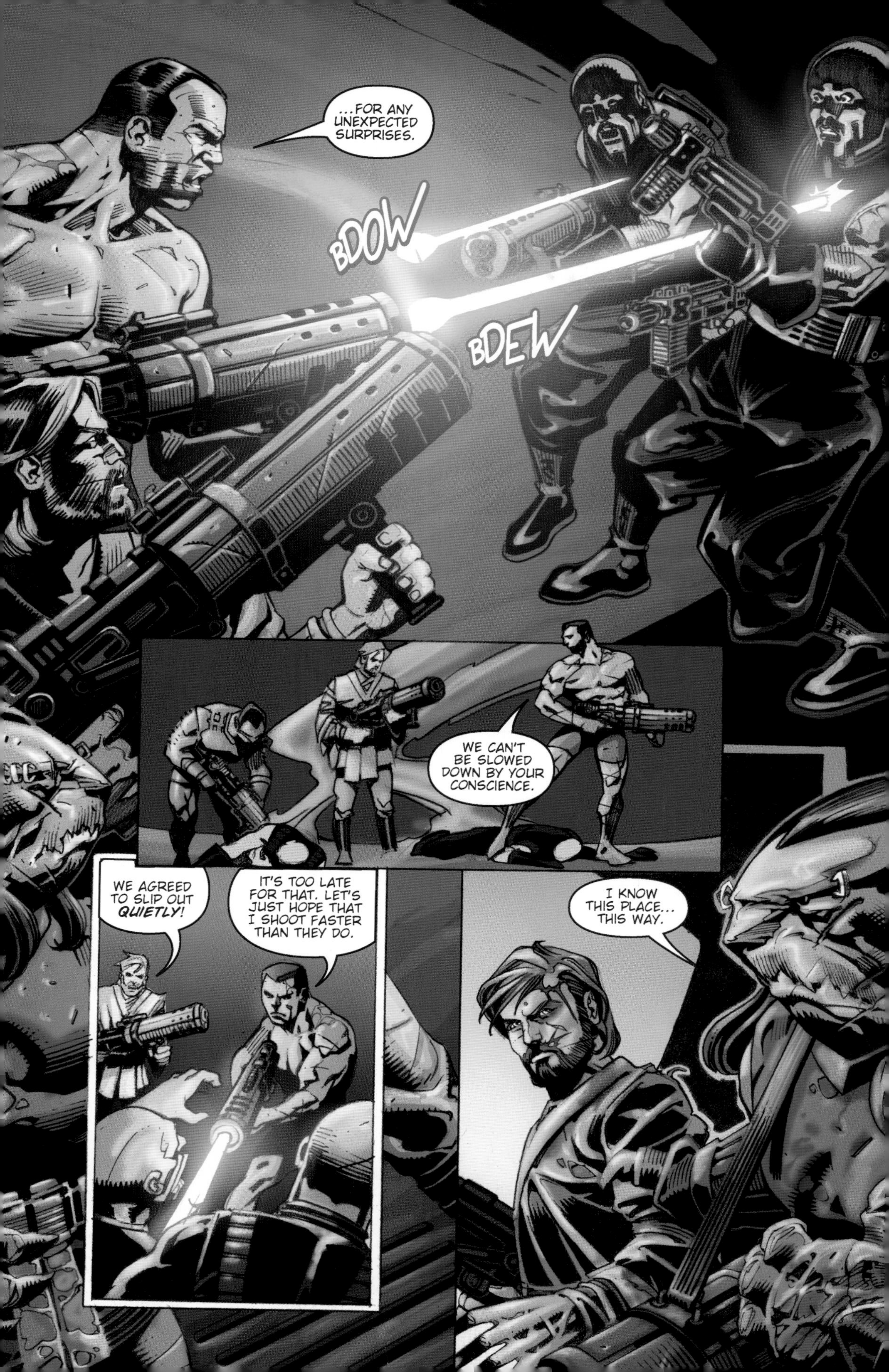
...FOR ANY UNEXPECTED SURPRISES.
BDOW
BDEW
WE CAN'T BE SLOWED DOWN BY YOUR CONSCIENCE.
WE AGREED TO SLIP OUT *QUIETLY*!
IT'S TOO LATE FOR THAT. LET'S JUST HOPE THAT I SHOOT FASTER THAN THEY DO.
I KNOW THIS PLACE... THIS WAY.

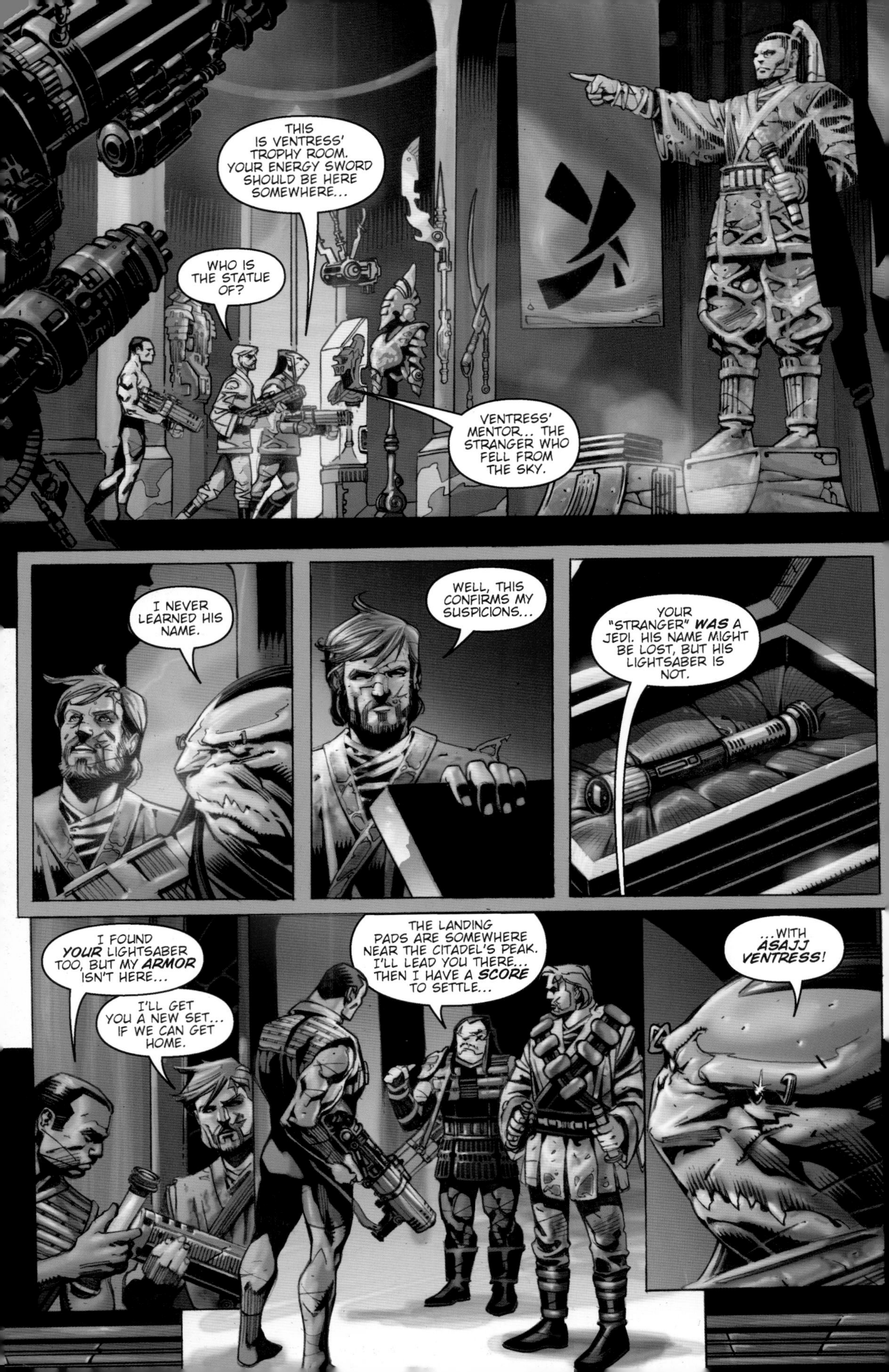

THIS IS VENTRESS' TROPHY ROOM. YOUR ENERGY SWORD SHOULD BE HERE SOMEWHERE...
WHO IS THE STATUE OF?
VENTRESS' MENTOR... THE STRANGER WHO FELL FROM THE SKY.
I NEVER LEARNED HIS NAME.
WELL, THIS CONFIRMS MY SUSPICIONS...
YOUR "STRANGER" WAS A JEDI. HIS NAME MIGHT BE LOST, BUT HIS LIGHTSABER IS NOT.
I FOUND YOUR LIGHTSABER TOO, BUT MY ARMOR ISN'T HERE...
I'LL GET YOU A NEW SET... IF WE CAN GET HOME.
THE LANDING PADS ARE SOMEWHERE NEAR THE CITADEL'S PEAK. I'LL LEAD YOU THERE... THEN I HAVE A SCORE TO SETTLE...
...WITH ASAJJ VENTRESS!

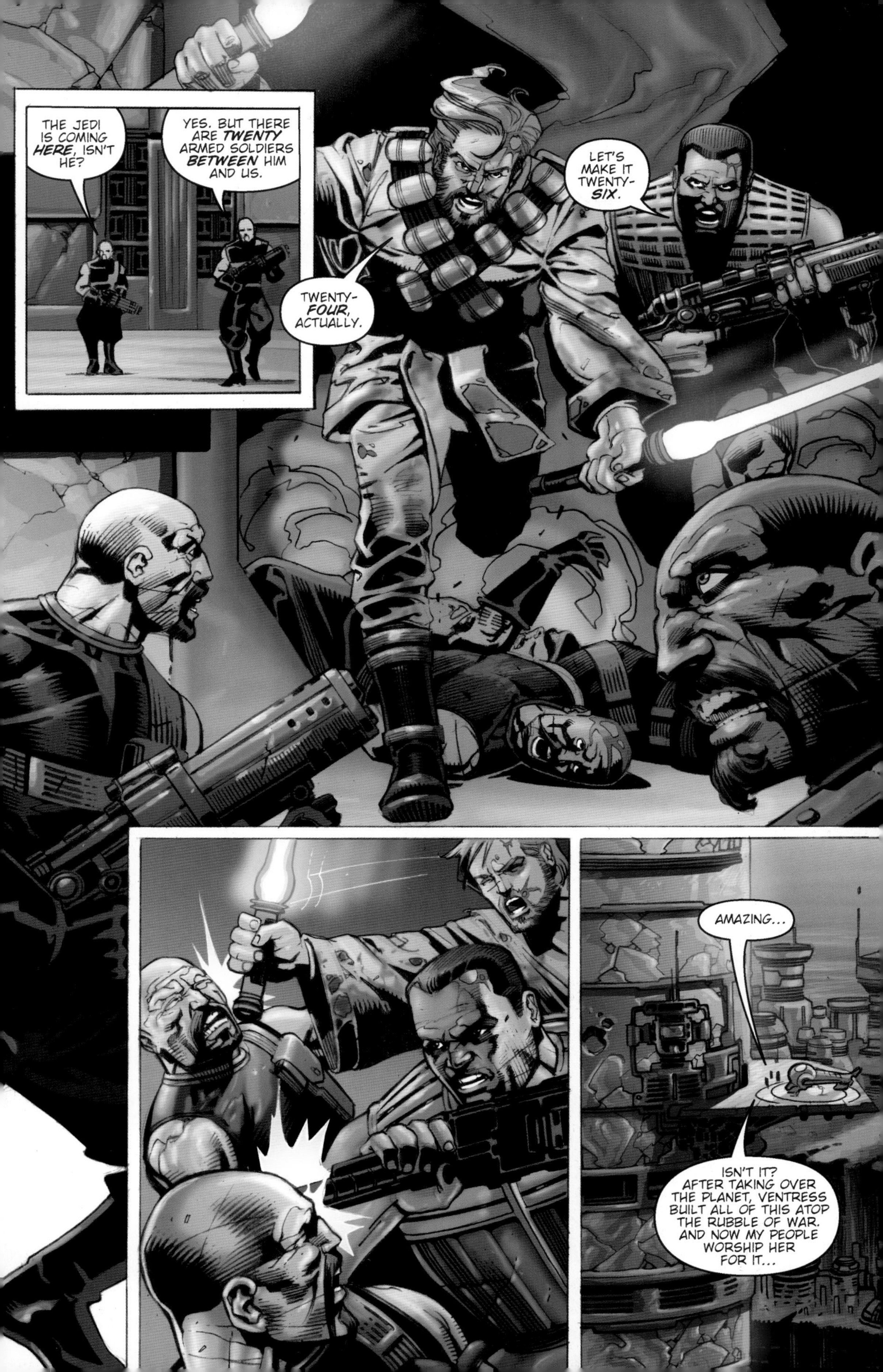
THE JEDI IS COMING *HERE*, ISN'T HE?
YES. BUT THERE ARE *TWENTY* ARMED SOLDIERS *BETWEEN* HIM AND US.
TWENTY-*FOUR*, ACTUALLY.
LET'S MAKE IT TWENTY-*SIX*.
AMAZING...
ISN'T IT? AFTER TAKING OVER THE PLANET, VENTRESS BUILT ALL OF THIS ATOP THE RUBBLE OF WAR. AND NOW MY PEOPLE WORSHIP HER FOR IT...

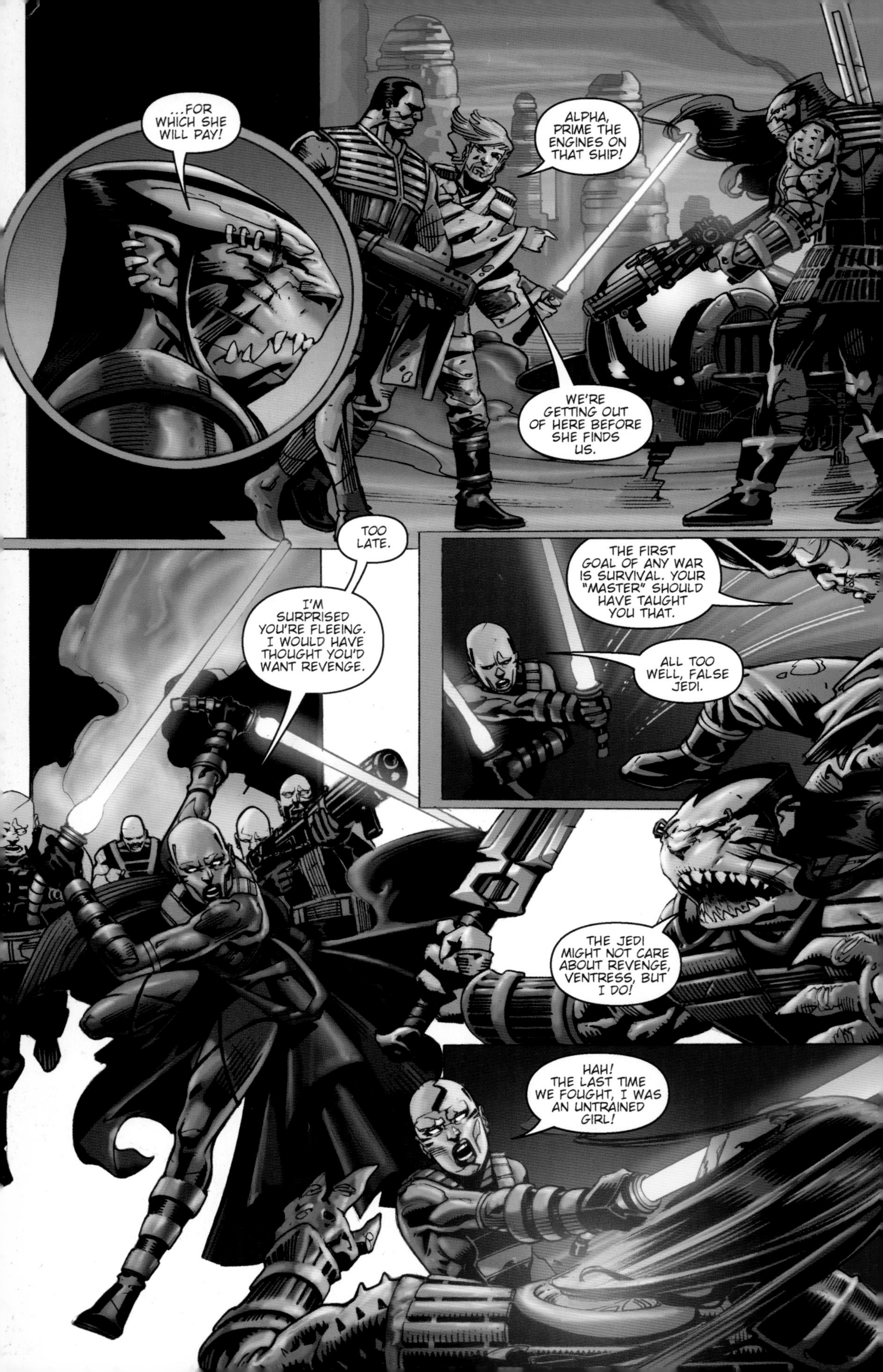
...FOR WHICH SHE WILL PAY!
ALPHA, PRIME THE ENGINES ON THAT SHIP!
WE'RE GETTING OUT OF HERE BEFORE SHE FINDS US.
TOO LATE.
I'M SURPRISED YOU'RE FLEEING. I WOULD HAVE THOUGHT YOU'D WANT REVENGE.
THE FIRST GOAL OF ANY WAR IS SURVIVAL. YOUR "MASTER" SHOULD HAVE TAUGHT YOU THAT.
ALL TOO WELL, FALSE JEDI.
THE JEDI MIGHT NOT CARE ABOUT REVENGE, VENTRESS, BUT I DO!
HAH! THE LAST TIME WE FOUGHT, I WAS AN UNTRAINED GIRL!

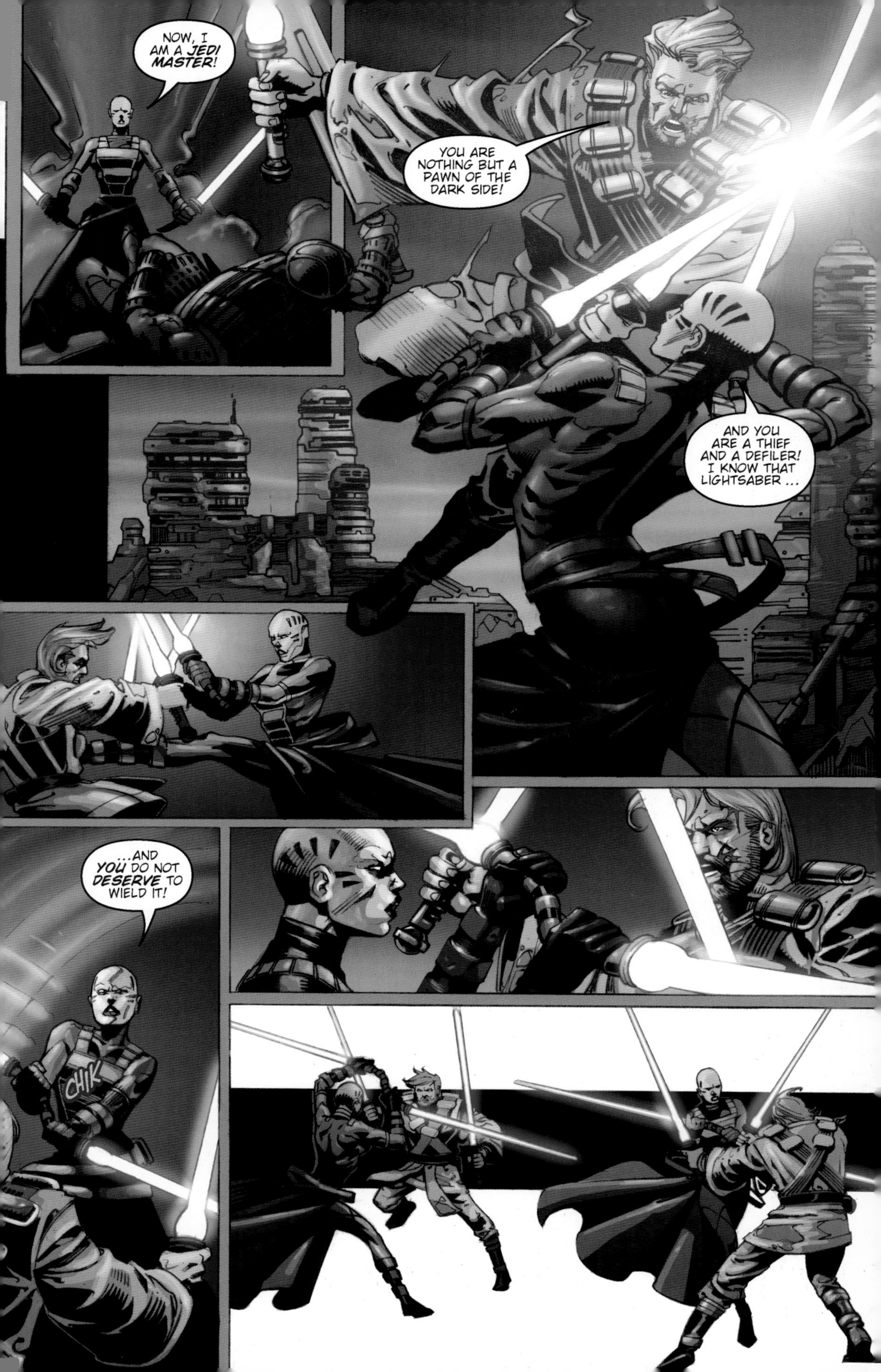
NOW, I AM A *JEDI MASTER!*
YOU ARE NOTHING BUT A PAWN OF THE DARK SIDE!
AND YOU ARE A THIEF AND A DEFILER! I KNOW THAT LIGHTSABER ...
...AND *YOU* DO NOT *DESERVE* TO WIELD IT!
CHIK

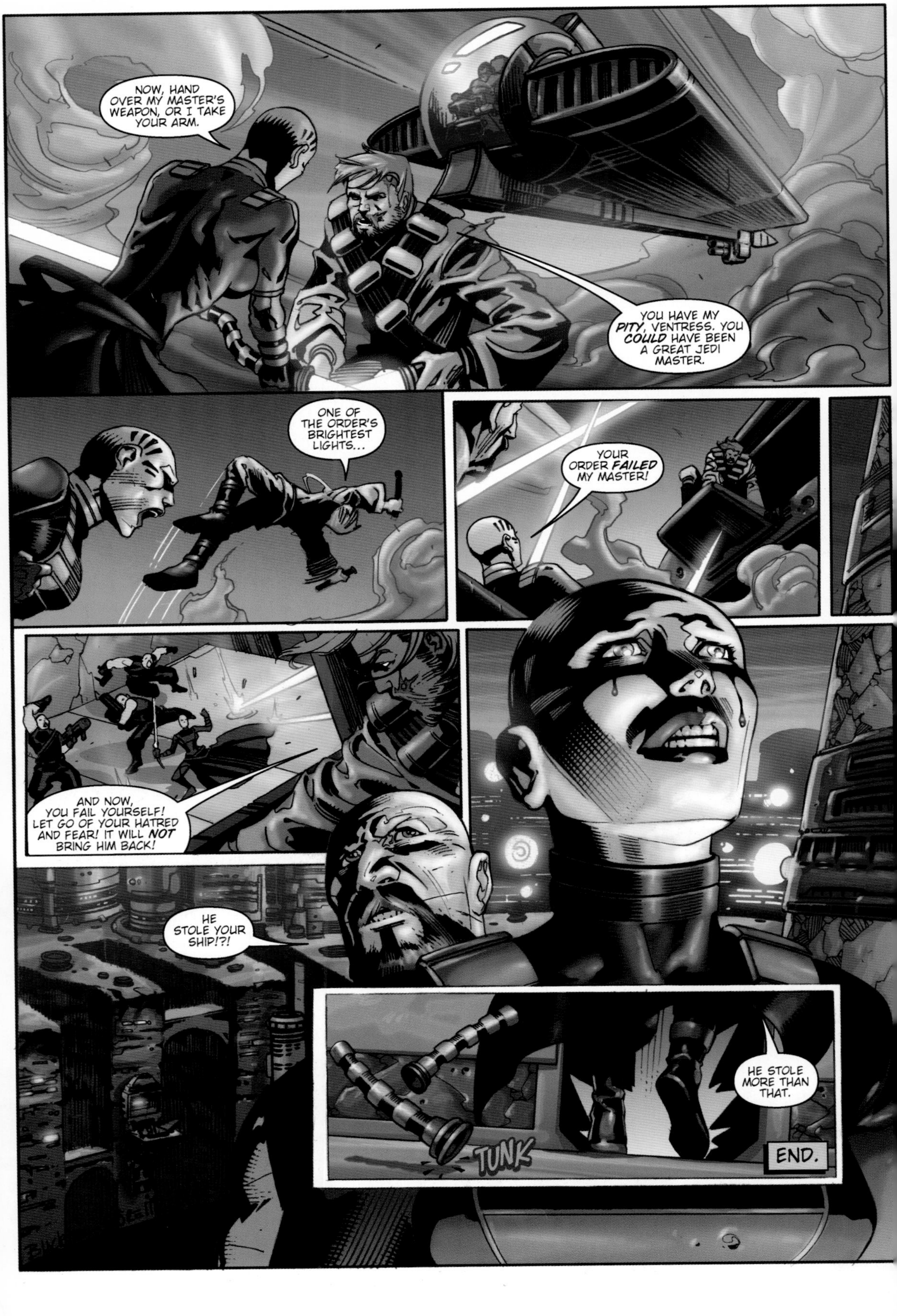
NOW, HAND OVER MY MASTER'S WEAPON, OR I TAKE YOUR ARM.
YOU HAVE MY PITY, VENTRESS. YOU COULD HAVE BEEN A GREAT JEDI MASTER.
ONE OF THE ORDER'S BRIGHTEST LIGHTS...
YOUR ORDER FAILED MY MASTER!
AND NOW, YOU FAIL YOURSELF! LET GO OF YOUR HATRED AND FEAR! IT WILL NOT BRING HIM BACK!
HE STOLE YOUR SHIP!?!
HE STOLE MORE THAN THAT.
TUNK
END.

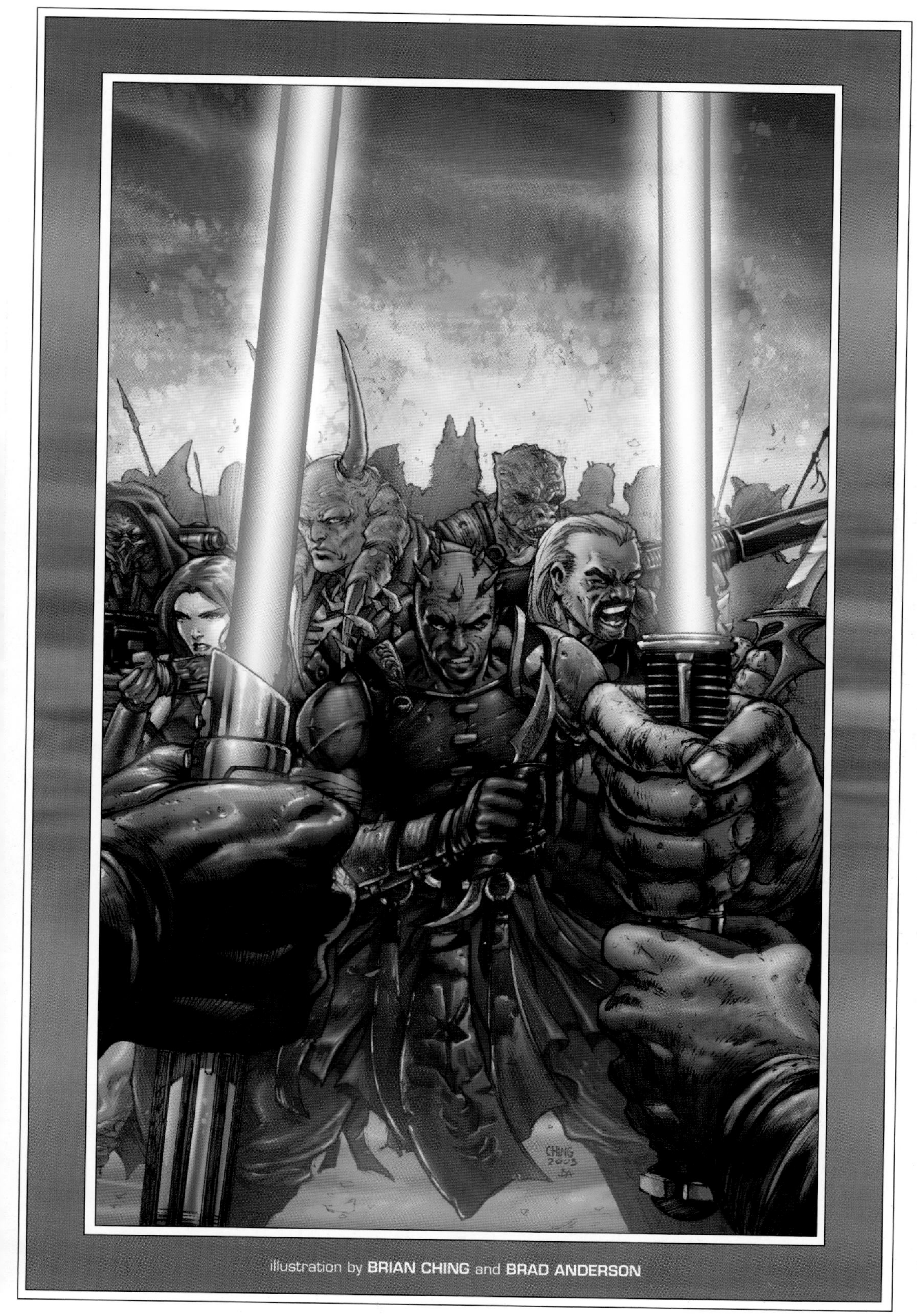
CHING
2003
BA

illustration by **BRIAN CHING** and **BRAD ANDERSON**

# NO MAN'S LAND

**"No Man's Land"**
written by **Haden Blackman**
art by **Tomás Giorello**

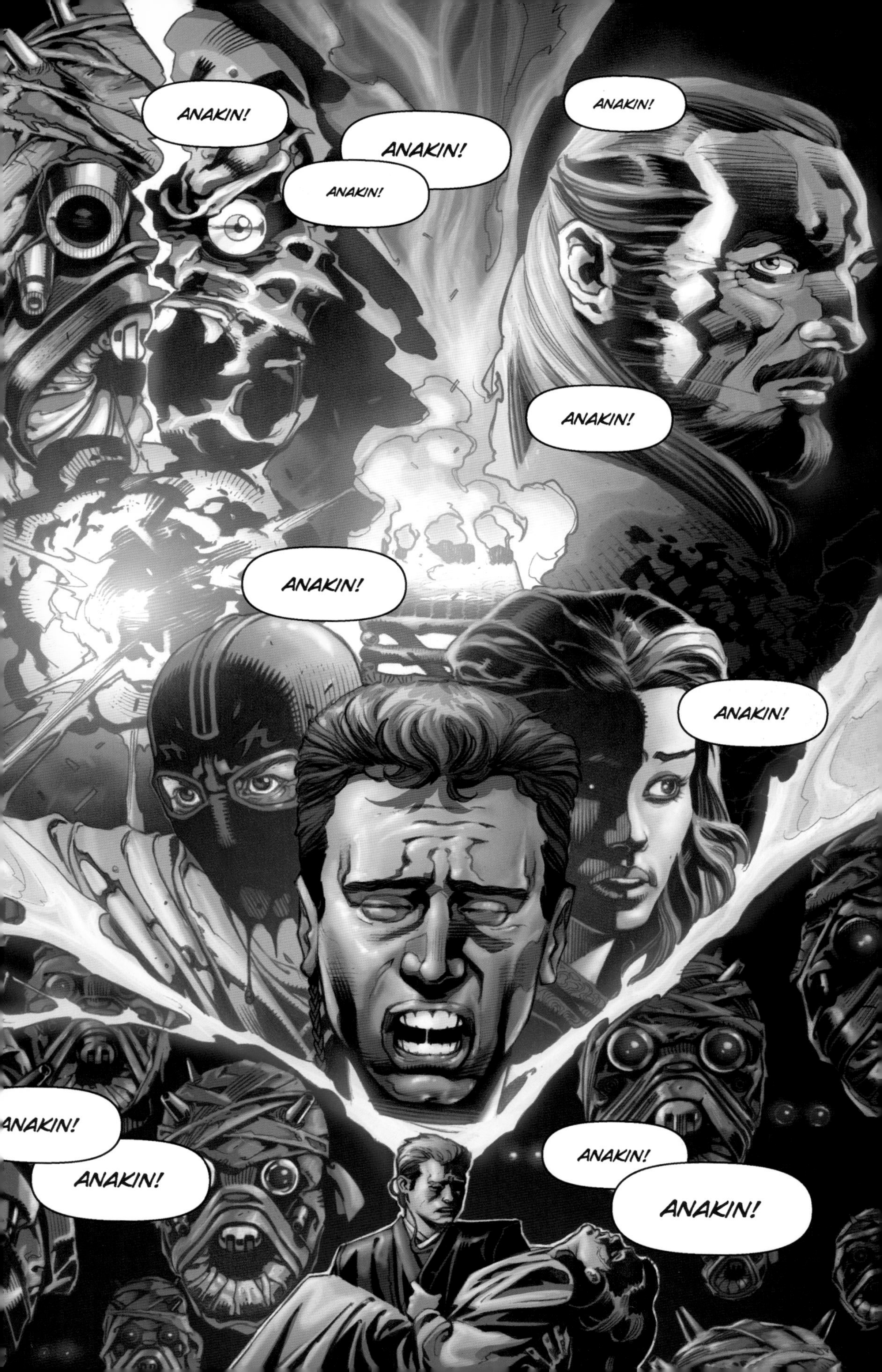
ANAKIN!
ANAKIN!
ANAKIN!
ANAKIN!
ANAKIN!
ANAKIN!
ANAKIN!
ANAKIN!
ANAKIN!
ANAKIN!
ANAKIN!

DREAMS.

HE HATES DREAMS.

AHHHH!

IF HE COULD, ANAKIN SKYWALKER THINKS HE WOULD NEVER SLEEP AGAIN.

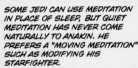

SOME JEDI CAN USE MEDITATION IN PLACE OF SLEEP, BUT QUIET MEDITATION HAS NEVER COME NATURALLY TO ANAKIN. HE PREFERS A "MOVING MEDITATION" SUCH AS MODIFYING HIS STARFIGHTER.

HANDS OCCUPIED, HIS MIND IS FREED AND FOCUSED. THINGS MAKE SENSE HERE. THERE ARE REASONS THINGS DON'T WORK AND STRAIGHTFORWARD WAYS TO MAKE THINGS BETTER.

YOU ARE DISTRESSED, YOUNG PADAWAN.

I FELT IT IN THE FORCE, ANAKIN. I SUSPECT THEY COULD HAVE FELT IT ON CORUSCANT.

I'M FINE, MASTER KI-ADI-MUNDI.

YOUR ASSIGNMENT AS MY PADAWAN IS NEW AND PERHAPS ONLY TEMPORARY. I UNDERSTAND THAT. TRUST TAKES TIME. STILL, I HOPE YOU WILL BE OPEN WITH ME. OBI-WAN'S DEATH CONTINUES TO TROUBLE YOU, DOESN'T IT?

THAT'S PART OF THE PROBLEM, MASTER -- I DON'T *FEEL* THAT OBI-WAN IS DEAD! MY *FEELINGS* TELL ME MASTER OBI-WAN IS STILL ALIVE! AND HE *NEEDS* ME!

IF THAT WERE SO, WOULDN'T HE HAVE MADE HIMSELF *KNOWN* BY NOW?

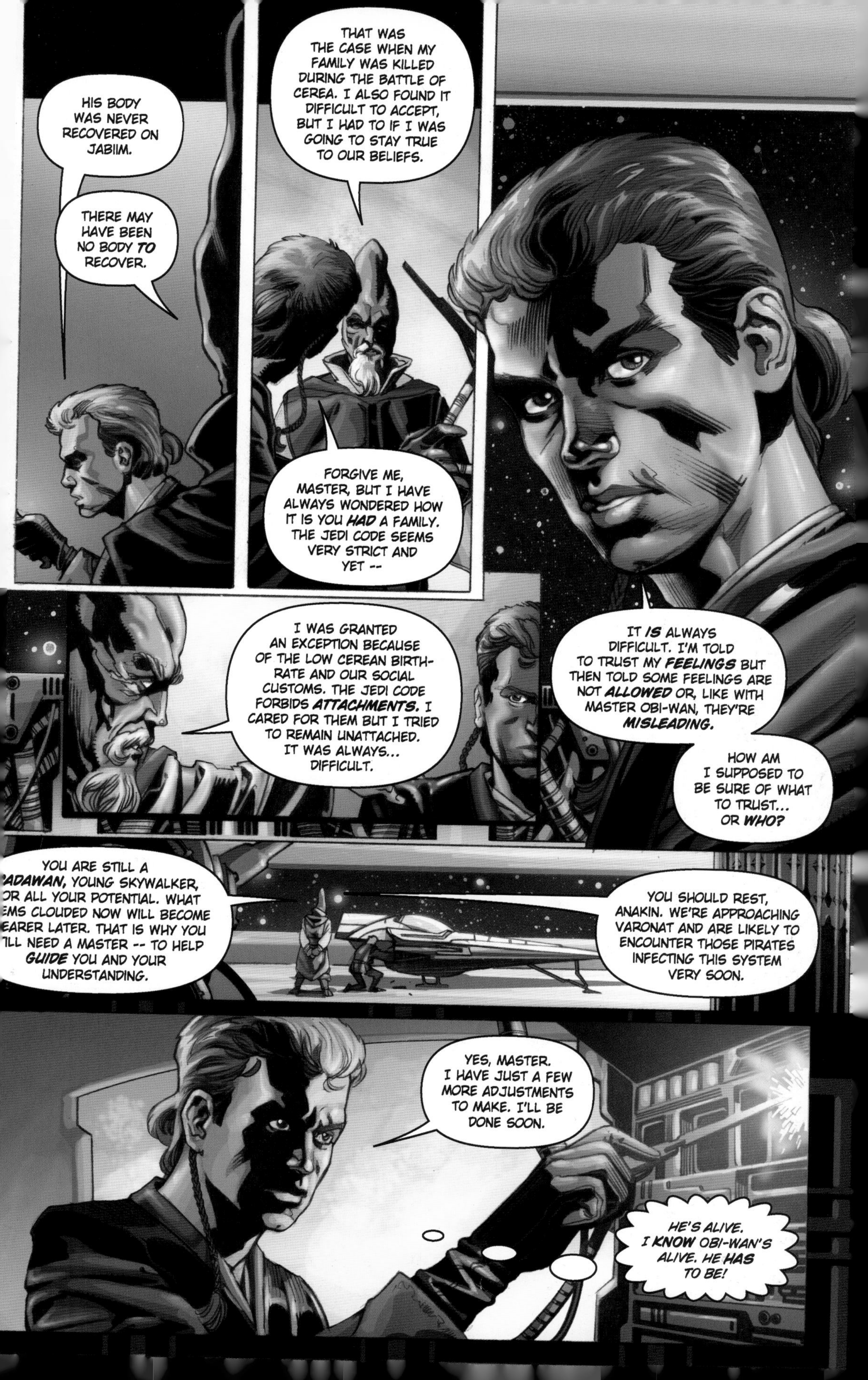
HIS BODY WAS NEVER RECOVERED ON JABIIM.
THERE MAY HAVE BEEN NO BODY *TO* RECOVER.
THAT WAS THE CASE WHEN MY FAMILY WAS KILLED DURING THE BATTLE OF CEREA. I ALSO FOUND IT DIFFICULT TO ACCEPT, BUT I HAD TO IF I WAS GOING TO STAY TRUE TO OUR BELIEFS.
FORGIVE ME, MASTER, BUT I HAVE ALWAYS WONDERED HOW IT IS YOU *HAD* A FAMILY. THE JEDI CODE SEEMS VERY STRICT AND YET --
I WAS GRANTED AN EXCEPTION BECAUSE OF THE LOW CEREAN BIRTH-RATE AND OUR SOCIAL CUSTOMS. THE JEDI CODE FORBIDS *ATTACHMENTS.* I CARED FOR THEM BUT I TRIED TO REMAIN UNATTACHED. IT WAS ALWAYS... DIFFICULT.
IT *IS* ALWAYS DIFFICULT. I'M TOLD TO TRUST MY *FEELINGS* BUT THEN TOLD SOME FEELINGS ARE NOT *ALLOWED* OR, LIKE WITH MASTER OBI-WAN, THEY'RE *MISLEADING.*
HOW AM I SUPPOSED TO BE SURE OF WHAT TO TRUST... OR *WHO?*
YOU ARE STILL A *ADAWAN,* YOUNG SKYWALKER, OR ALL YOUR POTENTIAL. WHAT EMS CLOUDED NOW WILL BECOME EARER LATER. THAT IS WHY YOU ILL NEED A MASTER -- TO HELP *GUIDE* YOU AND YOUR UNDERSTANDING.
YOU SHOULD REST, ANAKIN. WE'RE APPROACHING VARONAT AND ARE LIKELY TO ENCOUNTER THOSE PIRATES INFECTING THIS SYSTEM VERY SOON.
YES, MASTER. I HAVE JUST A FEW MORE ADJUSTMENTS TO MAKE. I'LL BE DONE SOON.
*HE'S ALIVE. I **KNOW** OBI-WAN'S ALIVE. HE **HAS** TO BE!*

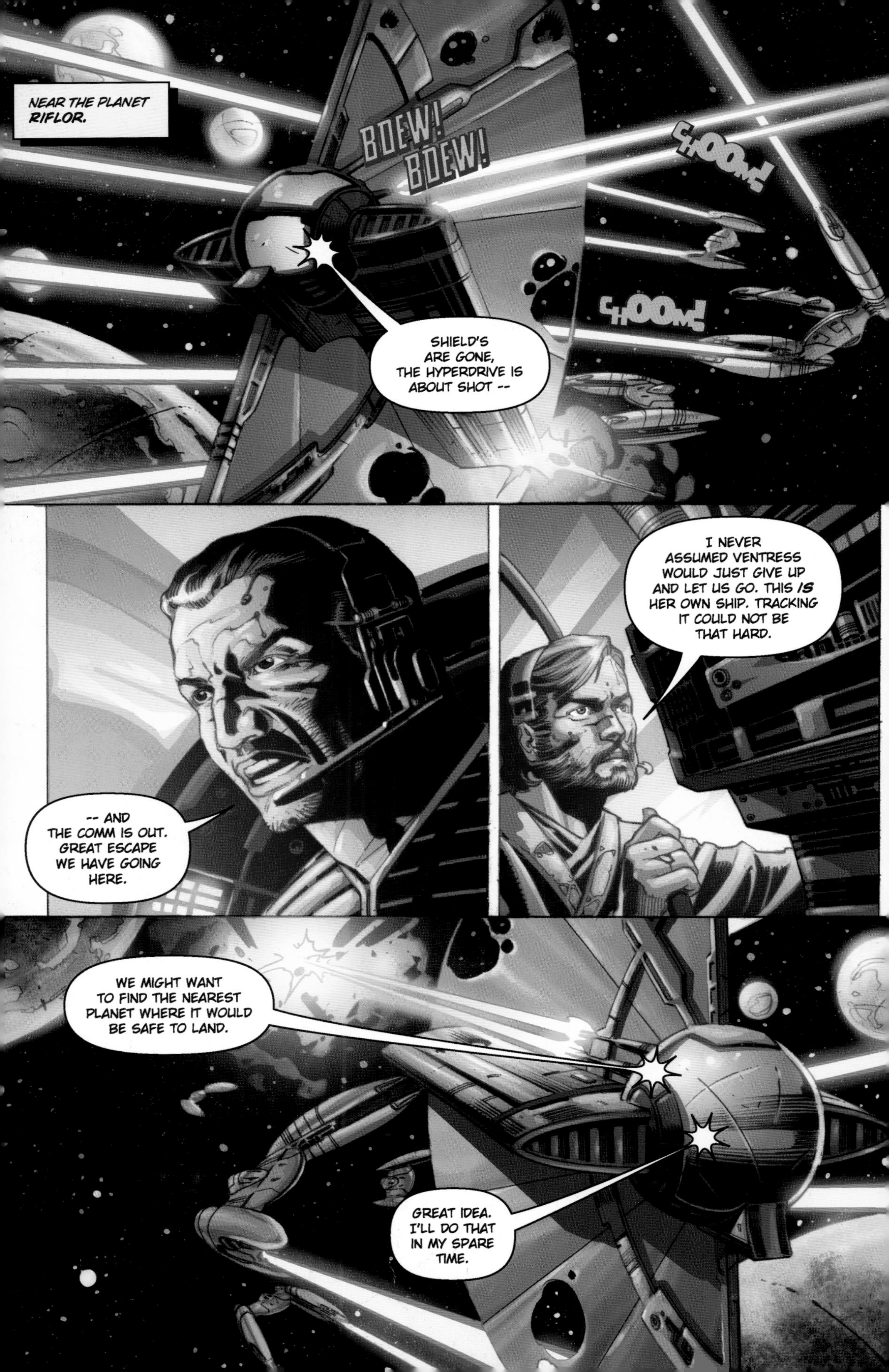

NEAR THE PLANET RIFLOR.
BDEW! BDEW!
CHOOM!
CHOOM!
SHIELD'S ARE GONE, THE HYPERDRIVE IS ABOUT SHOT --
-- AND THE COMM IS OUT. GREAT ESCAPE WE HAVE GOING HERE.
I NEVER ASSUMED VENTRESS WOULD JUST GIVE UP AND LET US GO. THIS *IS* HER OWN SHIP. TRACKING IT COULD NOT BE THAT HARD.
WE MIGHT WANT TO FIND THE NEAREST PLANET WHERE IT WOULD BE SAFE TO LAND.
GREAT IDEA. I'LL DO THAT IN MY SPARE TIME.

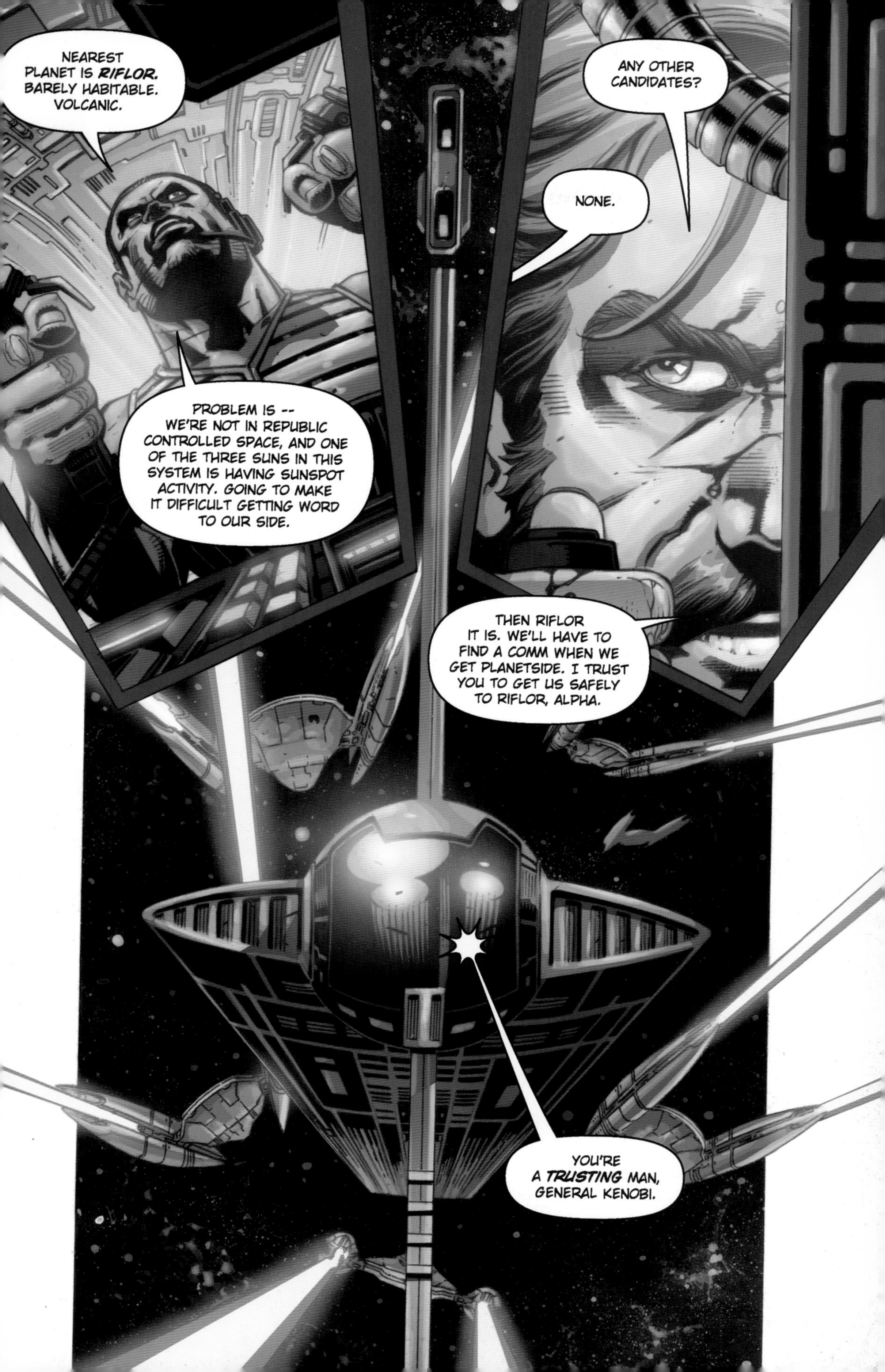
NEAREST PLANET IS *RIFLOR.* BARELY HABITABLE. VOLCANIC.
PROBLEM IS -- WE'RE NOT IN REPUBLIC CONTROLLED SPACE, AND ONE OF THE THREE SUNS IN THIS SYSTEM IS HAVING SUNSPOT ACTIVITY. GOING TO MAKE IT DIFFICULT GETTING WORD TO OUR SIDE.
ANY OTHER CANDIDATES?
NONE.
THEN RIFLOR IT IS. WE'LL HAVE TO FIND A COMM WHEN WE GET PLANETSIDE. I TRUST YOU TO GET US SAFELY TO RIFLOR, ALPHA.
YOU'RE A *TRUSTING* MAN, GENERAL KENOBI.

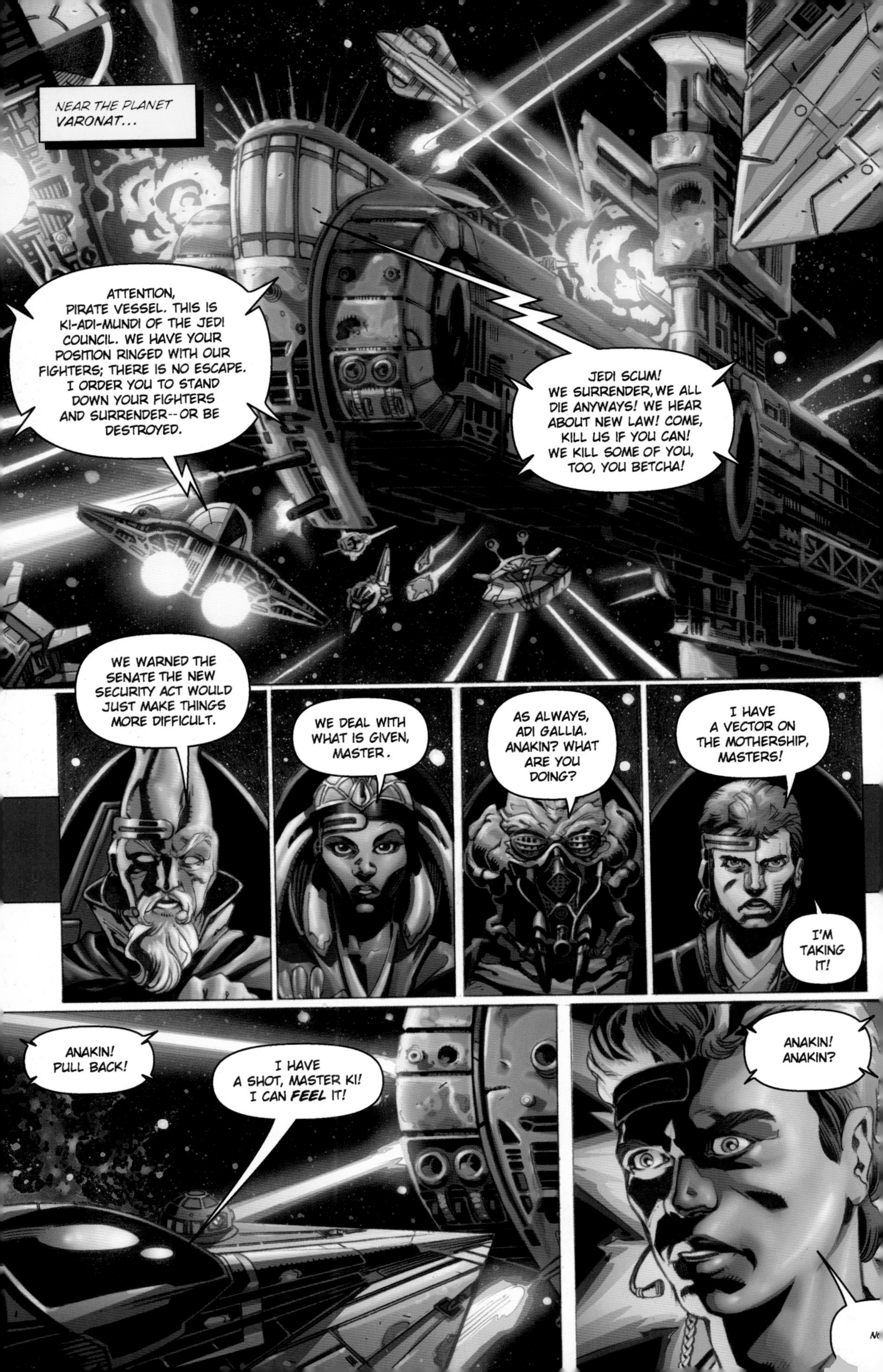
NEAR THE PLANET VARONAT...
ATTENTION, PIRATE VESSEL. THIS IS KI-ADI-MUNDI OF THE JEDI COUNCIL. WE HAVE YOUR POSITION RINGED WITH OUR FIGHTERS; THERE IS NO ESCAPE. I ORDER YOU TO STAND DOWN YOUR FIGHTERS AND SURRENDER--OR BE DESTROYED.
JEDI SCUM! WE SURRENDER, WE ALL DIE ANYWAYS! WE HEAR ABOUT NEW LAW! COME, KILL US IF YOU CAN! WE KILL SOME OF YOU, TOO, YOU BETCHA!
WE WARNED THE SENATE THE NEW SECURITY ACT WOULD JUST MAKE THINGS MORE DIFFICULT.
WE DEAL WITH WHAT IS GIVEN, MASTER.
AS ALWAYS, ADI GALLIA. ANAKIN? WHAT ARE YOU DOING?
I HAVE A VECTOR ON THE MOTHERSHIP, MASTERS!
I'M TAKING IT!
ANAKIN! PULL BACK!
I HAVE A SHOT, MASTER KI! I CAN FEEL IT!
ANAKIN! ANAKIN?

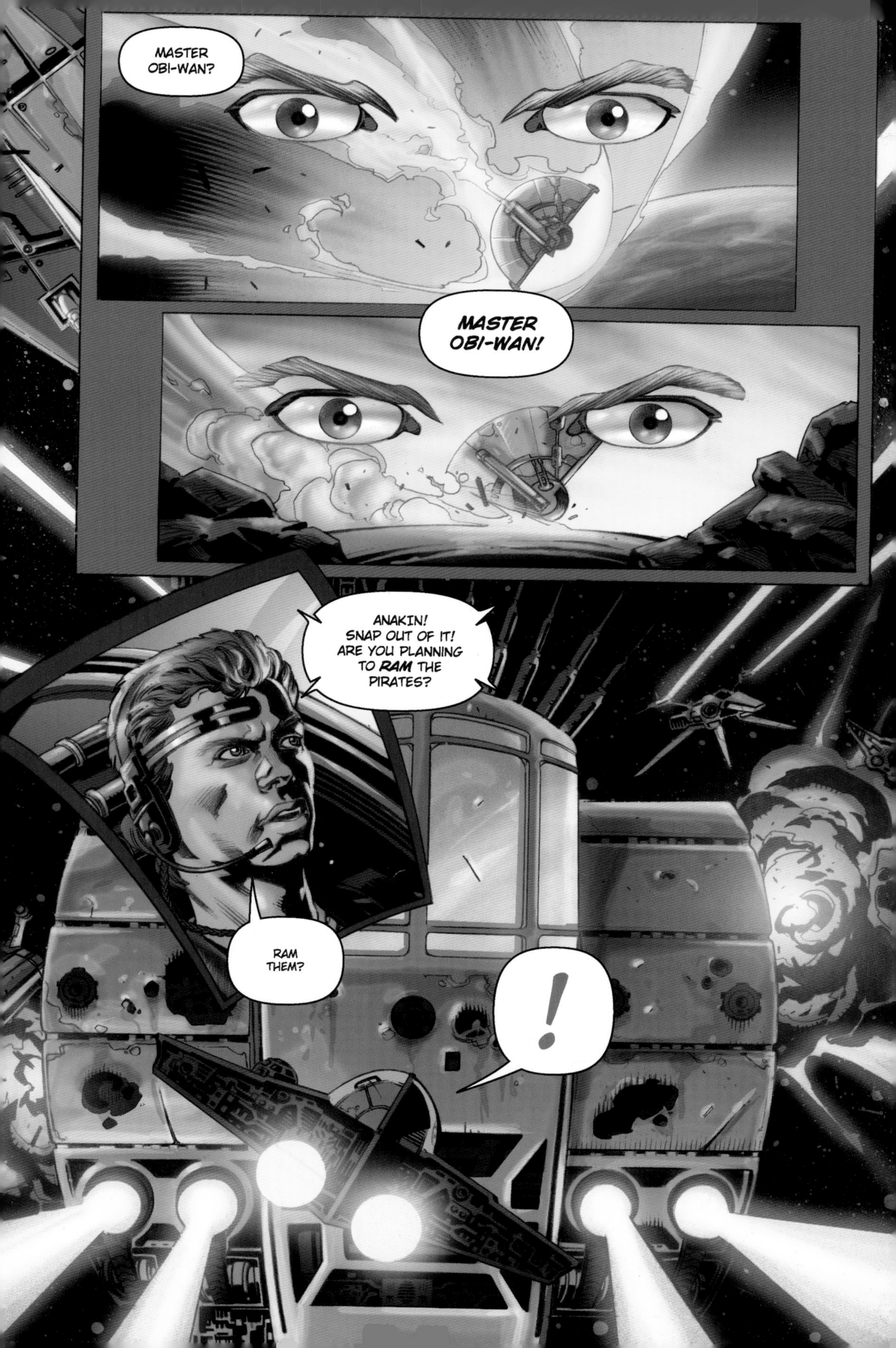
MASTER OBI-WAN?
MASTER OBI-WAN!
ANAKIN! SNAP OUT OF IT! ARE YOU PLANNING TO RAM THE PIRATES?
RAM THEM?
!

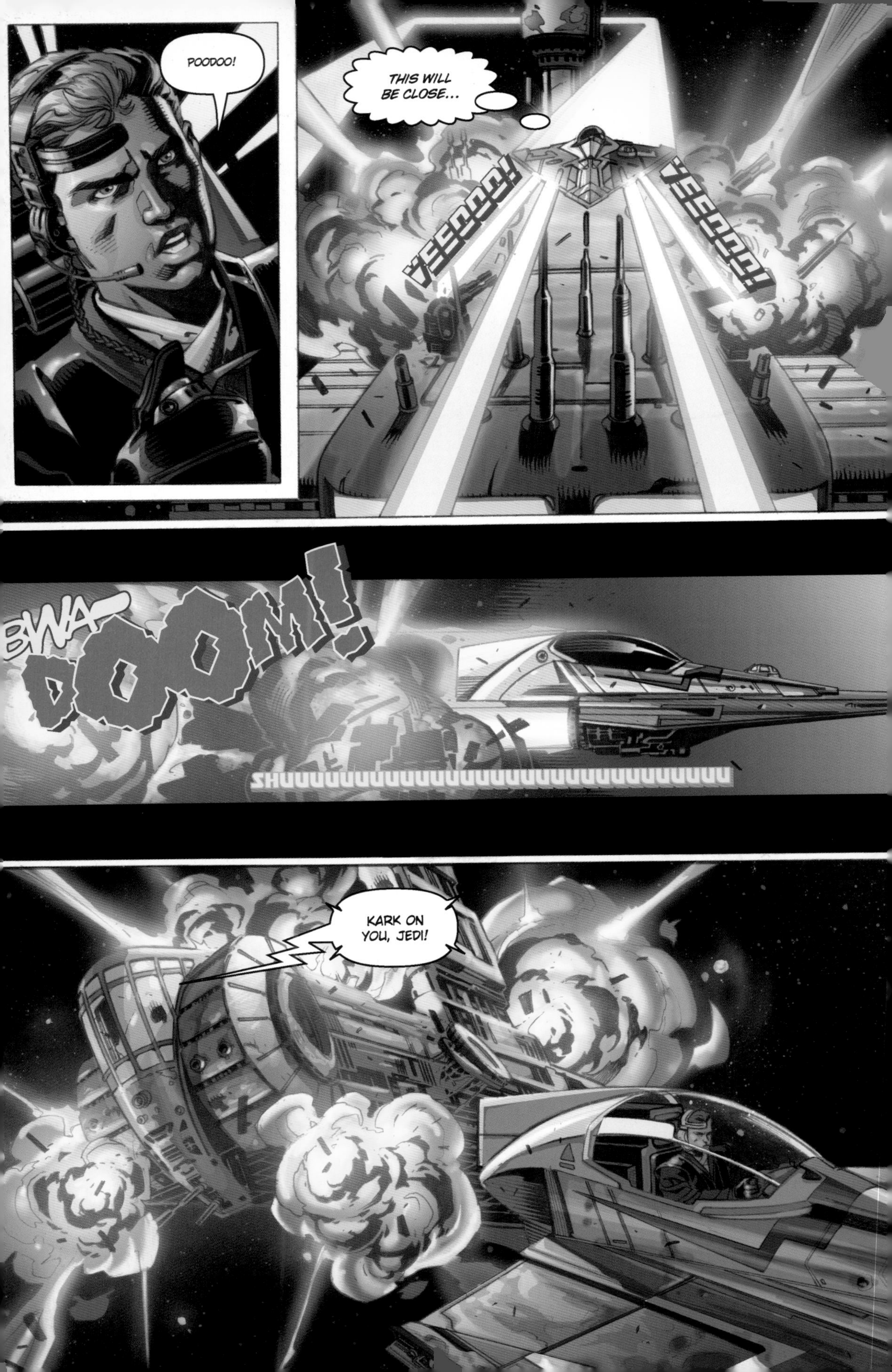
POODOO!
THIS WILL BE CLOSE...
BWA-DOOOM!
SHUUUUUUUUUUUUUUUUUUUUUUUUUUUUUUUUUUU
KARK ON YOU, JEDI!

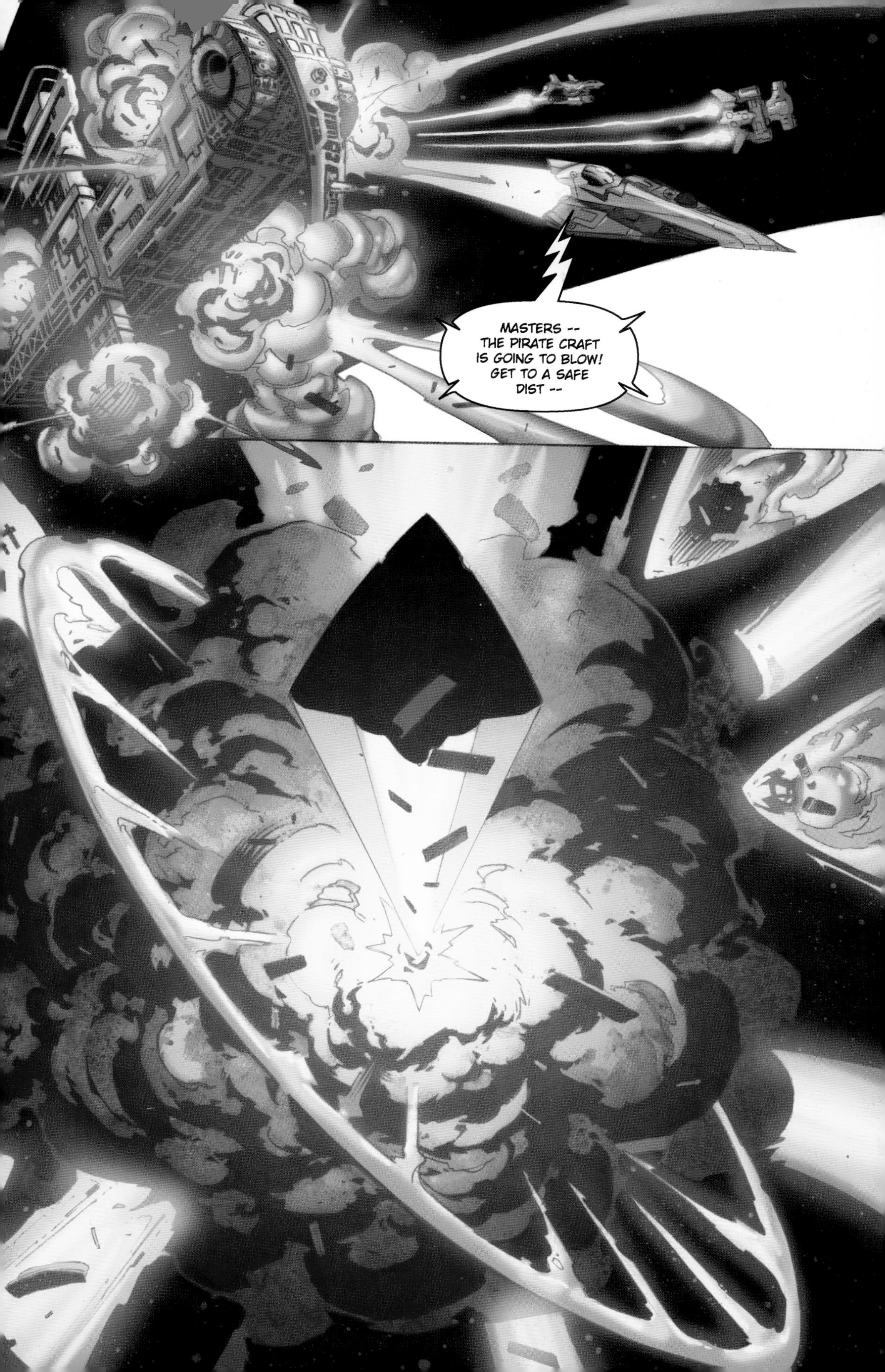
MASTERS -- THE PIRATE CRAFT IS GOING TO BLOW! GET TO A SAFE DIST --

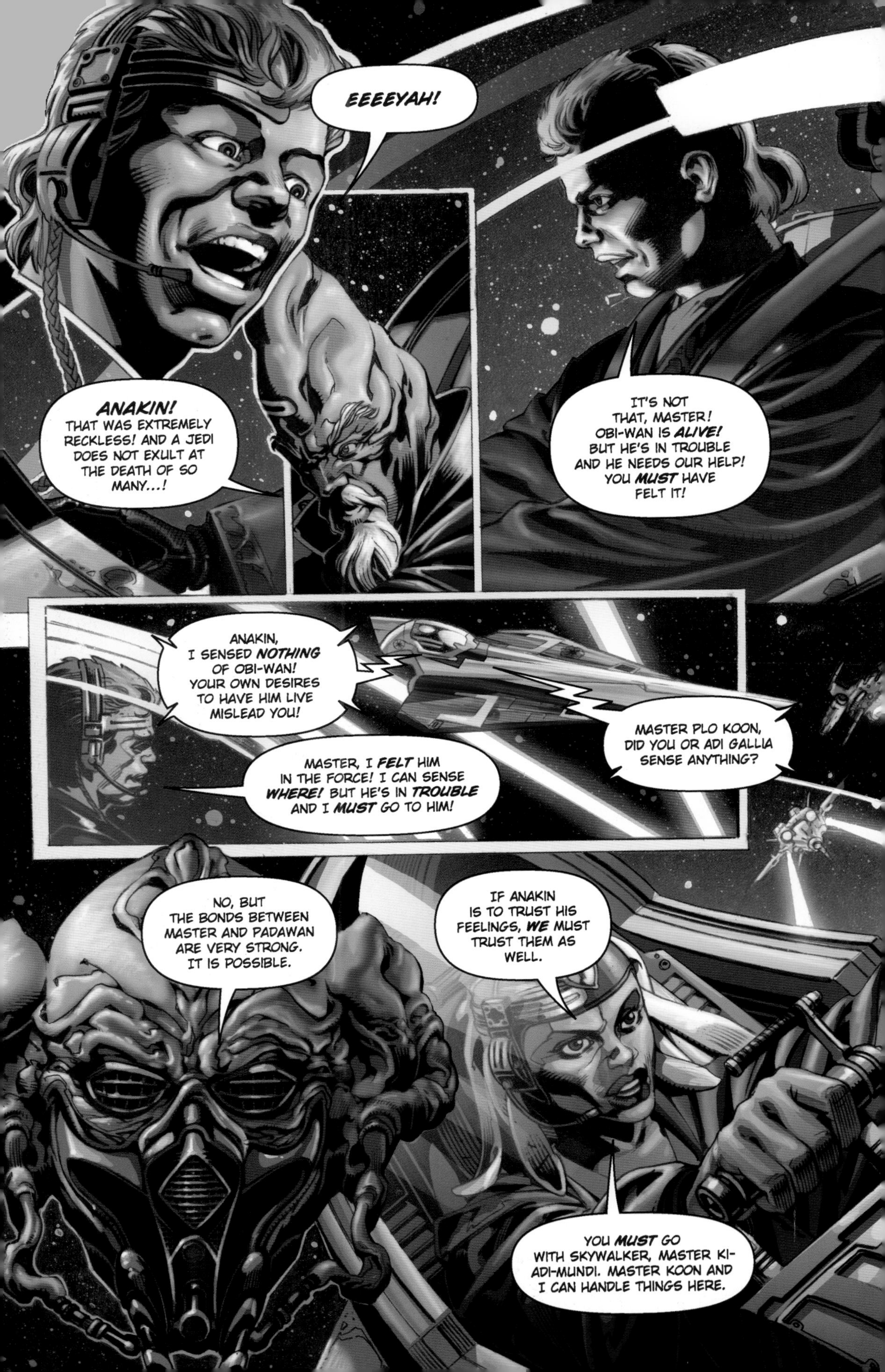
EEEEYAH!
ANAKIN! THAT WAS EXTREMELY RECKLESS! AND A JEDI DOES NOT EXULT AT THE DEATH OF SO MANY...!
IT'S NOT THAT, MASTER! OBI-WAN IS ALIVE! BUT HE'S IN TROUBLE AND HE NEEDS OUR HELP! YOU MUST HAVE FELT IT!
ANAKIN, I SENSED NOTHING OF OBI-WAN! YOUR OWN DESIRES TO HAVE HIM LIVE MISLEAD YOU!
MASTER, I FELT HIM IN THE FORCE! I CAN SENSE WHERE! BUT HE'S IN TROUBLE AND I MUST GO TO HIM!
MASTER PLO KOON, DID YOU OR ADI GALLIA SENSE ANYTHING?
NO, BUT THE BONDS BETWEEN MASTER AND PADAWAN ARE VERY STRONG. IT IS POSSIBLE.
IF ANAKIN IS TO TRUST HIS FEELINGS, WE MUST TRUST THEM AS WELL.
YOU MUST GO WITH SKYWALKER, MASTER KI-ADI-MUNDI. MASTER KOON AND I CAN HANDLE THINGS HERE.

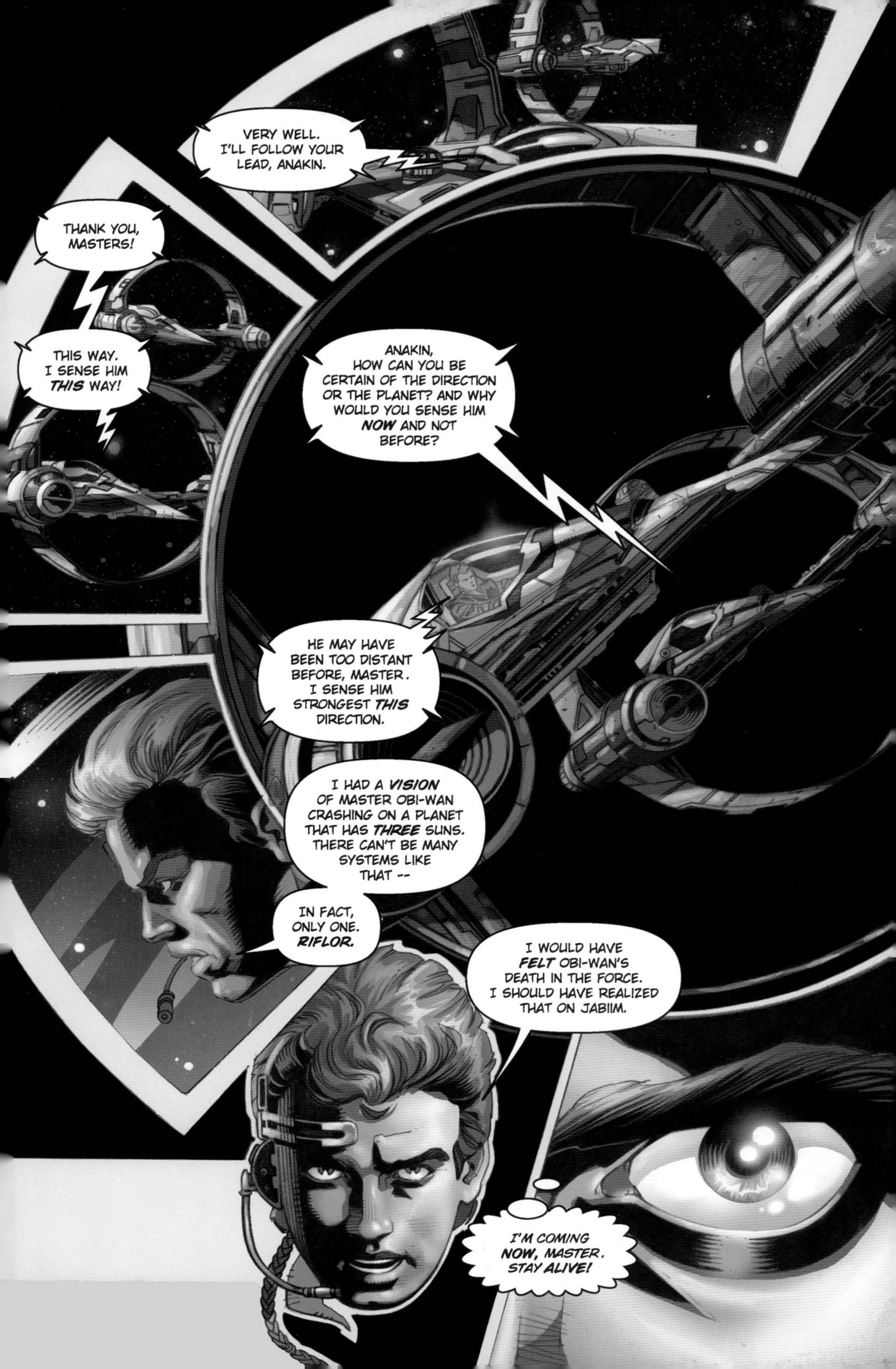
VERY WELL. I'LL FOLLOW YOUR LEAD, ANAKIN.
THANK YOU, MASTERS!
THIS WAY. I SENSE HIM THIS WAY!
ANAKIN, HOW CAN YOU BE CERTAIN OF THE DIRECTION OR THE PLANET? AND WHY WOULD YOU SENSE HIM NOW AND NOT BEFORE?
HE MAY HAVE BEEN TOO DISTANT BEFORE, MASTER. I SENSE HIM STRONGEST THIS DIRECTION.
I HAD A VISION OF MASTER OBI-WAN CRASHING ON A PLANET THAT HAS THREE SUNS. THERE CAN'T BE MANY SYSTEMS LIKE THAT --
IN FACT, ONLY ONE. RIFLOR.
I WOULD HAVE FELT OBI-WAN'S DEATH IN THE FORCE. I SHOULD HAVE REALIZED THAT ON JABIIM.
I'M COMING NOW, MASTER. STAY ALIVE!

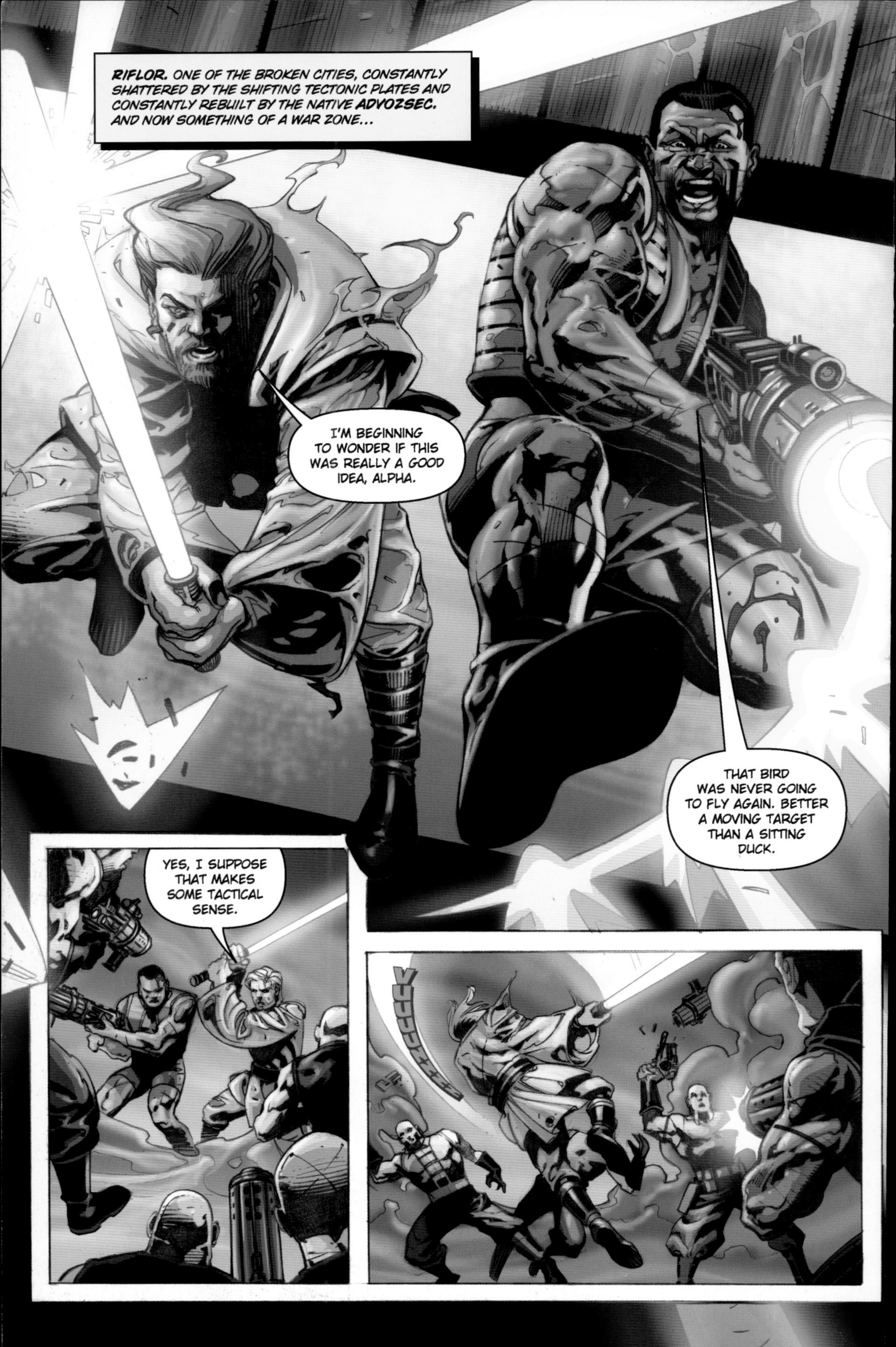
RIFLOR. ONE OF THE BROKEN CITIES, CONSTANTLY SHATTERED BY THE SHIFTING TECTONIC PLATES AND CONSTANTLY REBUILT BY THE NATIVE ADVOZSEC. AND NOW SOMETHING OF A WAR ZONE...
I'M BEGINNING TO WONDER IF THIS WAS REALLY A GOOD IDEA, ALPHA.
THAT BIRD WAS NEVER GOING TO FLY AGAIN. BETTER A MOVING TARGET THAN A SITTING DUCK.
YES, I SUPPOSE THAT MAKES SOME TACTICAL SENSE.

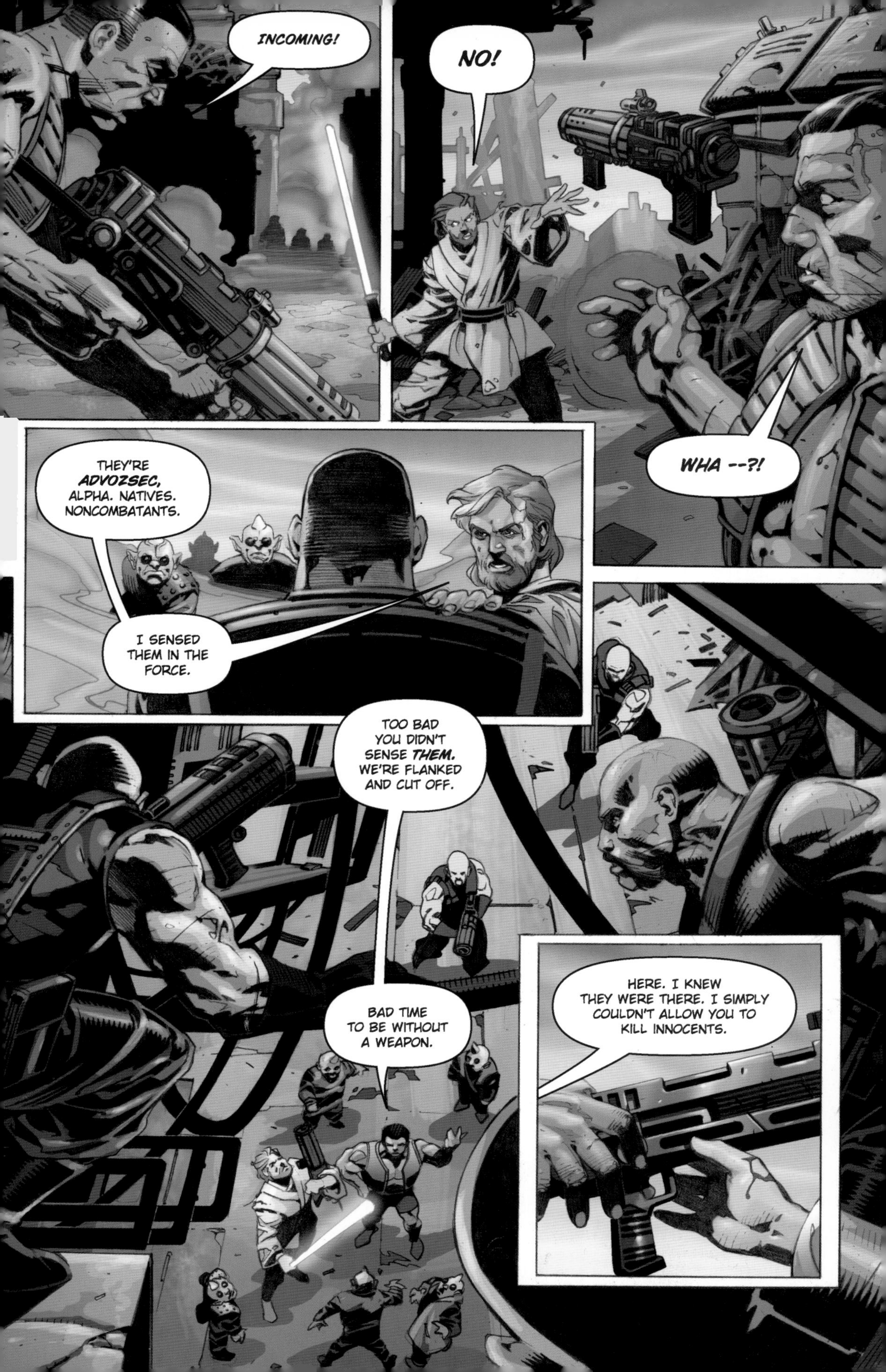
INCOMING!
NO!
WHA --?!
THEY'RE ADVOZSEC, ALPHA. NATIVES. NONCOMBATANTS.
I SENSED THEM IN THE FORCE.
TOO BAD YOU DIDN'T SENSE THEM. WE'RE FLANKED AND CUT OFF.
BAD TIME TO BE WITHOUT A WEAPON.
HERE. I KNEW THEY WERE THERE. I SIMPLY COULDN'T ALLOW YOU TO KILL INNOCENTS.

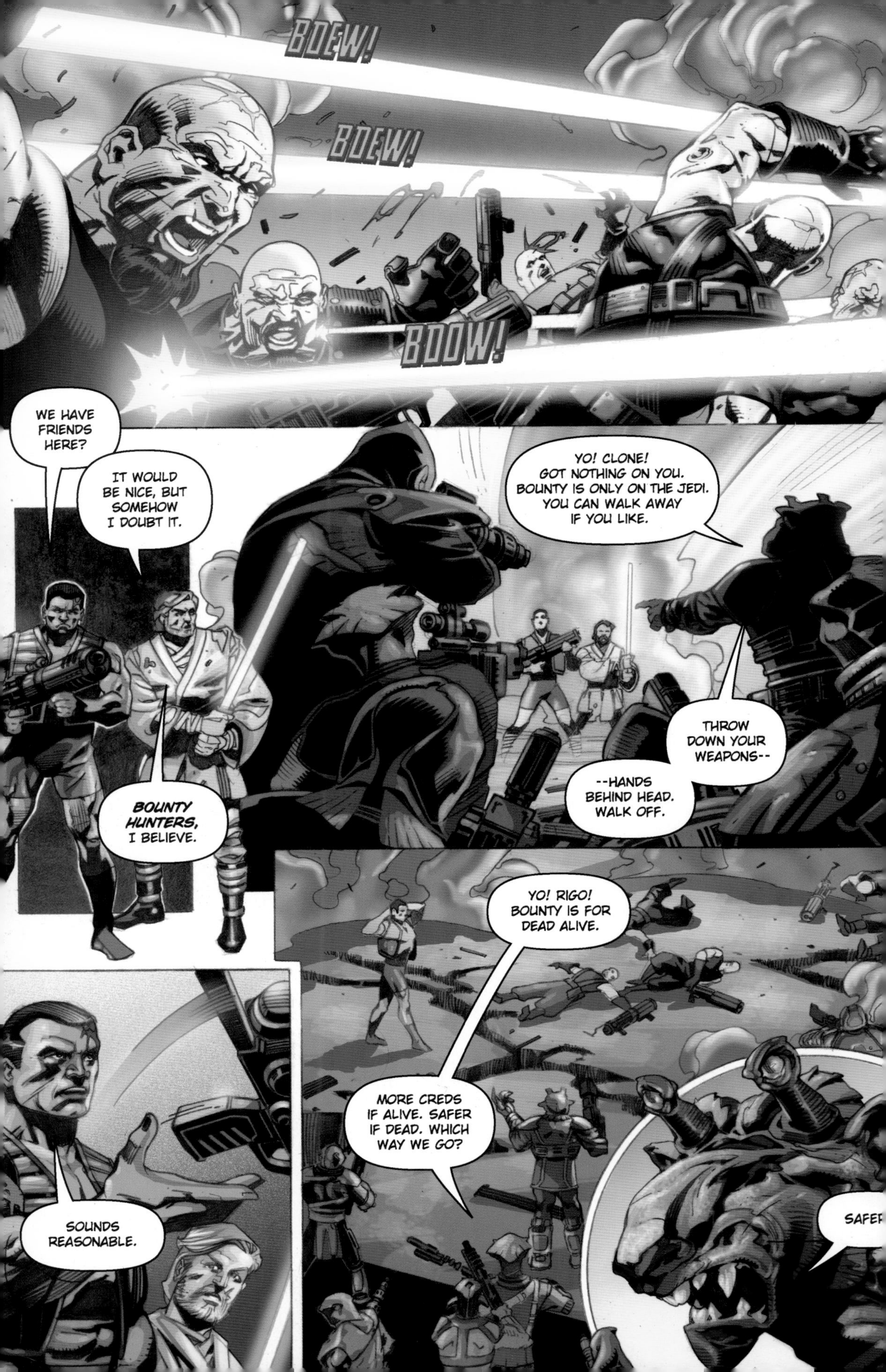
BDEW!
BDEW!
BDOW!
WE HAVE FRIENDS HERE?
IT WOULD BE NICE, BUT SOMEHOW I DOUBT IT.
YO! CLONE! GOT NOTHING ON YOU. BOUNTY IS ONLY ON THE JEDI. YOU CAN WALK AWAY IF YOU LIKE.
BOUNTY HUNTERS, I BELIEVE.
THROW DOWN YOUR WEAPONS--
--HANDS BEHIND HEAD. WALK OFF.
YO! RIGO! BOUNTY IS FOR DEAD ALIVE.
MORE CREDS IF ALIVE. SAFER IF DEAD. WHICH WAY WE GO?
SOUNDS REASONABLE.

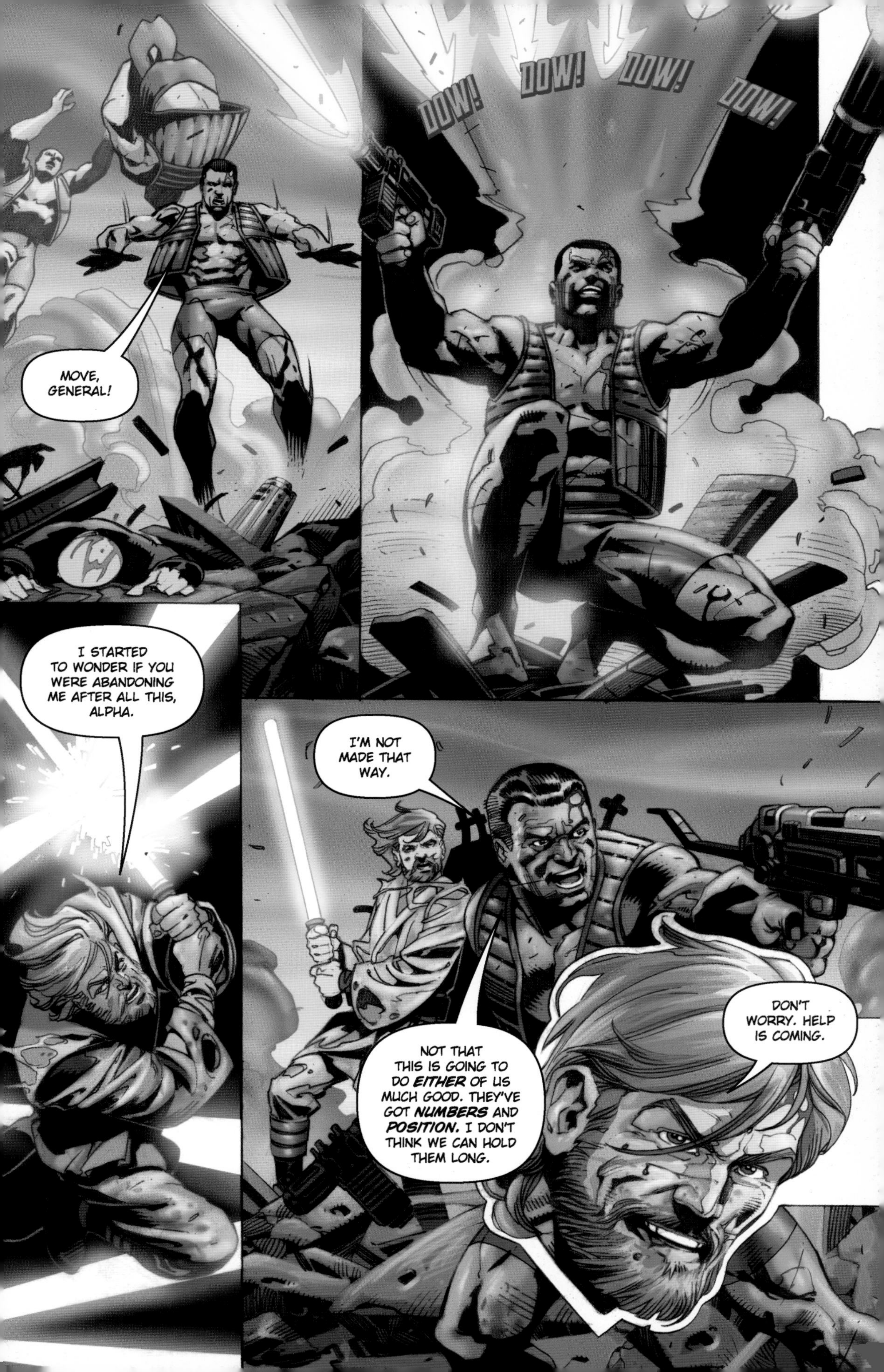

MOVE, GENERAL!
DOW!
DOW!
DOW!
DOW!
I STARTED TO WONDER IF YOU WERE ABANDONING ME AFTER ALL THIS, ALPHA.
I'M NOT MADE THAT WAY.
NOT THAT THIS IS GOING TO DO *EITHER* OF US MUCH GOOD. THEY'VE GOT *NUMBERS* AND *POSITION.* I DON'T THINK WE CAN HOLD THEM LONG.
DON'T WORRY. HELP IS COMING.

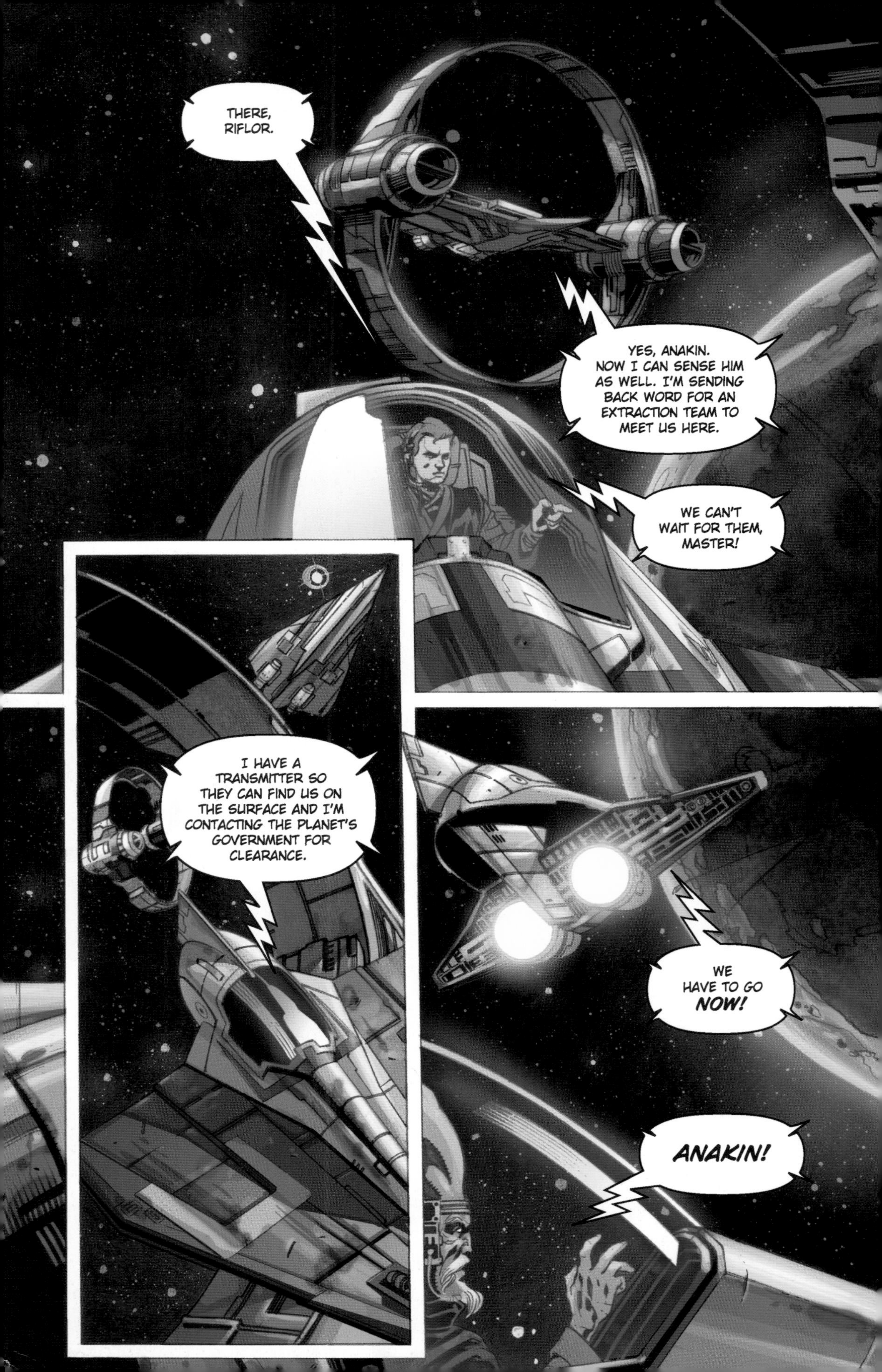
THERE, RIFLOR.
YES, ANAKIN. NOW I CAN SENSE HIM AS WELL. I'M SENDING BACK WORD FOR AN EXTRACTION TEAM TO MEET US HERE.
WE CAN'T WAIT FOR THEM, MASTER!
I HAVE A TRANSMITTER SO THEY CAN FIND US ON THE SURFACE AND I'M CONTACTING THE PLANET'S GOVERNMENT FOR CLEARANCE.
WE HAVE TO GO *NOW!*
*ANAKIN!*

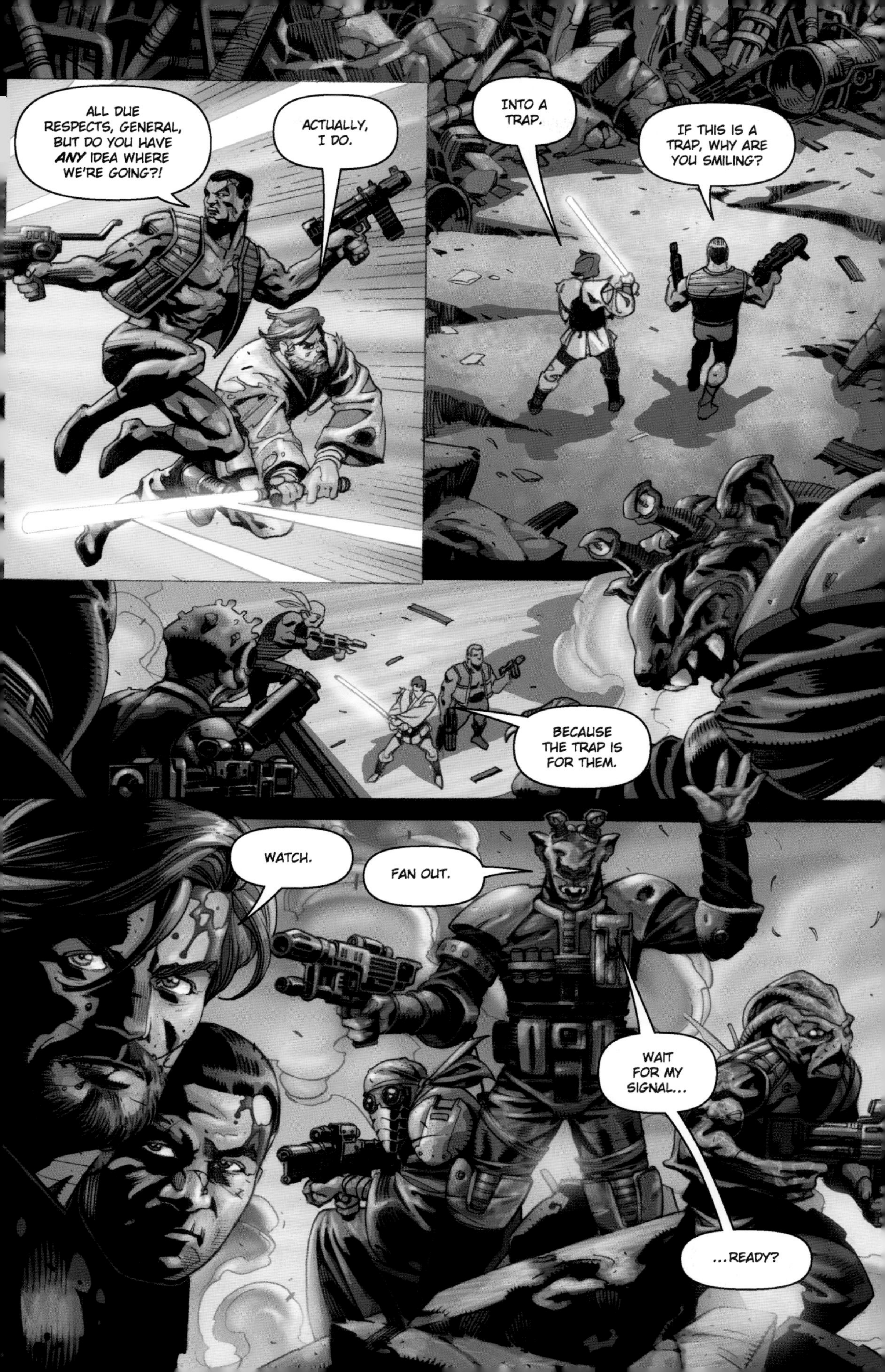
ALL DUE RESPECTS, GENERAL, BUT DO YOU HAVE ANY IDEA WHERE WE'RE GOING?!
ACTUALLY, I DO.
INTO A TRAP.
IF THIS IS A TRAP, WHY ARE YOU SMILING?
BECAUSE THE TRAP IS FOR THEM.
WATCH.
FAN OUT.
WAIT FOR MY SIGNAL...
...READY?

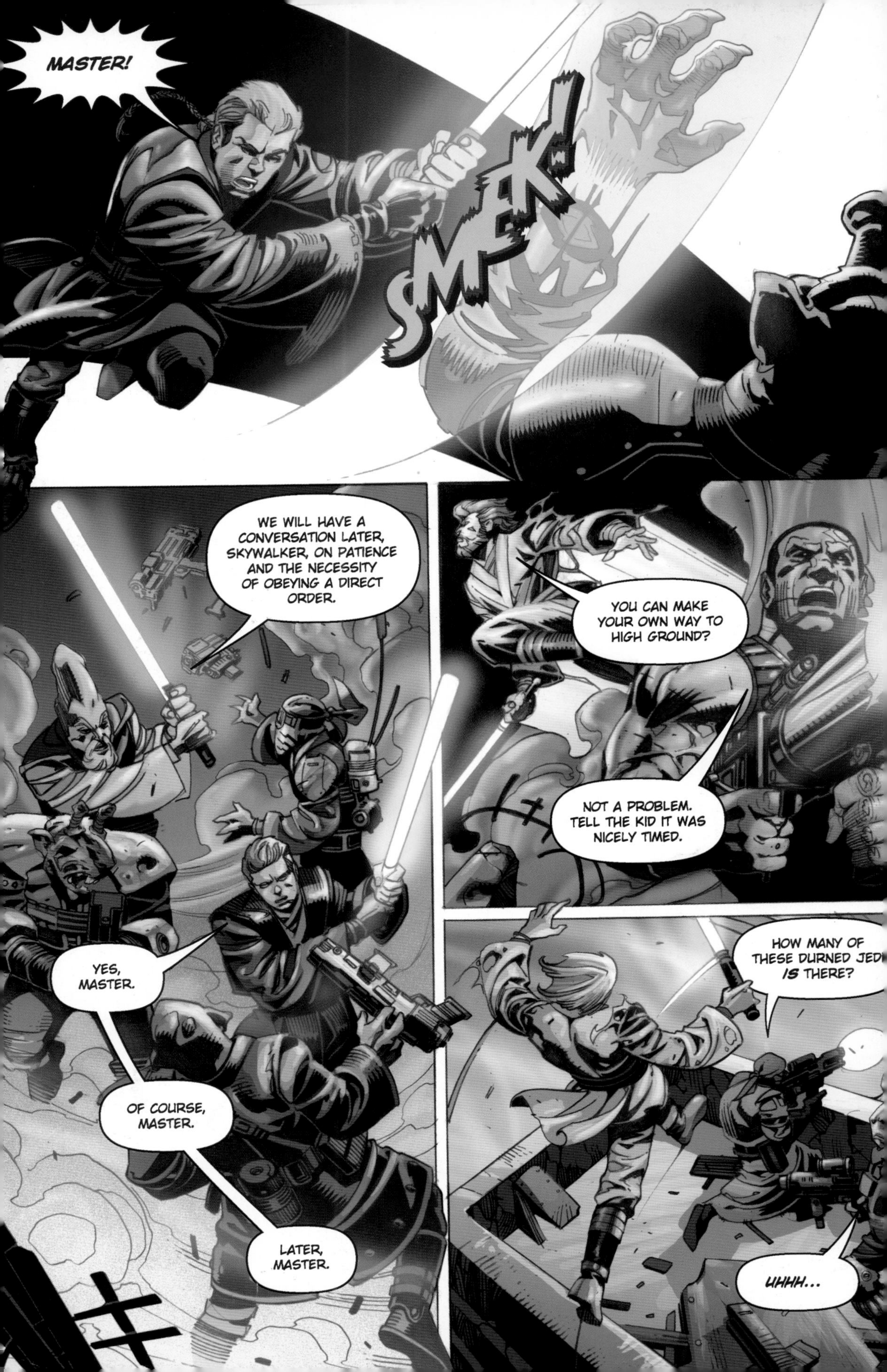
MASTER!
SMEK!
WE WILL HAVE A CONVERSATION LATER, SKYWALKER, ON PATIENCE AND THE NECESSITY OF OBEYING A DIRECT ORDER.
YES, MASTER.
OF COURSE, MASTER.
LATER, MASTER.
YOU CAN MAKE YOUR OWN WAY TO HIGH GROUND?
NOT A PROBLEM. TELL THE KID IT WAS NICELY TIMED.
HOW MANY OF THESE DURNED JEDI *IS* THERE?
UHHH...

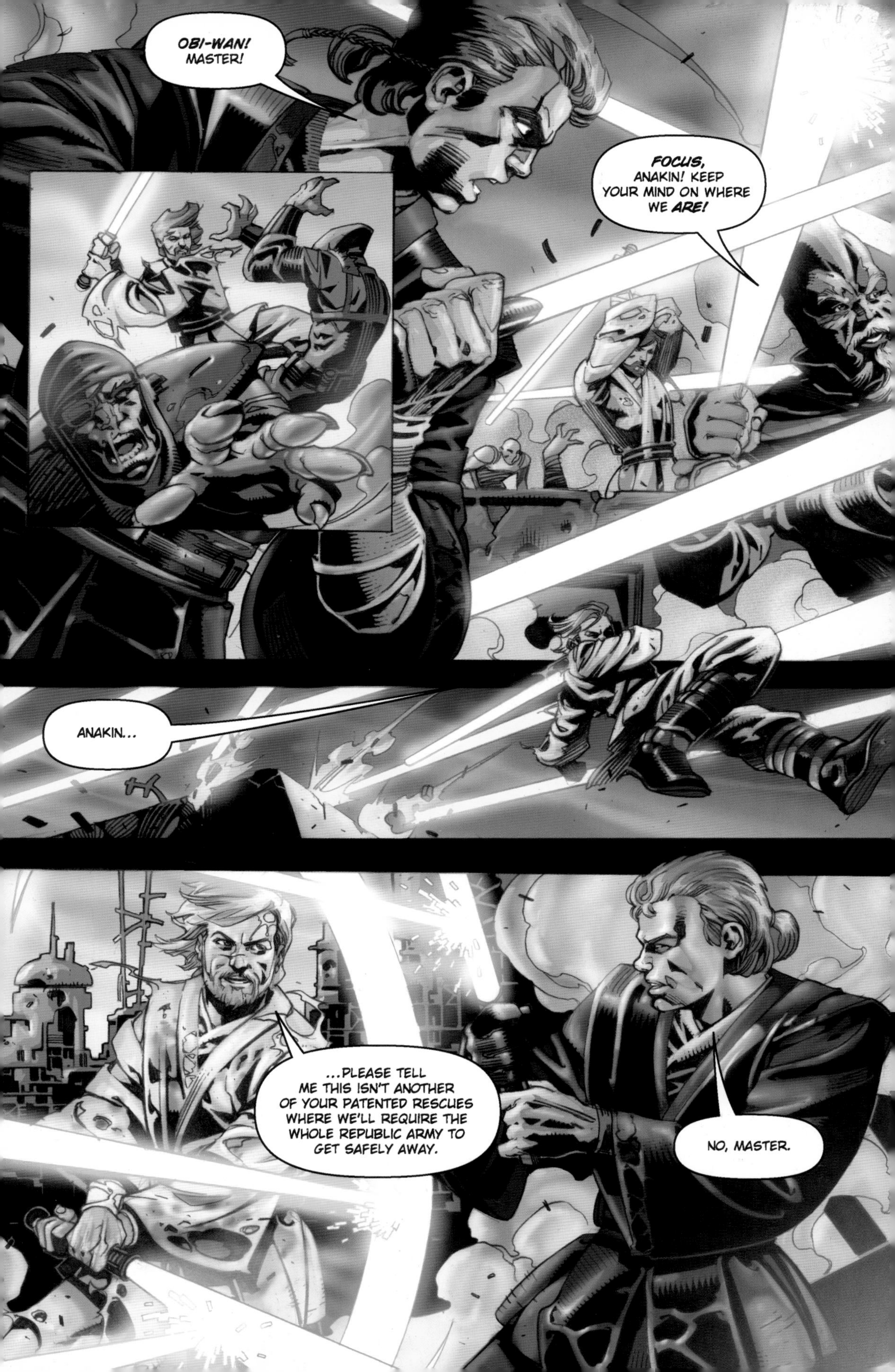
OBI-WAN! MASTER!
FOCUS, ANAKIN! KEEP YOUR MIND ON WHERE WE ARE!
ANAKIN...
...PLEASE TELL ME THIS ISN'T ANOTHER OF YOUR PATENTED RESCUES WHERE WE'LL REQUIRE THE WHOLE REPUBLIC ARMY TO GET SAFELY AWAY.
NO, MASTER.

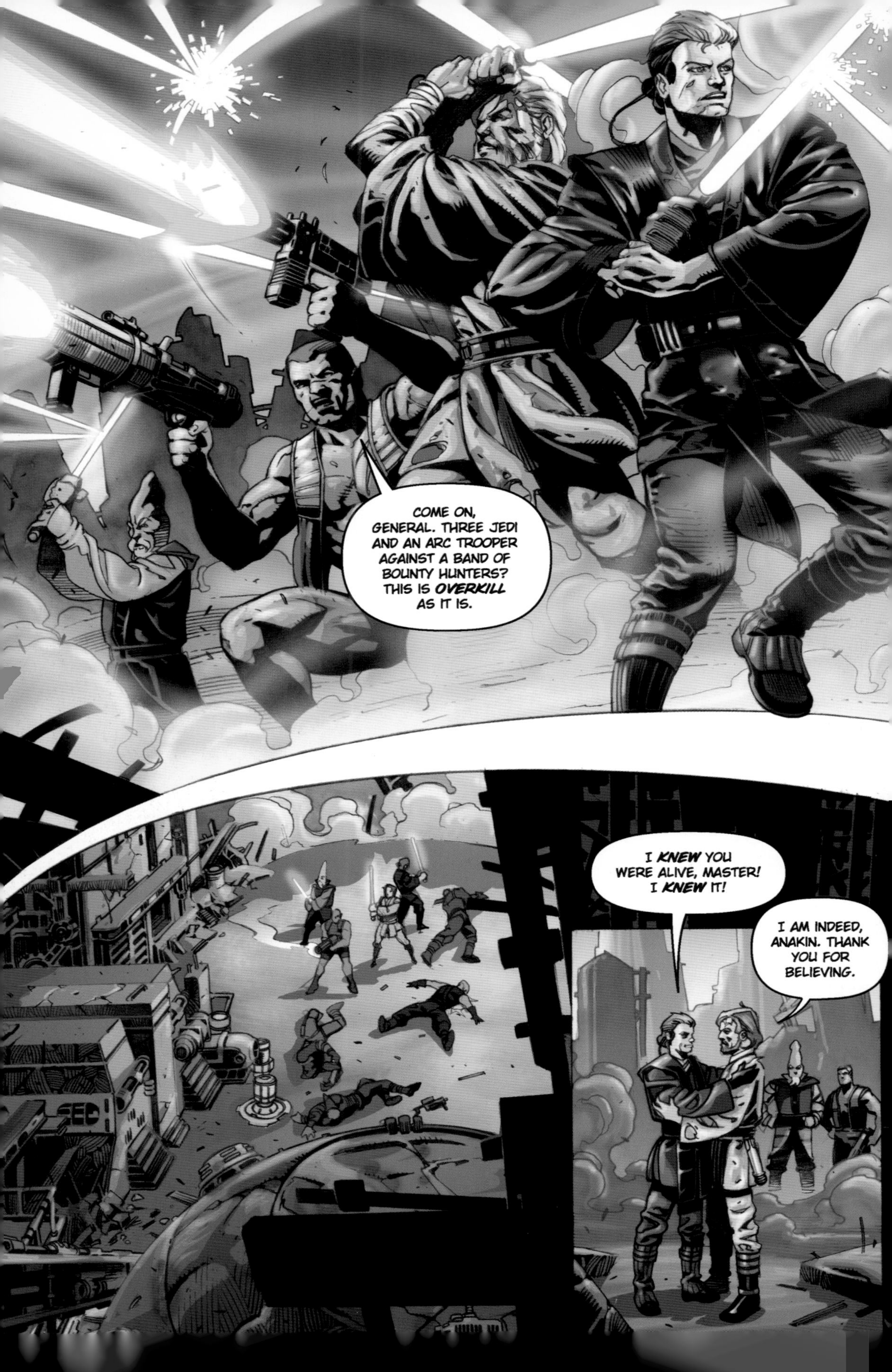
COME ON, GENERAL. THREE JEDI AND AN ARC TROOPER AGAINST A BAND OF BOUNTY HUNTERS? THIS IS OVERKILL AS IT IS.
I KNEW YOU WERE ALIVE, MASTER! I KNEW IT!
I AM INDEED, ANAKIN. THANK YOU FOR BELIEVING.

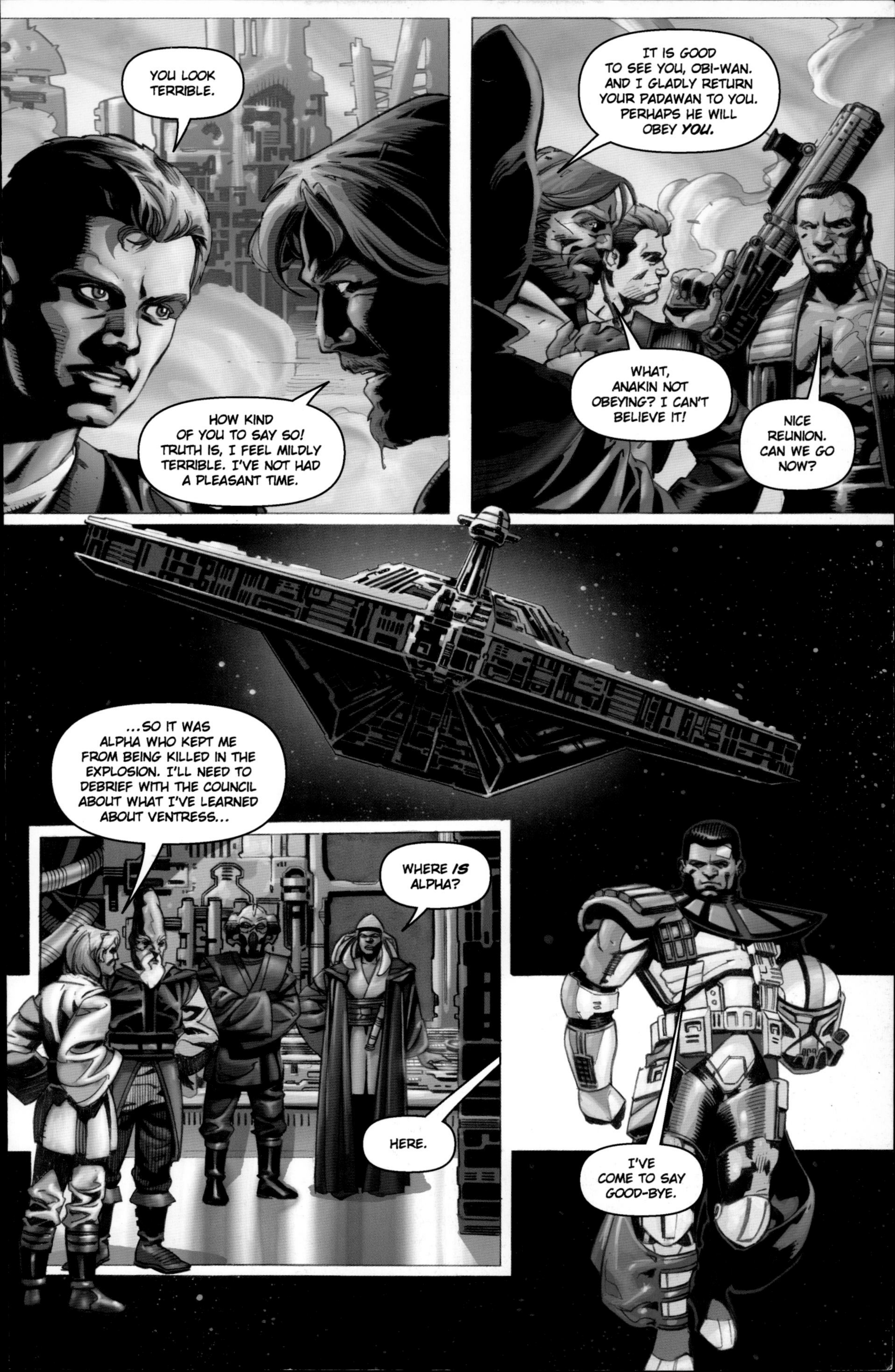
YOU LOOK TERRIBLE.
HOW KIND OF YOU TO SAY SO! TRUTH IS, I FEEL MILDLY TERRIBLE. I'VE NOT HAD A PLEASANT TIME.
IT IS GOOD TO SEE YOU, OBI-WAN. AND I GLADLY RETURN YOUR PADAWAN TO YOU. PERHAPS HE WILL OBEY *YOU.*
WHAT, ANAKIN NOT OBEYING? I CAN'T BELIEVE IT!
NICE REUNION. CAN WE GO NOW?
...SO IT WAS ALPHA WHO KEPT ME FROM BEING KILLED IN THE EXPLOSION. I'LL NEED TO DEBRIEF WITH THE COUNCIL ABOUT WHAT I'VE LEARNED ABOUT VENTRESS...
WHERE *IS* ALPHA?
HERE.
I'VE COME TO SAY GOOD-BYE.

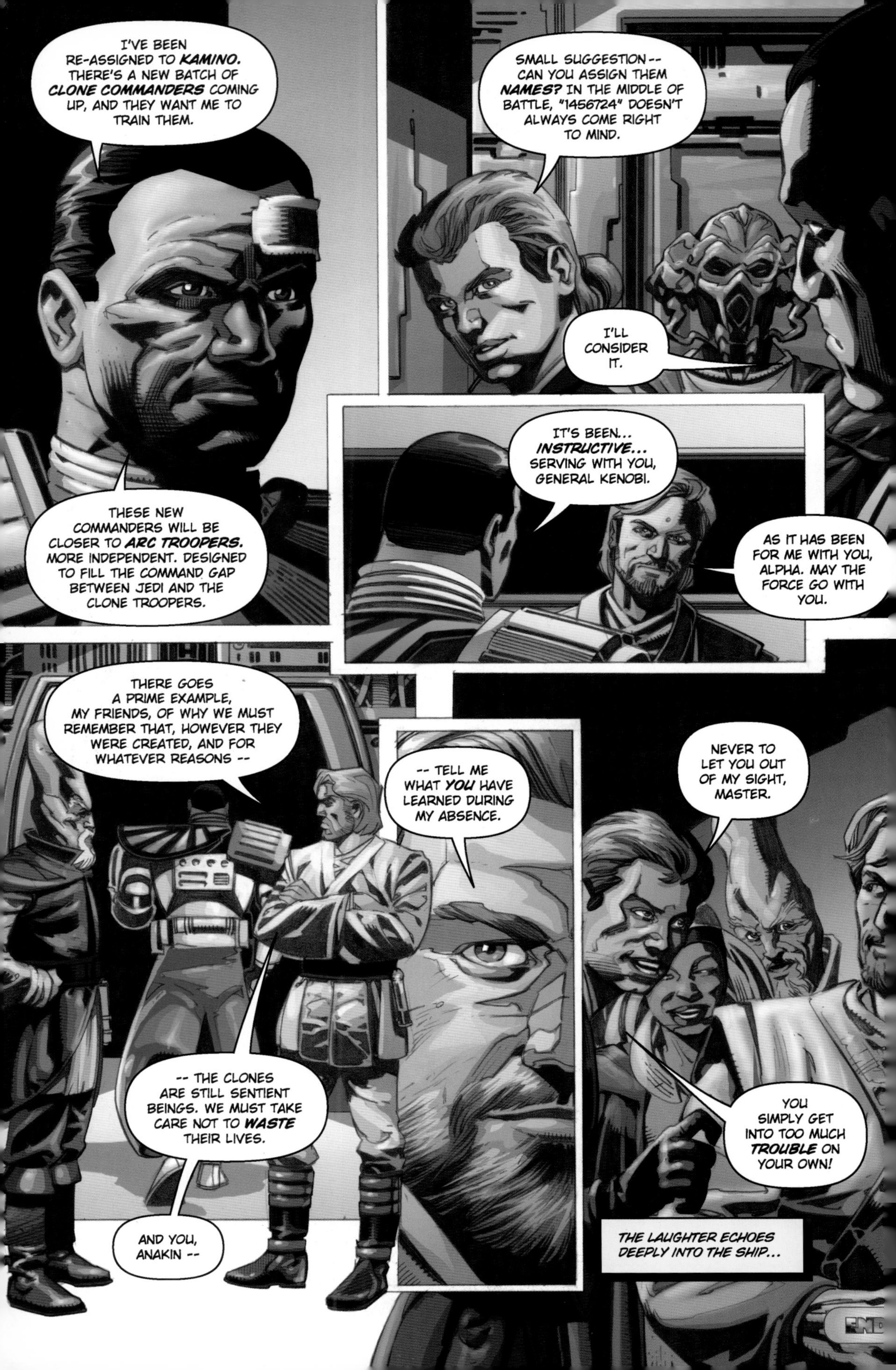
I'VE BEEN RE-ASSIGNED TO KAMINO. THERE'S A NEW BATCH OF CLONE COMMANDERS COMING UP, AND THEY WANT ME TO TRAIN THEM.
THESE NEW COMMANDERS WILL BE CLOSER TO ARC TROOPERS. MORE INDEPENDENT. DESIGNED TO FILL THE COMMAND GAP BETWEEN JEDI AND THE CLONE TROOPERS.
SMALL SUGGESTION -- CAN YOU ASSIGN THEM NAMES? IN THE MIDDLE OF BATTLE, "1456724" DOESN'T ALWAYS COME RIGHT TO MIND.
I'LL CONSIDER IT.
IT'S BEEN... INSTRUCTIVE... SERVING WITH YOU, GENERAL KENOBI.
AS IT HAS BEEN FOR ME WITH YOU, ALPHA. MAY THE FORCE GO WITH YOU.
THERE GOES A PRIME EXAMPLE, MY FRIENDS, OF WHY WE MUST REMEMBER THAT, HOWEVER THEY WERE CREATED, AND FOR WHATEVER REASONS --
-- THE CLONES ARE STILL SENTIENT BEINGS. WE MUST TAKE CARE NOT TO WASTE THEIR LIVES.
AND YOU, ANAKIN --
-- TELL ME WHAT YOU HAVE LEARNED DURING MY ABSENCE.
NEVER TO LET YOU OUT OF MY SIGHT, MASTER.
YOU SIMPLY GET INTO TOO MUCH TROUBLE ON YOUR OWN!
THE LAUGHTER ECHOES DEEPLY INTO THE SHIP...
END

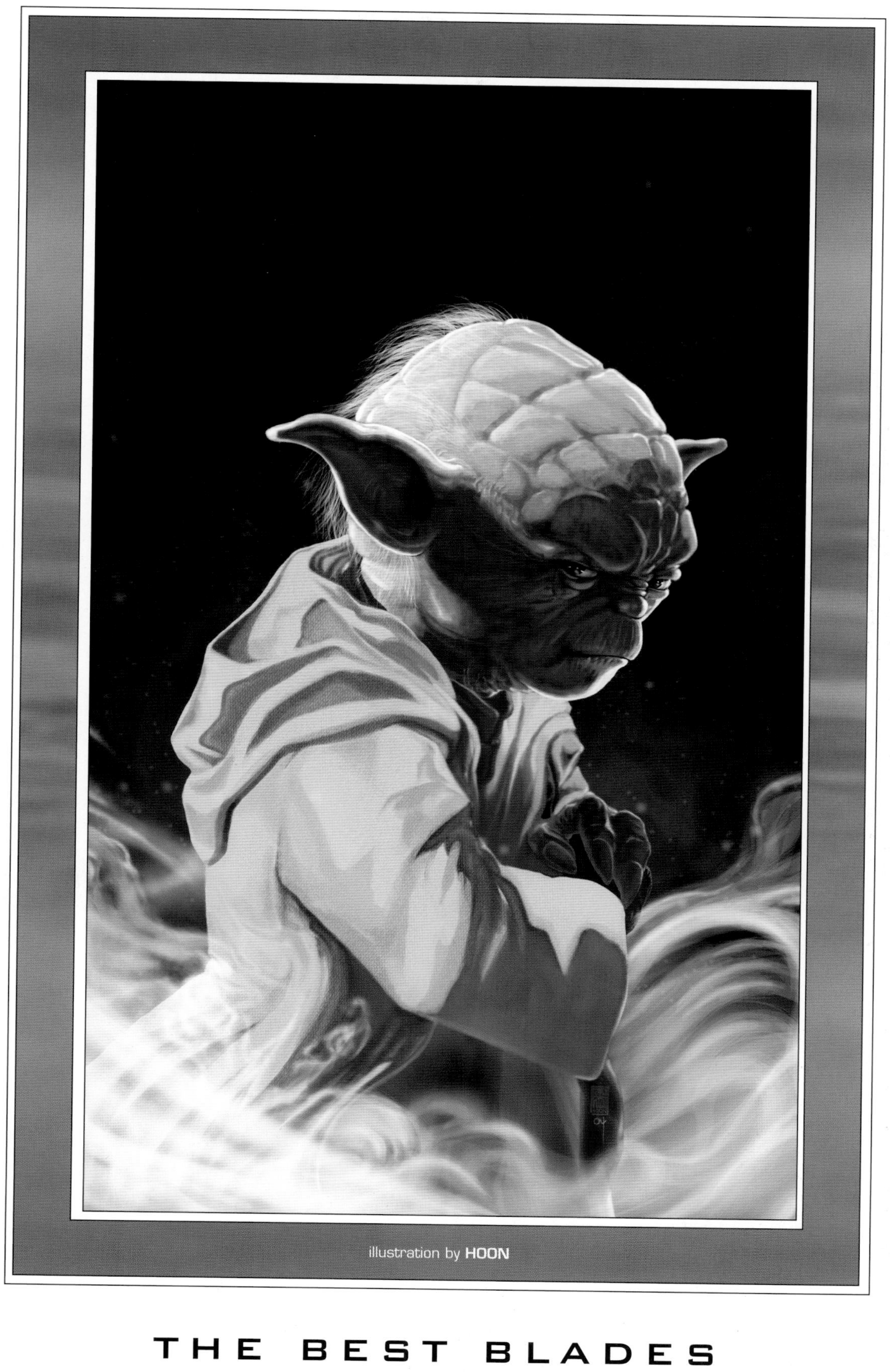

illustration by **HOON**

# THE BEST BLADES

**"The Best Blades"**
written by **Jeremy Barlow**
art by **HOON, Ramiro Montanez,**
and **Stacy Michalcewicz**

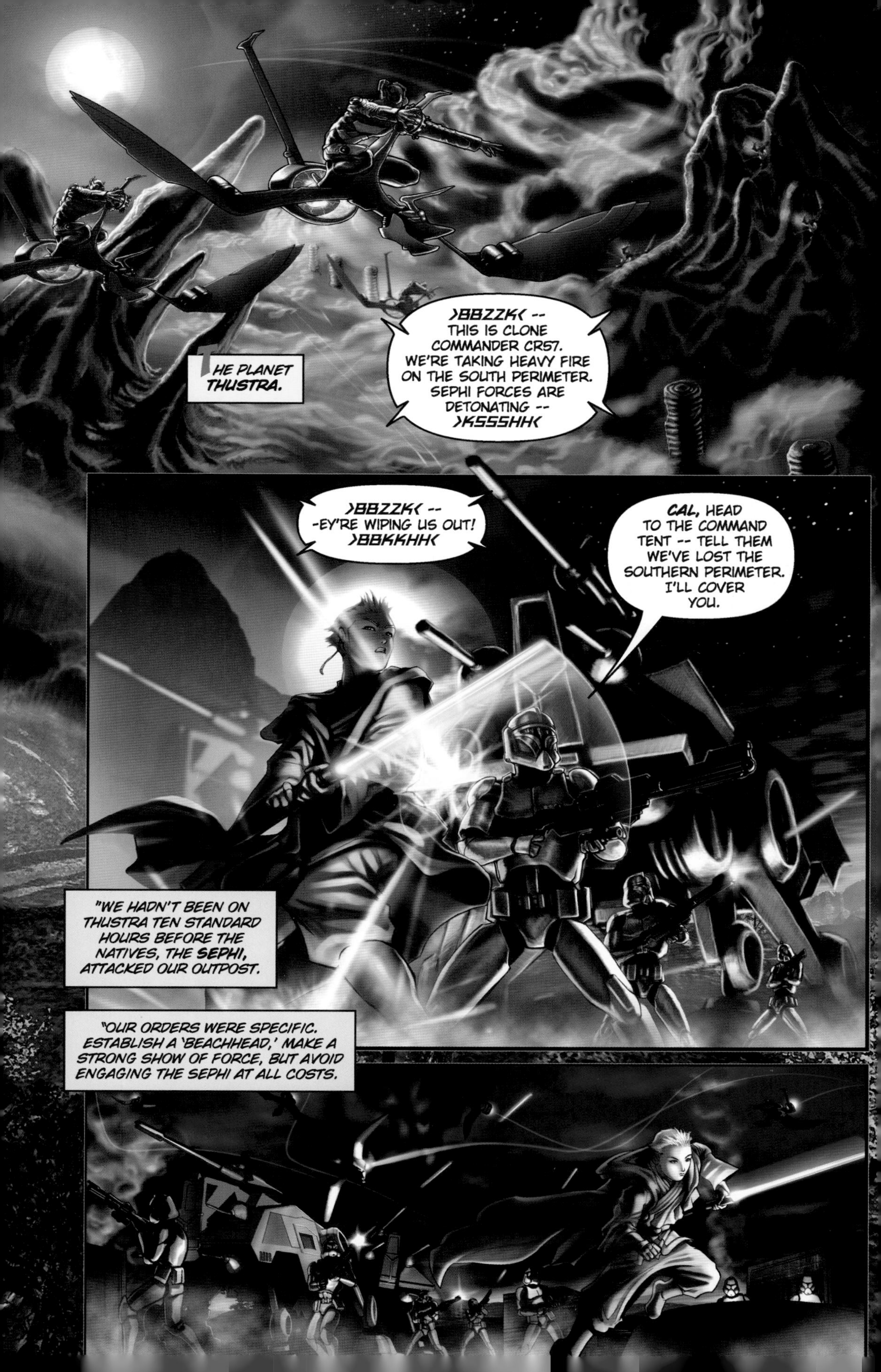
THE PLANET THUSTRA.
>BBZZK< -- THIS IS CLONE COMMANDER CR57. WE'RE TAKING HEAVY FIRE ON THE SOUTH PERIMETER. SEPHI FORCES ARE DETONATING -- >KSSSHH<
>BBZZK< -- -EY'RE WIPING US OUT! >BBKKHH<
CAL, HEAD TO THE COMMAND TENT -- TELL THEM WE'VE LOST THE SOUTHERN PERIMETER. I'LL COVER YOU.
"WE HADN'T BEEN ON THUSTRA TEN STANDARD HOURS BEFORE THE NATIVES, THE SEPHI, ATTACKED OUR OUTPOST.
"OUR ORDERS WERE SPECIFIC. ESTABLISH A 'BEACHHEAD,' MAKE A STRONG SHOW OF FORCE, BUT AVOID ENGAGING THE SEPHI AT ALL COSTS.

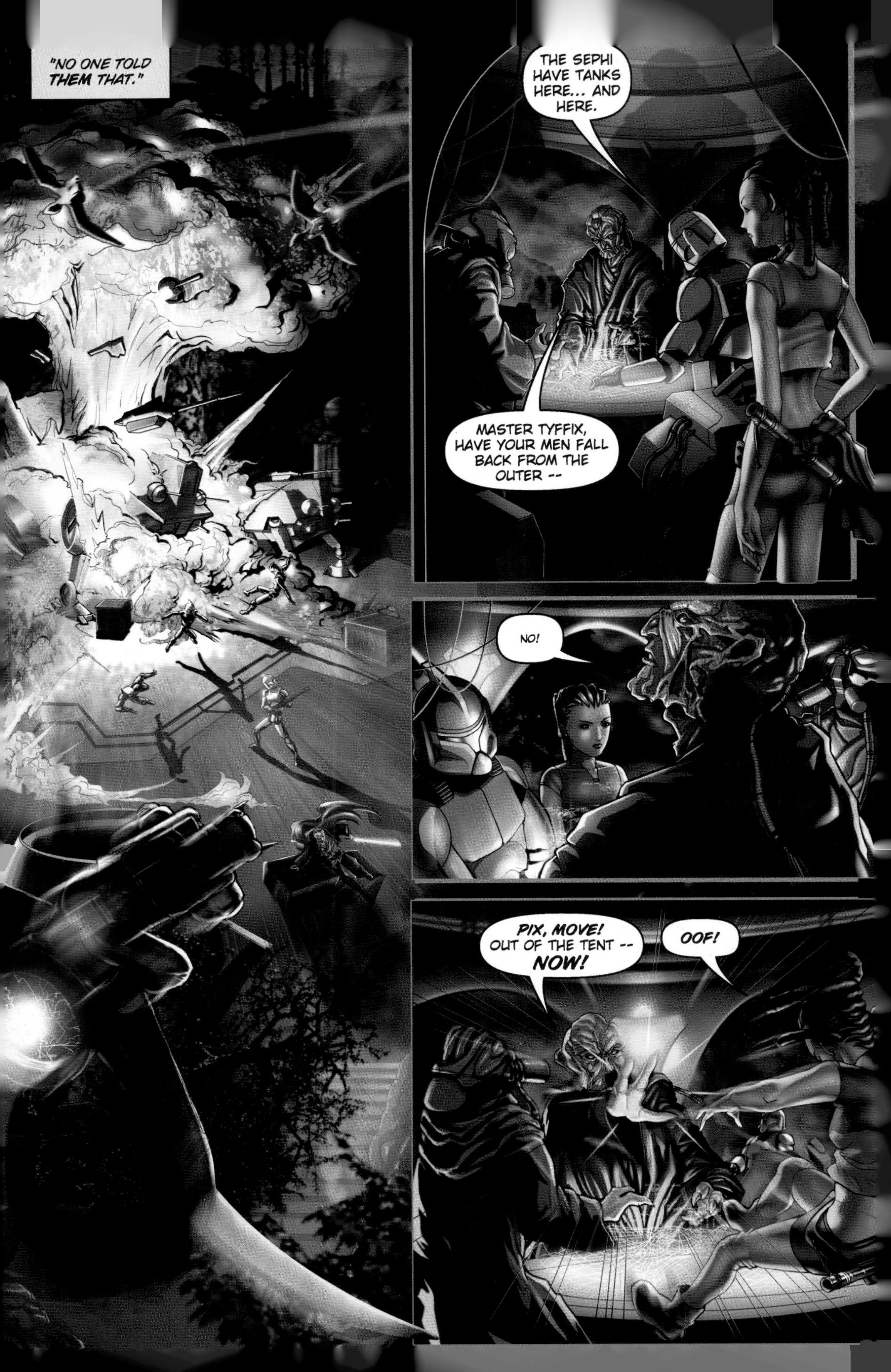
"NO ONE TOLD THEM THAT."
THE SEPHI HAVE TANKS HERE... AND HERE.
MASTER TYFFIX, HAVE YOUR MEN FALL BACK FROM THE OUTER --
NO!
PIX, MOVE! OUT OF THE TENT -- NOW!
OOF!

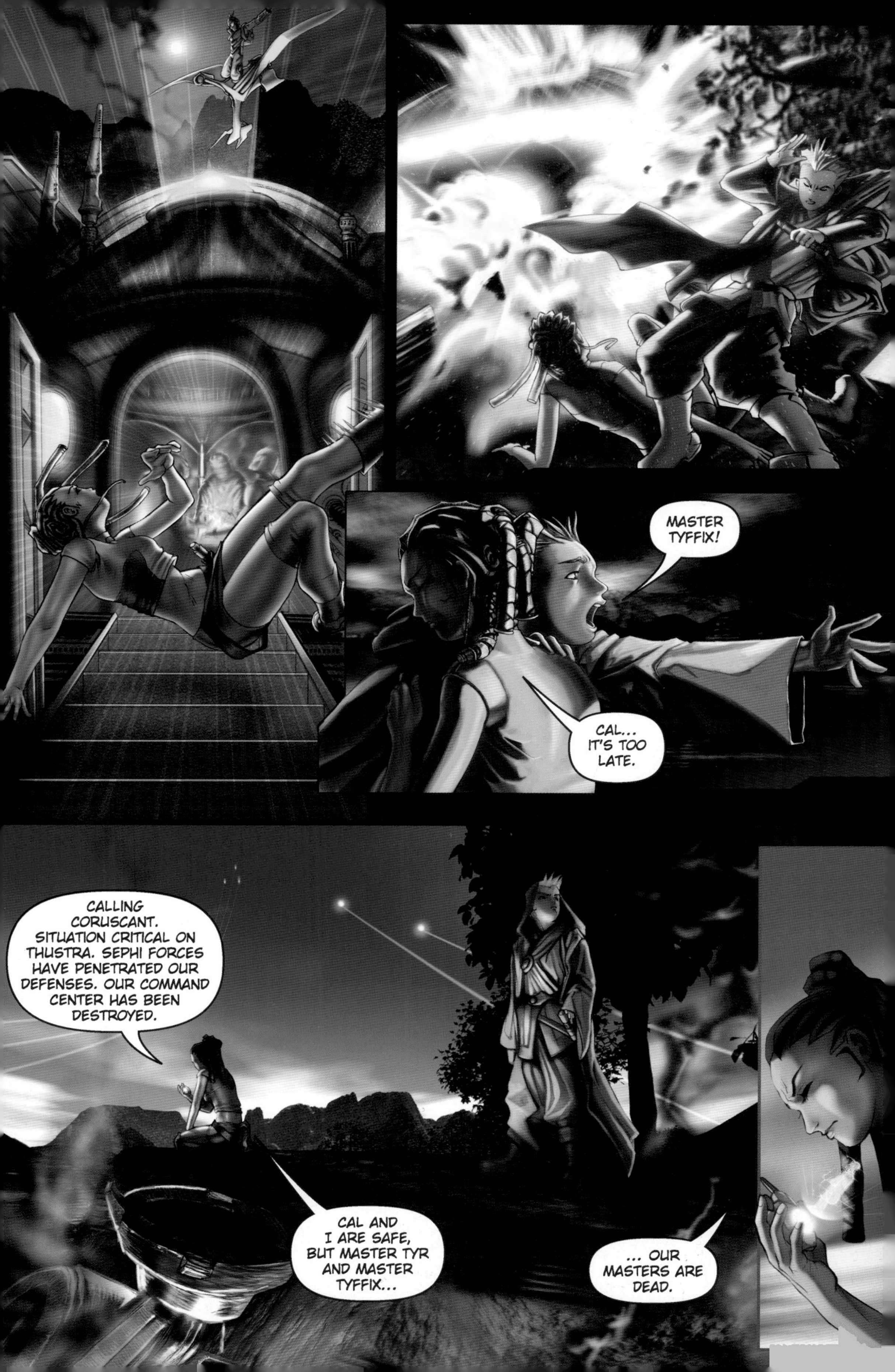
MASTER TYFFIX!
CAL... IT'S TOO LATE.
CALLING CORUSCANT. SITUATION CRITICAL ON THUSTRA. SEPHI FORCES HAVE PENETRATED OUR DEFENSES. OUR COMMAND CENTER HAS BEEN DESTROYED.
CAL AND I ARE SAFE, BUT MASTER TYR AND MASTER TYFFIX...
... OUR MASTERS ARE DEAD.

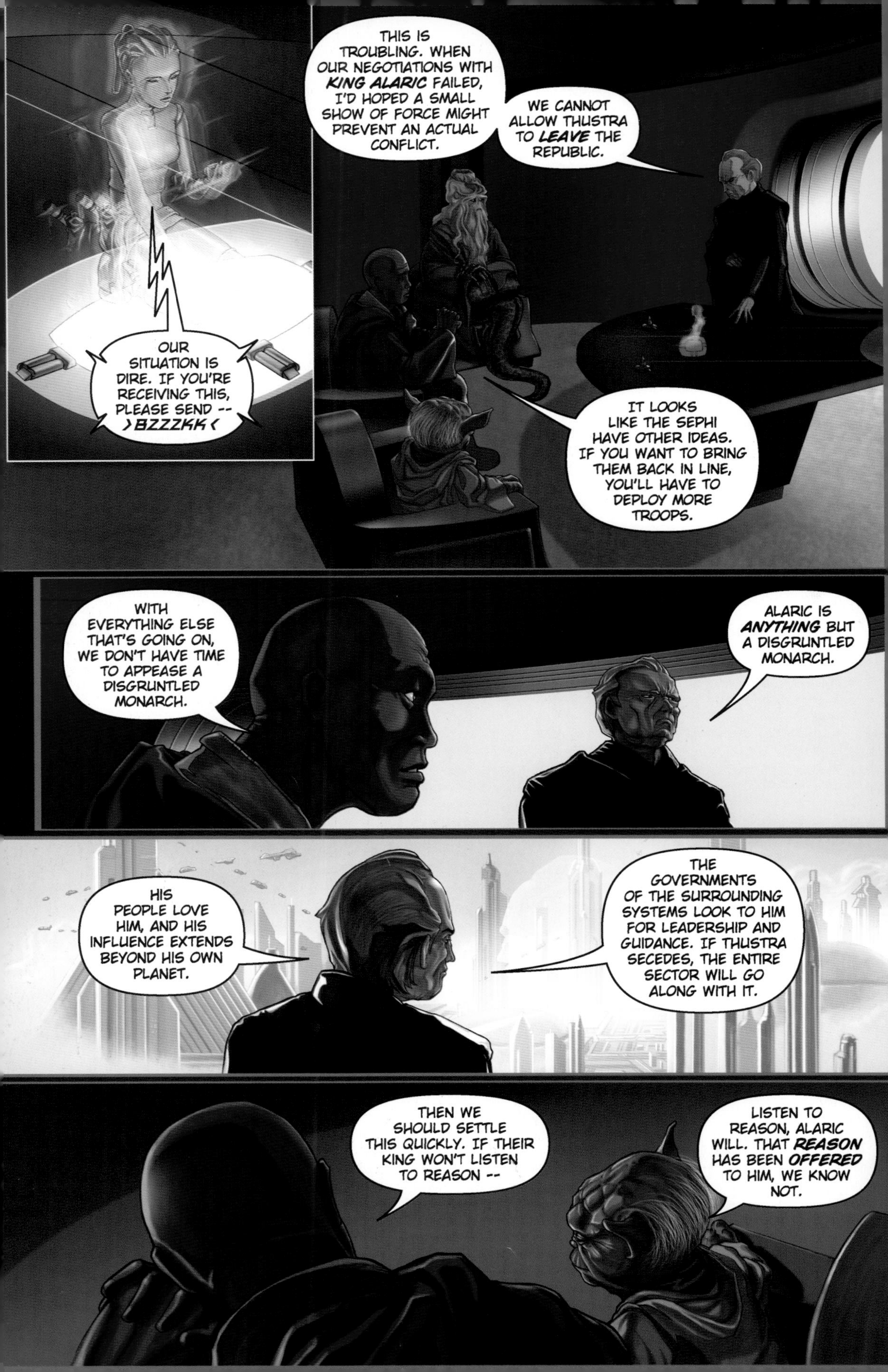
OUR SITUATION IS DIRE. IF YOU'RE RECEIVING THIS, PLEASE SEND -- >BZZZKK<
THIS IS TROUBLING. WHEN OUR NEGOTIATIONS WITH KING ALARIC FAILED, I'D HOPED A SMALL SHOW OF FORCE MIGHT PREVENT AN ACTUAL CONFLICT.
WE CANNOT ALLOW THUSTRA TO LEAVE THE REPUBLIC.
IT LOOKS LIKE THE SEPHI HAVE OTHER IDEAS. IF YOU WANT TO BRING THEM BACK IN LINE, YOU'LL HAVE TO DEPLOY MORE TROOPS.
WITH EVERYTHING ELSE THAT'S GOING ON, WE DON'T HAVE TIME TO APPEASE A DISGRUNTLED MONARCH.
ALARIC IS ANYTHING BUT A DISGRUNTLED MONARCH.
HIS PEOPLE LOVE HIM, AND HIS INFLUENCE EXTENDS BEYOND HIS OWN PLANET.
THE GOVERNMENTS OF THE SURROUNDING SYSTEMS LOOK TO HIM FOR LEADERSHIP AND GUIDANCE. IF THUSTRA SECEDES, THE ENTIRE SECTOR WILL GO ALONG WITH IT.
THEN WE SHOULD SETTLE THIS QUICKLY. IF THEIR KING WON'T LISTEN TO REASON --
LISTEN TO REASON, ALARIC WILL. THAT REASON HAS BEEN OFFERED TO HIM, WE KNOW NOT.

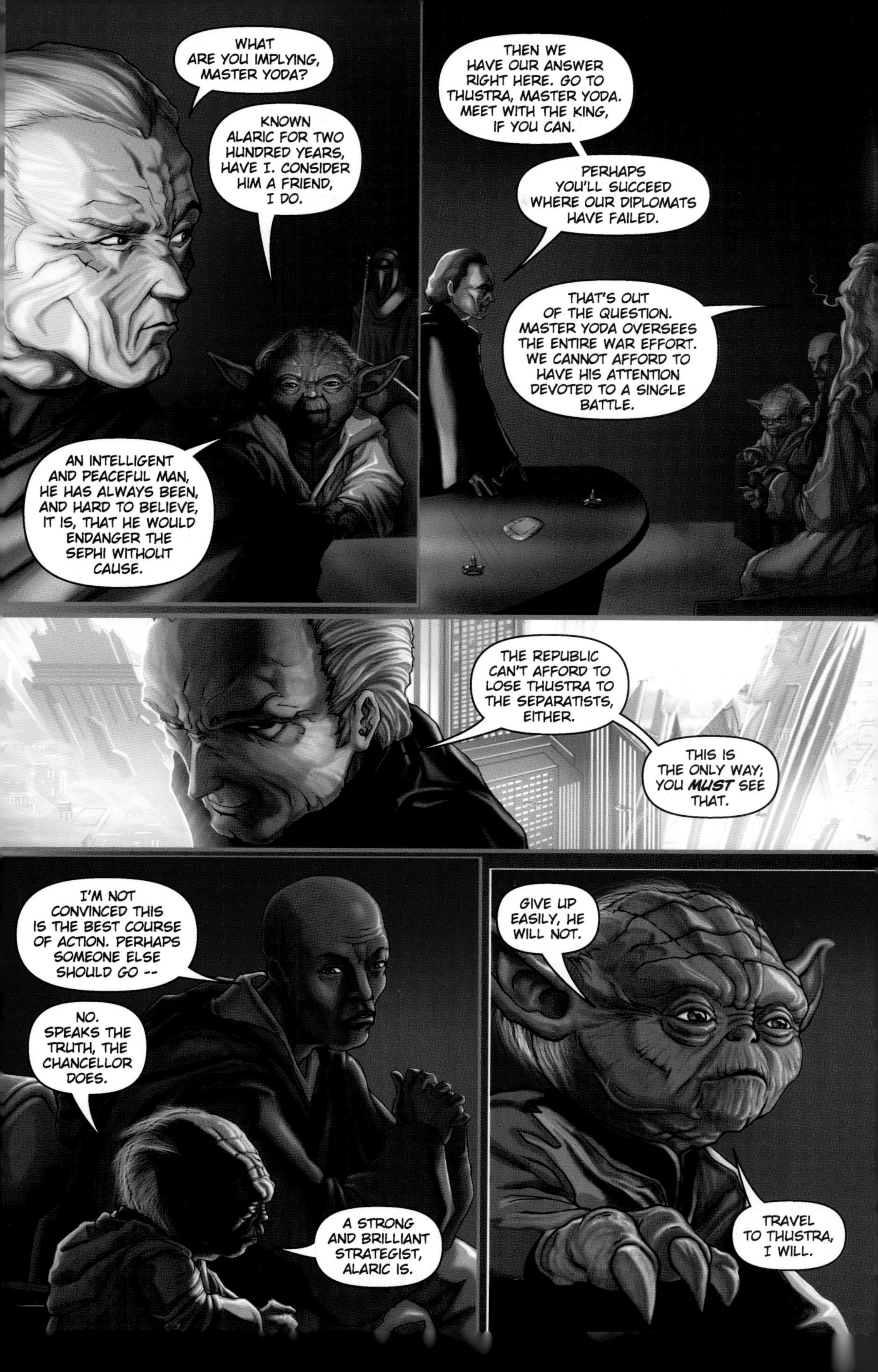
WHAT ARE YOU IMPLYING, MASTER YODA?
KNOWN ALARIC FOR TWO HUNDRED YEARS, HAVE I. CONSIDER HIM A FRIEND, I DO.
AN INTELLIGENT AND PEACEFUL MAN, HE HAS ALWAYS BEEN, AND HARD TO BELIEVE, IT IS, THAT HE WOULD ENDANGER THE SEPHI WITHOUT CAUSE.
THEN WE HAVE OUR ANSWER RIGHT HERE. GO TO THUSTRA, MASTER YODA. MEET WITH THE KING, IF YOU CAN.
PERHAPS YOU'LL SUCCEED WHERE OUR DIPLOMATS HAVE FAILED.
THAT'S OUT OF THE QUESTION. MASTER YODA OVERSEES THE ENTIRE WAR EFFORT. WE CANNOT AFFORD TO HAVE HIS ATTENTION DEVOTED TO A SINGLE BATTLE.
THE REPUBLIC CAN'T AFFORD TO LOSE THUSTRA TO THE SEPARATISTS, EITHER.
THIS IS THE ONLY WAY; YOU ***MUST*** SEE THAT.
I'M NOT CONVINCED THIS IS THE BEST COURSE OF ACTION. PERHAPS SOMEONE ELSE SHOULD GO --
NO. SPEAKS THE TRUTH, THE CHANCELLOR DOES.
A STRONG AND BRILLIANT STRATEGIST, ALARIC IS.
GIVE UP EASILY, HE WILL NOT.
TRAVEL TO THUSTRA, I WILL.

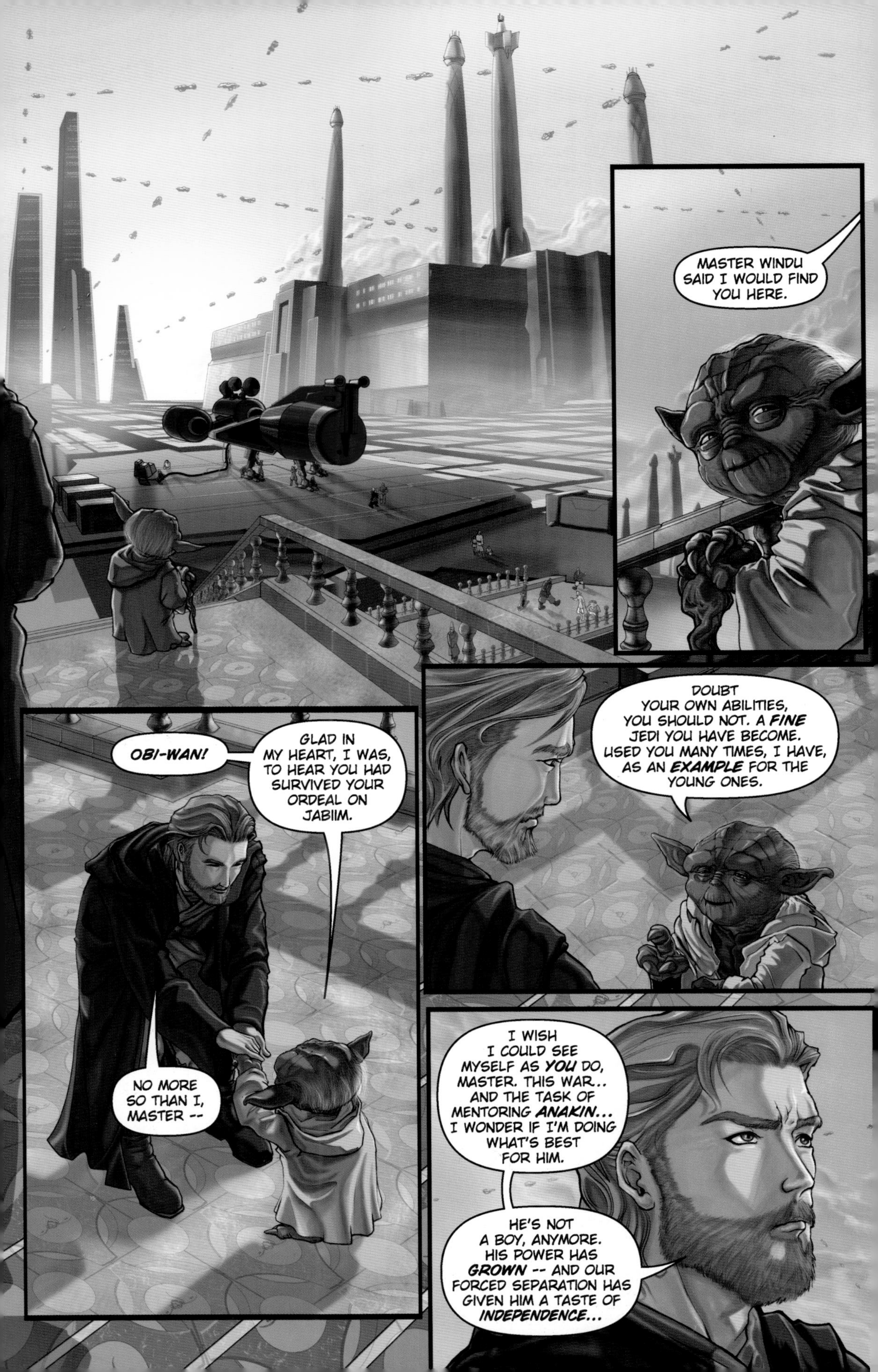
MASTER WINDU SAID I WOULD FIND YOU HERE.
OBI-WAN!
GLAD IN MY HEART, I WAS, TO HEAR YOU HAD SURVIVED YOUR ORDEAL ON JABIIM.
NO MORE SO THAN I, MASTER --
DOUBT YOUR OWN ABILITIES, YOU SHOULD NOT. A *FINE* JEDI YOU HAVE BECOME. USED YOU MANY TIMES, I HAVE, AS AN *EXAMPLE* FOR THE YOUNG ONES.
I WISH I COULD SEE MYSELF AS *YOU* DO, MASTER. THIS WAR.. AND THE TASK OF MENTORING *ANAKIN*... I WONDER IF I'M DOING WHAT'S BEST FOR HIM.
HE'S NOT A BOY, ANYMORE. HIS POWER HAS *GROWN* -- AND OUR FORCED SEPARATION HAS GIVEN HIM A TASTE OF *INDEPENDENCE*...

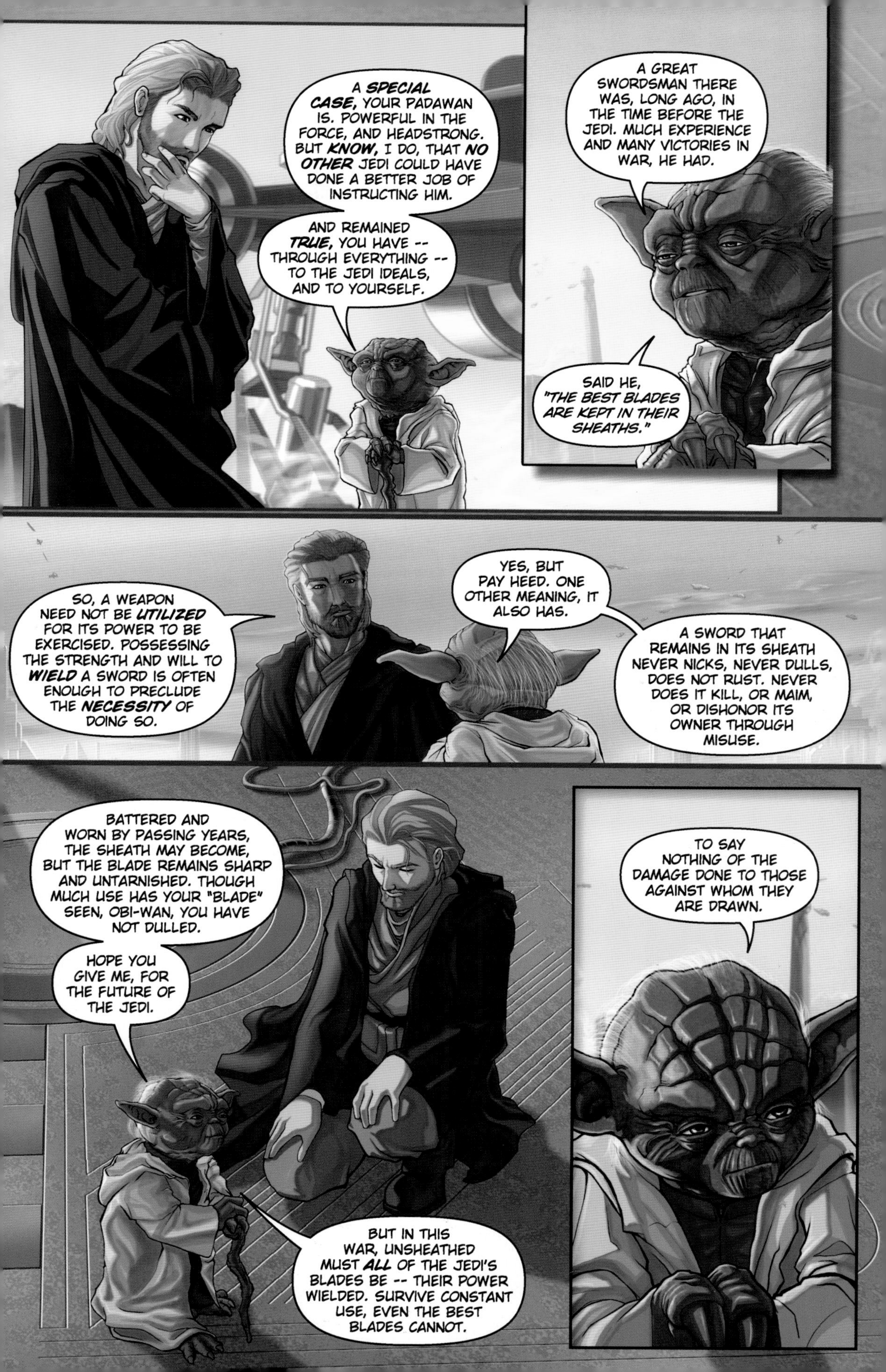

A SPECIAL CASE, YOUR PADAWAN IS. POWERFUL IN THE FORCE, AND HEADSTRONG. BUT KNOW, I DO, THAT NO OTHER JEDI COULD HAVE DONE A BETTER JOB OF INSTRUCTING HIM.
AND REMAINED TRUE, YOU HAVE -- THROUGH EVERYTHING -- TO THE JEDI IDEALS, AND TO YOURSELF.
A GREAT SWORDSMAN THERE WAS, LONG AGO, IN THE TIME BEFORE THE JEDI. MUCH EXPERIENCE AND MANY VICTORIES IN WAR, HE HAD.
SAID HE, "THE BEST BLADES ARE KEPT IN THEIR SHEATHS."
SO, A WEAPON NEED NOT BE UTILIZED FOR ITS POWER TO BE EXERCISED. POSSESSING THE STRENGTH AND WILL TO WIELD A SWORD IS OFTEN ENOUGH TO PRECLUDE THE NECESSITY OF DOING SO.
YES, BUT PAY HEED. ONE OTHER MEANING, IT ALSO HAS.
A SWORD THAT REMAINS IN ITS SHEATH NEVER NICKS, NEVER DULLS, DOES NOT RUST. NEVER DOES IT KILL, OR MAIM, OR DISHONOR ITS OWNER THROUGH MISUSE.
BATTERED AND WORN BY PASSING YEARS, THE SHEATH MAY BECOME, BUT THE BLADE REMAINS SHARP AND UNTARNISHED. THOUGH MUCH USE HAS YOUR "BLADE" SEEN, OBI-WAN, YOU HAVE NOT DULLED.
HOPE YOU GIVE ME, FOR THE FUTURE OF THE JEDI.
BUT IN THIS WAR, UNSHEATHED MUST ALL OF THE JEDI'S BLADES BE -- THEIR POWER WIELDED. SURVIVE CONSTANT USE, EVEN THE BEST BLADES CANNOT.
TO SAY NOTHING OF THE DAMAGE DONE TO THOSE AGAINST WHOM THEY ARE DRAWN.

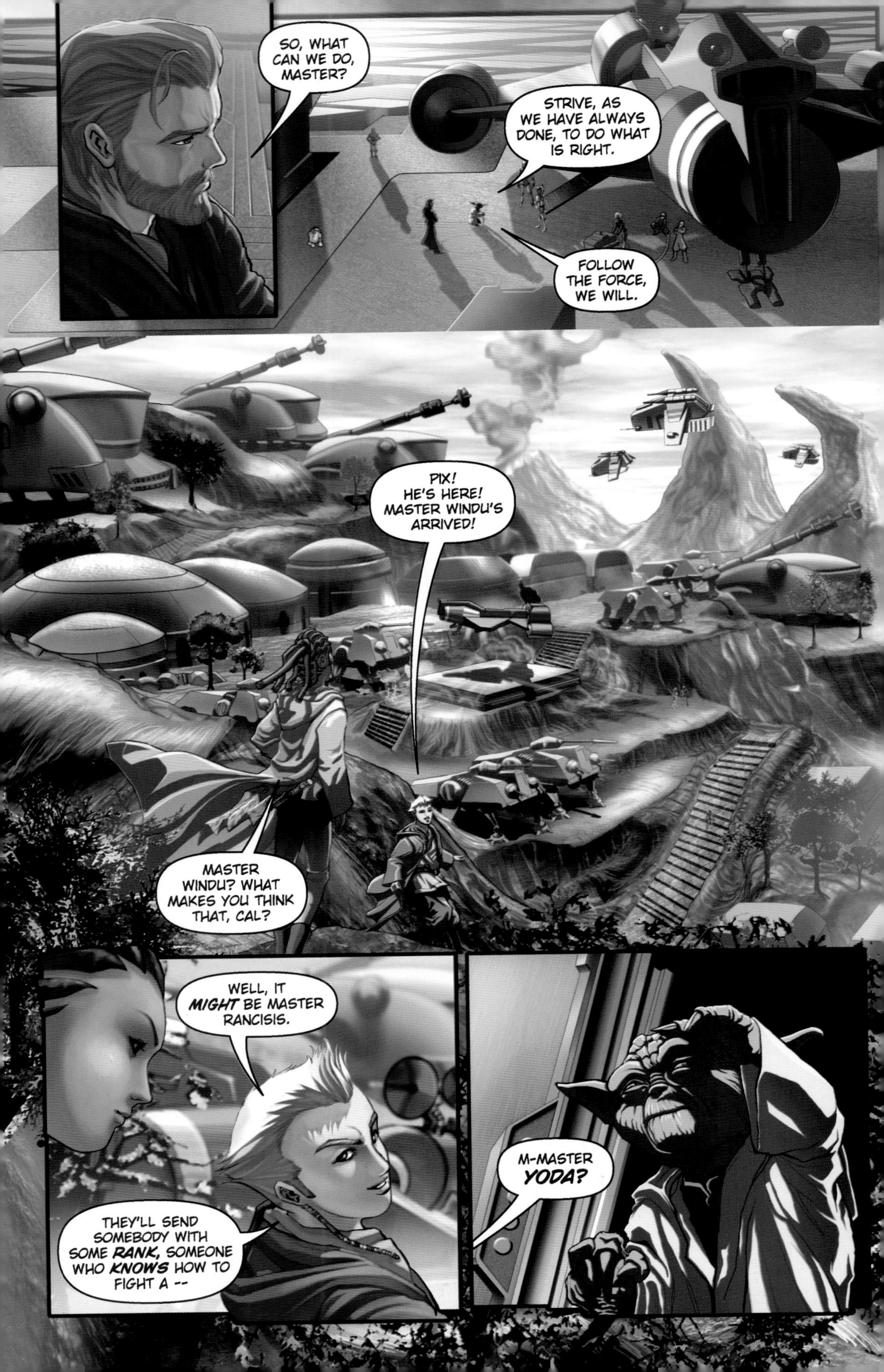

SO, WHAT CAN WE DO, MASTER?
STRIVE, AS WE HAVE ALWAYS DONE, TO DO WHAT IS RIGHT.
FOLLOW THE FORCE, WE WILL.
PIX! HE'S HERE! MASTER WINDU'S ARRIVED!
MASTER WINDU? WHAT MAKES YOU THINK THAT, CAL?
WELL, IT *MIGHT* BE MASTER RANCISIS.
THEY'LL SEND SOMEBODY WITH SOME *RANK*, SOMEONE WHO *KNOWS* HOW TO FIGHT A --
M-MASTER *YODA?*

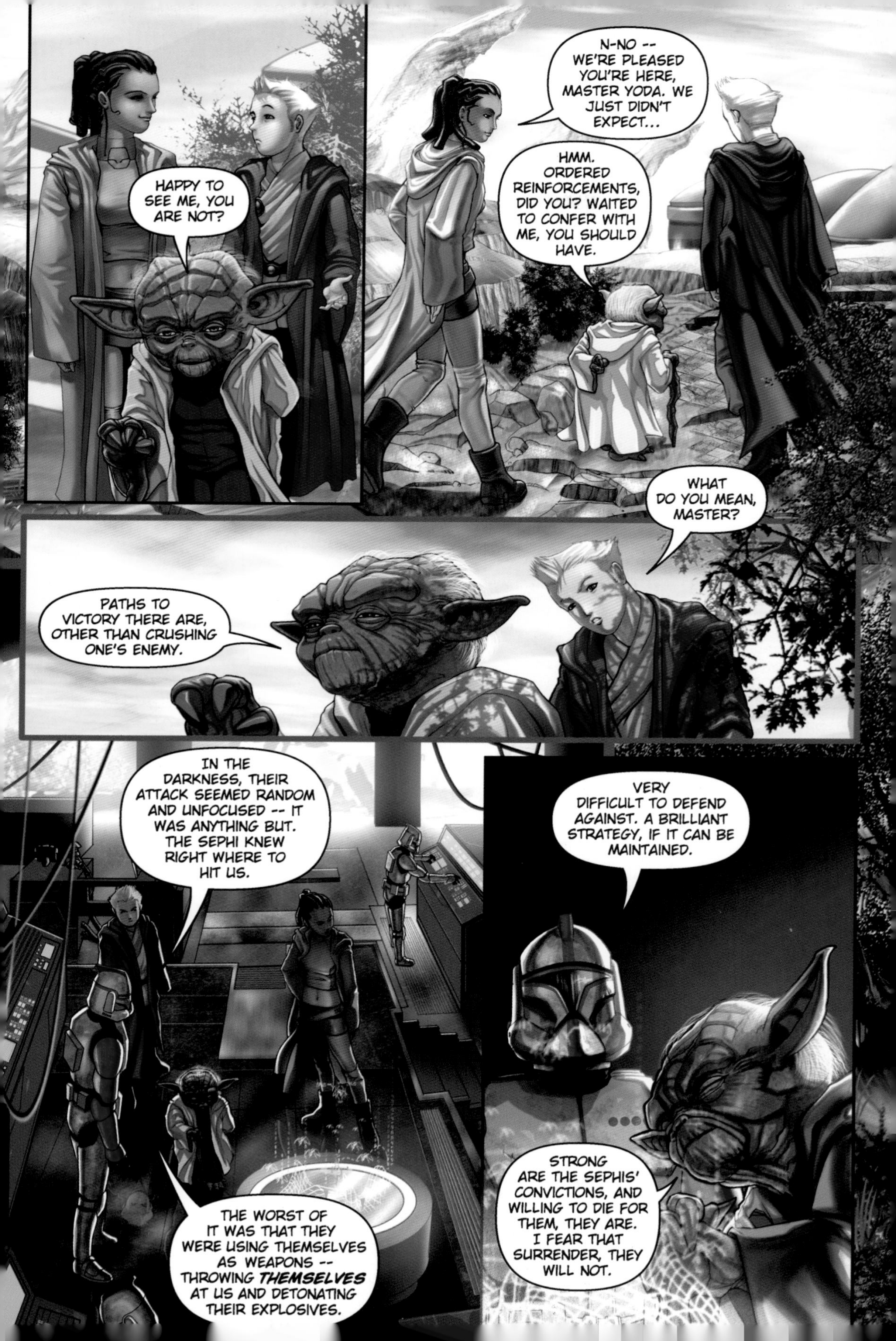
HAPPY TO SEE ME, YOU ARE NOT?
N-NO -- WE'RE PLEASED YOU'RE HERE, MASTER YODA. WE JUST DIDN'T EXPECT...
HMM. ORDERED REINFORCEMENTS, DID YOU? WAITED TO CONFER WITH ME, YOU SHOULD HAVE.
WHAT DO YOU MEAN, MASTER?
PATHS TO VICTORY THERE ARE, OTHER THAN CRUSHING ONE'S ENEMY.
IN THE DARKNESS, THEIR ATTACK SEEMED RANDOM AND UNFOCUSED -- IT WAS ANYTHING BUT. THE SEPHI KNEW RIGHT WHERE TO HIT US.
THE WORST OF IT WAS THAT THEY WERE USING THEMSELVES AS WEAPONS -- THROWING *THEMSELVES* AT US AND DETONATING THEIR EXPLOSIVES.
VERY DIFFICULT TO DEFEND AGAINST. A BRILLIANT STRATEGY, IF IT CAN BE MAINTAINED.
STRONG ARE THE SEPHIS' CONVICTIONS, AND WILLING TO DIE FOR THEM, THEY ARE. I FEAR THAT SURRENDER, THEY WILL NOT.

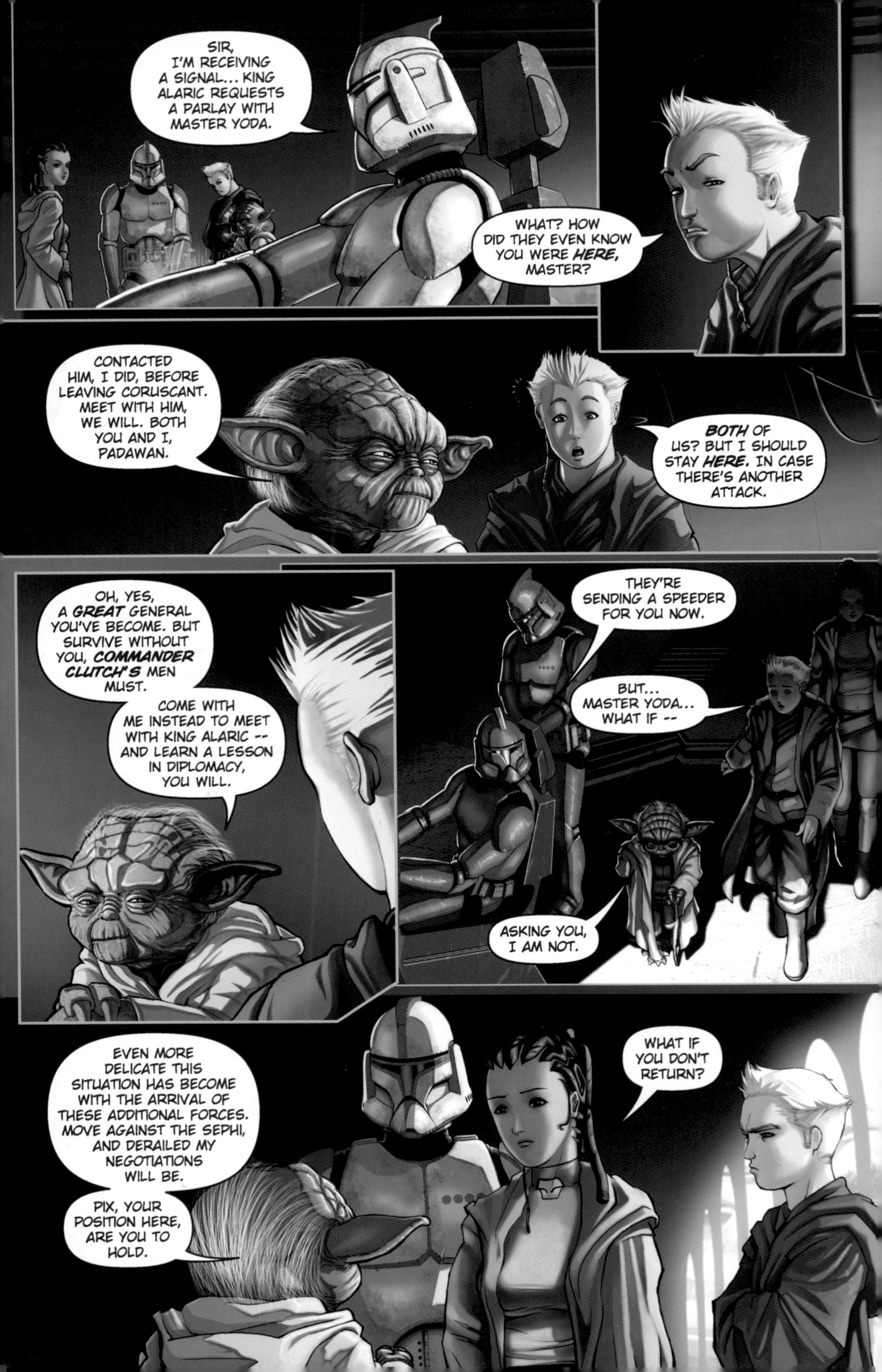
SIR, I'M RECEIVING A SIGNAL... KING ALARIC REQUESTS A PARLAY WITH MASTER YODA.
WHAT? HOW DID THEY EVEN KNOW YOU WERE *HERE,* MASTER?
CONTACTED HIM, I DID, BEFORE LEAVING CORUSCANT. MEET WITH HIM, WE WILL. BOTH YOU AND I, PADAWAN.
*BOTH* OF US? BUT I SHOULD STAY *HERE.* IN CASE THERE'S ANOTHER ATTACK.
OH, YES, A *GREAT* GENERAL YOU'VE BECOME. BUT SURVIVE WITHOUT YOU, *COMMANDER CLUTCH'S* MEN MUST.
COME WITH ME INSTEAD TO MEET WITH KING ALARIC -- AND LEARN A LESSON IN DIPLOMACY, YOU WILL.
THEY'RE SENDING A SPEEDER FOR YOU NOW.
BUT... MASTER YODA... WHAT IF --
ASKING YOU, I AM NOT.
EVEN MORE DELICATE THIS SITUATION HAS BECOME WITH THE ARRIVAL OF THESE ADDITIONAL FORCES. MOVE AGAINST THE SEPHI, AND DERAILED MY NEGOTIATIONS WILL BE.
PIX, YOUR POSITION HERE, ARE YOU TO HOLD.
WHAT IF YOU DON'T RETURN?

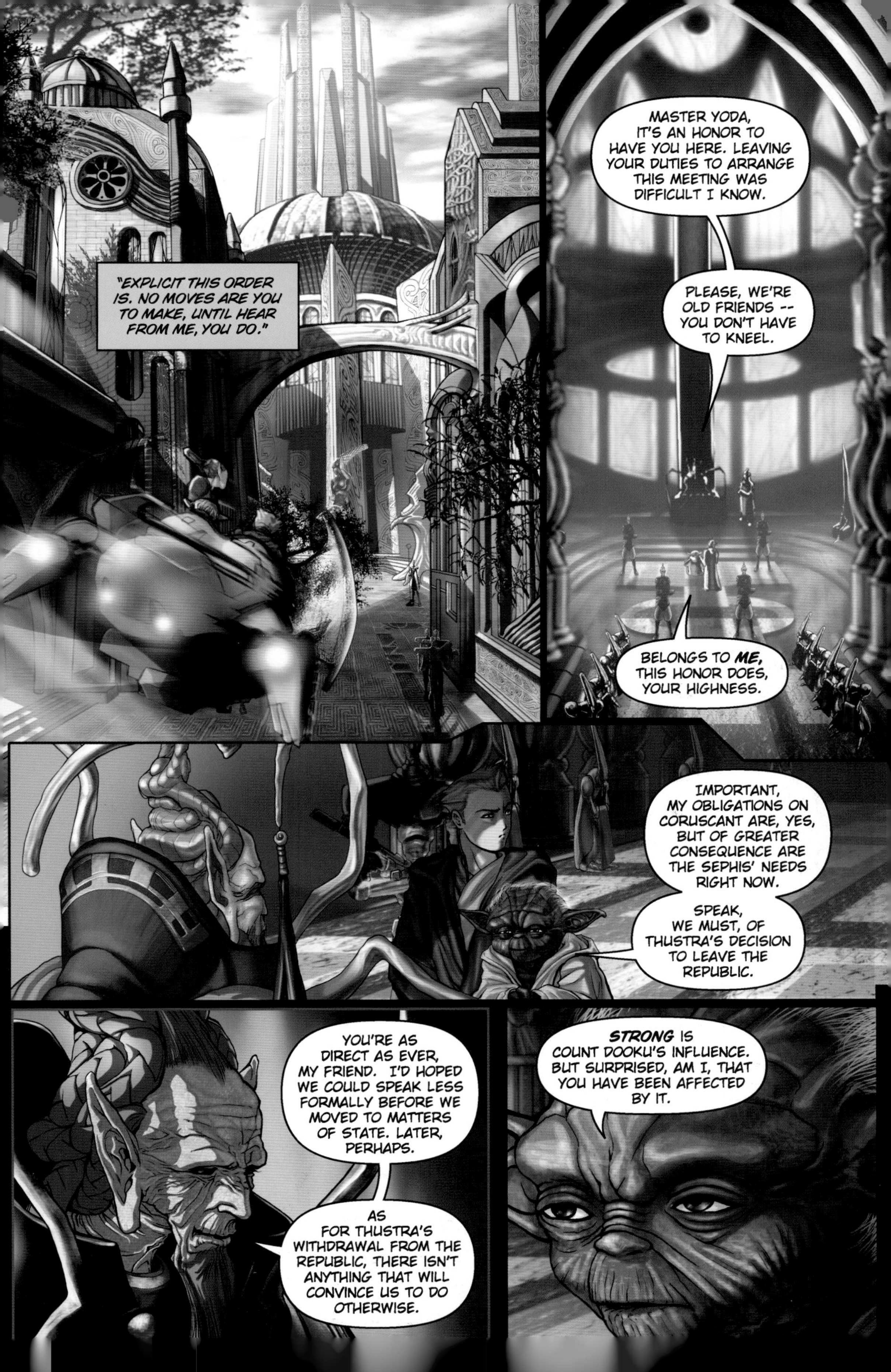
"EXPLICIT THIS ORDER IS. NO MOVES ARE YOU TO MAKE, UNTIL HEAR FROM ME, YOU DO."
MASTER YODA, IT'S AN HONOR TO HAVE YOU HERE. LEAVING YOUR DUTIES TO ARRANGE THIS MEETING WAS DIFFICULT I KNOW.
PLEASE, WE'RE OLD FRIENDS -- YOU DON'T HAVE TO KNEEL.
BELONGS TO ME, THIS HONOR DOES, YOUR HIGHNESS.
IMPORTANT, MY OBLIGATIONS ON CORUSCANT ARE, YES, BUT OF GREATER CONSEQUENCE ARE THE SEPHIS' NEEDS RIGHT NOW.
SPEAK, WE MUST, OF THUSTRA'S DECISION TO LEAVE THE REPUBLIC.
YOU'RE AS DIRECT AS EVER, MY FRIEND. I'D HOPED WE COULD SPEAK LESS FORMALLY BEFORE WE MOVED TO MATTERS OF STATE. LATER, PERHAPS.
AS FOR THUSTRA'S WITHDRAWAL FROM THE REPUBLIC, THERE ISN'T ANYTHING THAT WILL CONVINCE US TO DO OTHERWISE.
STRONG IS COUNT DOOKU'S INFLUENCE. BUT SURPRISED, AM I, THAT YOU HAVE BEEN AFFECTED BY IT.

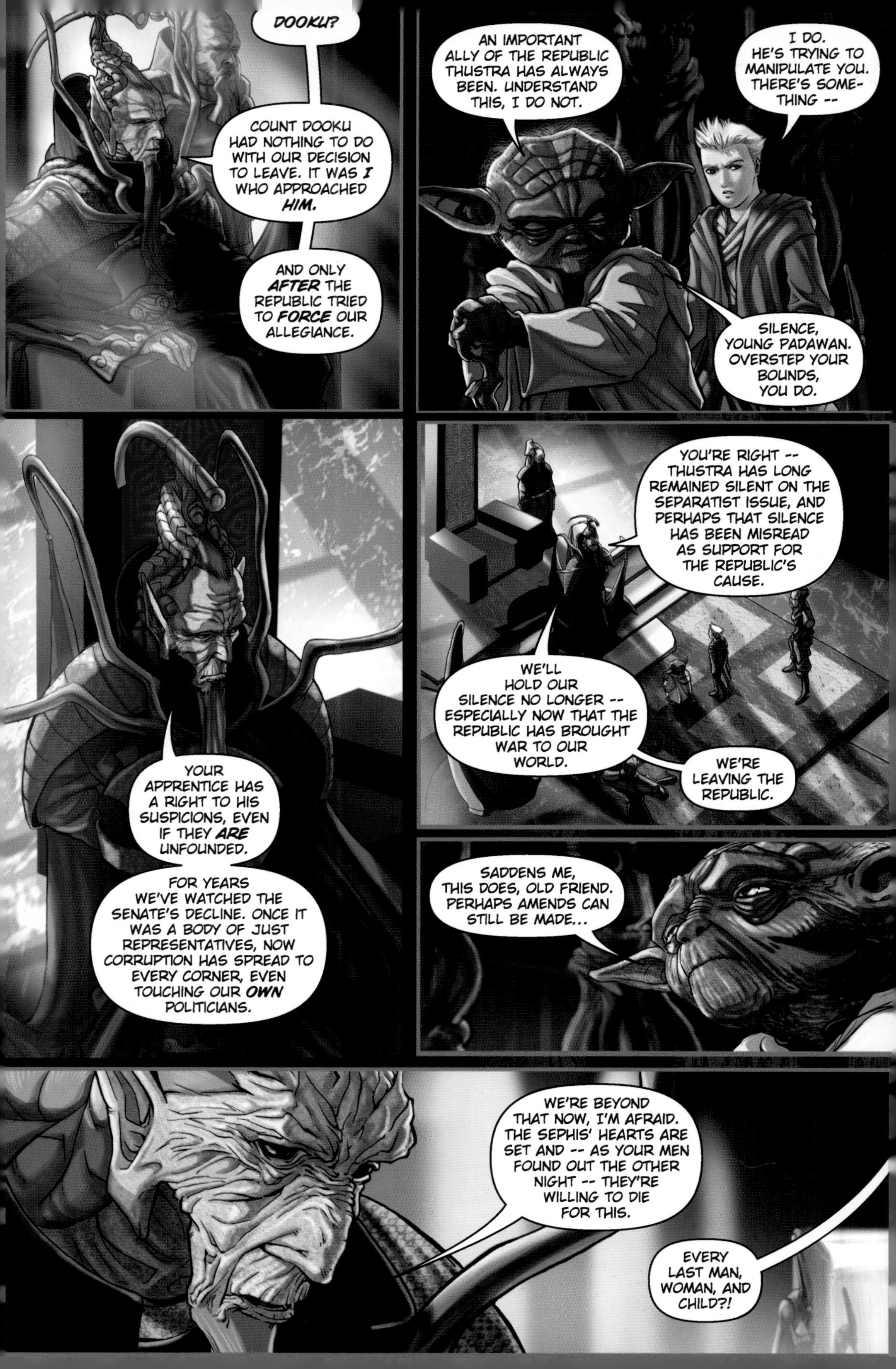
DOOKU?
COUNT DOOKU HAD NOTHING TO DO WITH OUR DECISION TO LEAVE. IT WAS *I* WHO APPROACHED *HIM.*
AND ONLY *AFTER* THE REPUBLIC TRIED TO *FORCE* OUR ALLEGIANCE.
AN IMPORTANT ALLY OF THE REPUBLIC THUSTRA HAS ALWAYS BEEN. UNDERSTAND THIS, I DO NOT.
I DO. HE'S TRYING TO MANIPULATE YOU. THERE'S SOMETHING --
SILENCE, YOUNG PADAWAN. OVERSTEP YOUR BOUNDS, YOU DO.
YOUR APPRENTICE HAS A RIGHT TO HIS SUSPICIONS, EVEN IF THEY *ARE* UNFOUNDED.
FOR YEARS WE'VE WATCHED THE SENATE'S DECLINE. ONCE IT WAS A BODY OF JUST REPRESENTATIVES, NOW CORRUPTION HAS SPREAD TO EVERY CORNER, EVEN TOUCHING OUR *OWN* POLITICIANS.
YOU'RE RIGHT -- THUSTRA HAS LONG REMAINED SILENT ON THE SEPARATIST ISSUE, AND PERHAPS THAT SILENCE HAS BEEN MISREAD AS SUPPORT FOR THE REPUBLIC'S CAUSE.
WE'LL HOLD OUR SILENCE NO LONGER -- ESPECIALLY NOW THAT THE REPUBLIC HAS BROUGHT WAR TO OUR WORLD.
WE'RE LEAVING THE REPUBLIC.
SADDENS ME, THIS DOES, OLD FRIEND. PERHAPS AMENDS CAN STILL BE MADE...
WE'RE BEYOND THAT NOW, I'M AFRAID. THE SEPHIS' HEARTS ARE SET AND -- AS YOUR MEN FOUND OUT THE OTHER NIGHT -- THEY'RE WILLING TO DIE FOR THIS.
EVERY LAST MAN, WOMAN, AND CHILD?!

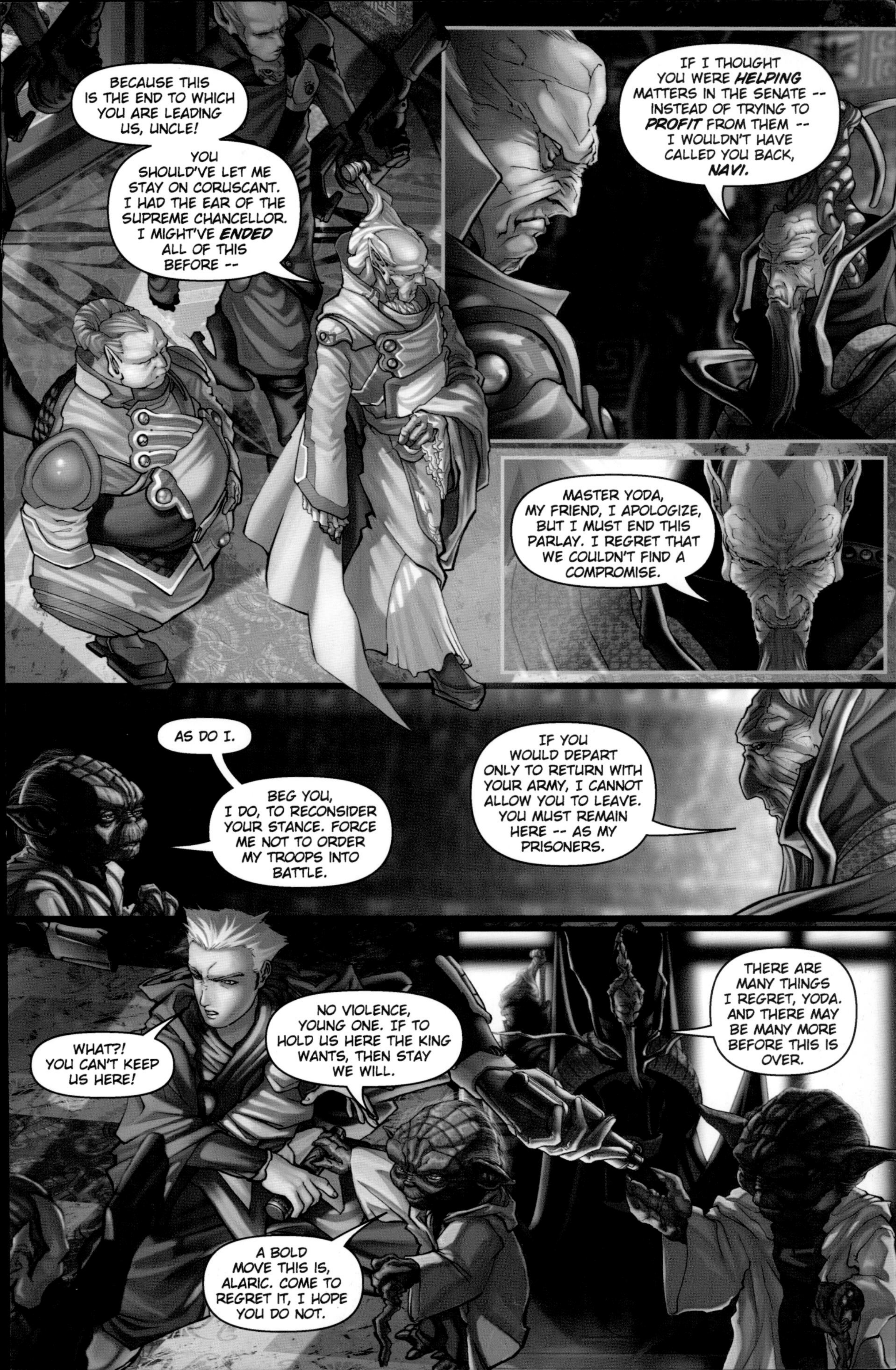
BECAUSE THIS IS THE END TO WHICH YOU ARE LEADING US, UNCLE!
YOU SHOULD'VE LET ME STAY ON CORUSCANT. I HAD THE EAR OF THE SUPREME CHANCELLOR. I MIGHT'VE *ENDED* ALL OF THIS BEFORE --
IF I THOUGHT YOU WERE *HELPING* MATTERS IN THE SENATE -- INSTEAD OF TRYING TO *PROFIT* FROM THEM -- I WOULDN'T HAVE CALLED YOU BACK, *NAVI.*
MASTER YODA, MY FRIEND, I APOLOGIZE, BUT I MUST END THIS PARLAY. I REGRET THAT WE COULDN'T FIND A COMPROMISE.
AS DO I.
BEG YOU, I DO, TO RECONSIDER YOUR STANCE. FORCE ME NOT TO ORDER MY TROOPS INTO BATTLE.
IF YOU WOULD DEPART ONLY TO RETURN WITH YOUR ARMY, I CANNOT ALLOW YOU TO LEAVE. YOU MUST REMAIN HERE -- AS MY PRISONERS.
WHAT?! YOU CAN'T KEEP US HERE!
NO VIOLENCE, YOUNG ONE. IF TO HOLD US HERE THE KING WANTS, THEN STAY WE WILL.
A BOLD MOVE THIS IS, ALARIC. COME TO REGRET IT, I HOPE YOU DO NOT.
THERE ARE MANY THINGS I REGRET, YODA. AND THERE MAY BE MANY MORE BEFORE THIS IS OVER.

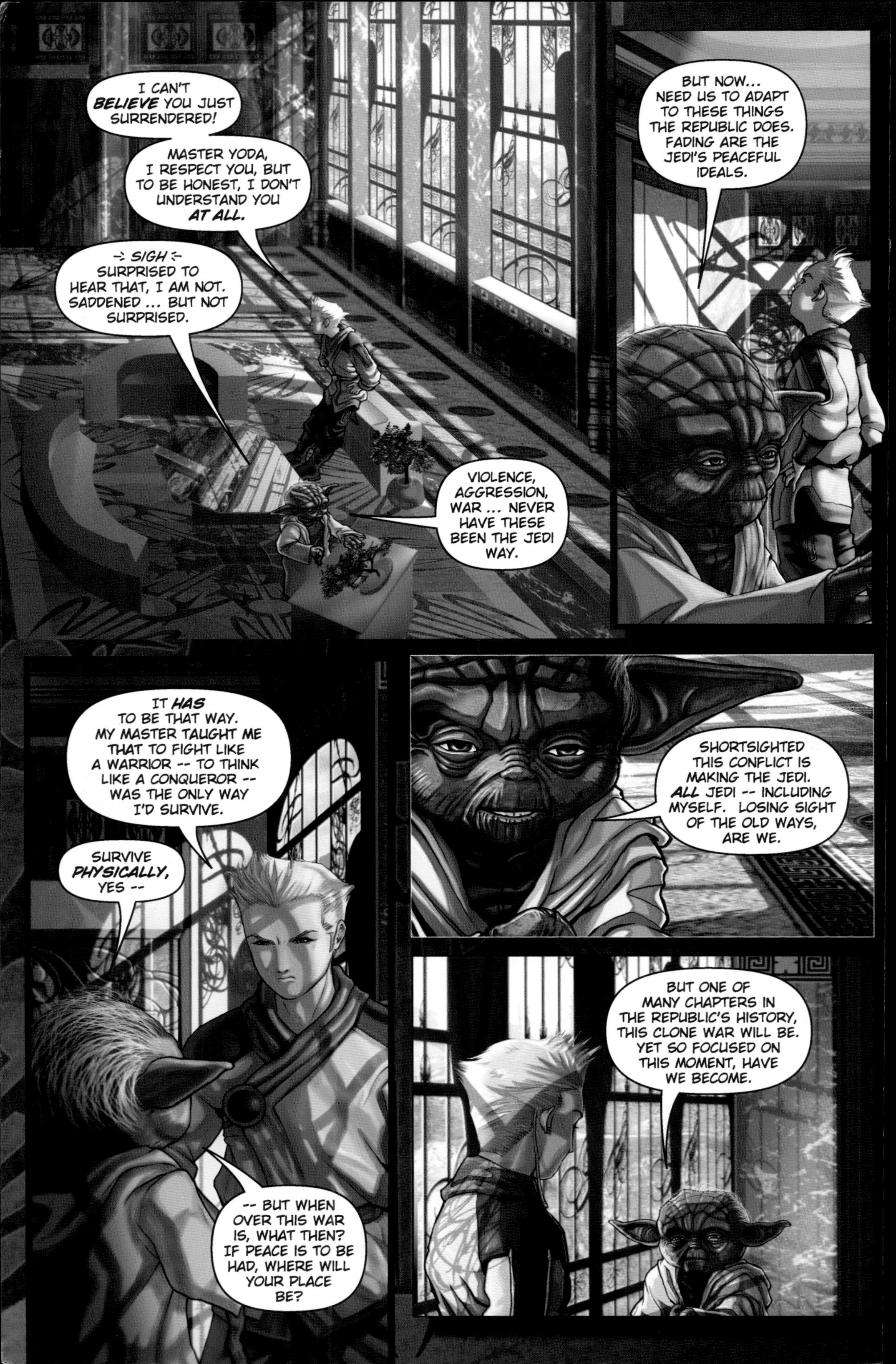
I CAN'T BELIEVE YOU JUST SURRENDERED!
MASTER YODA, I RESPECT YOU, BUT TO BE HONEST, I DON'T UNDERSTAND YOU AT ALL.
SIGH
SURPRISED TO HEAR THAT, I AM NOT. SADDENED ... BUT NOT SURPRISED.
VIOLENCE, AGGRESSION, WAR ... NEVER HAVE THESE BEEN THE JEDI WAY.
BUT NOW... NEED US TO ADAPT TO THESE THINGS THE REPUBLIC DOES. FADING ARE THE JEDI'S PEACEFUL IDEALS.
IT HAS TO BE THAT WAY. MY MASTER TAUGHT ME THAT TO FIGHT LIKE A WARRIOR -- TO THINK LIKE A CONQUEROR -- WAS THE ONLY WAY I'D SURVIVE.
SURVIVE PHYSICALLY, YES --
-- BUT WHEN OVER THIS WAR IS, WHAT THEN? IF PEACE IS TO BE HAD, WHERE WILL YOUR PLACE BE?
SHORTSIGHTED THIS CONFLICT IS MAKING THE JEDI. ALL JEDI -- INCLUDING MYSELF. LOSING SIGHT OF THE OLD WAYS, ARE WE.
BUT ONE OF MANY CHAPTERS IN THE REPUBLIC'S HISTORY, THIS CLONE WAR WILL BE. YET SO FOCUSED ON THIS MOMENT, HAVE WE BECOME.

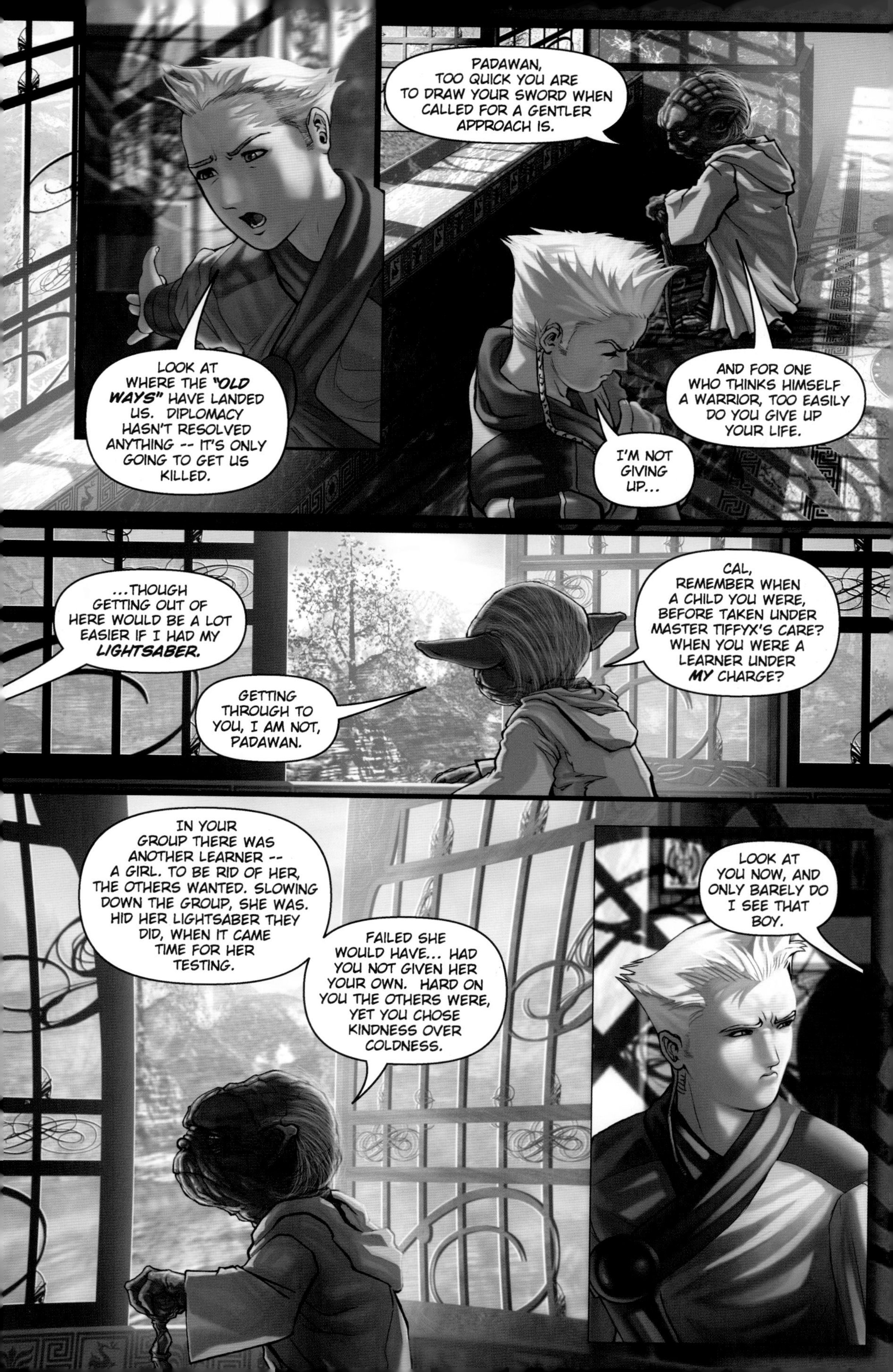
LOOK AT WHERE THE "OLD WAYS" HAVE LANDED US. DIPLOMACY HASN'T RESOLVED ANYTHING -- IT'S ONLY GOING TO GET US KILLED.
PADAWAN, TOO QUICK YOU ARE TO DRAW YOUR SWORD WHEN CALLED FOR A GENTLER APPROACH IS.
AND FOR ONE WHO THINKS HIMSELF A WARRIOR, TOO EASILY DO YOU GIVE UP YOUR LIFE.
I'M NOT GIVING UP...
...THOUGH GETTING OUT OF HERE WOULD BE A LOT EASIER IF I HAD MY LIGHTSABER.
GETTING THROUGH TO YOU, I AM NOT, PADAWAN.
CAL, REMEMBER WHEN A CHILD YOU WERE, BEFORE TAKEN UNDER MASTER TIFFYX'S CARE? WHEN YOU WERE A LEARNER UNDER MY CHARGE?
IN YOUR GROUP THERE WAS ANOTHER LEARNER -- A GIRL. TO BE RID OF HER, THE OTHERS WANTED. SLOWING DOWN THE GROUP, SHE WAS. HID HER LIGHTSABER THEY DID, WHEN IT CAME TIME FOR HER TESTING.
FAILED SHE WOULD HAVE... HAD YOU NOT GIVEN HER YOUR OWN. HARD ON YOU THE OTHERS WERE, YET YOU CHOSE KINDNESS OVER COLDNESS.
LOOK AT YOU NOW, AND ONLY BARELY DO I SEE THAT BOY.

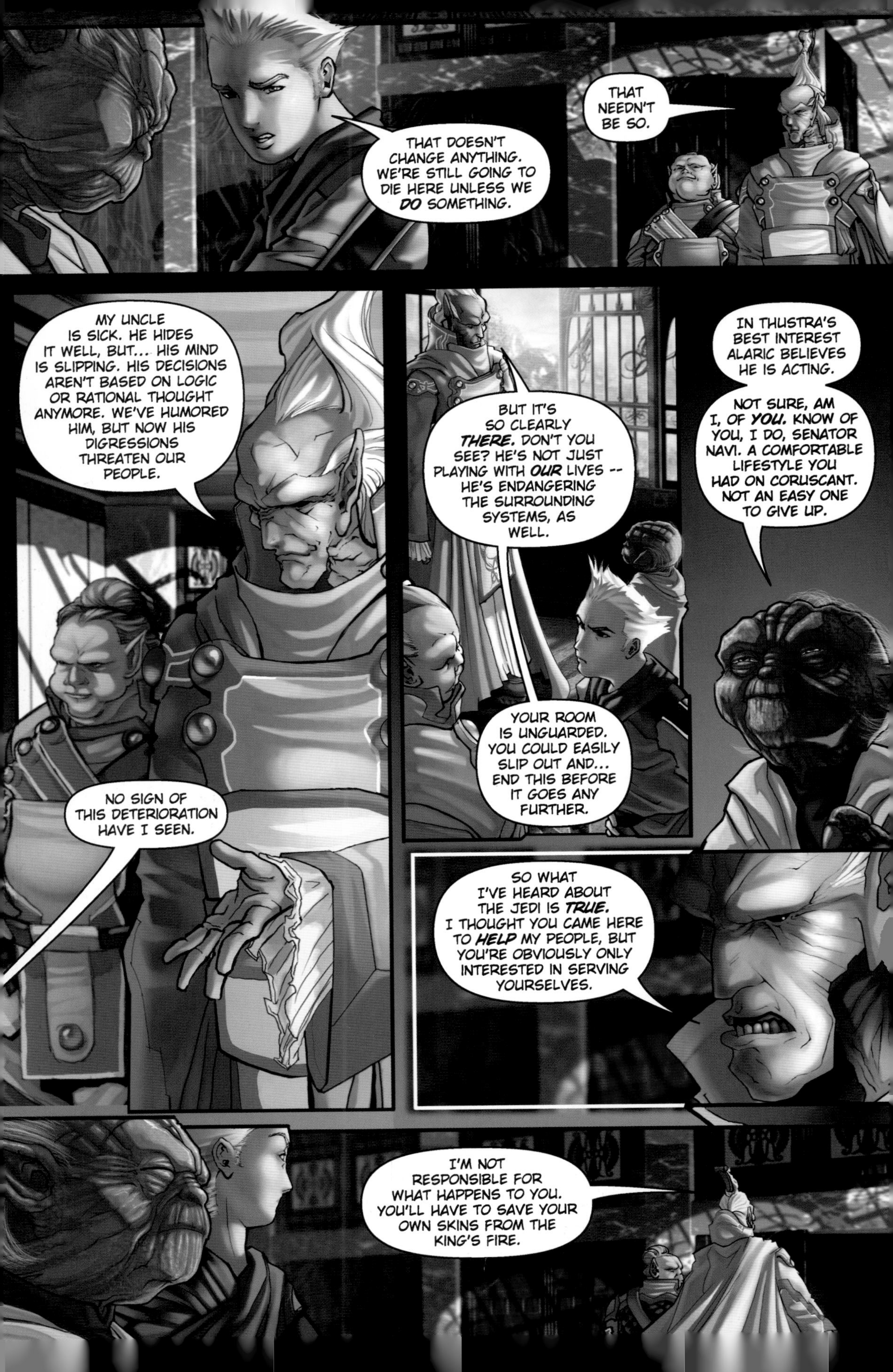

THAT DOESN'T CHANGE ANYTHING. WE'RE STILL GOING TO DIE HERE UNLESS WE *DO* SOMETHING.
THAT NEEDN'T BE SO.
MY UNCLE IS SICK. HE HIDES IT WELL, BUT... HIS MIND IS SLIPPING. HIS DECISIONS AREN'T BASED ON LOGIC OR RATIONAL THOUGHT ANYMORE. WE'VE HUMORED HIM, BUT NOW HIS DIGRESSIONS THREATEN OUR PEOPLE.
NO SIGN OF THIS DETERIORATION HAVE I SEEN.
BUT IT'S SO CLEARLY *THERE.* DON'T YOU SEE? HE'S NOT JUST PLAYING WITH *OUR* LIVES -- HE'S ENDANGERING THE SURROUNDING SYSTEMS, AS WELL.
YOUR ROOM IS UNGUARDED. YOU COULD EASILY SLIP OUT AND... END THIS BEFORE IT GOES ANY FURTHER.
IN THUSTRA'S BEST INTEREST ALARIC BELIEVES HE IS ACTING.
NOT SURE, AM I, OF *YOU.* KNOW OF YOU, I DO, SENATOR NAVI. A COMFORTABLE LIFESTYLE YOU HAD ON CORUSCANT. NOT AN EASY ONE TO GIVE UP.
SO WHAT I'VE HEARD ABOUT THE JEDI IS *TRUE.* I THOUGHT YOU CAME HERE TO *HELP* MY PEOPLE, BUT YOU'RE OBVIOUSLY ONLY INTERESTED IN SERVING YOURSELVES.
I'M NOT RESPONSIBLE FOR WHAT HAPPENS TO YOU. YOU'LL HAVE TO SAVE YOUR OWN SKINS FROM THE KING'S FIRE.

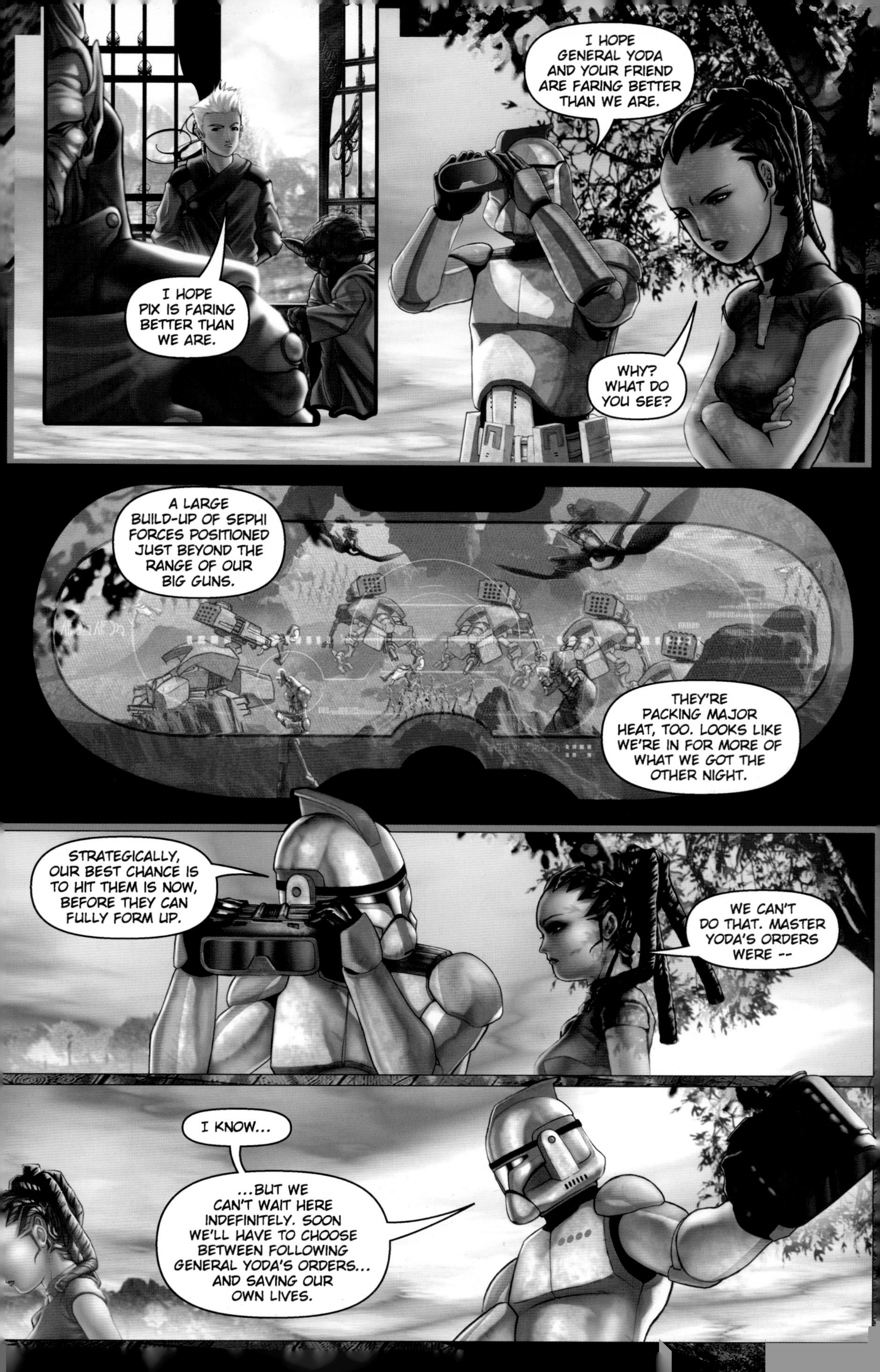
I HOPE PIX IS FARING BETTER THAN WE ARE.
I HOPE GENERAL YODA AND YOUR FRIEND ARE FARING BETTER THAN WE ARE.
WHY? WHAT DO YOU SEE?
A LARGE BUILD-UP OF SEPHI FORCES POSITIONED JUST BEYOND THE RANGE OF OUR BIG GUNS.
THEY'RE PACKING MAJOR HEAT, TOO. LOOKS LIKE WE'RE IN FOR MORE OF WHAT WE GOT THE OTHER NIGHT.
STRATEGICALLY, OUR BEST CHANCE IS TO HIT THEM IS NOW, BEFORE THEY CAN FULLY FORM UP.
WE CAN'T DO THAT. MASTER YODA'S ORDERS WERE --
I KNOW...
...BUT WE CAN'T WAIT HERE INDEFINITELY. SOON WE'LL HAVE TO CHOOSE BETWEEN FOLLOWING GENERAL YODA'S ORDERS... AND SAVING OUR OWN LIVES.

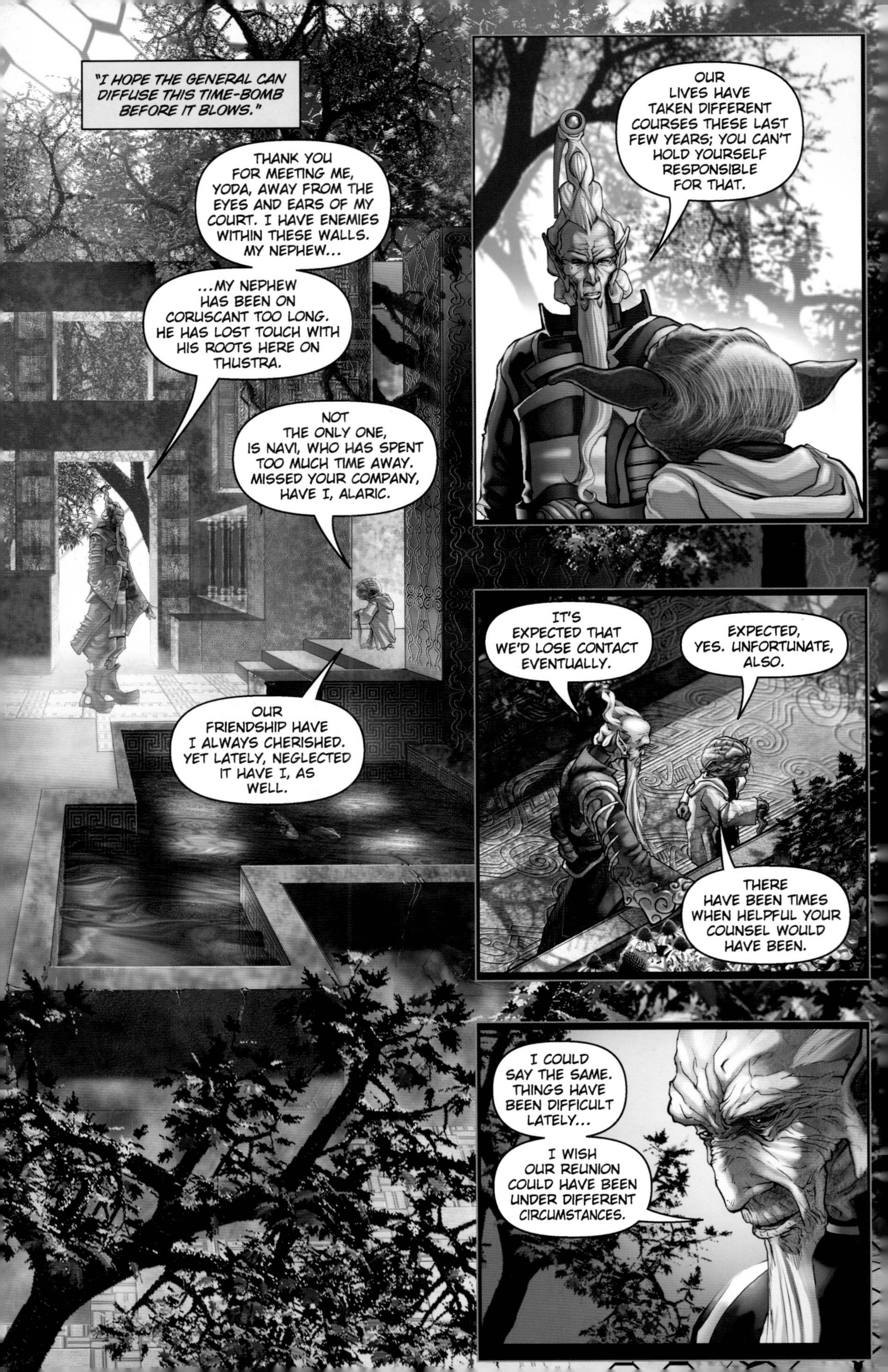
"I HOPE THE GENERAL CAN DIFFUSE THIS TIME-BOMB BEFORE IT BLOWS."
THANK YOU FOR MEETING ME, YODA, AWAY FROM THE EYES AND EARS OF MY COURT. I HAVE ENEMIES WITHIN THESE WALLS. MY NEPHEW...
...MY NEPHEW HAS BEEN ON CORUSCANT TOO LONG. HE HAS LOST TOUCH WITH HIS ROOTS HERE ON THUSTRA.
NOT THE ONLY ONE, IS NAVI, WHO HAS SPENT TOO MUCH TIME AWAY. MISSED YOUR COMPANY, HAVE I, ALARIC.
OUR FRIENDSHIP HAVE I ALWAYS CHERISHED. YET LATELY, NEGLECTED IT HAVE I, AS WELL.
OUR LIVES HAVE TAKEN DIFFERENT COURSES THESE LAST FEW YEARS; YOU CAN'T HOLD YOURSELF RESPONSIBLE FOR THAT.
IT'S EXPECTED THAT WE'D LOSE CONTACT EVENTUALLY.
EXPECTED, YES. UNFORTUNATE, ALSO.
THERE HAVE BEEN TIMES WHEN HELPFUL YOUR COUNSEL WOULD HAVE BEEN.
I COULD SAY THE SAME. THINGS HAVE BEEN DIFFICULT LATELY...
I WISH OUR REUNION COULD HAVE BEEN UNDER DIFFERENT CIRCUMSTANCES.

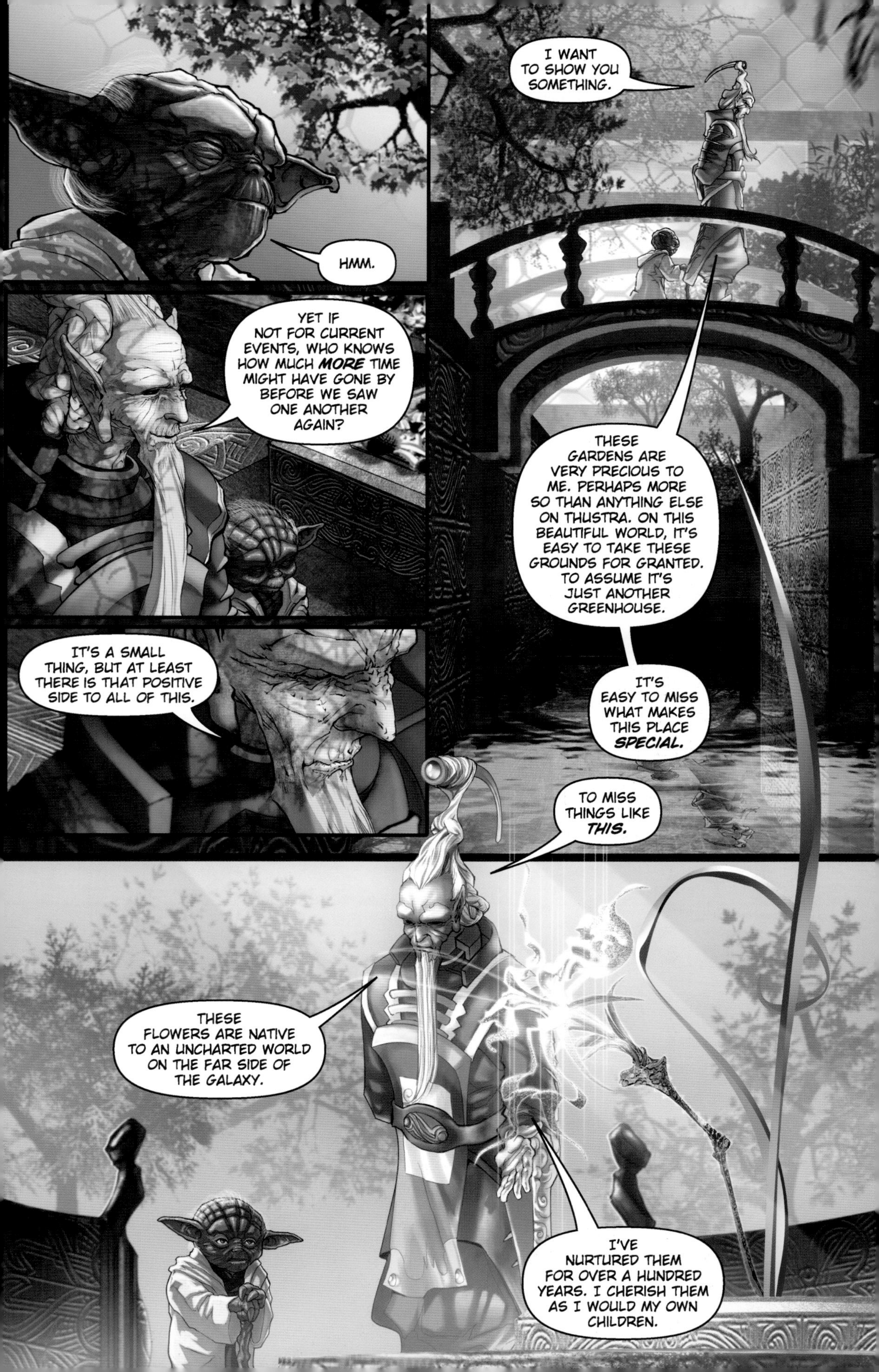
HMM.
I WANT TO SHOW YOU SOMETHING.
YET IF NOT FOR CURRENT EVENTS, WHO KNOWS HOW MUCH MORE TIME MIGHT HAVE GONE BY BEFORE WE SAW ONE ANOTHER AGAIN?
IT'S A SMALL THING, BUT AT LEAST THERE IS THAT POSITIVE SIDE TO ALL OF THIS.
THESE GARDENS ARE VERY PRECIOUS TO ME. PERHAPS MORE SO THAN ANYTHING ELSE ON THUSTRA. ON THIS BEAUTIFUL WORLD, IT'S EASY TO TAKE THESE GROUNDS FOR GRANTED. TO ASSUME IT'S JUST ANOTHER GREENHOUSE.
IT'S EASY TO MISS WHAT MAKES THIS PLACE SPECIAL.
TO MISS THINGS LIKE THIS.
THESE FLOWERS ARE NATIVE TO AN UNCHARTED WORLD ON THE FAR SIDE OF THE GALAXY.
I'VE NURTURED THEM FOR OVER A HUNDRED YEARS. I CHERISH THEM AS I WOULD MY OWN CHILDREN.

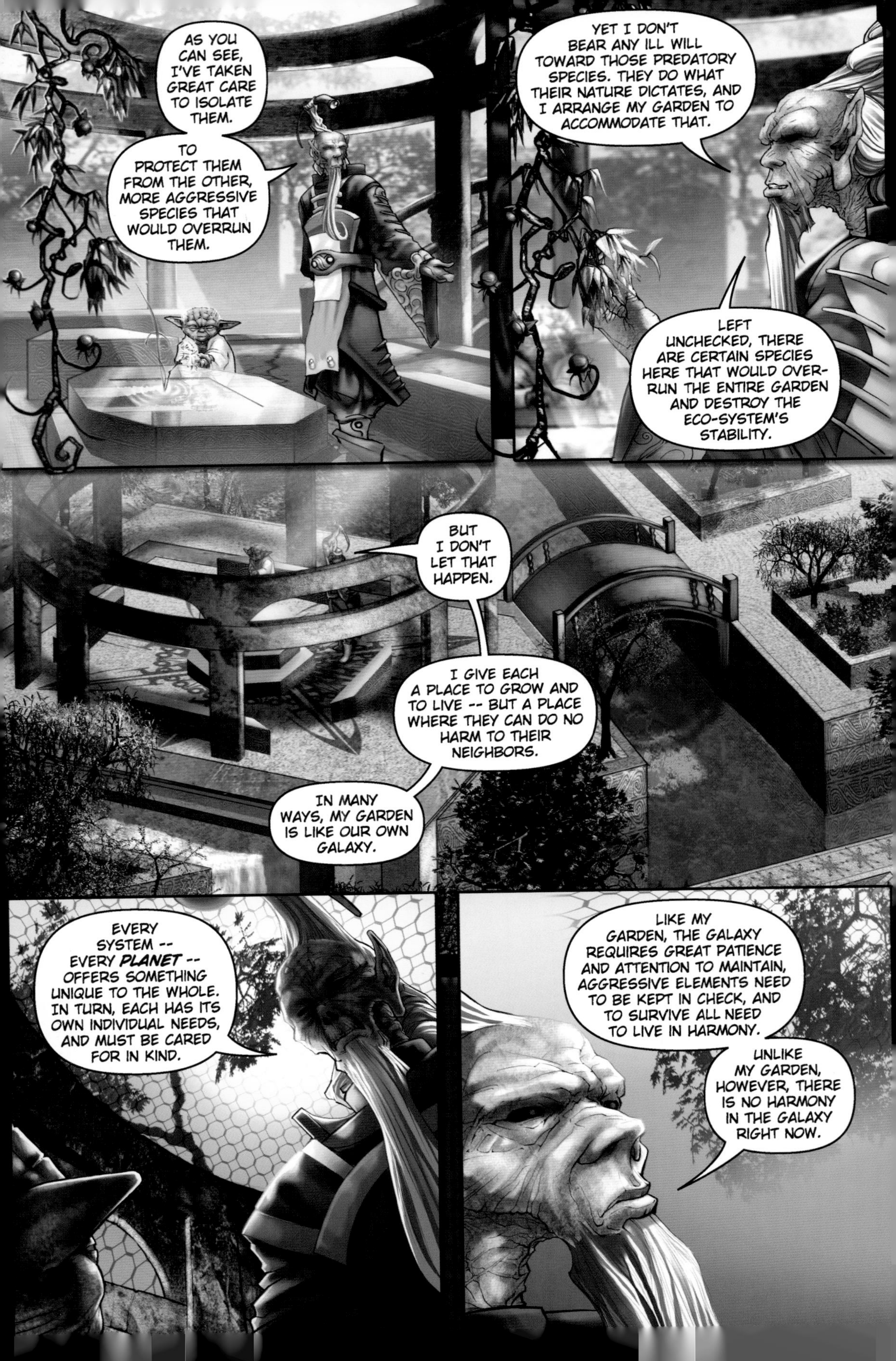
AS YOU CAN SEE, I'VE TAKEN GREAT CARE TO ISOLATE THEM.
TO PROTECT THEM FROM THE OTHER, MORE AGGRESSIVE SPECIES THAT WOULD OVERRUN THEM.
YET I DON'T BEAR ANY ILL WILL TOWARD THOSE PREDATORY SPECIES. THEY DO WHAT THEIR NATURE DICTATES, AND I ARRANGE MY GARDEN TO ACCOMMODATE THAT.
LEFT UNCHECKED, THERE ARE CERTAIN SPECIES HERE THAT WOULD OVER-RUN THE ENTIRE GARDEN AND DESTROY THE ECO-SYSTEM'S STABILITY.
BUT I DON'T LET THAT HAPPEN.
I GIVE EACH A PLACE TO GROW AND TO LIVE -- BUT A PLACE WHERE THEY CAN DO NO HARM TO THEIR NEIGHBORS.
IN MANY WAYS, MY GARDEN IS LIKE OUR OWN GALAXY.
EVERY SYSTEM -- EVERY ***PLANET*** -- OFFERS SOMETHING UNIQUE TO THE WHOLE. IN TURN, EACH HAS ITS OWN INDIVIDUAL NEEDS, AND MUST BE CARED FOR IN KIND.
LIKE MY GARDEN, THE GALAXY REQUIRES GREAT PATIENCE AND ATTENTION TO MAINTAIN, AGGRESSIVE ELEMENTS NEED TO BE KEPT IN CHECK, AND TO SURVIVE ALL NEED TO LIVE IN HARMONY.
UNLIKE MY GARDEN, HOWEVER, THERE IS NO HARMONY IN THE GALAXY RIGHT NOW.

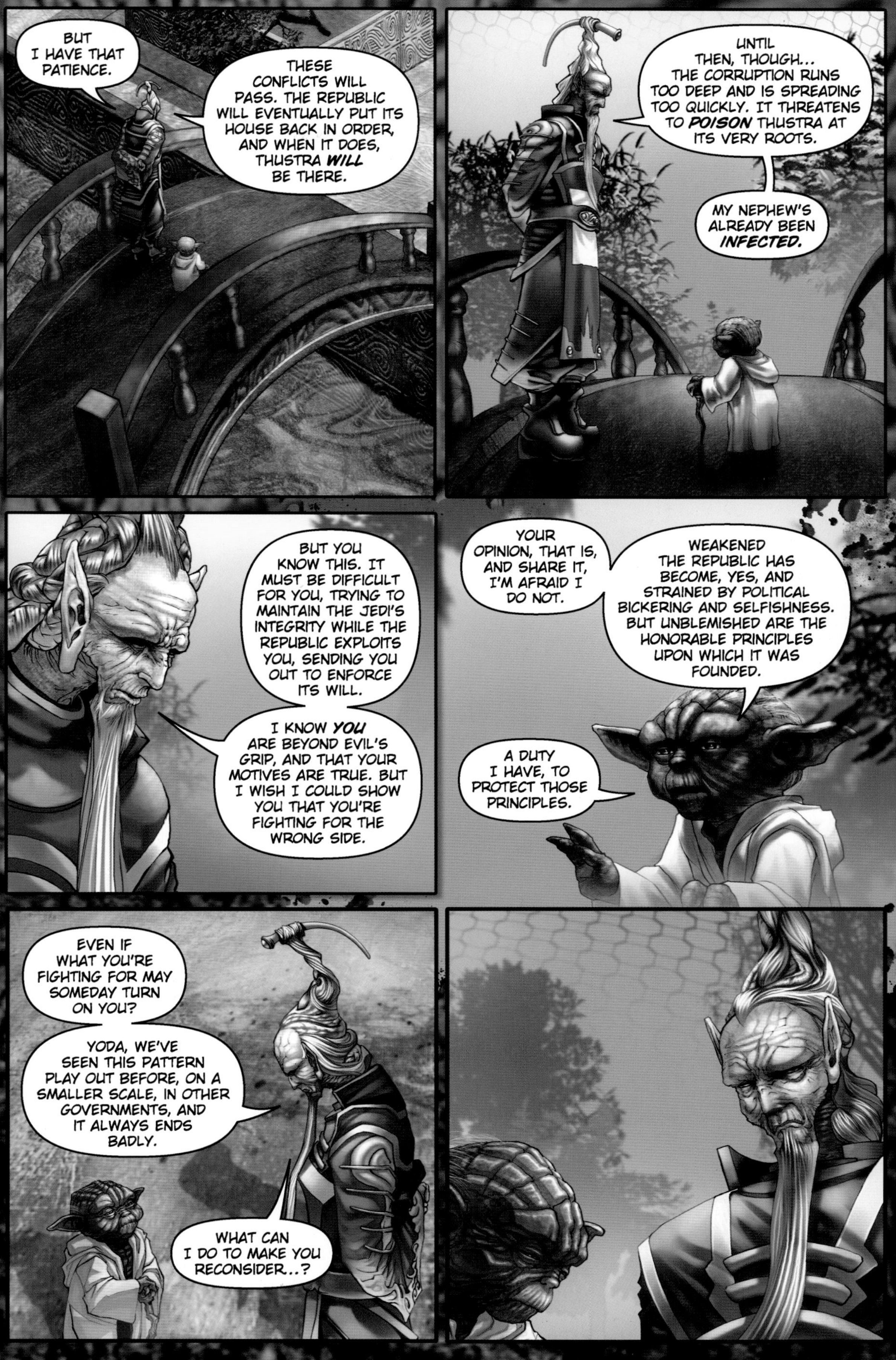
BUT I HAVE THAT PATIENCE.
THESE CONFLICTS WILL PASS. THE REPUBLIC WILL EVENTUALLY PUT ITS HOUSE BACK IN ORDER, AND WHEN IT DOES, THUSTRA ***WILL*** BE THERE.
UNTIL THEN, THOUGH... THE CORRUPTION RUNS TOO DEEP AND IS SPREADING TOO QUICKLY. IT THREATENS TO ***POISON*** THUSTRA AT ITS VERY ROOTS.
MY NEPHEW'S ALREADY BEEN ***INFECTED.***
BUT YOU KNOW THIS. IT MUST BE DIFFICULT FOR YOU, TRYING TO MAINTAIN THE JEDI'S INTEGRITY WHILE THE REPUBLIC EXPLOITS YOU, SENDING YOU OUT TO ENFORCE ITS WILL.
I KNOW ***YOU*** ARE BEYOND EVIL'S GRIP, AND THAT YOUR MOTIVES ARE TRUE. BUT I WISH I COULD SHOW YOU THAT YOU'RE FIGHTING FOR THE WRONG SIDE.
YOUR OPINION, THAT IS, AND SHARE IT, I'M AFRAID I DO NOT.
WEAKENED THE REPUBLIC HAS BECOME, YES, AND STRAINED BY POLITICAL BICKERING AND SELFISHNESS. BUT UNBLEMISHED ARE THE HONORABLE PRINCIPLES UPON WHICH IT WAS FOUNDED.
A DUTY I HAVE, TO PROTECT THOSE PRINCIPLES.
EVEN IF WHAT YOU'RE FIGHTING FOR MAY SOMEDAY TURN ON YOU?
YODA, WE'VE SEEN THIS PATTERN PLAY OUT BEFORE, ON A SMALLER SCALE, IN OTHER GOVERNMENTS, AND IT ALWAYS ENDS BADLY.
WHAT CAN I DO TO MAKE YOU RECONSIDER..?

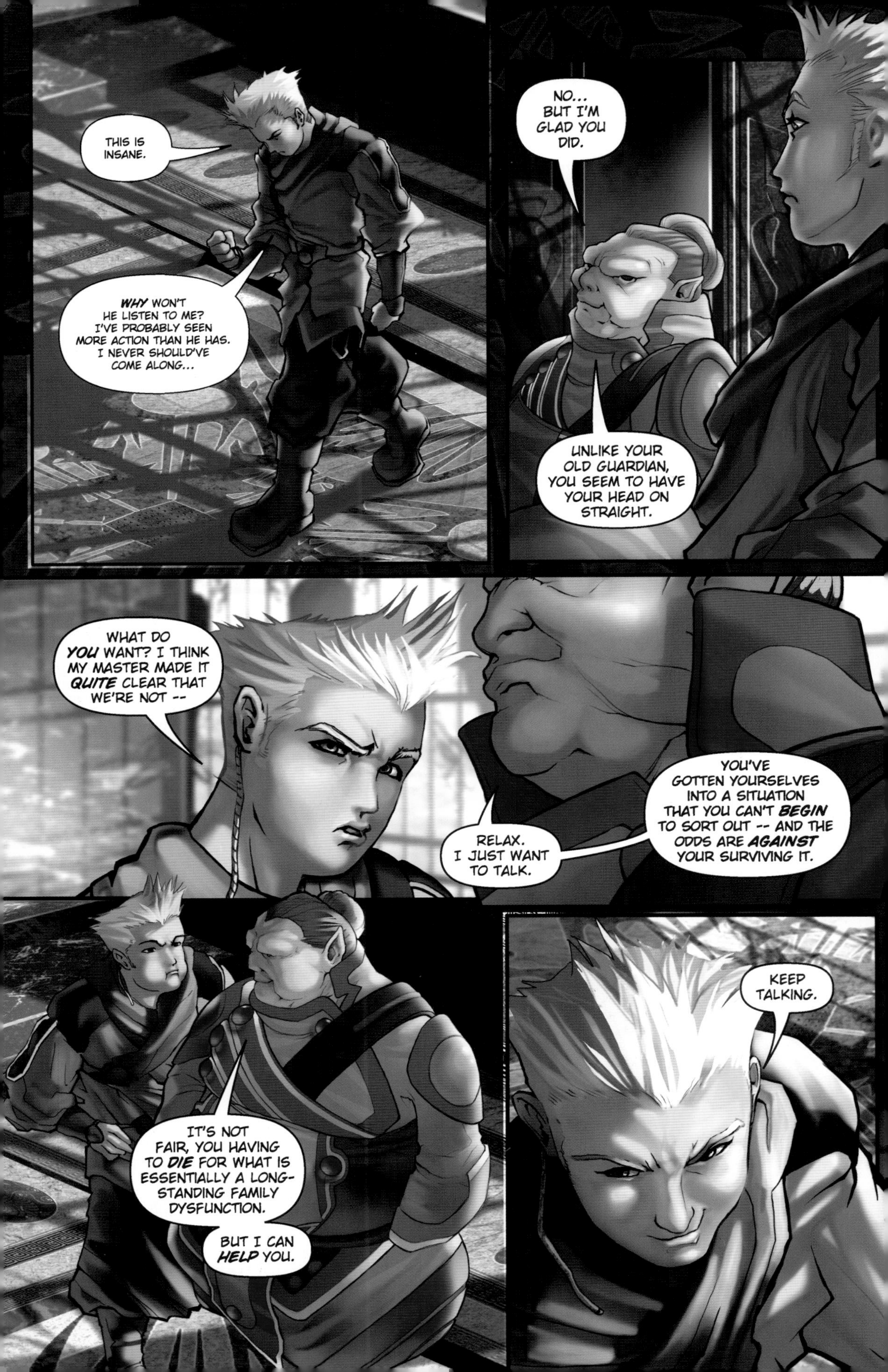
THIS IS INSANE.
*WHY* WON'T HE LISTEN TO ME? I'VE PROBABLY SEEN MORE ACTION THAN HE HAS. I NEVER SHOULD'VE COME ALONG...
NO... BUT I'M GLAD YOU DID.
UNLIKE YOUR OLD GUARDIAN, YOU SEEM TO HAVE YOUR HEAD ON STRAIGHT.
WHAT DO *YOU* WANT? I THINK MY MASTER MADE IT *QUITE* CLEAR THAT WE'RE NOT --
RELAX. I JUST WANT TO TALK.
YOU'VE GOTTEN YOURSELVES INTO A SITUATION THAT YOU CAN'T *BEGIN* TO SORT OUT -- AND THE ODDS ARE *AGAINST* YOUR SURVIVING IT.
IT'S NOT FAIR, YOU HAVING TO *DIE* FOR WHAT IS ESSENTIALLY A LONG-STANDING FAMILY DYSFUNCTION.
BUT I CAN *HELP* YOU.
KEEP TALKING.

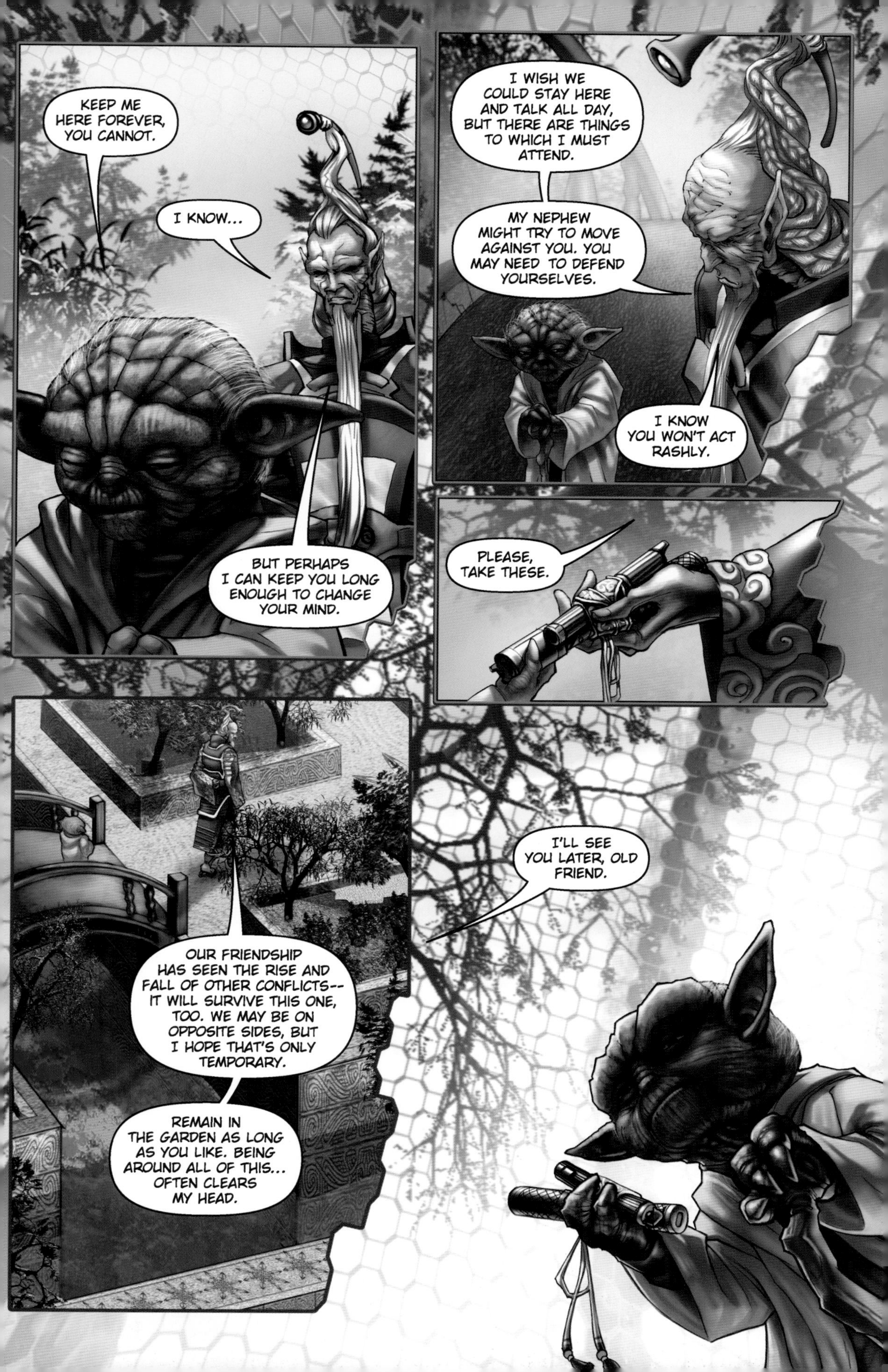
KEEP ME HERE FOREVER, YOU CANNOT.
I KNOW...
BUT PERHAPS I CAN KEEP YOU LONG ENOUGH TO CHANGE YOUR MIND.
I WISH WE COULD STAY HERE AND TALK ALL DAY, BUT THERE ARE THINGS TO WHICH I MUST ATTEND.
MY NEPHEW MIGHT TRY TO MOVE AGAINST YOU. YOU MAY NEED TO DEFEND YOURSELVES.
I KNOW YOU WON'T ACT RASHLY.
PLEASE, TAKE THESE.
OUR FRIENDSHIP HAS SEEN THE RISE AND FALL OF OTHER CONFLICTS-- IT WILL SURVIVE THIS ONE, TOO. WE MAY BE ON OPPOSITE SIDES, BUT I HOPE THAT'S ONLY TEMPORARY.
REMAIN IN THE GARDEN AS LONG AS YOU LIKE. BEING AROUND ALL OF THIS... OFTEN CLEARS MY HEAD.
I'LL SEE YOU LATER, OLD FRIEND.

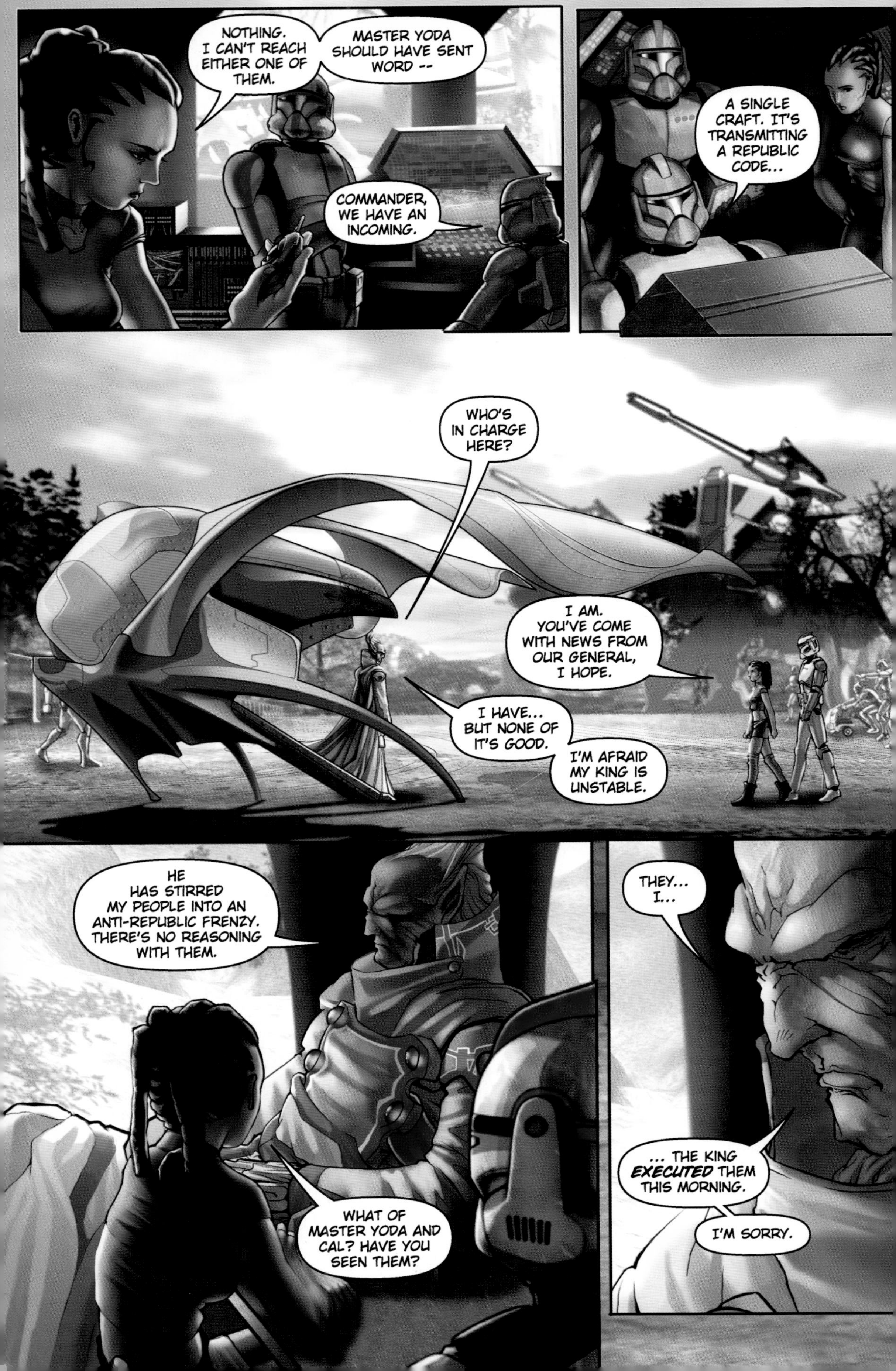
NOTHING. I CAN'T REACH EITHER ONE OF THEM.
MASTER YODA SHOULD HAVE SENT WORD --
COMMANDER, WE HAVE AN INCOMING.
A SINGLE CRAFT. IT'S TRANSMITTING A REPUBLIC CODE...
WHO'S IN CHARGE HERE?
I AM. YOU'VE COME WITH NEWS FROM OUR GENERAL, I HOPE.
I HAVE... BUT NONE OF IT'S GOOD.
I'M AFRAID MY KING IS UNSTABLE.
HE HAS STIRRED MY PEOPLE INTO AN ANTI-REPUBLIC FRENZY. THERE'S NO REASONING WITH THEM.
WHAT OF MASTER YODA AND CAL? HAVE YOU SEEN THEM?
THEY... I...
... THE KING EXECUTED THEM THIS MORNING.
I'M SORRY.

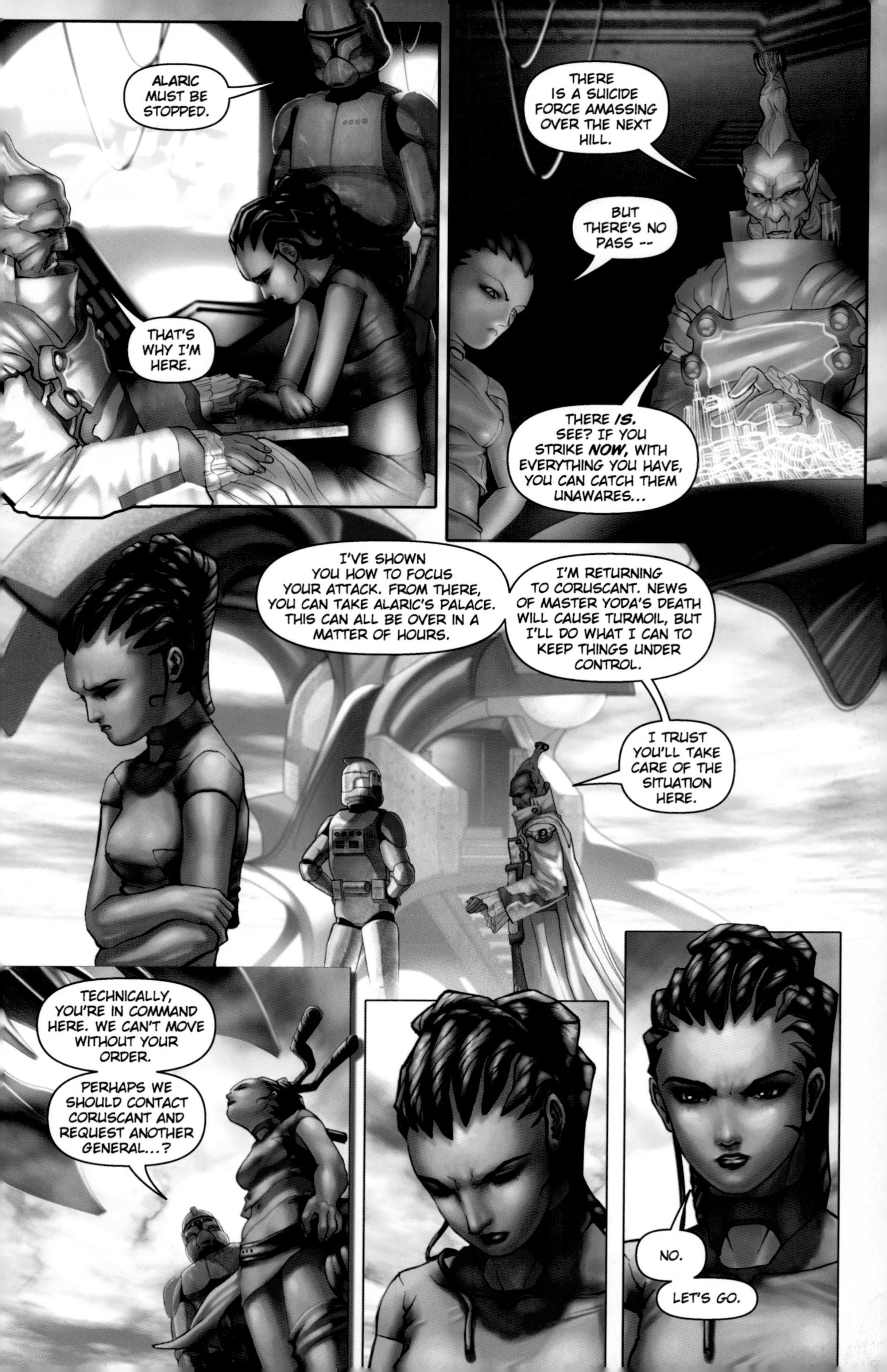
ALARIC MUST BE STOPPED.
THAT'S WHY I'M HERE.
THERE IS A SUICIDE FORCE AMASSING OVER THE NEXT HILL.
BUT THERE'S NO PASS --
THERE *IS.* SEE? IF YOU STRIKE *NOW,* WITH EVERYTHING YOU HAVE, YOU CAN CATCH THEM UNAWARES...
I'VE SHOWN YOU HOW TO FOCUS YOUR ATTACK. FROM THERE, YOU CAN TAKE ALARIC'S PALACE. THIS CAN ALL BE OVER IN A MATTER OF HOURS.
I'M RETURNING TO CORUSCANT. NEWS OF MASTER YODA'S DEATH WILL CAUSE TURMOIL, BUT I'LL DO WHAT I CAN TO KEEP THINGS UNDER CONTROL.
I TRUST YOU'LL TAKE CARE OF THE SITUATION HERE.
TECHNICALLY, YOU'RE IN COMMAND HERE. WE CAN'T MOVE WITHOUT YOUR ORDER.
PERHAPS WE SHOULD CONTACT CORUSCANT AND REQUEST ANOTHER GENERAL...?
NO.
LET'S GO.

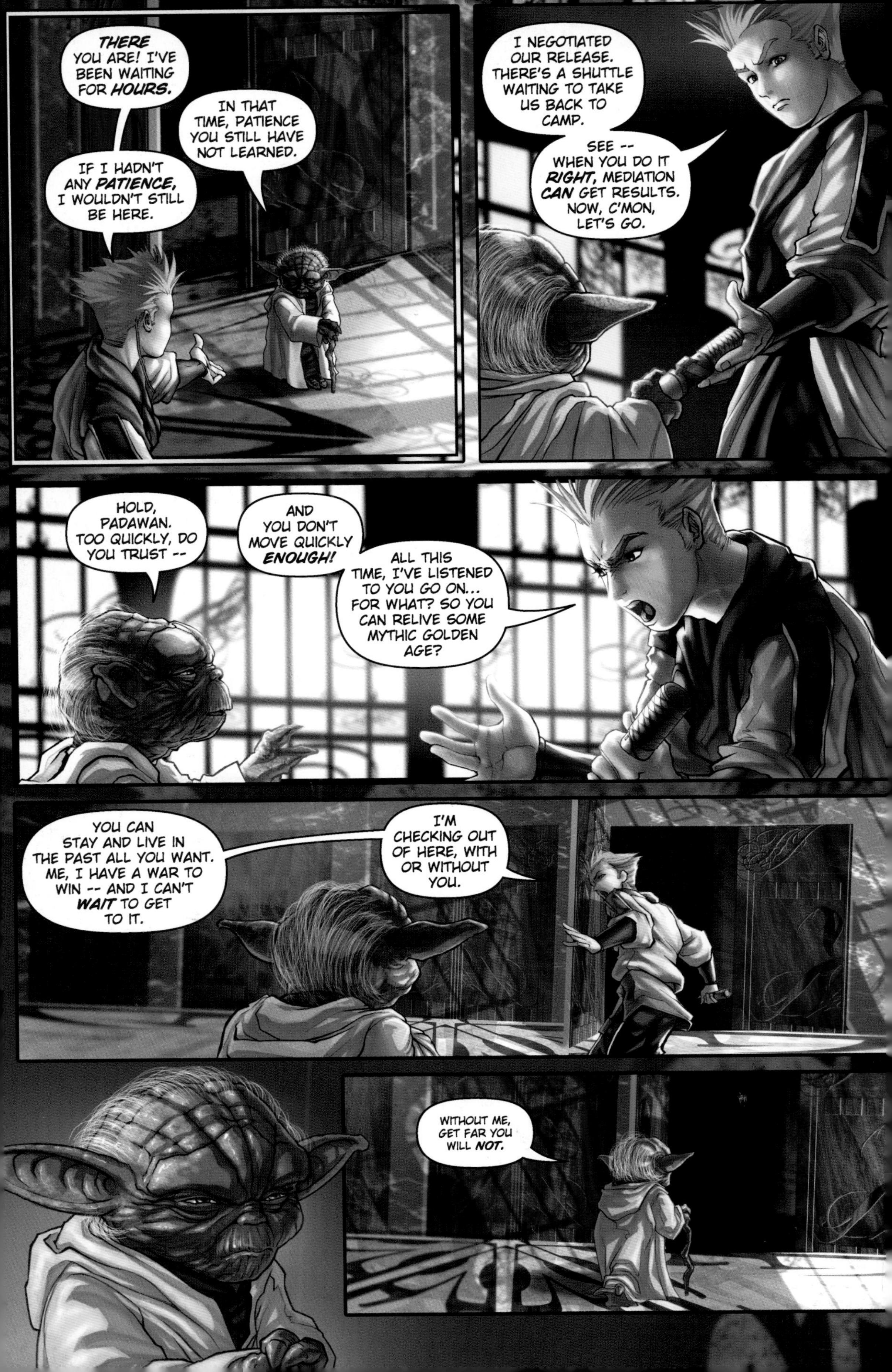
THERE YOU ARE! I'VE BEEN WAITING FOR HOURS.
IN THAT TIME, PATIENCE YOU STILL HAVE NOT LEARNED.
IF I HADN'T ANY PATIENCE, I WOULDN'T STILL BE HERE.
I NEGOTIATED OUR RELEASE. THERE'S A SHUTTLE WAITING TO TAKE US BACK TO CAMP.
SEE -- WHEN YOU DO IT RIGHT, MEDIATION CAN GET RESULTS. NOW, C'MON, LET'S GO.
HOLD, PADAWAN. TOO QUICKLY, DO YOU TRUST --
AND YOU DON'T MOVE QUICKLY ENOUGH!
ALL THIS TIME, I'VE LISTENED TO YOU GO ON... FOR WHAT? SO YOU CAN RELIVE SOME MYTHIC GOLDEN AGE?
YOU CAN STAY AND LIVE IN THE PAST ALL YOU WANT. ME, I HAVE A WAR TO WIN -- AND I CAN'T WAIT TO GET TO IT.
I'M CHECKING OUT OF HERE, WITH OR WITHOUT YOU.
WITHOUT ME, GET FAR YOU WILL NOT.

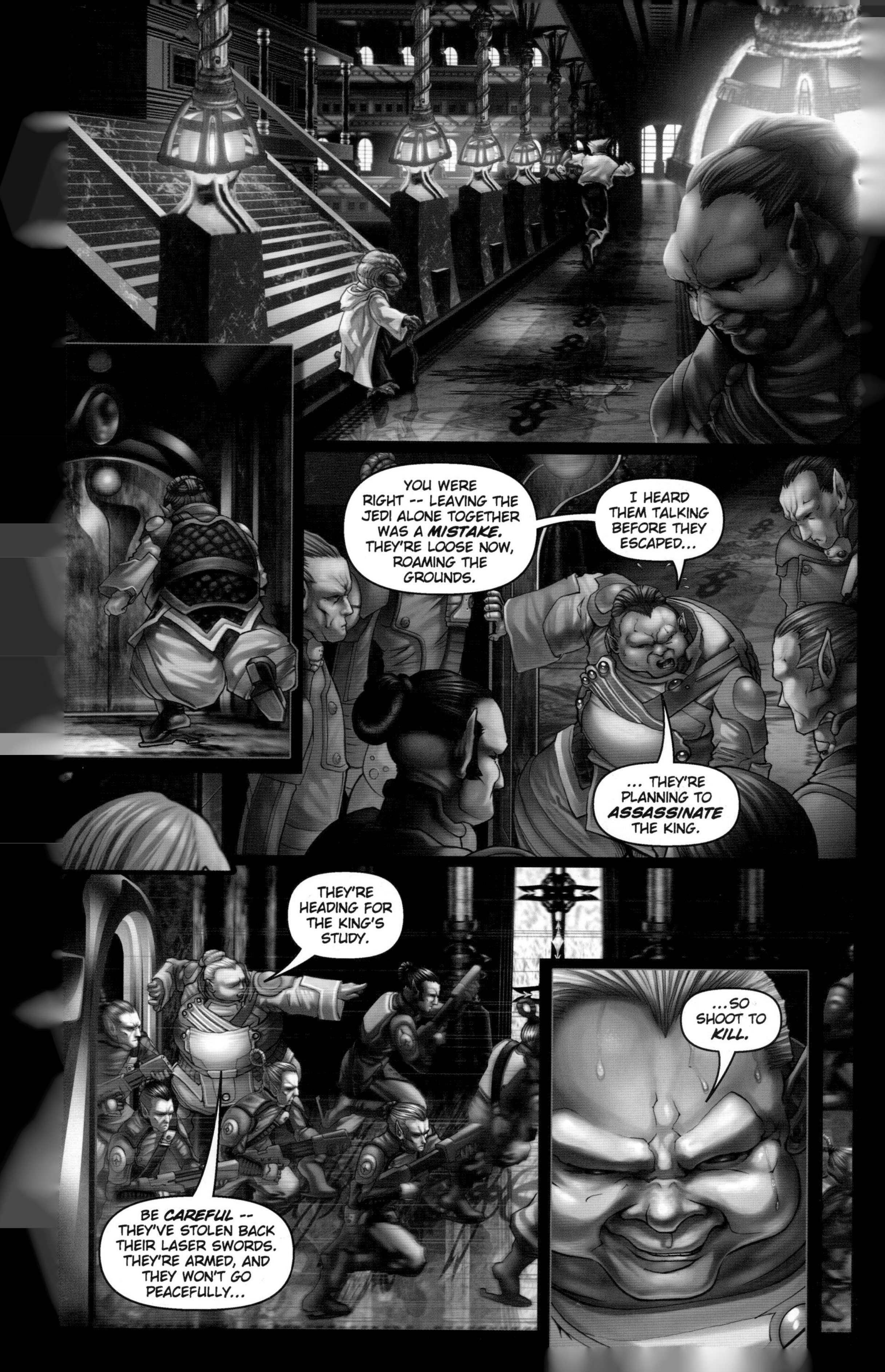

YOU WERE RIGHT -- LEAVING THE JEDI ALONE TOGETHER WAS A ***MISTAKE.*** THEY'RE LOOSE NOW, ROAMING THE GROUNDS.
I HEARD THEM TALKING BEFORE THEY ESCAPED...
... THEY'RE PLANNING TO ***ASSASSINATE*** THE KING.
THEY'RE HEADING FOR THE KING'S STUDY.
BE ***CAREFUL*** -- THEY'VE STOLEN BACK THEIR LASER SWORDS. THEY'RE ARMED, AND THEY WON'T GO PEACEFULLY...
...SO SHOOT TO ***KILL.***

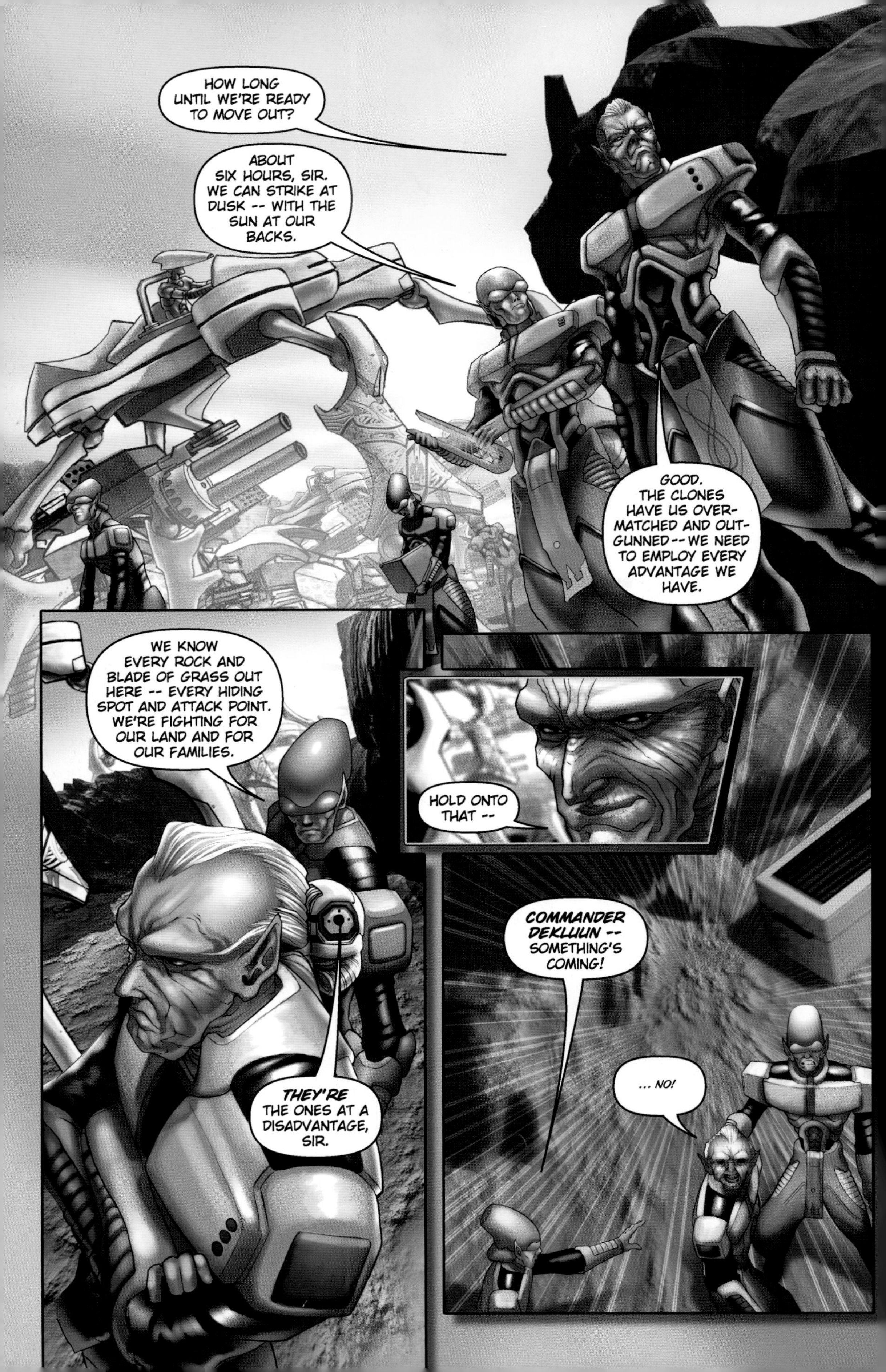
HOW LONG UNTIL WE'RE READY TO MOVE OUT?
ABOUT SIX HOURS, SIR. WE CAN STRIKE AT DUSK -- WITH THE SUN AT OUR BACKS.
GOOD. THE CLONES HAVE US OVER-MATCHED AND OUT-GUNNED -- WE NEED TO EMPLOY EVERY ADVANTAGE WE HAVE.
WE KNOW EVERY ROCK AND BLADE OF GRASS OUT HERE -- EVERY HIDING SPOT AND ATTACK POINT. WE'RE FIGHTING FOR OUR LAND AND FOR OUR FAMILIES.
THEY'RE THE ONES AT A DISADVANTAGE, SIR.
HOLD ONTO THAT --
COMMANDER DEKLUUN -- SOMETHING'S COMING!
... NO!

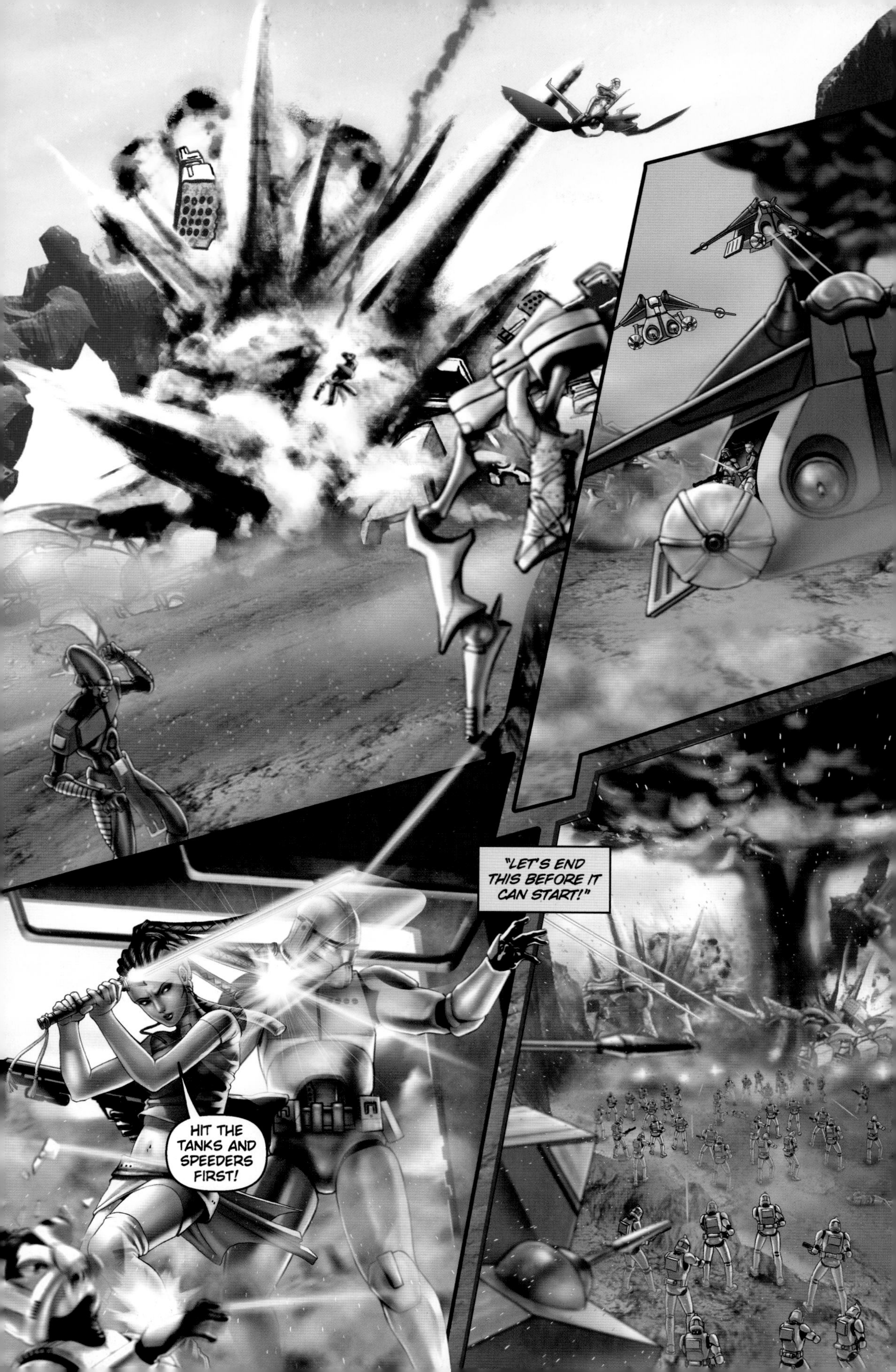
"LET'S END THIS BEFORE IT CAN START!"
HIT THE TANKS AND SPEEDERS FIRST!

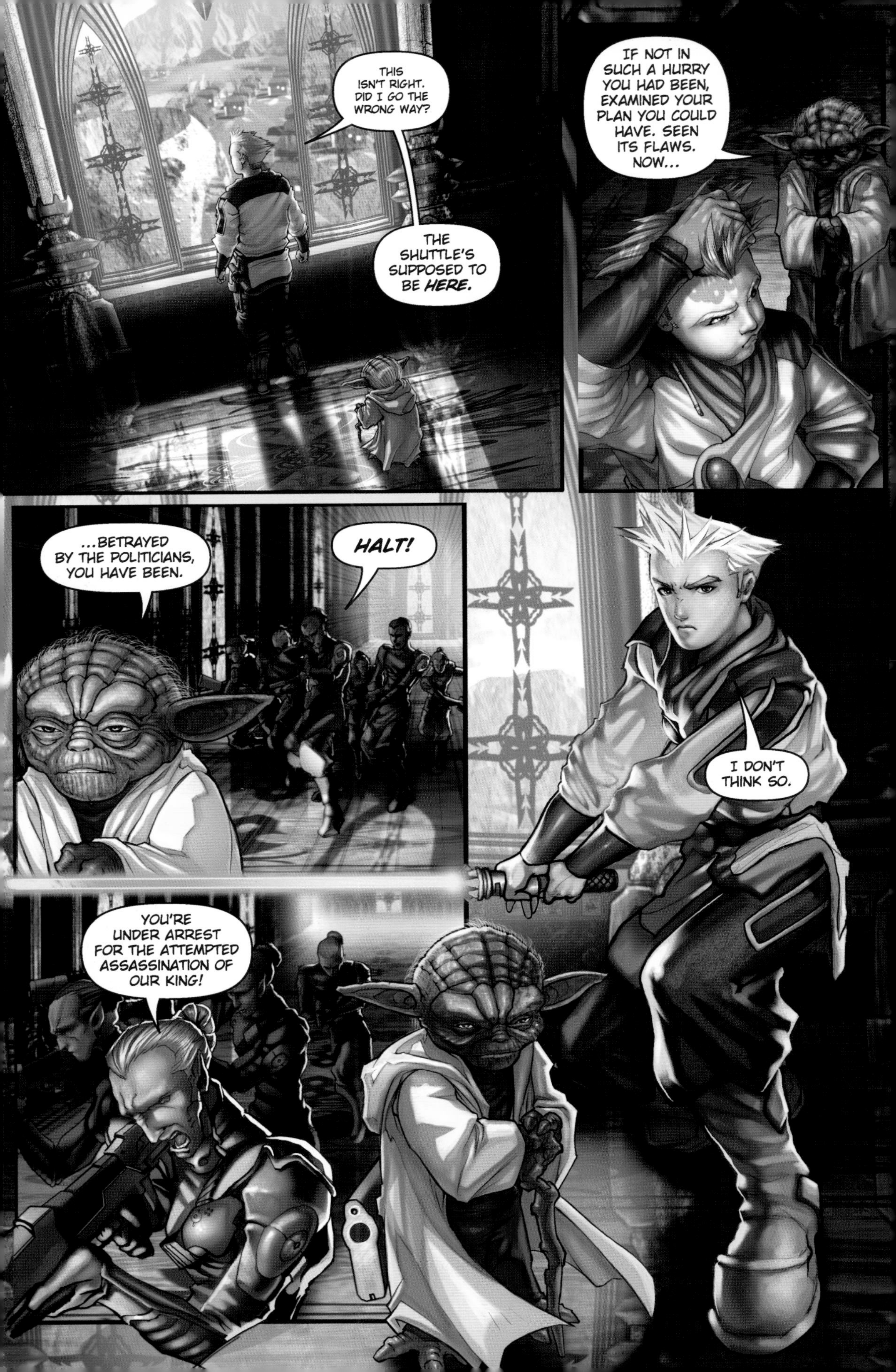
THIS ISN'T RIGHT. DID I GO THE WRONG WAY?
THE SHUTTLE'S SUPPOSED TO BE *HERE.*
IF NOT IN SUCH A HURRY YOU HAD BEEN, EXAMINED YOUR PLAN YOU COULD HAVE. SEEN ITS FLAWS. NOW...
...BETRAYED BY THE POLITICIANS, YOU HAVE BEEN.
*HALT!*
I DON'T THINK SO.
YOU'RE UNDER ARREST FOR THE ATTEMPTED ASSASSINATION OF OUR KING!

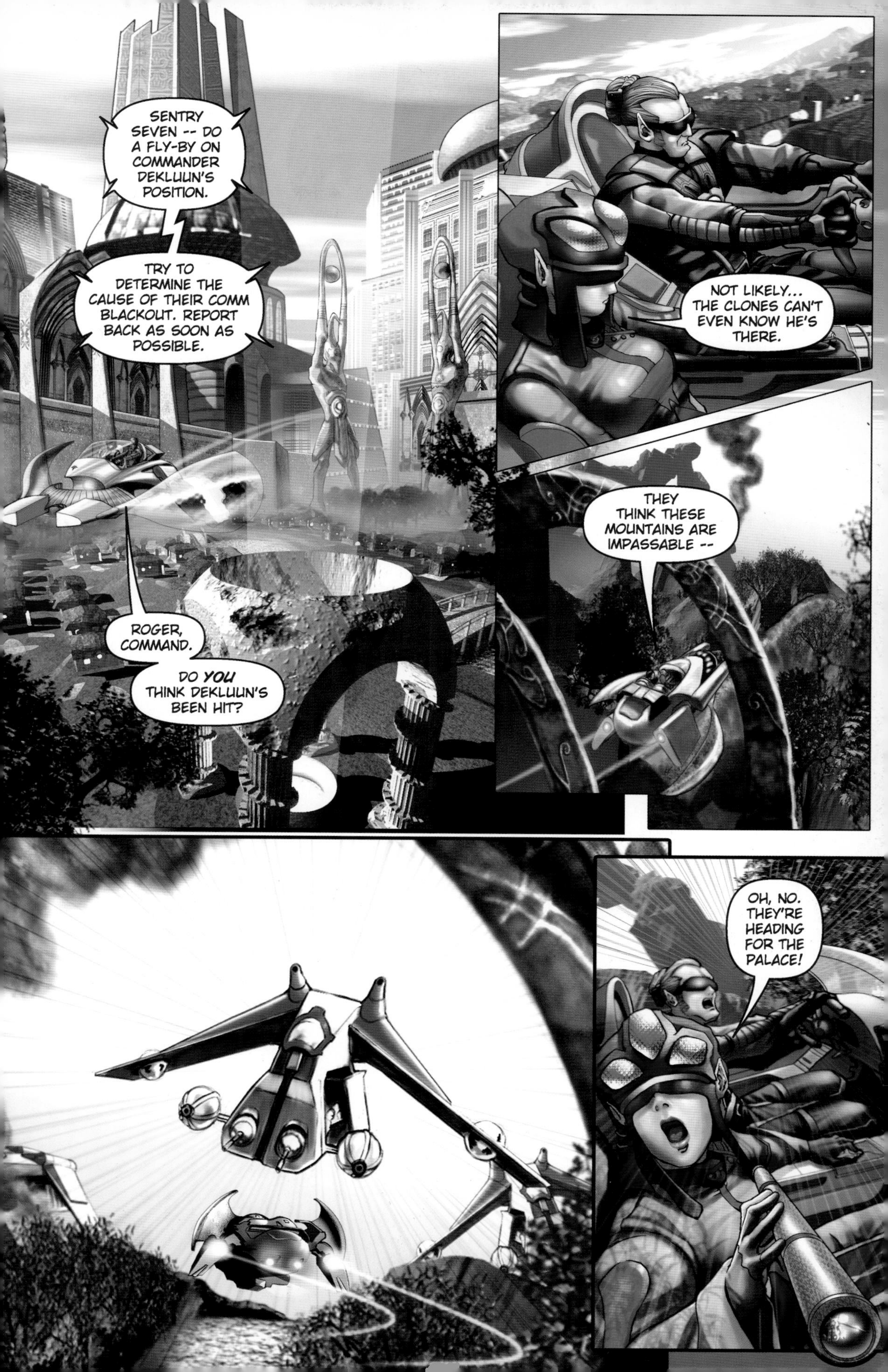
SENTRY SEVEN -- DO A FLY-BY ON COMMANDER DEKLUUN'S POSITION.
TRY TO DETERMINE THE CAUSE OF THEIR COMM BLACKOUT. REPORT BACK AS SOON AS POSSIBLE.
ROGER, COMMAND.
DO *YOU* THINK DEKLUUN'S BEEN HIT?
NOT LIKELY... THE CLONES CAN'T EVEN KNOW HE'S THERE.
THEY THINK THESE MOUNTAINS ARE IMPASSABLE --
OH, NO. THEY'RE HEADING FOR THE PALACE!

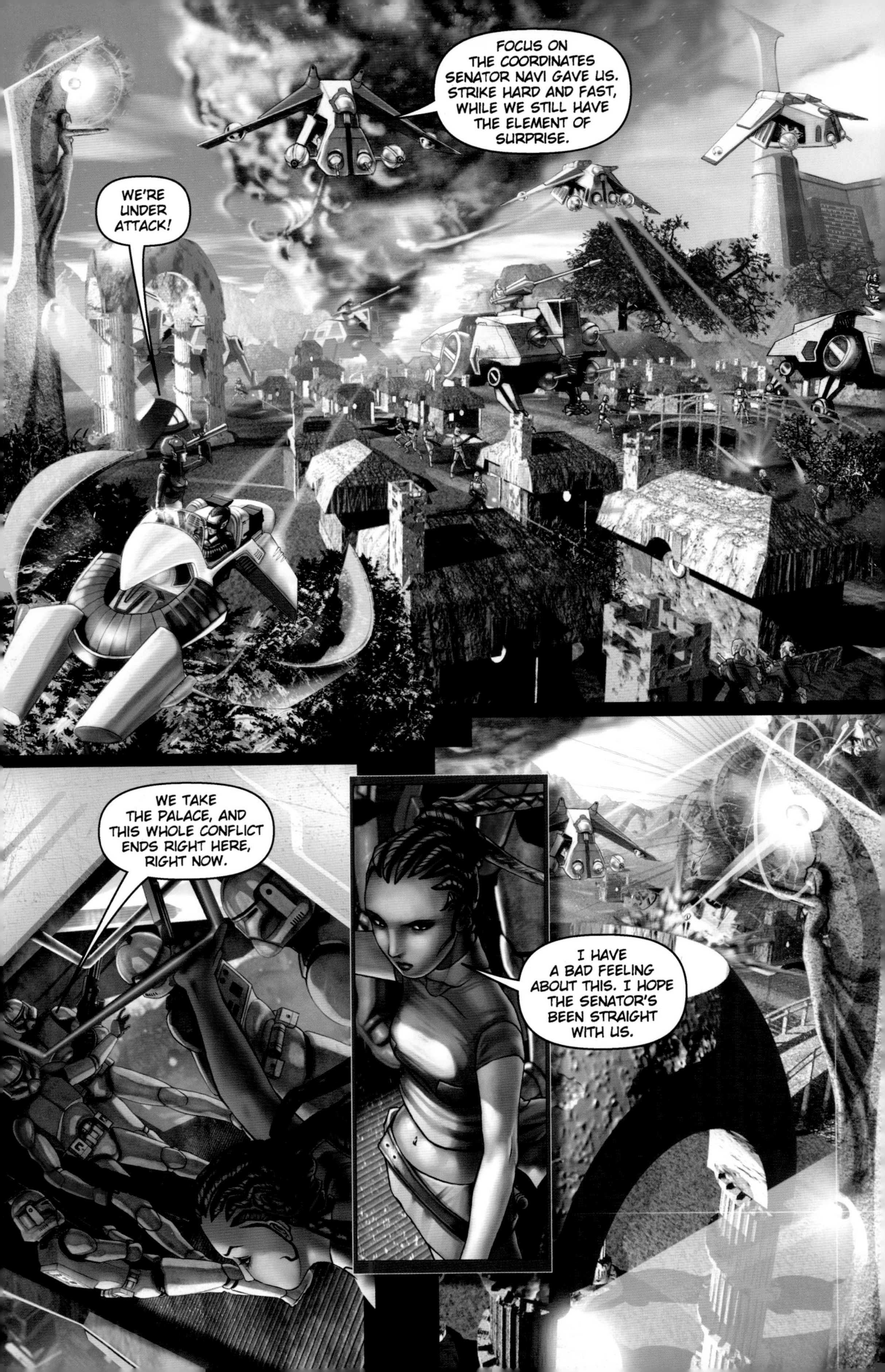
FOCUS ON THE COORDINATES SENATOR NAVI GAVE US. STRIKE HARD AND FAST, WHILE WE STILL HAVE THE ELEMENT OF SURPRISE.
WE'RE UNDER ATTACK!
WE TAKE THE PALACE, AND THIS WHOLE CONFLICT ENDS RIGHT HERE, RIGHT NOW.
I HAVE A BAD FEELING ABOUT THIS. I HOPE THE SENATOR'S BEEN STRAIGHT WITH US.

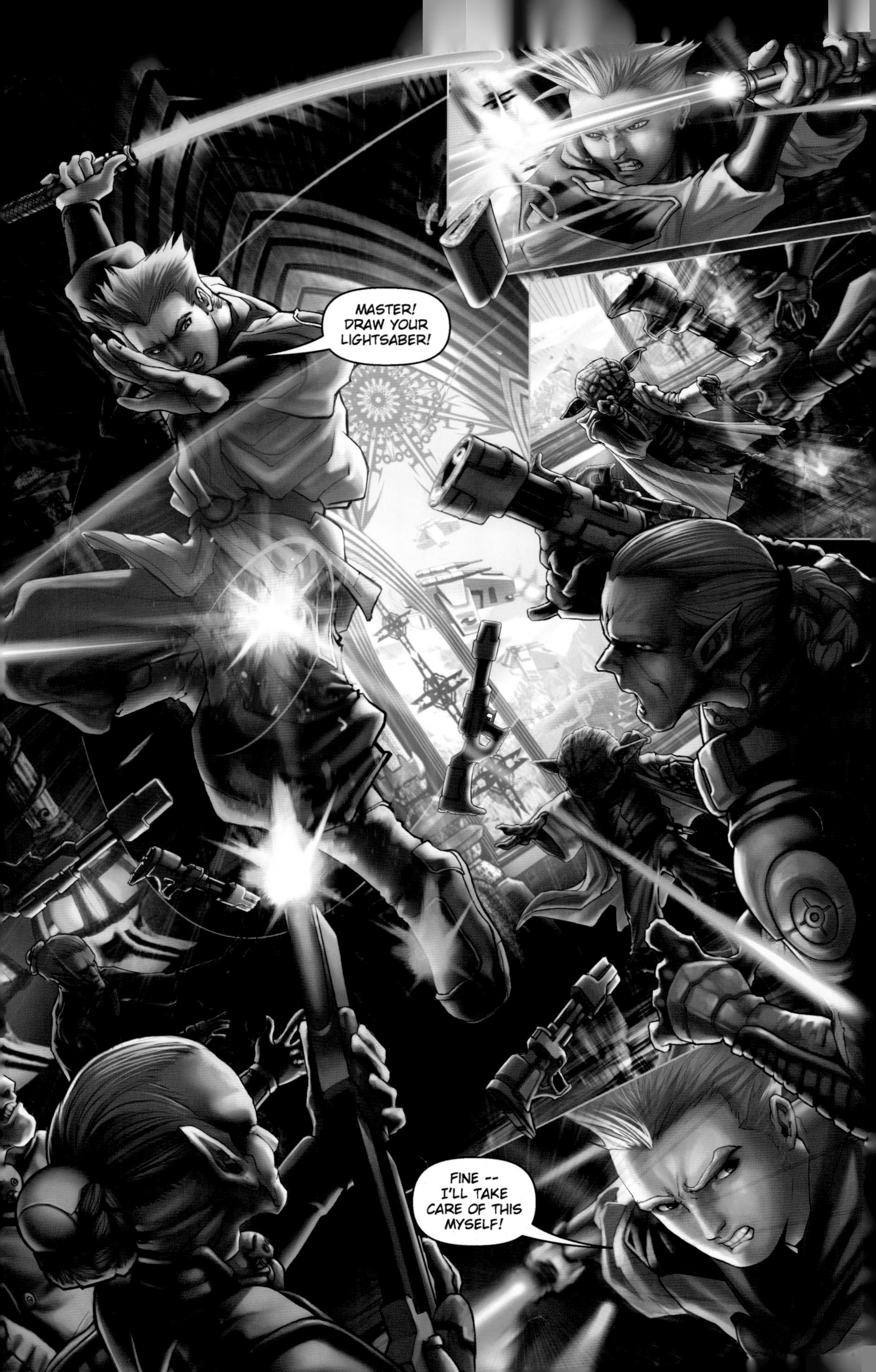
MASTER! DRAW YOUR LIGHTSABER!
FINE -- I'LL TAKE CARE OF THIS MYSELF!

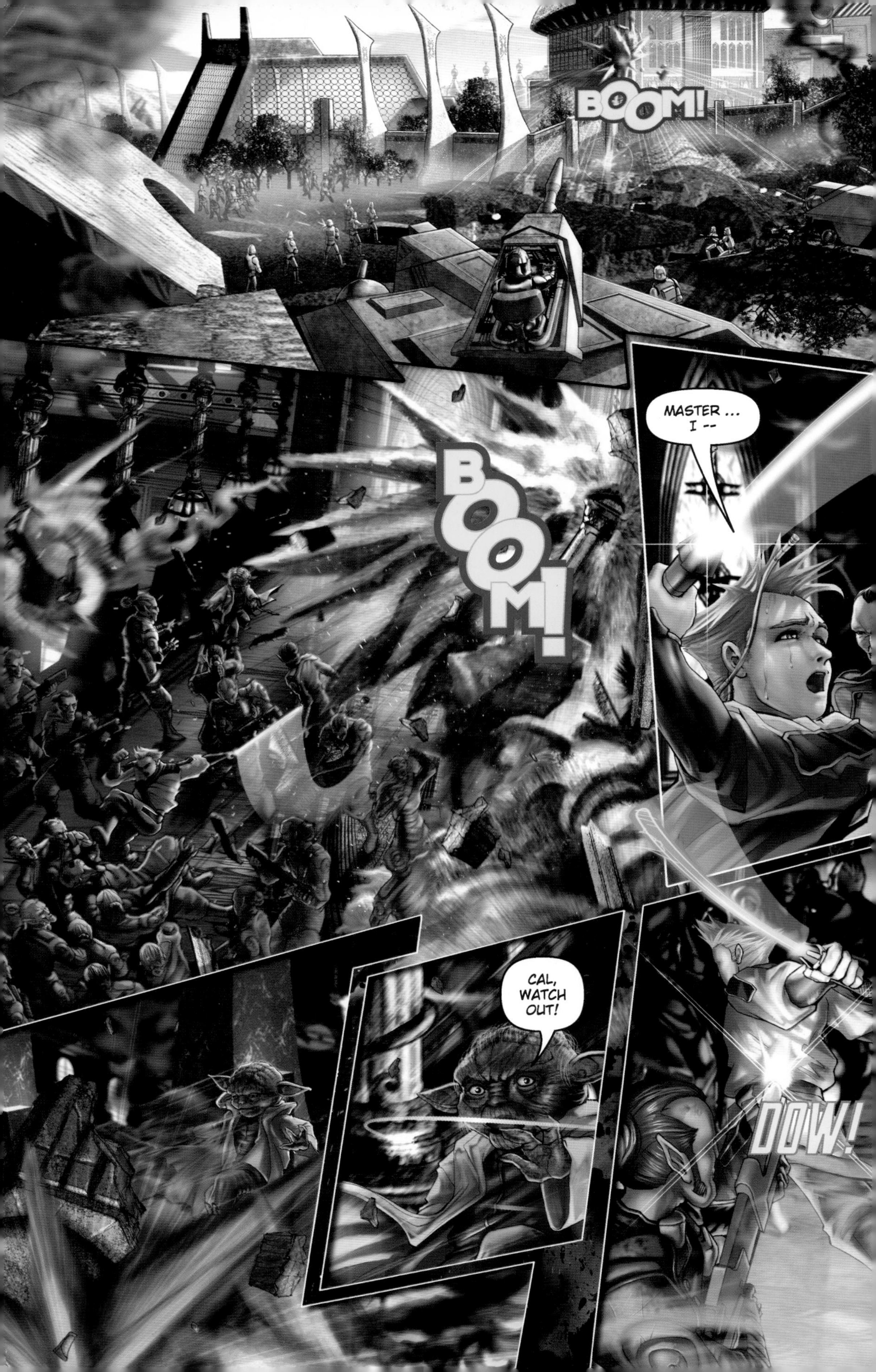
BOOM!
BOOM!
MASTER ... I --
CAL, WATCH OUT!
DOW!

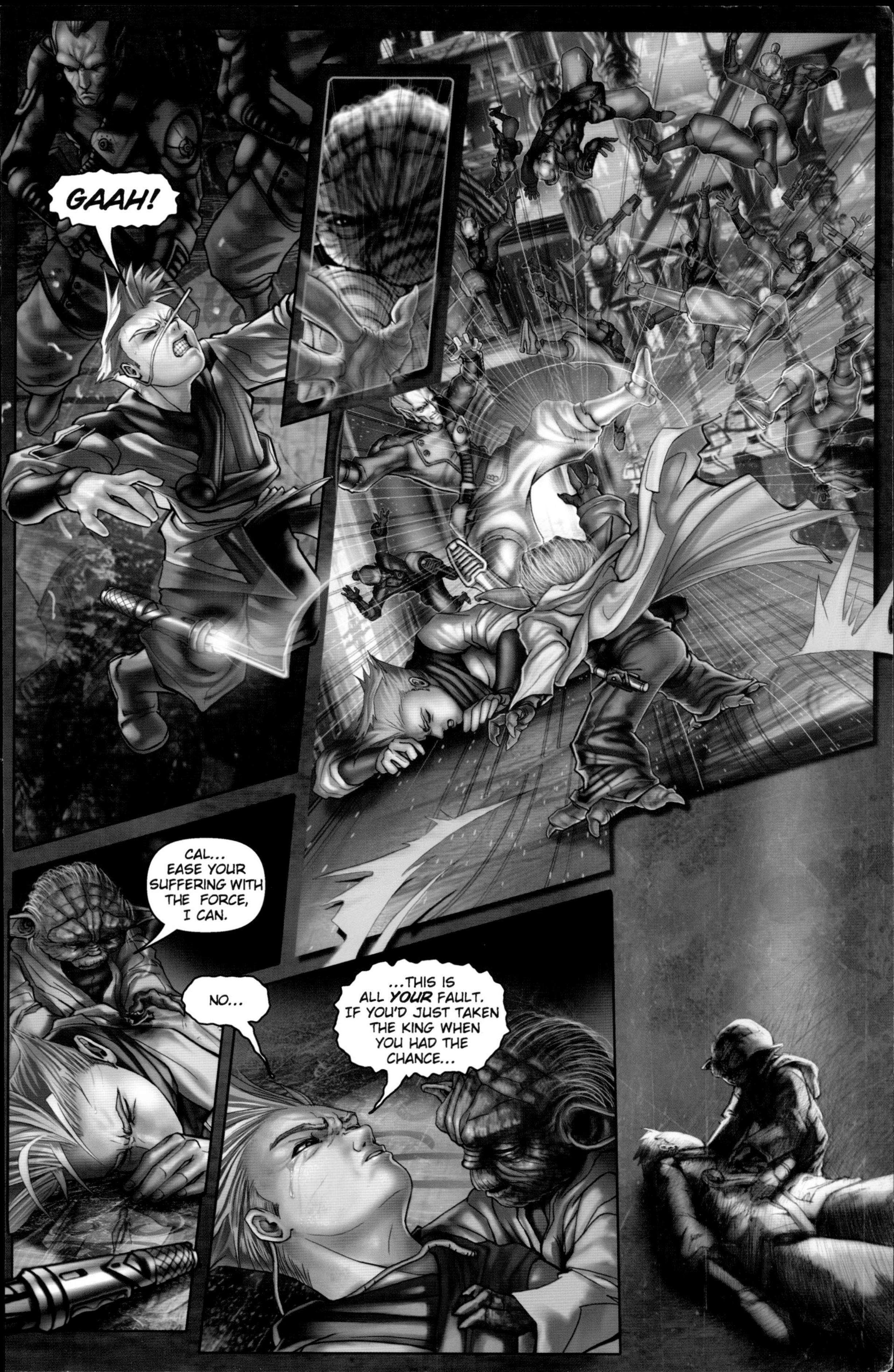
GAAH!
CAL... EASE YOUR SUFFERING WITH THE FORCE, I CAN.
NO...
...THIS IS ALL YOUR FAULT. IF YOU'D JUST TAKEN THE KING WHEN YOU HAD THE CHANCE...

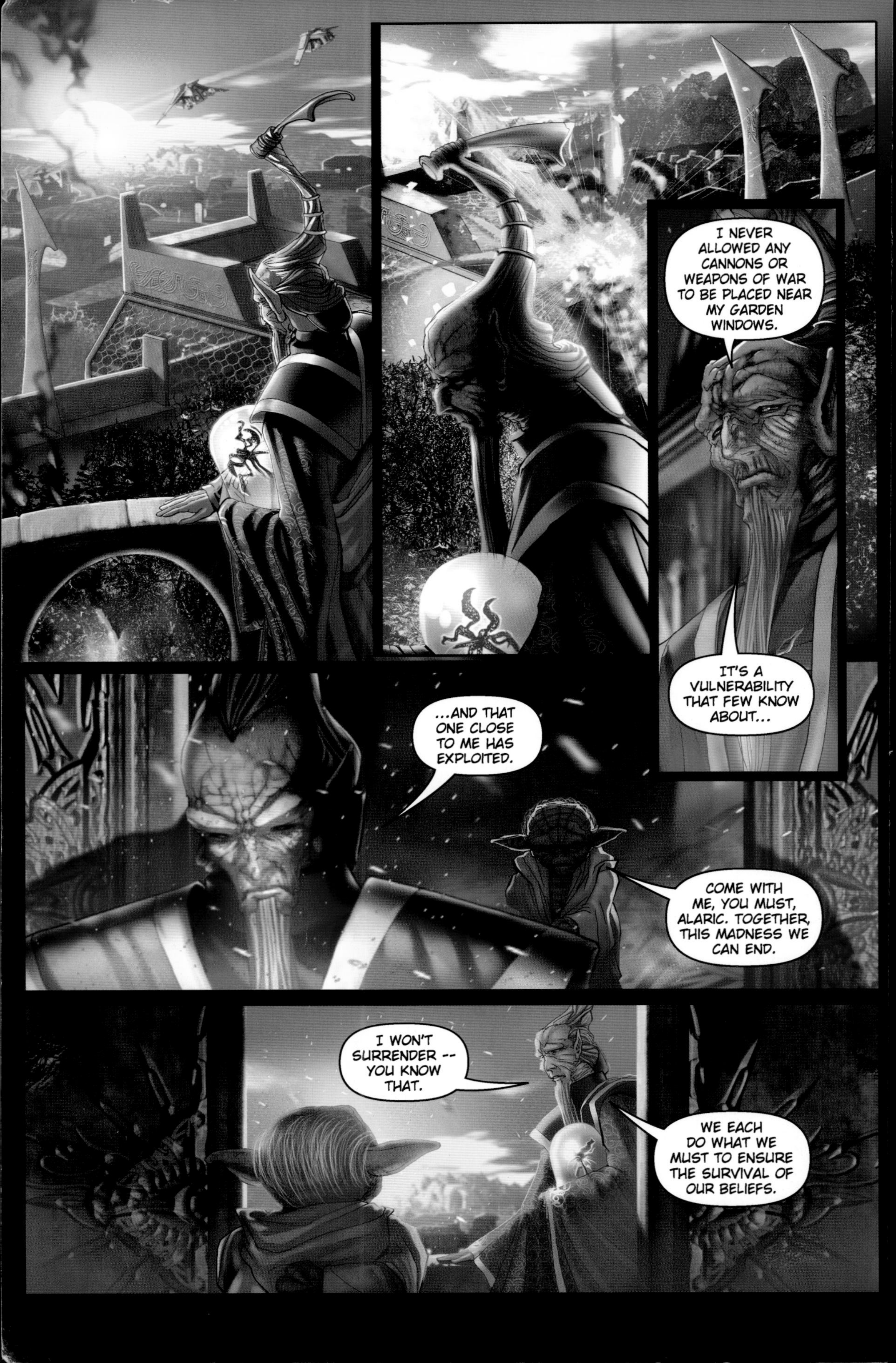
I NEVER ALLOWED ANY CANNONS OR WEAPONS OF WAR TO BE PLACED NEAR MY GARDEN WINDOWS.
IT'S A VULNERABILITY THAT FEW KNOW ABOUT...
...AND THAT ONE CLOSE TO ME HAS EXPLOITED.
COME WITH ME, YOU MUST, ALARIC. TOGETHER, THIS MADNESS WE CAN END.
I WON'T SURRENDER -- YOU KNOW THAT.
WE EACH DO WHAT WE MUST TO ENSURE THE SURVIVAL OF OUR BELIEFS.

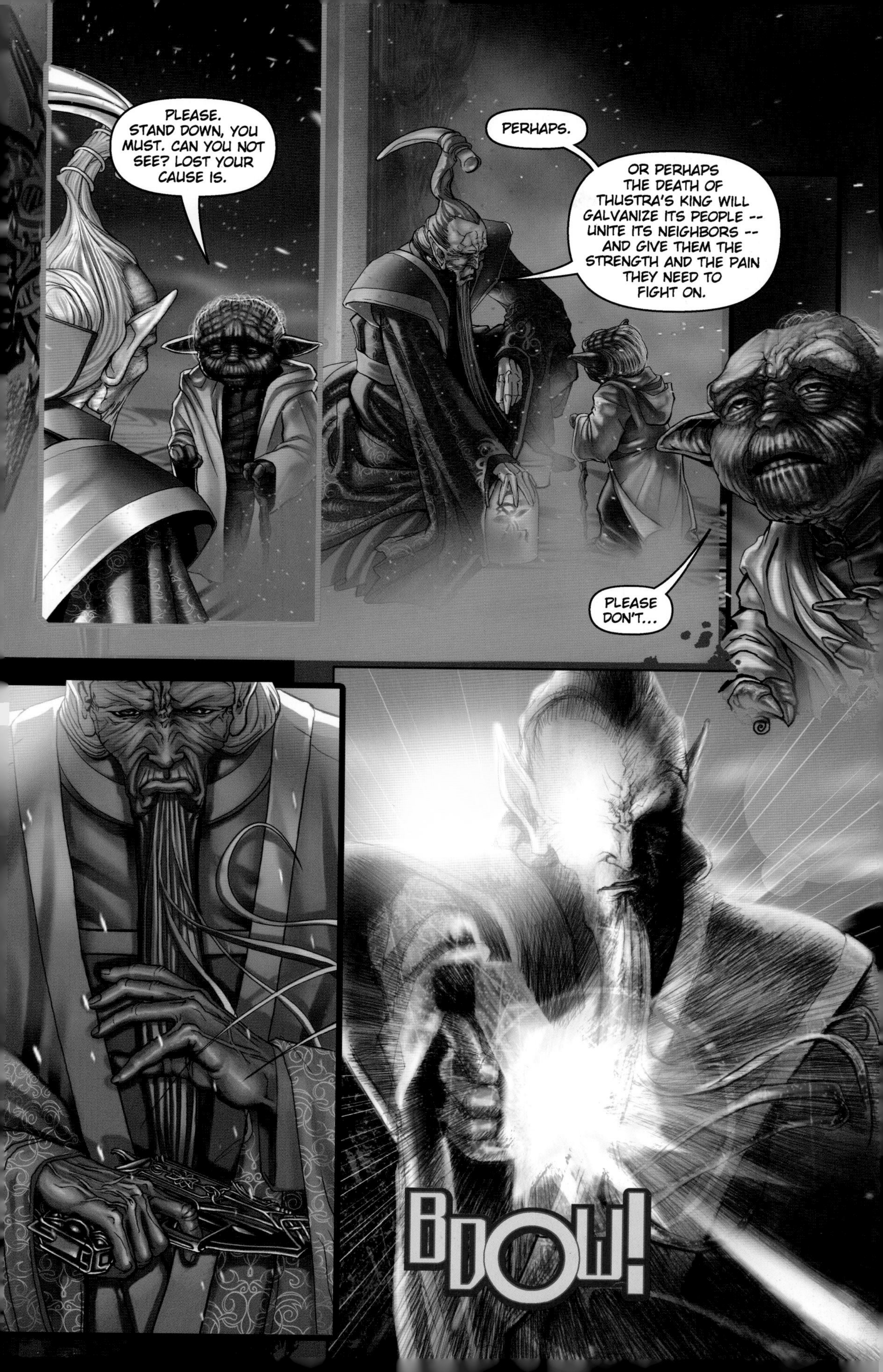
PLEASE. STAND DOWN, YOU MUST. CAN YOU NOT SEE? LOST YOUR CAUSE IS.
PERHAPS.
OR PERHAPS THE DEATH OF THUSTRA'S KING WILL GALVANIZE ITS PEOPLE -- UNITE ITS NEIGHBORS -- AND GIVE THEM THE STRENGTH AND THE PAIN THEY NEED TO FIGHT ON.
PLEASE DON'T...
BDOW!

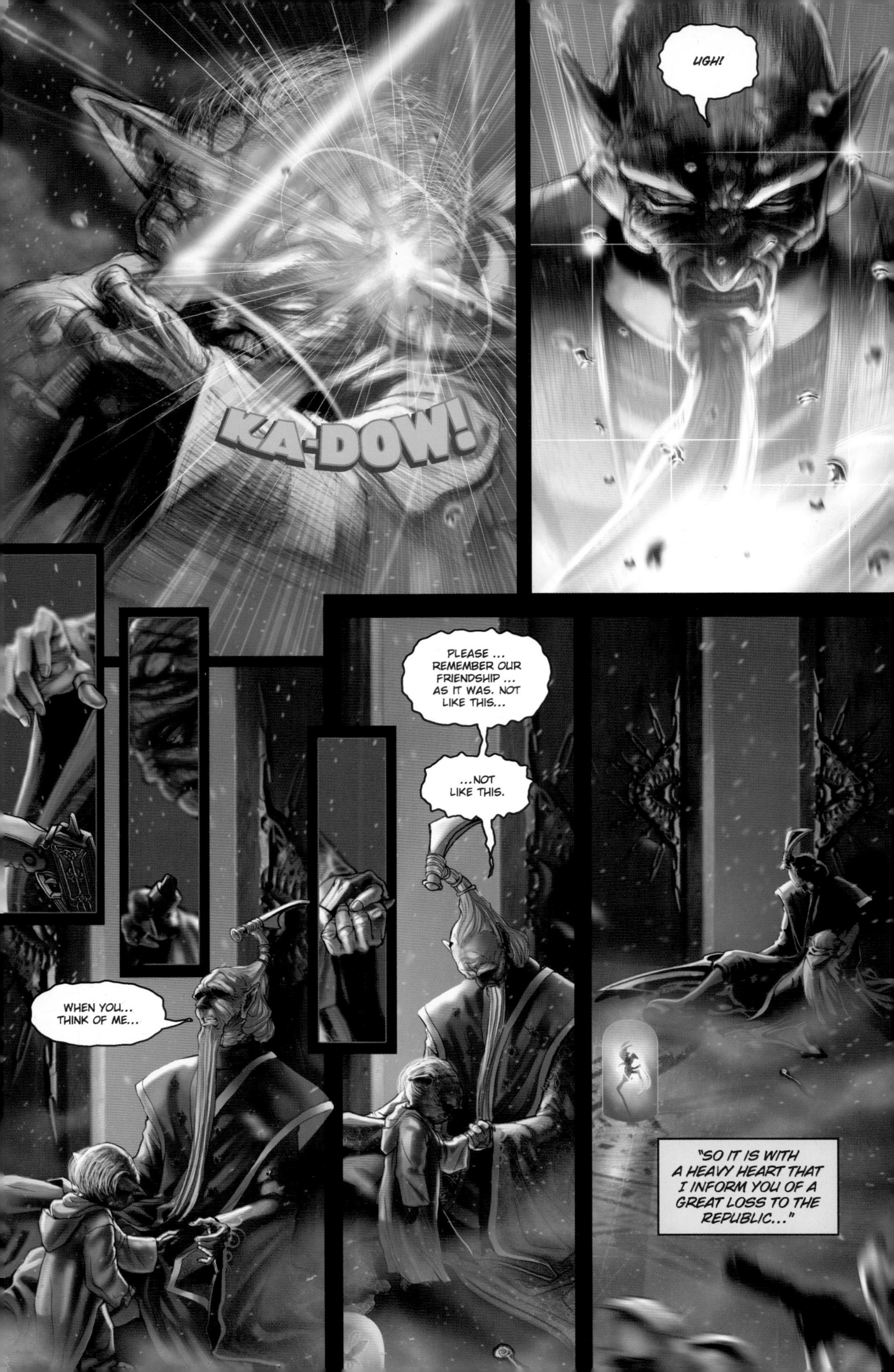
KA-DOW!
UGH!
WHEN YOU... THINK OF ME...
PLEASE ... REMEMBER OUR FRIENDSHIP ... AS IT WAS. NOT LIKE THIS...
...NOT LIKE THIS.
"SO IT IS WITH A HEAVY HEART THAT I INFORM YOU OF A GREAT LOSS TO THE REPUBLIC..."

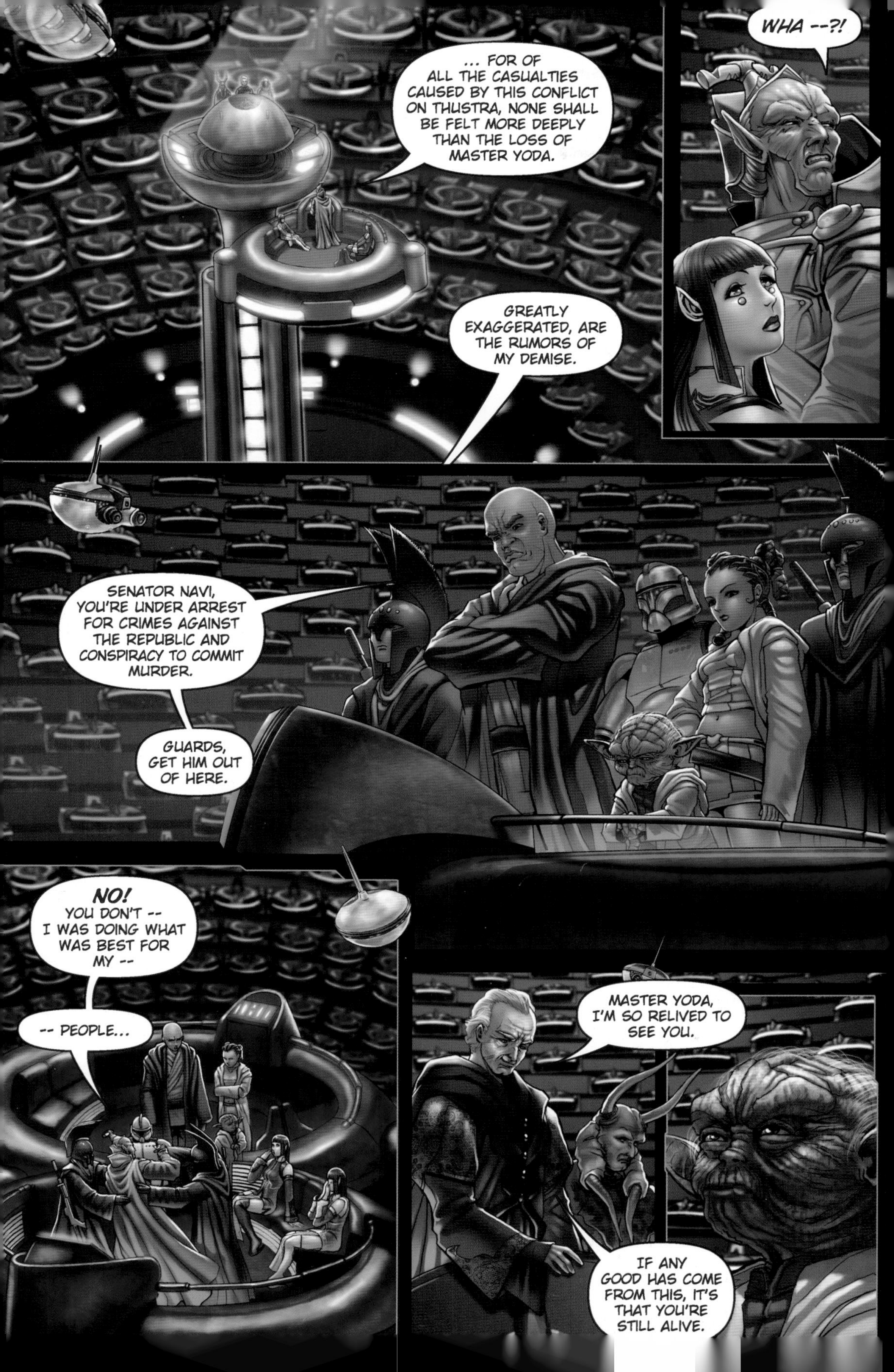
... FOR OF ALL THE CASUALTIES CAUSED BY THIS CONFLICT ON THUSTRA, NONE SHALL BE FELT MORE DEEPLY THAN THE LOSS OF MASTER YODA.
GREATLY EXAGGERATED, ARE THE RUMORS OF MY DEMISE.
WHA --?!
SENATOR NAVI, YOU'RE UNDER ARREST FOR CRIMES AGAINST THE REPUBLIC AND CONSPIRACY TO COMMIT MURDER.
GUARDS, GET HIM OUT OF HERE.
NO! YOU DON'T -- I WAS DOING WHAT WAS BEST FOR MY --
-- PEOPLE...
MASTER YODA, I'M SO RELIVED TO SEE YOU.
IF ANY GOOD HAS COME FROM THIS, IT'S THAT YOU'RE STILL ALIVE.

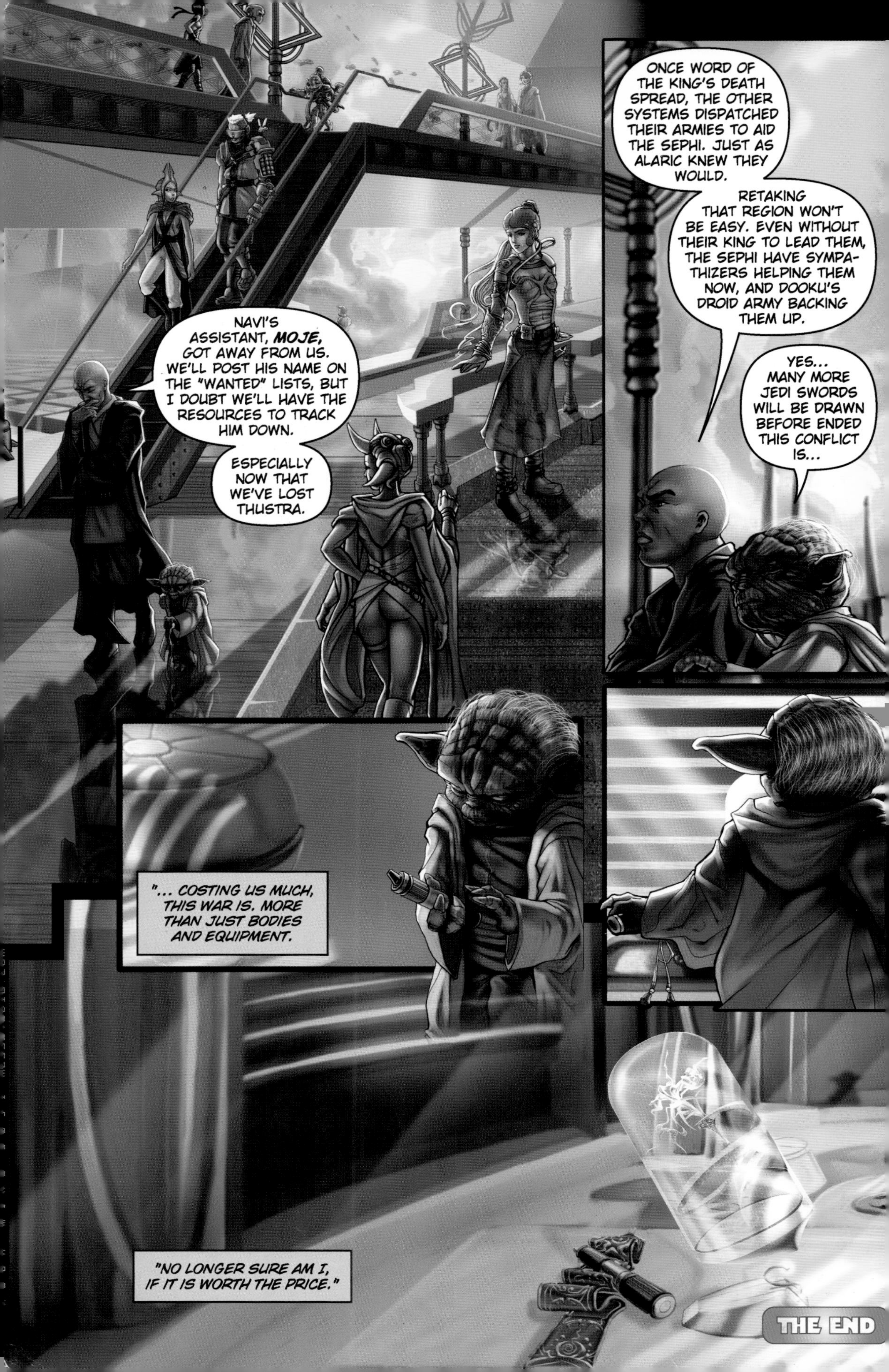
NAVI'S ASSISTANT, **MOJE,** GOT AWAY FROM US. WE'LL POST HIS NAME ON THE "WANTED" LISTS, BUT I DOUBT WE'LL HAVE THE RESOURCES TO TRACK HIM DOWN.
ESPECIALLY NOW THAT WE'VE LOST THUSTRA.
ONCE WORD OF THE KING'S DEATH SPREAD, THE OTHER SYSTEMS DISPATCHED THEIR ARMIES TO AID THE SEPHI. JUST AS ALARIC KNEW THEY WOULD.
RETAKING THAT REGION WON'T BE EASY. EVEN WITHOUT THEIR KING TO LEAD THEM, THE SEPHI HAVE SYMPATHIZERS HELPING THEM NOW, AND DOOKU'S DROID ARMY BACKING THEM UP.
YES... MANY MORE JEDI SWORDS WILL BE DRAWN BEFORE ENDED THIS CONFLICT IS...
*"... COSTING US MUCH, THIS WAR IS. MORE THAN JUST BODIES AND EQUIPMENT.*
*"NO LONGER SURE AM I, IF IT IS WORTH THE PRICE."*
THE END

# STAR WARS ®

## TIMELINE OF TRADE PAPERBACKS AND GRAPHIC NOVELS!

**OLD REPUBLIC ERA:**
25,000-1000 YEARS BEFORE
*STAR WARS: A NEW HOPE*

**Tales of the Jedi—**
**Knights of the Old Republic**
ISBN: 1-56971-020-1          $14.95

**Dark Lords of the Sith**
ISBN: 1-56971-095-3          $17.95

**The Sith War**
ISBN: 1-56971-173-9          $17.95

**The Golden Age of the Sith**
ISBN: 1-56971-229-8          $16.95

**The Freedon Nadd Uprising**
ISBN: 1-56971-307-3          $5.95

**The Fall of the Sith Empire**
ISBN: 1-56971-320-0          $15.95

**Redemption**
ISBN: 1-56971-535-1          $14.95

**Jedi vs. Sith**
ISBN: 1-56971-649-8          $17.95

**RISE OF THE EMPIRE ERA:**
1000-0 YEARS BEFORE
*STAR WARS: A NEW HOPE*

**The Stark Hyperspace War**
ISBN: 1-56971-985-3          $12.95

**Prelude to Rebellion**
ISBN: 1-56971-448-7          $14.95

**Jedi Council—Acts of War**
ISBN: 1-56971-539-4          $12.95

**Darth Maul**
ISBN: 1-56971-542-4          $12.95

**Jedi Council—**
**Emissaries to Malastare**
ISBN: 1-56971-545-9          $15.95

**Episode I—**
**The Phantom Menace**
ISBN: 1-56971-359-6          $12.95

**Episode I—**
**The Phantom Menace Adventures**
ISBN: 1-56971-443-6          $12.95

**Outlander**
ISBN: 1-56971-514-9          $14.95

**Star Wars: Jango Fett—**
**Open Seasons**
ISBN: 1-56971-671-4          $12.95

**The Bounty Hunters**
ISBN: 1-56971-467-3          $12.95

**Twilight**
ISBN: 1-56971-558-0          $12.95

**The Hunt for Aurra Sing**
ISBN: 1-56971-651-X          $12.95

**Darkness**
ISBN: 1-56971-659-5          $12.95

**The Rite of Passage**
ISBN: 1-59307-042-X          $12.95

**Episode II—Attack of the Clones**
ISBN: 1-56971-609-9          $17.95

**Clone Wars Volume 1:**
**The Defense of Kamino**
ISBN: 1-56971-962-4          $14.95

**Clone Wars Volume 2:**
**Victories and Sacrifices**
ISBN: 1-56971-969-1          $14.95

**Clone Wars Adventures Volume 1**
ISBN: 1-59307-243-0          $6.95

**Clone Wars Volume 3:**
**Last Stand on Jabiim**
ISBN: 1-59307-006-3          $14.95

**Clone Wars Volume 4: Light and Dark**
ISBN: 1-59307-195-7          $16.95

**Droids—The Kalarba Adventures**
ISBN: 1-56971-064-3          $17.95

**Droids—Rebellion**
ISBN: 1-56971-224-7          $14.95

**Classic Star Wars—**
**Han Solo At Stars' End**
ISBN: 1-56971-254-9          $6.95

**Boba Fett—Enemy of The Empire**
ISBN: 1-56971-407-X          $12.95

**Dark Forces—**
**Soldier for the Empire GSA**
ISBN: 1-56971-348-0          $14.95

**Mara Jade—By the Emperor's Hand**
ISBN: 1-56971-401-0          $15.95

**Underworld**
ISBN: 1-56971-618-8          $15.95

**Empire Volume 1: Betrayal**
ISBN: 1-56971-964-0          $12.95

**Empire Volume 2: Darklighter**
ISBN: 1-56971-975-6          $17.95

**REBELLION ERA:**
0-5 YEARS AFTER
*STAR WARS: A NEW HOPE*

**Classic Star Wars, Volume 1:**
**In Deadly Pursuit**
ISBN: 1-56971-109-7          $16.95

**Classic Star Wars, Volume 2:**
**The Rebel Storm**
ISBN: 1-56971-106-2          $16.95

**Classic Star Wars, Volume 3:**
**Escape to Hoth**
ISBN: 1-56971-093-7          $16.95

**Classic Star Wars—**
**The Early Adventures**
ISBN: 1-56971-178-X          $19.95

**Jabba the Hutt—The Art of the Deal**
ISBN: 1-56971-310-3          $9.95

**Vader's Quest**
ISBN: 1-56971-415-0          $11.95

**Splinter of the Mind's Eye**
ISBN: 1-56971-223-9          $14.95

**A Long Time Ago... Volume 1:**
**Doomworld**
ISBN: 1-56971-754-0          $29.95

**A Long Time Ago... Volume 2:**
**Dark Encounters**
ISBN: 1-56971-785-0          $29.95

**A Long Time Ago... Volume 3:**
**Resurrection of Evil**
ISBN: 1-56971-786-9          $29.95

**A Long Time Ago... Volume 4: Screams in the Void**
ISBN: 1-56971-787-7 $29.95

**A Long Time Ago... Volume 5: Fool's Bounty**
ISBN: 1-56971-906-3 $29.95

**A Long Time Ago... Volume 6: Wookiee World**
ISBN: 1-56971-907-1 $29.95

**A Long Time Ago... Volume 7: Far, Far Away**
ISBN: 1-56971-908-X $29.95

**Battle of the Bounty Hunters Pop-Up Book**
ISBN: 1-56971-129-1 $17.95

**Shadows of the Empire**
ISBN: 1-56971-183-6 $17.95

**The Empire Strikes Back— The Special Edition**
ISBN: 1-56971-234-4 $9.95

**Return of the Jedi—The Special Edition**
ISBN: 1-56971-235-2 $9.95

**NEW REPUBLIC ERA:**
5-25 YEARS AFTER
*STAR WARS: A NEW HOPE*

**X-Wing Rouge Squadron The Phantom Affair**
ISBN: 1-56971-251-4 $12.95

**Battleground Tatooine**
ISBN: 1-56971-276-X $12.95

**The Warrior Princess**
ISBN: 1-56971-330-8 $12.95

**Requiem for a Rogue**
ISBN: 1-56971-331-6 $12.95

**In the Empire's Service**
ISBN: 1-56971-383-9 $12.95

**Blood and Honor**
ISBN: 1-56971-387-1 $12.95

**Masquerade**
ISBN: 1-56971-487-8 $12.95

**Mandatory Retirement**
ISBN: 1-56971-492-4 $12.95

**Shadows of the Empire Evolution**
ISBN: 1-56971-441-X $14.95

**Heir to the Empire**
ISBN: 1-56971-202-6 $19.95

**Dark Force Rising**
ISBN: 1-56971-269-7 $17.95

**The Last Command**
ISBN: 1-56971-378-2 $17.95

**Dark Empire**
ISBN: 1-59307-039-X $16.95

**Dark Empire II**
ISBN: 1-56971-119-4 $17.95

**Empire's End**
ISBN: 1-56971-306-5 $5.95

**Boba Fett—Death, Lies, & Treachery**
ISBN: 1-56971-311-1 $12.95

**Crimson Empire**
ISBN: 1-56971-355-3 $17.95

**Crimson Empire II—Council of Blood**
ISBN: 1-56971-410-X $17.95

**Jedi Academy—Leviathan**
ISBN: 1-56971-456-8 $11.95

**Union**
ISBN: 1-56971-464-9 $12.95

**NEW JEDI ORDER ERA:**
25+ YEARS AFTER
*STAR WARS: A NEW HOPE*

**Chewbacca**
ISBN: 1-56971-515-7 $12.95

**INFINITIES:**
DOES NOT APPLY TO TIMELINE

**Infinities — A New Hope**
ISBN: 1-56971-648-X $12.95

**Infinities—The Empire Strikes Back**
ISBN: 1-56971-904-7 $12.95

**Infinities—Return of the Jedi**
ISBN: 1-59307-206-6 $12.95

**Star Wars Tales Volume 1**
ISBN: 1-56971-619-6 $19.95

**Star Wars Tales Volume 2**
ISBN: 1-56971-757-5 $19.95

**Star Wars Tales Volume 3**
ISBN: 1-56971-836-9 $19.95

**Star Wars Tales Volume 4**
ISBN: 1-56971-989-6 $19.95

**AVAILABLE AT YOUR LOCAL COMICS SHOP OR BOOKSTORE**

To find a comics shop in your area, call 1-888-266-4226

For more information or to order direct: • On the web: www.darkhorse.com • E-mail: mailorder@darkhorse.com
• Phone: 1-800-862-0052 or (503) 652-9701 Mon.-Sat. 9 A.M. to 5 P.M. Pacific Time

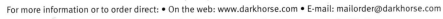

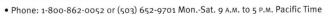